My People's Passover Haggadah

My People's Passover Haggadah
Volume 2

TRADITIONAL TEXTS,
MODERN COMMENTARIES

EDITED BY
RABBI LAWRENCE A. HOFFMAN, PhD
AND DAVID ARNOW, PhD

CONTRIBUTORS

DAVID ARNOW, PhD

RABBI CAROLE B. BALIN, PhD

MARC BRETTLER, PhD

RABBI NEIL GILLMAN, PhD

ALYSSA GRAY, PhD

RABBI ARTHUR GREEN, PhD

JOEL M. HOFFMAN, PhD

RABBI LAWRENCE A. HOFFMAN, PhD

RABBI LAWRENCE KUSHNER

RABBI DANIEL LANDES

RABBI NEHEMIA POLEN, PhD

WENDY I. ZIERLER, PhD

Jewish Lights Publishing

My People's Passover Haggadah, Volume 2:
Traditional Texts, Modern Commentaries

2008 First Printing
© 2008 by Lawrence A. Hoffman and David Arnow

Library of Congress Cataloging-in-Publication Data
Haggadah. English & Hebrew.
My people's Passover Haggadah : traditional texts, modern commentaries / edited by Lawrence A. Hoffman and David Arnow.—1st ed.
v. cm.
Text of Haggadah in Hebrew with English translation; commentaries in English.
Includes bibliographical references and index.
ISBN: 978-1-58023-354-5 (hardcover : v. 1)
ISBN: 978-1-68336-204-3 (paperback : v. 1)
ISBN: 978-1-58023-346-0 (hardcover : v. 2)
ISBN: 978-1-68336-205-0 (paperback: v. 2)
1. Haggadot—Texts. 2. Seder—Liturgy—Texts. 3. Judaism—Liturgy—Texts. 4. Haggadah.
I. Hoffman, Lawrence A., 1942– II. Arnow, David. III. Title.
BM674.643.H64 2008
296.4'5371—dc22
2007048984

First Edition

Published by Jewish Lights Publishing

www.jewishlights.com

Contents:
Volume 2

COMMENTATORS:

DAVID ARNOW: *The World of Midrash*

CAROLE B. BALIN: *Modern Haggadot*

MARC BRETTLER: *Our Biblical Heritage*

NEIL GILLMAN: *Theologically Speaking*

ALYSSA GRAY: *Medieval Commentators*

ARTHUR GREEN: *Personal Spirituality*

JOEL M. HOFFMAN: *Translating the Haggadah*

LAWRENCE A. HOFFMAN: *History of the Haggadah*

LAWRENCE KUSHNER AND NEHEMIA POLEN: *Chasidic Voices*

DANIEL LANDES: *The Halakhah of the Seder*

WENDY I. ZIERLER: *Feminist Voices*

9. A LONG ANSWER: A MIDRASH ON "MY FATHER WAS A WANDERING ARAMEAN ..." 1

10. THE ROLE OF GOD 29
    A. "GOD BROUGHT US OUT OF EGYPT—NOT BY AN ANGEL ..." 29
    B. GOD'S PUNISHING MIGHT: THE PLAGUES IN EGYPT AND AT THE SEA 30
    C. GOD'S SAVING MIGHT: *DAYYENU* 32

11. SUMMING IT ALL UP 72
    A. SYMBOLS OF THE NIGHT: PASSOVER, MATZAH, BITTER HERBS 72
    B. THE ESSENCE OF THE NIGHT: "IN EACH AND EVERY GENERATION ..." 73

C. ... TO PRAISE AND REDEMPTION 93

12. "PRAISE"—HALLEL, PART ONE, PSALMS 113–114 93
    A. AN INTRODUCTION TO *HALLEL* 93

B. PSALM 113 93

C. PSALM 114 94

13. REDEMPTION: BLESSING AND MEAL **109**

A. THE BLESSING OF REDEMPTION AND THE SECOND CUP 109

B. BLESSINGS OVER THE MEAL: THE SECOND WASHING (*ROCHTSAH*); *MOTSI*;
MATZAH; *MAROR*; AND HILLEL'S SANDWICH (*KOREKH*). *110*

C. THE MEAL *111*

D. CODA TO THE MEAL: THE "HIDDEN" *AFIKOMAN* (*TSAFUN*); GRACE AFTER
MEALS (*BAREKH*); AND THE THIRD CUP *111*

D. YEARNINGS AND HOPES **137**

14. MEDIEVAL ADDITIONS **137**

A. WELCOMING ELIJAH. 137

B. GOD'S TRIUMPH OVER EVIL: "POUR OUT YOUR WRATH …" 137

15. "PRAISE"—HALLEL, PART TWO, PSALMS 115–118, 136 . . . . . **154**

A. PSALMS 115–118 AND CONCLUSION. 154

B. PSALM 136 (THE GREAT *HALLEL*) AND CONCLUSION 157

16. FORMAL CONCLUSION **186**

A. THE FOURTH CUP AND FINAL BLESSING. 186

B. PRAYER FOR "ACCEPTANCE" OF THE SEDER (*NIRTSAH*) 187

C. A MESSIANIC HOPE: "NEXT YEAR IN JERUSALEM!" 187

17. FOUR SEDER SONGS **198**

A. *KI LO NA'EH, KI LO YA'EH* ("FOR IT FITS AND BEFITS HIM") . . . 198

B. *ADIR HU* ("HE IS MIGHTY") 198

C. *ECHAD MI YODE'A* ("WHO KNOWS ONE?") 199

D. *CHAD GADYA* ("ONE KID") 202

APPENDIX I
Two Early Seders: Mishnah and Tosefta **225**

APPENDIX II
A Haggadah from the Cairo Genizah **235**

Notes 249

List of Abbreviations 257

Glossary 259

Annotated Select Bibliography 275

About the Contributors 283

Index 287

Here's What You'll Find in Volume 1

ACKNOWLEDGMENTS xi

INTRODUCTION: HOW TO GET THE MOST OUT OF THIS BOOK
    Lawrence A. Hoffman and David Arnow xiii

PART I CELEBRATING PASSOVER: CONTEXTUAL REFLECTIONS

1. WHAT IS THE HAGGADAH ANYWAY? 3
    Lawrence A. Hoffman

2. PASSOVER IN THE BIBLE AND BEFORE. 9
    David Arnow

3. PASSOVER FOR THE EARLY RABBIS: FIXED AND FREE 15
    David Arnow

4. THIS BREAD: CHRISTIANITY AND THE SEDER 21
    Lawrence A. Hoffman

5. THE SEDER PLATE: THE WORLD ON A DISH. 37
    David Arnow

CONTENTS

6. PEOPLEHOOD WITH PURPOSE: THE AMERICAN SEDER AND
   CHANGING JEWISH IDENTITY. 47
   Lawrence A. Hoffman

7. WHERE HAVE ALL THE WOMEN GONE? FEMINIST QUESTIONS
   ABOUT THE HAGGADAH 71
   Wendy I. Zierler

8. MOVING THROUGH THE MOVEMENTS: AMERICAN DENOMINATIONS
   AND THEIR HAGGADOT. 79
   Carole B. Balin

9. "GOOD TO THE LAST DROP": THE PROLIFERATION OF
   THE MAXWELL HOUSE HAGGADAH 85
   Carole B. Balin

PART II THE PASSOVER HAGGADAH

A. SETTING THE STAGE

1. PREPARING THE HOME. 92
   A. "THE CHECKING OF LEAVEN" (B'DIKAT CHAMETS) 92
   B. PERMISSION TO COOK FOR SHABBAT: "THE MIXING OF FOODS"
      (ERUV TAVSHILIN) 92
   C. ARRANGING THE SEDER PLATE 93

2. THE ORDER OF THE SEDER: KADESH URCHATS 107

3. BEGINNING THE SEDER 111
   A. LIGHTING CANDLES 111
   B. DEFINING SACRED TIME (KIDDUSH AND THE FIRST CUP) 111
   C. DISTINGUISHING TIMES OF HOLINESS (HAVDALAH) 112
   D. GRATITUDE FOR BEING HERE (SHEHECHEYANU) 113
   E. THE FIRST WASHING (URCHATS) AND DIPPING KARPAS 113
   F. "BREAKING THE MATZAH" (YACHATS) AND RESERVING THE AFIKOMAN . . 113
   G. "BREAD OF AFFLICTION," HA LACHMA ANYA: (BEGIN MAGGID: "TELLING") . . 113

4. QUESTIONS OF THE NIGHT: MAH NISHTANAH,
   "WHY IS THIS NIGHT DIFFERENT?" 147

B. FROM ENSLAVEMENT ...

5. A SHORT ANSWER: ENSLAVEMENT IS PHYSICAL—
AVADIM HAYYINU, "WE WERE SLAVES" *161*

6. HOW WE TELL THE TALE *169*

    A. EVERYONE TELLS THE STORY: "EVEN IF ALL OF US WERE SMART ..." 169

    B. TELLING AT LENGTH: THE FIVE SAGES' SEDER 169

    C. TELLING AT NIGHT? "ALL THE DAYS OF YOUR LIFE ..." 169

    D. TELLING THE NEXT GENERATION: THE FOUR CHILDREN 170

    E. TELLING AT THE PROPER TIME: AT THE BEGINNING OF THE MONTH? 171

7. A SHORT ANSWER: ENSLAVEMENT IS SPIRITUAL—
WE WORSHIPED IDOLS *213*

8. PROMISES—PAST AND PRESENT *221*

    A. THE PROMISE TO ABRAHAM: "BLESSED IS THE ONE WHO KEEPS HIS PROMISE ..." 221

    B. THE PROMISE TO US: "THIS KEPT OUR ANCESTORS AND US GOING ..." 221

Part II

The Passover
Haggadah

(continued)

9. A LONG ANSWER: A MIDRASH ON "MY FATHER WAS A WANDERING ARAMEAN ..."

[1]Note well what Laban the Aramean wanted to do to our father Jacob, for Pharaoh's decree only concerned the males, while Laban wanted to uproot everyone, as it says, [2]"My father was a wandering Aramean. He descended to Egypt and lived there in small numbers, and there he became a large, mighty, and populous nation."

[3]"Descended to Egypt"—this means compelled by the word of God.

[4]"Lived there"—this teaches that our ancestor Jacob didn't go down to Egypt to plant himself there, but rather to live there, as it says, [5]"They told Pharaoh, 'We have only come to live in this land because there is no pasture for your servants' flocks and because the famine in the Land of Canaan is severe. So now, sir, let your servants stay in the Land of Goshen.'"

[6]"In small numbers"—as it says, "Numbering seventy people, your ancestors went down to Egypt, and now Adonai your God has made you populous like the stars of the sky."

[7]"Became a nation"—this teaches that Israel was distinct there.

[8]"Large, mighty"—as it says, "The children of Israel were fertile and multiplied and became very, very populous and mighty, and the land was filled with them."

[9]"Populous"—as it says, "I made your population like wildflowers, and you were populous and large, and you grew into a woman. Your breasts grew and your hair sprouted, yet you remained naked and bare."

[10]"I passed by you and I saw you wallowing in your blood. And I said to you, live in your blood. And I said to you, live in your blood."

[11]"The Egyptians were evil toward us and afflicted us and imposed harsh labor upon us."

צֵא[1] וּלְמַד מַה־בִּקֵּשׁ לָבָן הָאֲרַמִּי לַעֲשׂוֹת לְיַעֲקֹב אָבִינוּ. שֶׁפַּרְעֹה לֹא גָזַר אֶלָּא עַל הַזְּכָרִים וְלָבָן בִּקֵּשׁ לַעֲקֹר אֶת־הַכֹּל. שֶׁנֶּאֱמַר: [2]אֲרַמִּי אֹבֵד אָבִי וַיֵּרֶד מִצְרַיְמָה וַיָּגָר שָׁם בִּמְתֵי מְעָט וַיְהִי־שָׁם לְגוֹי גָּדוֹל עָצוּם וָרָב: [3]וַיֵּרֶד מִצְרַיְמָה. אָנוּס עַל פִּי הַדִּבּוּר: [4]וַיָּגָר שָׁם. מְלַמֵּד שֶׁלֹּא יָרַד יַעֲקֹב אָבִינוּ לְהִשְׁתַּקֵּעַ בְּמִצְרַיִם אֶלָּא לָגוּר שָׁם. שֶׁנֶּאֱמַר: [5]וַיֹּאמְרוּ אֶל פַּרְעֹה לָגוּר בָּאָרֶץ בָּאנוּ כִּי אֵין מִרְעֶה לַצֹּאן אֲשֶׁר לַעֲבָדֶיךָ כִּי כָבֵד הָרָעָב בְּאֶרֶץ כְּנָעַן וְעַתָּה יֵשְׁבוּ נָא עֲבָדֶיךָ בְּאֶרֶץ גֹּשֶׁן: [6]בִּמְתֵי מְעָט. כְּמָה שֶׁנֶּאֱמַר: בְּשִׁבְעִים נֶפֶשׁ יָרְדוּ אֲבֹתֶיךָ מִצְרַיְמָה וְעַתָּה שָׂמְךָ יְיָ אֱלֹהֶיךָ כְּכוֹכְבֵי הַשָּׁמַיִם לָרֹב: [7]וַיְהִי־שָׁם לְגוֹי. מְלַמֵּד שֶׁהָיוּ יִשְׂרָאֵל מְצֻיָּנִים שָׁם: [8]גָּדוֹל עָצוּם. כְּמָה שֶׁנֶּאֱמַר: וּבְנֵי יִשְׂרָאֵל פָּרוּ וַיִּשְׁרְצוּ וַיִּרְבּוּ וַיַּעַצְמוּ בִּמְאֹד מְאֹד וַתִּמָּלֵא הָאָרֶץ אֹתָם: [9]וָרָב. כְּמָה שֶׁנֶּאֱמַר: רְבָבָה כְּצֶמַח הַשָּׂדֶה נְתַתִּיךְ וַתִּרְבִּי וַתִּגְדְּלִי וַתָּבֹאִי בַּעֲדִי עֲדָיִים שָׁדַיִם נָכֹנוּ וּשְׂעָרֵךְ צִמֵּחַ וְאַתְּ עֵרֹם וְעֶרְיָה: [10]וָאֶעֱבֹר עָלַיִךְ וָאֶרְאֵךְ מִתְבּוֹסֶסֶת בְּדָמָיִךְ וָאֹמַר לָךְ בְּדָמַיִךְ חֲיִי וָאֹמַר לָךְ בְּדָמַיִךְ חֲיִי: [11]וַיָּרֵעוּ אֹתָנוּ הַמִּצְרִים וַיְעַנּוּנוּ וַיִּתְּנוּ עָלֵינוּ עֲבֹדָה קָשָׁה:

1

12"The Egyptians were evil toward us"—as it says, "Let us be clever about them lest they multiply and in the event of a war they be added to those who hate us and, having waged war, leave this land."

13"Afflicted us"—as it says, "They put taskmasters over them to afflict them in their suffering. They built garrison cities for Pharaoh: Pithom and Rameses."

14"Imposed harsh labor upon us"—as it says, "With severity the Egyptians made the children of Israel work."

15"We cried out to Adonai our ancestors' God, and Adonai heard our voice and saw our misery and our work and our distress."

16"We cried out to Adonai our ancestors' God"—as it says, "After a long time, the king of Egypt died, and the children of Israel sighed because of their work and cried out, and their plea rose to God because of the work."

17"Adonai heard our voice"—as it says, "God heard their groaning, and God remembered His covenant with Abraham, with Isaac, and with Jacob."

18"Saw our misery"—this is the separation from worldly ways, as it says, "God saw the children of Israel and God knew."

19"And our work"—this is the boys, as it says, "You shall throw every boy who is born into the Nile, while you shall let every girl live."

20"And our distress"—this is the persecution, as it says, "I also saw the distress that the Egyptians inflict upon them."

12 וַיָּרֵעוּ אֹתָנוּ הַמִּצְרִים. כְּמָה שֶׁנֶּאֱמַר: הָבָה נִתְחַכְּמָה לוֹ פֶּן יִרְבֶּה וְהָיָה כִּי תִקְרֶאנָה מִלְחָמָה וְנוֹסַף גַּם הוּא עַל שֹׂנְאֵינוּ וְנִלְחַם־בָּנוּ וְעָלָה מִן הָאָרֶץ: 13 וַיְעַנּוּנוּ. כְּמָה שֶׁנֶּאֱמַר: וַיָּשִׂימוּ עָלָיו שָׂרֵי מִסִּים לְמַעַן עַנֹּתוֹ בְּסִבְלֹתָם וַיִּבֶן עָרֵי מִסְכְּנוֹת לְפַרְעֹה אֶת־פִּתֹם וְאֶת־ רַעַמְסֵס: 14 וַיִּתְּנוּ עָלֵינוּ עֲבֹדָה קָשָׁה. כְּמָה שֶׁנֶּאֱמַר: וַיַּעֲבִדוּ מִצְרַיִם אֶת־בְּנֵי יִשְׂרָאֵל בְּפָרֶךְ:

15 וַנִּצְעַק אֶל יְיָ אֱלֹהֵי אֲבֹתֵינוּ וַיִּשְׁמַע יְיָ אֶת־קֹלֵנוּ וַיַּרְא אֶת־עָנְיֵנוּ וְאֶת־ עֲמָלֵנוּ וְאֶת־לַחֲצֵנוּ: 16 וַנִּצְעַק אֶל יְיָ אֱלֹהֵי אֲבֹתֵינוּ. כְּמָה שֶׁנֶּאֱמַר: וַיְהִי בַיָּמִים הָרַבִּים הָהֵם וַיָּמָת מֶלֶךְ מִצְרַיִם וַיֵּאָנְחוּ בְנֵי יִשְׂרָאֵל מִן הָעֲבֹדָה וַיִּזְעָקוּ וַתַּעַל שַׁוְעָתָם אֶל הָאֱלֹהִים מִן הָעֲבֹדָה: 17 וַיִּשְׁמַע יְיָ אֶת־קֹלֵנוּ. כְּמָה שֶׁנֶּאֱמַר: וַיִּשְׁמַע אֱלֹהִים אֶת־נַאֲקָתָם וַיִּזְכֹּר אֱלֹהִים אֶת־בְּרִיתוֹ אֶת־אַבְרָהָם אֶת־יִצְחָק וְאֶת־יַעֲקֹב: 18 וַיַּרְא אֶת־ עָנְיֵנוּ. זוֹ פְּרִישׁוּת דֶּרֶךְ אֶרֶץ. כְּמָה שֶׁנֶּאֱמַר: וַיַּרְא אֱלֹהִים אֶת־בְּנֵי יִשְׂרָאֵל וַיֵּדַע אֱלֹהִים: 19 וְאֶת־עֲמָלֵנוּ. אֵלּוּ הַבָּנִים. כְּמָה שֶׁנֶּאֱמַר: כָּל־הַבֵּן הַיִּלּוֹד הַיְאֹרָה תַּשְׁלִיכֻהוּ וְכָל־הַבַּת תְּחַיּוּן: 20 וְאֶת־לַחֲצֵנוּ. זֶה הַדְּחַק. כְּמָה שֶׁנֶּאֱמַר: וְגַם רָאִיתִי אֶת־הַלַּחַץ אֲשֶׁר מִצְרַיִם לֹחֲצִים אֹתָם:

From Enslavement to Redemption ... from Darkness to Great Light
American Jewish Historical Society, Newton Center, Massachusetts, and New York, New York
Frontispiece to Tractate Pesachim of the Babylonian Talmud. Published in 1949 in Munich and
Heidelberg by the Rabbinical Council of Ashkenaz (Germany) in the American Sector with the
assistance of the Military Government of the United States and the Joint Distribution Committee.
This edition of the Talmud was dedicated to the U.S. Army.
Bottom: A labor camp in Germany in the era of the Nazis. Above lower drawing: "Though they
almost wiped me off the earth, I did not abandon Your precepts" (Psalm 119:87).
Beneath upper drawing: "From enslavement to redemption ... from darkness to great light." From
the Babylonian Talmud, Pesachim 116b and the Haggadah. The customary Ashkenazi order is
"darkness to great light" and then "enslavement to redemption" (see My People's Passover
Haggadah, Volume 2, p. 93). Here, the order is reversed, so as to end with "great light."
Maimonides, the Yemenite and the Sefardi traditions also end with "darkness to great light."

ARNOW (THE WORLD OF MIDRASH)

[1] *"Laban wanted to uproot everyone"* The Haggadah's particular animus toward Laban reflects the physical and spiritual threat he posed to the Jewish future. The *Sifre on Deuteronomy* (*Piska* 301) notes that "Laban is considered as if he had destroyed [Jacob]." According to *Pirkei D'rabbi Eliezer*, "Laban took all the men of his city, mighty men, and pursued [Jacob], seeking to slay him."[1] And although Laban did not in fact harm Jacob—they made a treaty with one another—a talmudic tradition holds that God counted his evil thoughts as if they had been carried out (PT Peah 5a, 1:16:b). Had Laban destroyed Jacob and his family, it would indeed have ended the Jewish story. *(p. 8)*

BALIN (MODERN HAGGADOT)

[2] *"My father was a wandering Aramean"*[1] The requirement to recount the story of the Exodus by means of midrashic elaboration on several verses from the Book of Deuteronomy (26:5–8) dates back to one of the very earliest post-Temple descriptions of a Passover *(p. 12)*

BRETTLER (OUR BIBLICAL HERITAGE)

[1] *"Laban the Aramean"* Laban, father of Rachel and Leah and thus father-in-law of Jacob, is depicted negatively in Genesis—as conniving and miserly—but the sentiment expressed here goes far beyond the biblical text.

[2] *"My father was a wandering Aramean"* This begins another *(p. 13)*

GILLMAN (THEOLOGICALLY SPEAKING)

[1] *"What Laban the Aramean wanted to do to our father Jacob"* This is the third beginning of the story, the third form of the disgrace or the "bad things," the one that the Mishnah (Pes. 10:4) suggests we use as the skeleton for telling the story. We are to expound the biblical passage that begins "My father was a wandering Aramean …" (Deut. 26:5). In order to turn it into a form of disgrace, the Haggadah reinterprets the verse to mean "an Aramean sought to destroy my father." This *(p. 15)*

9. A LONG ANSWER: A MIDRASH ON "MY FATHER WAS A WANDERING ARAMEAN …"

[1] Note well what Laban the Aramean wanted to do to our father Jacob, for Pharaoh's decree only concerned the males, while Laban wanted to uproot everyone, as it says, [2] "My father was a wandering Aramean. He descended to Egypt and lived there in small numbers, and there he became a large, mighty, and populous nation." [3] "Descended to Egypt"—this means compelled by the word of God. [4] "Lived there"—this teaches that our ancestor Jacob didn't go down

GRAY (MEDIEVAL COMMENTATORS)

[1] *"Note well what Laban the Aramean wanted to do"* Mishnah Pesachim 10:4 closes with the direction that the Seder leader must "expound" *(doresh)* beginning with the verse "My father was a wandering Aramean" (Deut. 26:5) until the "end of the *parashah*." Abudarham explains *"parashah"* here to mean the four verses (Deut. 26:5–8) that deal with the Exodus story. The Mishnah says that the leader is to "expound" these verses but leaves open the issue of how he is to do so. Abudarham points out *(p. 16)*

GREEN (PERSONAL SPIRITUALITY)

[11] *"The Egyptians were evil toward us"* This unusual phrase, read literally, can also mean "The Egyptians made us evil" or "brought out the bad in us." There is much in our tradition that talks about the nobility of the Hebrew slaves, their loyalty to the ways of their ancestors, and so forth. But it is also important to remember that oppression evokes qualities in ourselves that do not make us proud: anger, hatred, fear of outsiders, a desire for revenge, and a bitterness about our fate that makes

(p. 20)

WE HAVE RECEIVED TWO BRIEF ANSWERS TO THE CENTRAL QUESTION OF WHAT THIS NIGHT IS ALL ABOUT: ENSLAVEMENT MAY BE PHYSICAL (SEE MY PEOPLE'S PASSOVER HAGGADAH, VOLUME 1, P. 161) OR SPIRITUAL (VOLUME 1, P. 213). WE NOW PLUNGE INTO FULFILLING AN ANCIENT INJUNCTION TO TELL THE STORY OF OUR ENSLAVEMENT AND FREEDOM THROUGH A COMPLEX MIDRASH ON DEUTERONOMY 26:5–8. WE ARE CHALLENGED TO FIND ITS ORIGINAL INTENT AND WHAT IT MIGHT MEAN FOR US TODAY.

L. HOFFMAN (HISTORY)

[1] *"Note well"* [*the central midrash*] The Mishnah's barebones instructions for the Haggadah's essential plot line are very old—probably reaching back to whenever it was that a rabbinic Seder was first inaugurated. They were (as we saw in *My People's Passover Haggadah*, Volume 1, "Why ... different [*Mah nishtanah*]"; p. 154):

(p. 24)

צֵא וּלְמַד מַה־בִּקֵּשׁ לָבָן הָאֲרַמִּי לַעֲשׂוֹת לְיַעֲקֹב [1]
אָבִינוּ. שֶׁפַּרְעֹה לֹא גָזַר אֶלָּא עַל הַזְּכָרִים וְלָבָן בִּקֵּשׁ
לַעֲקֹר אֶת־הַכֹּל. שֶׁנֶּאֱמַר: אֲרַמִּי אֹבֵד אָבִי וַיֵּרֶד [2]
מִצְרַיְמָה וַיָּגָר שָׁם בִּמְתֵי מְעָט וַיְהִי־שָׁם לְגוֹי גָּדוֹל
עָצוּם וָרָב: וַיֵּרֶד מִצְרַיְמָה. אָנוּס עַל פִּי הַדִּבּוּר: [3]
וַיָּגָר שָׁם. מְלַמֵּד שֶׁלֹּא יָרַד יַעֲקֹב אָבִינוּ [4]

J. HOFFMAN (TRANSLATION)

[1] *"Note well"* Literally, "Go and learn."

[2] *"Wandering Aramean"* This is one common translation of the enigmatic Hebrew from Deuteronomy 26:5. *JPS* gives us "fugitive Aramean," while the Septuagint—the third-century BCE Greek translation of the Bible—offers instead "my father abandoned Aram." At issue is the verb *oved*, variously, "wandering" (as here), "abandoned" (in the Septuagint), or "perish" (as in King James's "a Syrian ready to

(p. 20)

ZIERLER (FEMINIST VOICES)

[1] *"Note well what Laban the Aramean wanted to do"* Why is Laban presented here as the arch evildoer? Laban attempts "to uproot [*la'akor*] everyone." Elsewhere in Genesis, the same root, *ayin, kuf, resh*, is used to represent a divinely ordained condition of barrenness. The matriarchs are barren until God grants them their sought-after progeny. Laban's evil-doing consists in his attempt to make himself fruitful and everyone else

(p. 28)

to Egypt to plant himself there, but rather to live there, as it says, [5]"They told Pharaoh, 'We have only come to live in this land because there is no pasture for your servants' flocks and because the famine in the Land of Canaan is severe. So now, sir, let your servants stay in the Land of Goshen.'"

[6]"In small numbers"—as it says, "Numbering seventy people, your ancestors went down to Egypt, and now Adonai your God has made you populous like the stars of the sky."

[7]"Became a nation"—this teaches that Israel was distinct there.

[8]"Large, mighty"—as it says, "The children of Israel were fertile and multiplied and became very, very populous and mighty, and the land was filled with them."

[9]"Populous"—as it says, "I made your population like wildflowers, and you were populous and large, and you grew into a woman. Your breasts grew and your hair sprouted, yet you remained naked and bare." [10]"I passed by you and I saw you wallowing in your blood. And I said to you, live in your blood. And I said to you, live in your blood."

[11]"The Egyptians were evil toward us and afflicted us and imposed harsh labor upon us."

לְהִשְׁתַּקֵּעַ בְּמִצְרַיִם אֶלָּא לָגוּר שָׁם. שֶׁנֶּאֱמַר: [5]וַיֹּאמְרוּ אֶל פַּרְעֹה לָגוּר בָּאָרֶץ בָּאנוּ כִּי אֵין מִרְעֶה לַצֹּאן אֲשֶׁר לַעֲבָדֶיךָ כִּי כָבֵד הָרָעָב בְּאֶרֶץ כְּנָעַן וְעַתָּה יֵשְׁבוּ נָא עֲבָדֶיךָ בְּאֶרֶץ גֹּשֶׁן:

[6]בִּמְתֵי מְעָט. כְּמָה שֶׁנֶּאֱמַר: בְּשִׁבְעִים נֶפֶשׁ יָרְדוּ אֲבֹתֶיךָ מִצְרָיְמָה וְעַתָּה שָׂמְךָ יְיָ אֱלֹהֶיךָ כְּכוֹכְבֵי הַשָּׁמַיִם לָרֹב:

[7]וַיְהִי־שָׁם לְגוֹי. מְלַמֵּד שֶׁהָיוּ יִשְׂרָאֵל מְצֻיָּנִים שָׁם:

[8]גָּדוֹל עָצוּם. כְּמָה שֶׁנֶּאֱמַר: וּבְנֵי יִשְׂרָאֵל פָּרוּ וַיִּשְׁרְצוּ וַיִּרְבּוּ וַיַּעַצְמוּ בִּמְאֹד מְאֹד וַתִּמָּלֵא הָאָרֶץ אֹתָם:

[9]וָרָב. כְּמָה שֶׁנֶּאֱמַר: רְבָבָה כְּצֶמַח הַשָּׂדֶה נְתַתִּיךְ וַתִּרְבִּי וַתִּגְדְּלִי וַתָּבֹאִי בַּעֲדִי עֲדָיִים שָׁדַיִם נָכֹנוּ וּשְׂעָרֵךְ צִמֵּחַ וְאַתְּ עֵרֹם וְעֶרְיָה: [10]וָאֶעֱבֹר עָלַיִךְ וָאֶרְאֵךְ מִתְבּוֹסֶסֶת בְּדָמָיִךְ וָאֹמַר לָךְ בְּדָמַיִךְ חֲיִי וָאֹמַר לָךְ בְּדָמַיִךְ חֲיִי:

[11]וַיָּרֵעוּ אֹתָנוּ הַמִּצְרִים וַיְעַנּוּנוּ וַיִּתְּנוּ עָלֵינוּ עֲבֹדָה קָשָׁה:

[12]"The Egyptians were evil toward us"—as it says, "Let us be clever about them lest they multiply and in the event of a war they be added to those who hate us and, having waged war, leave this land."

[13]"Afflicted us"—as it says, "They put taskmasters over them to afflict them in their suffering. They built garrison cities for Pharaoh: Pithom and Rameses."

[14]"Imposed harsh labor upon us"—as it says, "With severity the Egyptians made the children of Israel work."

[15]"We cried out to Adonai our ancestors' God, and Adonai heard our voice and saw our misery and our work and our distress."

[16]"We cried out to Adonai our ancestors' God"—as it says, "After a long time, the king of Egypt died, and the children of Israel sighed because of their work and cried out, and their plea rose to God because of the work."

[17]"Adonai heard our voice"—as it says, "God heard their groaning, and God remembered His covenant with Abraham, with Isaac, and with Jacob."

[18]"Saw our misery"—this is the separation from worldly ways, as it says, "God saw the children of Israel and God knew."

[12] וַיָּרֵעוּ אֹתָנוּ הַמִּצְרִים. כְּמָה שֶׁנֶּאֱמַר: הָבָה נִתְחַכְּמָה לוֹ פֶּן יִרְבֶּה וְהָיָה כִּי תִקְרֶאנָה מִלְחָמָה וְנוֹסַף גַּם הוּא עַל שׂנְאֵינוּ וְנִלְחַם־בָּנוּ וְעָלָה מִן הָאָרֶץ:

[13] וַיְעַנּוּנוּ. כְּמָה שֶׁנֶּאֱמַר: וַיָּשִׂימוּ עָלָיו שָׂרֵי מִסִּים לְמַעַן עַנֹּתוֹ בְּסִבְלֹתָם וַיִּבֶן עָרֵי מִסְכְּנוֹת לְפַרְעֹה אֶת־פִּתֹם וְאֶת־רַעַמְסֵס:

[14] וַיִּתְּנוּ עָלֵינוּ עֲבֹדָה קָשָׁה. כְּמָה שֶׁנֶּאֱמַר: וַיַּעֲבִדוּ מִצְרַיִם אֶת־בְּנֵי יִשְׂרָאֵל בְּפָרֶךְ:

[15] וַנִּצְעַק אֶל יְיָ אֱלֹהֵי אֲבֹתֵינוּ וַיִּשְׁמַע יְיָ אֶת־קֹלֵנוּ וַיַּרְא אֶת־עָנְיֵנוּ וְאֶת־עֲמָלֵנוּ וְאֶת־לַחֲצֵנוּ:

[16] וַנִּצְעַק אֶל יְיָ אֱלֹהֵי אֲבֹתֵינוּ. כְּמָה שֶׁנֶּאֱמַר: וַיְהִי בַיָּמִים הָרַבִּים הָהֵם וַיָּמָת מֶלֶךְ מִצְרַיִם וַיֵּאָנְחוּ בְנֵי יִשְׂרָאֵל מִן הָעֲבֹדָה וַיִּזְעָקוּ וַתַּעַל שַׁוְעָתָם אֶל הָאֱלֹהִים מִן הָעֲבֹדָה:

[17] וַיִּשְׁמַע יְיָ אֶת־קֹלֵנוּ. כְּמָה שֶׁנֶּאֱמַר: וַיִּשְׁמַע אֱלֹהִים אֶת־נַאֲקָתָם וַיִּזְכֹּר אֱלֹהִים אֶת־בְּרִיתוֹ אֶת־אַבְרָהָם אֶת־יִצְחָק וְאֶת־יַעֲקֹב:

[18] וַיַּרְא אֶת־עָנְיֵנוּ. זוֹ פְּרִישׁוּת דֶּרֶךְ אֶרֶץ. כְּמָה שֶׁנֶּאֱמַר: וַיַּרְא אֱלֹהִים אֶת־בְּנֵי יִשְׂרָאֵל וַיֵּדַע אֱלֹהִים:

[19]"And our work"—this is the boys, as it says, "You shall throw every boy who is born into the Nile, while you shall let every girl live."

[20]"And our distress"—this is the persecution, as it says, "I also saw the distress that the Egyptians inflict upon them."

[19] וְאֶת־עֲמָלֵנוּ. אֵלּוּ הַבָּנִים. כְּמָה שֶׁנֶּאֱמַר: כָּל־הַבֵּן הַיִּלּוֹד הַיְאֹרָה תַּשְׁלִיכֻהוּ וְכָל־הַבַּת תְּחַיּוּן:

[20] וְאֶת־לַחֲצֵנוּ. זֶה הַדְּחַק. כְּמָה שֶׁנֶּאֱמַר: וְגַם רָאִיתִי אֶת־הַלַּחַץ אֲשֶׁר מִצְרַיִם לֹחֲצִים אֹתָם:

ARNOW (THE WORLD OF MIDRASH)

On the other hand, had Jacob returned to live with Laban, the outcome may have been the termination of Jacob's spiritual legacy through the adoption of his father-in-law's idolatry.

[3] *"Compelled by the word of God"* The Bible itself hints at Jacob's discomfort about going to Egypt. Why else would God suddenly appear to reassure him: "Fear not to go down to Egypt …" (Gen. 46:3). According to an ancient legend, without God's intervention, it would have required chains to drag Jacob down to Egypt. "This may be compared to a cow that resisted being dragged to the slaughterhouse. What did they do? They drew her calf before her, whereupon she followed, albeit unwillingly. Similarly, God brought Joseph there first, to entice Jacob to go despite himself."[2]

[4] *"Lived there"* The *Sifre on Deuteronomy* (*Piska* 301), an early parallel to the Haggadah's midrash, makes an intriguing comment: "Should you say that [Jacob] went [to Egypt] in order to assume the crown of kingship for himself, the Bible goes on to say [he only went to live there temporarily]." The term "crown of kingship *(keter malkhut)*, appears three times in the Bible, all in the Book of Esther, all in reference to figures—Vashti, Esther, and the king's horse—who wear the *keter malkhut* but whose real power is limited, to say the least.[3] The midrash puts a damper on any hope that Jacob or his descendants would long enjoy Joseph's quasi-regal status.

[6] *"Numbering seventy people"* The listing of the clan that went down to Egypt with Jacob totals sixty-six souls. Adding Joseph and his two sons brings the figure to sixty-nine and sets the midrashic stage for identifying the party who would bring the total to seventy. *Pirkei D'rabbi Eliezer* (eighth century) avers that it was God, as God says: "I Myself will go down with you …" (Gen. 46:4). Other traditions implicitly argue against the Bible's general exclusion of Jacob's female descendants from the list. One midrash

identifies the seventieth soul as Yocheved, mother of Moses, who "was born by the gates of Egypt." Another holds that Serach, daughter of Asher and the only female mentioned in the enumeration, was counted twice due to her extraordinary longevity! (*Gen. Rab.* 94:9).

⁷ *"Israel was distinct"* The second-century *Mekhilta D'rabbi Yishmael* attributes four virtues for which Israel merited redemption: they abstained from sexual relations with the Egyptians, refrained from tale-bearing, did not change their names, and did not give up their language.⁴ A twelfth-century midrash offers a different perspective on this passage: "Their clothing, food, and language were different from those of the Egyptians. They were marked and known as a nation apart and separate from the Egyptians" (*Lekach Tov, Ki Tavo*, 46a). This may allude to the realities of Jewish life in Islamic countries where Jews (and Christians) had to wear identifying clothing.

⁸ *"Very, very populous"* Midrashic sources make much of the fecundity of Jacob's descendants. *Exodus Rabbah* (1:8) imagines women giving birth to six or even a dozen children at once! More modestly, the ninth-century *Midrash on Proverbs* (19) interprets the phrase "very, very populous" *(bim'od m'od)* to mean "double the number there had been." A medieval Yemenite source (*Midrash Hagadol* on Exod. 1:7) reads that phrase to mean that as Israel "increased very greatly in the past, so it will again in the future." *Exodus Rabbah* connects Israel's fruitfulness with the preceding verse about the death of Joseph and his brothers: "Although Joseph and his brothers were dead, *their God was not dead.*" They might have thought God was dead because about two hundred years had elapsed between God's last appearance in the Book of Genesis (46:4) and Moses' encounter with God at the burning bush. But, as Israel fell into slavery, the miracle of procreation provided a glimmer of God's otherwise distant presence.

"The Children of Israel Were Fertile ..."
The Moriah Haggadah, Israel, 2005
Avner Moriah, illuminator

[9-10] *"Naked and bare ... live in your blood"* The allegorical interpretation of these verses from Ezekiel first appears in *Mekhilta D'rabbi Yishmael,* among the most ancient of all midrashim. The time had come for God to fulfill the promise of redemption made to Abraham at the "splitting covenant" or the Covenant between the Pieces (Gen. 15; see *My People's Passover Haggadah,* Volume 1, p. 221): "But as yet the Israelites had no religious duties to perform by which to merit redemption, as it says: '... you remained naked and bare (Ezek. 16:7),'" which means bare of any religious deeds. Therefore [God] assigned them two duties [*mitzvot*], the paschal sacrifice and circumcision, with which to merit redemption. For thus is it said, 'I passed by you and I saw you wallowing in your blood. And when I passed by you, and saw you wallowing in your blood [literally, "in your bloods," i.e., the blood of the paschal sacrifice and of circumcision], I said to you, Live!' ... (Ezek. 16:6).... For one cannot obtain rewards except for deeds."[5] This midrash anchors the Exodus in a covenantal context: God and humanity each play a role in bringing about redemption—then and now!

[12] *"The Egyptians were evil"* The midrash attributes a measure of responsibility for Israel's ordeal to "the Egyptians," not just Pharaoh. One view holds that the Pharaoh of the Exodus was not a new king—"A new king arose over Egypt who did not know Joseph" (Exod. 1:8)—but the same ruler just issuing new decrees. "[His court] said to him: Come and let us team up against this people. Pharaoh objected ... 'Were it not for Joseph [the Egyptian population] would be dead. How can you team up against them?' Since Pharaoh would not go along with them, they immediately dethroned him for three months. When Pharaoh saw that they had brought him down, he conceded: 'I will do whatever you say'" (*Tanchuma* on Exod. 1:8).

[12] *"Let us be clever about them"* Ever careful readers of the Bible, the Sages noticed that Pharaoh says, "Come let us deal craftily with *him,*" not "*them.*" Reading "him" as "Him," the third-century talmudic sage Rabbi Chamah bar Chaninah imagines Pharaoh strategizing how to outwit God. Knowing that God punishes measure for measure and that God had promised Noah never to destroy the entire world by a flood, Pharaoh "craftily" reckons that the Egyptians can drown the newborn Israelite males with impunity. But Pharaoh fails to appreciate that God's promise to Noah would not prevent God from visiting a flood upon a particular people, that is, drowning the Egyptians in the Red Sea (Sot. 11a). Trying to outwit God is not so smart after all.

[13] *"Taskmasters over them"* Again the singular rather than the plural ("taskmasters over *him*" instead of "*them*") provided an opportunity for midrash. "It should have read 'over them'! [The midrash now identifies "him" as Pharaoh.] It indicates that they brought a brick-mold and hung it round Pharaoh's neck; and every Israelite who complained that he was weak was told, 'Are you weaker than Pharaoh?' [As if to say, Pharaoh's not complaining, so why are you!]" (Sot. 11b). To humiliate the Israelites, clever Pharaoh winds up doing the work of a slave.

[14] *"With severity"* The Talmud (Sot. 11b) interprets *b'farekh,* "with severity," as *b'feh rakh,* "with a tender mouth"—"sweet words," as it were. *Midrash Aggadah* (twelfth century) elaborates: "The Egyptians said to them, 'For every brick you make each of

you will receive payment in gold.' So the Israelites worked quickly: one made a hundred bricks and another made two hundred. It was immediately decreed that from then on everyone had to produce that same number of bricks [without pay]." Another interpretation of "with severity": "They gave the men's work to the women and the women's work to the men" (Sot. 11b).

16 *"After a long time"* Sekhel Tov, a thirteenth-century midrash, highlights a subtle, subjective aspect of Israel's servitude in Egypt. "The period when the Israelites groaned under their burdens is called 'after a long time,' literally 'many days.' Thus Scripture says, 'Israel has gone for many days without the true God, without a priest to give instruction and without Torah' (2 Chronicles 15:3). When the Israelites serve in joy it is 'but a few days.' As it says, 'So Jacob served seven years for Rachel and they seemed to him but a few days because of his love for her' (Gen. 29:20)" (*Sekhel Tov* on Exod. 2:23). Work, even slavish, for a finite period and for a valued goal, speeds the passage of time. Labor with no end in sight and without purpose—devoid of spiritual content, as in the verse from Chronicles—slows time to a crawl.

17 *"God heard their groaning"* A wordless cry initiates the process of redemption. *Midrash Tanchuma* finds an unyielding, stubborn hope in that cry: "Rabbi Pinchas Hakohen son of Chamah said, 'If your hope is not fulfilled, hope again.' David said, 'Hope in God, be strong and strengthen your heart, hope in God' (Ps. 27:14). If your hope is fulfilled, great. If not, return and "hope in God" again. And David said, 'I put my hope [*kavo kiviti*] in God' (Ps. 40:2).[6] On account of hope 'God inclined toward me and heeded my cry' (Ps. 40:2). 'God heard their groaning, and God remembered His covenant with Abraham, with Isaac, and with Jacob' (Exod. 2:24)."[7] The Israelites cry out—in pain, but in hope.

18 *"Separation from worldly ways"* According to one legend, Moses' father, Amram, decreed the "separation from worldly ways,"[8] i.e. from conjugal relations, but he had the good sense to take the advice of his daughter, Miriam, and revoke the decree! "Amram was the greatest man of his generation; when he saw that the wicked Pharaoh had decreed, 'You shall throw every boy who is born into the Nile, while every girl you shall let live (Exod. 1:22), Amram said, 'In vain do we labor.' He divorced his wife. When the Israelites saw this, then all divorced their wives. His daughter said to him, 'Father, your decree is more severe than Pharaoh's; because Pharaoh decreed only against the males, whereas you have decreed against the males and females.... In the case of the wicked Pharaoh there is a doubt whether his decree will be fulfilled or not, whereas in your case, because you are righteous, your decree will certainly be fulfilled.... He remarried his wife; and the other men remarried theirs" (Sot. 12a).

19 *"The boys"* Pharaoh's drowning of "the boys" reminds us of Moses, a survivor, as it were, of Pharaoh's genocide. *Pirkei D'rabbi Eliezer* elaborates on the role Pharaoh's daughter plays as a rescuer. "The daughter of Pharaoh suffered terribly from leprosy. Unable to bathe in hot water, she came for a bath in the river. There she saw the baby Moses. She stretched out her hand, touched him and was healed. She said: 'This child is

righteous and I will preserve his life. One who preserves a life is as though one had kept alive the whole world' (Mishnah Sanhedrin 4:5). Therefore she merited life in this world and in the world to come."[9] *Midrash Hagadol* (on Gen. 23:1) counts Bithyah, or Batya as she is sometimes known, among the Bible's twenty-two most righteous women. Hence her name—daughter of God.

[20] *"The distress"* The *Midrash on Psalms* (42:5 and 43:1) poignantly illustrates the angry disappointment Jews have expressed over the generations when bereft of a redeeming hand—divine or human. It pictures Jews in later generations saying, "Why don't You work miracles for us as You did for our ancestors.... In Egypt, they obeyed just one commandment [slaying the paschal offering] and went free that very night; but what of me? I have obeyed all the commandments.... From what did You redeem our ancestors from Egypt? Was it not from the oppression of the Egyptians of which God said, 'And I have also seen the distress ...'? (Exod. 3:9). For me too, life is nothing but oppression by an enemy. Did You not send redemption via two redeemers [Moses and Aaron] to that generation...? Send two redeemers like them to this generation!"

———◆———

BALIN (MODERN HAGGADOT)

Seder, that found in the Mishnah. Mishnah Pesachim 10:4 instructs the Seder leader to gear his midrash to the level of the youngest present at the Seder: "The father instructs the son according to the understanding of his son ... he expounds from 'My father was a wandering Aramean' to the end of the passage." The Conservative Movement's 1982 Haggadah, *The Feast of Freedom*, takes this guidance to heart. It uses the prescribed verses from Deuteronomy as the basis for a midrash on the Exodus that elaborates on contemporary issues affecting the younger generation, namely the role of women. *The Feast of Freedom*'s midrash tells a talmudic story attributing the Exodus "to the merit of the righteous women of that generation" (Sot. 11b). The presence of this statement in the Conservative Haggadah coincided with the movement's embrace of egalitarianism. Work on the Haggadah began in 1977, the year the Jewish Theological Seminary created a commission to study the ordination of women. It adopted that position—not without some conflict—in 1979, the same year in which the movement published a preliminary draft of its new Haggadah.

[20] *"And our distress"* This bourgeois ideal is inscribed in *Seder Hagadah: Domestic Service for the Eve of Passover* (1898), a precursor to the Reform movement's first self-contained *Union Haggadah: Home Service for the Passover Eve* (1907), as in the following passage to be uttered by "the Mother of the house" in empathy with her Israelite foremothers in Egypt:

And oh, how void of comfort was the lot of the loving wives and mothers in Israel. While the men went out to heavy tasks, they were waiting at home with fear in their hearts, lest their loved ones should never return, and they become widowed and childless![2]

♦

BRETTLER (OUR BIBLICAL HERITAGE)

reprise of the early history of Israel (see *My People's Passover Haggadah*, Volume 1, p. 213), from Deuteronomy 26:5–8. (It continues through 26:9, with the gift of the land, but this is not relevant to the Haggadah.) The phrase explicated here, *arami oved avi*, has both syntactic and semantic difficulties, though most scholars understand it in its biblical context as "My father [= Jacob] was a fugitive Aramean" (so *NJPS*), and thus having nothing to do with Laban. It is very striking that in the Haggadah's reworking of these biblical passages, Moses, the human hero of the Haggadah, is never mentioned by name. The Bible sometimes depicts Moses as God's partner in redeeming Israel; for example, it is noteworthy that immediately before the Song of the Sea, Exodus 14:31 notes, "They believed in Adonai and in Moses His servant." It is likely that in the biblical period there was a cult of Moses, which is why the biblical text polemically states in Deuteronomy 34:6 concerning Moses, "And no one knows his burial place to this day." The Rabbis, like some biblical authors, are trying to ensure that Adonai, rather than Moses, remains the hero of the story.

[3] *"Compelled by the word of God"* This modifies the plain meaning of the text in Deuteronomy, which may suggest that Jacob left the Land of Israel voluntarily and makes it fit with Genesis 46:4, "I Myself [= Adonai] will go down with you to Egypt, and I Myself will also bring you back...."

[5] *"To live"* Quoting Genesis 47:4, which also uses the root *g-(w)-r*, "to sojourn," thereby showing that Deuteronomy and Genesis tell the same story.

[6] *"Seventy"* Citing Deuteronomy 10:22, which specifies exactly how "few in number" they were: seventy.

[7] *"Became a nation"* This follows an implicit assumption of the biblical story, that Israel maintained its ethnic identity in Egypt; how this was accomplished is not narrated in the biblical text.

[8] *"Fertile and multiplied"* Here the end of Deuteronomy 26:5 is filled in using Exodus 1:7; the latter uses language of Genesis 1 in describing the fertility of Israel, suggesting that Israel (rather than all of humanity) has fulfilled the divine blessing of Genesis 1:28, and thus has a special relationship with God.

[9–10] *"I made your population ... your blood"* Citing Ezekiel 16:7 and then 16:6. This difficult chapter from the prophet describes how Adonai found Israel as an abandoned foundling, wallowing in blood from birth, and then adopted Israel, and eventually married her when she attained puberty, described in 16:7–8. Uncharacteristically, the order of the verses in the biblical source is changed here (from vv. 6–7 to v. 7 and then v. 6). This allows the author to end with the section about "blood," further anchoring these verses to Passover, where blood plays a crucial role. This passage from Ezekiel needs to be connected to Deuteronomy 26, since it too is a short history of Israel, albeit in parable form. The connection between the word *varav*, "and numerous," of Deuteronomy 26:5, and *r'vavah*, "populous," of Ezekiel 16:7, facilitates this connection.

[11] *"The Egyptians were evil"* Deuteronomy 26:6, which will now be explicated phrase by phrase.

[12] *"Let us be clever"* Here the phrase is filled in by Exodus 1:10.

[13] *"They put taskmasters"* From Exodus 1:11.

[14] *"With severity"* From Exodus 1:13.

[15] *"We cried"* Deuteronomy 26:7, which will now be explicated phrase by phrase.

[16] *"And cried out"* From Exodus 2:23, which uses the verb *z-'-k* rather than Deuteronomy's *ts-'-k*. The two verbs seem identical in meaning, and this reflects a case where letters pronounced similarly may sometimes interchange.

[17] *"God heard"* Exodus 2:24.

[18] *"God saw the children of Israel and God knew"* Exodus 2:25. This is the last of three consecutive verses in Exodus used to explicate three consecutive phrases from the base text in Deuteronomy. Its appropriateness to this context is not obvious and is probably based on a sexual understanding of "affliction" (*'-n-h*) and of *yada*, "to know in the biblical sense."

[19] *"'And our work'—This is the boys"* The Hebrew word *amal* may refer to hard labor of the type typically performed by men, as in Ecclesiastes 2:22, "For what does a man get for all the toiling and worrying he does under the sun?" It is thus understood here to refer to males.

[19] *"You shall throw"* From the second half of Exodus 1:22.

[20] *"The distress"* The second half of Exodus 3:9, which uses the same word, *lachats*, as Deuteronomy.

———◆———

GILLMAN (THEOLOGICALLY SPEAKING)

passage (Deut. 26:5–8), interpreted word for word, now becomes the text for the telling of the story.

We have, then, three versions of the disgrace that marks the point of departure for the telling of the story of the Exodus: our ancestors' enslavement in Egypt, our pre-Abrahamic ancestors' idol worshiping, and Jacob's oppression at the hands of Laban. In contrast, there will be only one agreed-upon theme for the glory or the praise that will conclude the story. That theme will be redemption, mainly the redemption from Egypt, but with adumbrations of the ultimate, messianic redemption to come.

Of the three versions of disgrace, the second has nothing to do with our origins as a people and the third demands a tortuous translation of a biblical passage. The first, however, "We were slaves to Pharaoh in Egypt ..." is a clear and unambiguous biblical verse (Deut. 6:20). We can only wonder why the Mishnah did not choose this passage to recommend as the basic text with which to tell our story.

[6] *"Numbering seventy people"* The Hebrew word *nefesh*, "people," in this passage, is often mistranslated as "soul." The Bible itself does not know of a disembodied spiritual entity that is separate and distinct from the material body. In the Bible, *nefesh* and its parallel term *n'shamah* mean a living human being, a person. This passage indicates that a total of seventy people went down to Egypt. (See the more extended reference in Gen. 46:26–27.)

Only in the post-biblical tradition do these terms come to mean what we today refer to as "soul," distinct from body. That usage stems from Greek philosophy, which had a dualistic view of the human person: we are constituted as two separate entities: a material body, and a nonmaterial spirit or soul. In the Bible itself, the view is that the human person is a single, vivified body. Genesis 2:7 teaches that God created the human being by breathing "the breath of life" into a clod of earth. That "breath of life" is not a separate entity, but rather a spark that vivifies the clod of earth. When we die, that spark is simply extinguished. In the later tradition, death is the separation of soul from the body.

[17] *"Adonai heard our voice"* To theologians who believe that all of our God-talk is metaphorical, God does not literally "hear," nor does God literally "speak." But there is an added dimension to the relationship between speaking and hearing that is appropriate in this context. I find myself frequently speaking even when there is no one to hear me, or even when there are potential hearers present but I still feel that I am not being "heard."

There are many purposes to speaking. Sometimes, speaking is a form of doing. "I now pronounce you man and wife" is a doing; the couple are now married because of something that I have said/done. Sometimes, speaking is a form of self-expression; I speak, not to be heard, but to get something off my chest. In other instances, I often feel that I have been heard even though I have not uttered a word, because of my body language, for example. Dancers, musicians, and artists say a great deal without using words or uttering a sound.

The important implication of this statement is less that God "heard" but more that God "noticed."

[17] *"And God remembered His covenant"* Covenant, in Hebrew *b'rit*, is the linchpin of the Jewish religion. In its origins, it was an institution borrowed from ancient Near Eastern jurisprudence. It signified a treaty binding two kingdoms. The Bible transformed it into a commitment binding God and first Abraham, then Isaac, later still Jacob, and ultimately at Sinai, the Jewish people as a whole. In this final iteration, the covenant signified God and Israel's mutual commitment of loyalty to each other for eternity. The demands of the covenant were that Israel would obey God's commands, and God would protect Israel. But beyond these formal criteria, the covenant was also an expression of affection between the two parties. "I will be your God and you will be My people" is the biblical formulation. A more extended formulation of that intimate relationship is in Deuteronomy 26:16–19.

For God to remember the covenant with Abraham, Isaac, and Jacob, then, was to signify that God was now prepared to fulfill God's promise to protect and save Israel. The burning question, of course, is why now? Where was God during the years of enslavement and oppression? That question is not addressed, either in the Bible or in the Haggadah. See, for example, Exodus 6:4–5, where God is referred to as "now" hearing the moans of the oppressed Israelites and of remembering the covenant. Again, we can ask, "Why now?"

———◆———

GRAY (MEDIEVAL COMMENTATORS)

that at least some of the exposition of these verses in our Haggadah was ultimately drawn from the third-century *Sifre on Deuteronomy* (*Piska* 301).

[1] *"Laban the Aramean"* *Rashbetz* notes that we begin here not with Pharaoh, but with the first of the evildoers who plotted to destroy Israel—Laban, Jacob's father-in-law. *Rashbetz* explains that the Haggadah's understanding that "Laban attempted to uproot all" is drawn from Onkelos's Aramaic translation/commentary to Deuteronomy 26:5: "Laban the Aramean wished to destroy Father." Laban was worse than Pharaoh: while Pharaoh wished only to destroy the Israelite males (Exod. 1:22), Laban wished to destroy everyone, thus preventing the nation of Israel from ever coming into existence. Laban revealed this alleged preemptive genocidal intention to Jacob when he stated that, had God not warned him to speak neither "good nor evil" to Jacob, he could have done Jacob great evil (Gen. 31:29). Laban obviously did not succeed in his plan. But Abudarham explains that as to idolatrous nations, God considers even their evil *intentions* as if these were fully completed actions; they get no benefit of the doubt. (See Arnow, *My People's Passover Haggadah*, Volume 2, p. 4.) Hence, Deuteronomy 26:5 literally says that "an Aramean destroyed [*oved*] my father," instead of "an Aramean *wished* [no such word appears in the Hebrew] to destroy my father."

² *"He descended to Egypt"* *Ritba* logically asks what the connection is between Laban's desire to destroy Jacob and the latter's descent to Egypt. He explains that all the bad experiences the patriarchs had after the Covenant between the Pieces were part and parcel of the oppressions God warned Abraham about at the making of the covenant. Indeed, as *Ritba* points out, the patriarchs' lives were all very difficult after that covenant was made.

³ *"Compelled by the word of God"* The Hebrew phrase translated as "compelled by the word of God" is *anus al pi hadibbur* or, in some medieval versions, *anus al pi hadiber* ("compelled by the [divine] speaker"). This phrase, however worded, is a small midrash on the scriptural phrase "descended to Egypt." Abarbanel points out that many versions of the Haggadah known to him include this phrase, but others do not, notably *Rambam*'s Haggadah.

Abudarham—whose Haggadah did include the phrase—explains that Jacob went unwillingly to Egypt, as we can see from God's instruction to him not to be afraid of going there (Gen. 46:3). Hence, his descent to Egypt was "compelled by the word of God." *Ritba*, on the other hand, explains this reference to divine compulsion as a point in Jacob's favor: although Jacob knew about the oppression and slavery that his descendants would suffer, he did not refrain from going to Egypt in fulfillment of the divine decree.

⁷ *"'Became a nation'—This teaches that Israel was distinct there"* *Ritba*, Abudarham, and *Rashbetz* all maintain that the Israelites in Egypt were able to congregate, live together, and form themselves into one people distinct from the Egyptians. *Ritba* describes this as a "miracle of the Holy Blessed One," because by living together, the Israelites were able to help and strengthen each other. These commentators also focus on the literal meaning of *m'tsuyanim* (translated "distinct" in the Haggadah) as "distinguished": *Ritba* points out that the Israelites were distinguished in physical appearance, while *Rashbetz* holds that the Israelites were distinguished in that they did not conduct themselves like strangers while in Egypt, but like an honorable and proud nation. *Rashbetz* also claims that the Israelites were distinguished in that they did not cease studying Torah while in Egypt and continued to see themselves as descendants of Abraham.

⁹ *"I made your population like wildflowers"* This is from Ezekiel 16:7. Abudarham offers two interpretations of this verse: (1) The Israelites increased the way vegetation does, with scarcely any effort or trouble; or (2) just as vegetation grows back more thickly once it has been cut, so did Israel increase and multiply the more the Egyptians oppressed them.

⁹ *"You remained naked and bare"* Here the Haggadah quotes Ezekiel 16:7. Abudarham interprets this on the basis of the *Mekhilta D'rabbi Yishmael*—that at the time of the Exodus, the Israelites were "naked" of *mitzvot*.[1] Therefore God gave them two *mitzvot*—the blood of the Passover sacrifice and the blood of circumcision—so that they could "clothe" themselves with at least these two *mitzvot*. Abudarham claims that the reference in Ezekiel 16:6 to *damayikh* (literally, "your bloods," in the plural) alludes

to these two blood-oriented *mitzvot,* because the minimum plural is two. The two "bloods" thus alludes to the blood of the Passover sacrifice and the blood of circumcision.

[10] *"Wallowing in your blood"* Radak (R. David Kimchi Provence, c. 1160–1235) interprets this as a metaphor. The Israelites were actually "wallowing" in the mud and clay that they used to make bricks. The Egyptians were so demanding of the daily quota of bricks that the Israelites had no time to clean themselves but were constantly covered with mud. Nevertheless, God commanded them, "Live!" meaning that the Israelites should not think that this degrading, backbreaking labor would kill them, but should realize that despite all the filth and toil, they would still flourish like plants in the field.

[12] *"'The Egyptians were evil toward us'—as it says, let us be clever about them"* Rashbetz points out that in Deuteronomy 26:6, the verse reading "the Egyptians were evil toward us" is *vayare'u otanu hamitsrim,* while in Numbers 20:15, the similar verse reads *vayare'u lanu mitsrayim.* In Numbers, "us" is expressed as *lanu* (literally, "to us"), while in Deuteronomy it is *otanu. Rashbetz* explains the difference as follows: the point in Numbers 20:15 is that the evil the Egyptians did touched the Israelites' bodies directly (such as by working them mercilessly). Thus the verse uses *lanu* for "us," emphasizing that the evil happened directly *to* the Israelites. The point of the word *otanu* as "us" in Deuteronomy 26:6 is that the Egyptians thought the Israelites to be evil in and of themselves, even without doing anything *to* them. The Egyptians consequently plotted how to deal "cleverly" with the Israelites so as to neutralize their "evil." The plot they initially hatched, as noted by the Haggadah's quotation of Exodus 1:10, was to throw the Israelite baby boys into the Nile.

[12] *"Let us be clever about them"* (See J. Hoffman, *My People's Passover Haggadah,* Volume 2, p. 23.) Exodus 1:10 reads *havah nitchakmah lo,* which literally means "Come let us be clever about *him.*" If the verse refers to Israel, as seems to be the case, why is a singular pronoun used instead of the plural *lahem,* meaning "them"? *Rashbetz, Ritba,* and Abudarham all refer to the Talmud's discussion of this question at Sotah 11a. R. Chama b. R. Chanina responds that the Torah uses the singular *lo* to emphasize that the Egyptians' real desire was to settle accounts with God, not with Israel (see Arnow, *My People's Passover Haggadah,* Volume 2, p. 10). They were persecuting Israel in order to rebel against God—the ultimate "singular."

Rashbam explains the need for being clever as being that the Egyptians did not want the Israelites to take advantage of a hypothetical "fog of war" to leave Egypt. The Egyptians felt that it would be very damaging for Egypt to lose its slave population, which would result in their being a "cut-off [meaning 'diminished'] empire." *Rashbam's* reference to the Egyptians' fear of being a "cut-off empire" is an interesting allusion to Avodah Zarah 10b, where a Roman nobleman convinces a Roman emperor not to murder all the empire's Jews on the grounds that doing so will render Rome an impotent "cut-off empire." *Ramban* explains that Pharaoh had to be crafty in dealing with the Israelites for internal political reasons. He could not attack the Israelites directly with the sword, as that would be a flagrant breach of trust to a people who had been invited to Egypt by a previous Pharaoh. Moreover, the Egyptian public likely would not stand for it. Pharaoh thus began slowly and gradually to deprive the Israelites of freedom and life: he began with heavy taxes, moved on to secret commands to the midwives to murder Jewish baby boys, and then finally commanded the murder of the children publicly. From *Ramban's* description one gets acute psychological insight into how even a public that may be initially disinclined to sanction the sort of cruelty to which the Israelites were subjected could gradually become accustomed to it and eventually even participate in it with alacrity.

13 *"'[The Egyptians] afflicted us'—as it says, 'They put taskmasters over them to afflict them in their suffering'"* Ritba explains that the Israelites' servitude began in a most devious way. At first, the Egyptians began to erect fortified buildings for Pharaoh and asked the Israelites to help them.

16 *"'We cried out to Adonai our ancestor's God' ... the king of Egypt died, and the children of Israel sighed"* Rashbetz explains that the children of Israel, in their suffering, were hoping for the death of the "new king" of Egypt (Exod. 1:8) who had enslaved them. They hoped that perhaps with the accession of a new king they could return to the good old days of living in freedom. But when they saw that the king who succeeded the enslaving king was even worse than his predecessor, they realized they had no choice but to rely on God for deliverance.

17 *"'Adonai heard our voice' ... covenant with Abraham, with Isaac, and with Jacob"* Ritba and Rashbetz both point out that the Haggadah quotes verses about God's recollection of the patriarchs because the Israelites were not worthy by themselves to be redeemed. God redeemed them because God recalled the merit of the patriarchs. *Ritba* quotes *Exodus Rabbah* 1:36 and 17:3 to drive home this point: the *mashkof* or top beam over the door on which blood was to be placed stands for Abraham, while the *sh'tei hamezuzot* (two doorposts) placed perpendicular to it represent Isaac and Jacob. Yet the question remains: why didn't the Israelites deserve to be redeemed for their own sakes? *Rashbetz* points to Ezekiel 20:7–9, in which the prophet recalls that while in Egypt, the Israelites had begun to worship Egyptian gods. This serious breach of the Abrahamic covenant did not cause God to break the promise to redeem them, but did cause God to redeem them for reasons other than their own merit.

20 *"'And our distress'—this is the persecution"* Abudarham sensibly interprets the word *dochak* (persecution), which more literally means "pressure," as referring to the ongoing pressure of having to produce a fixed number of bricks. *Ritba*, however, has a more interesting explanation that is related to *Rashbetz's* reference to Ezekiel 20:7–9 (which refers to Israelite idolatry in Egypt). He points out that when the Egyptians saw that they could not put an end to the Israelites physically, they began to exert pressure on them so that the Israelites would take on the Egyptian religion and assimilate into Egyptian society. *Ritba* explicitly links *dochak* to *sh'mad*, the rabbinic term for a persecution calculated to cause Jews to apostatize out of Judaism. When God saw what

was happening, He realized that He had better redeem them before the process of assimilation went too far, given that the Israelites had already begun to adopt some Egyptian ways (as in Ezek. 20:7–9).

———◆———

GREEN (PERSONAL SPIRITUALITY)

change very slow and painful. All these can be found in the tale of Exodus and its aftermath. It is important to recognize these as the legacy of enslavement and not to let them dominate us even after we are free. We also need to recall them when dealing with other groups that are still struggling with the long aftermath of oppression. Suffering "brings out the bad in us" that often takes many generations to overcome.

———◆———

J. HOFFMAN (TRANSLATION)

perish was my father"). An additional complication comes from the way word order works in Hebrew. "X verbed Y" can also be written as "Y verbed X" (with the same meaning). For example, the Hebrew equivalent of "a cat saw Isaac" can also mean "Isaac saw a cat." Here, then, in addition to "my father was…," the Hebrew also supports a reading along the lines of "an Aramean destroyed my father." But context makes this (popular) translation unlikely. (Regarding Aram, Genesis notes that Rebekah and her family come from Aram—in modern-day Syria.)

2 *"Lived"* Commonly, "sojourned," to reinforce the notion that the Hebrews never considered Egypt "home," as taught by the Haggadah immediately below. The point of the midrash is that, here, the verb "live" refers to "sojourned." It is common for a word to mean different things in the same sentence. A similar example would be: "When I said my uncle builds houses, I didn't mean that he actually builds houses. He pays other people to build them." Similarly, here, we have something along the lines of "when it says he lived there, it doesn't mean he planted himself, it just means he lived there."

2 *"In small numbers"* This looks like a misplaced modifier (in Hebrew, so also in our English). Did he "live there in small numbers" or "descend there in small numbers"?

2 *"Large, mighty, and populous"* There are three adjectives in Hebrew. We assume that each represents a different aspect of the nation. *JPS*, by contrast ("great and very populous nation") interprets one of the adjectives as an adverb. The word for "populous" is more accurately translated "many," but "a many nation" is not English.

3 *"This means"* We add this phrase to help make the English clearer. See "Word of God," immediately below.

[3] *"Word of God"* Literally, just "the word." In general, in translating these passages, we face the dilemma of converting purposely terse Hebrew into prose that a modern English reader can understand. When we do, we create a clearer translation, but at the expense of the flavor of the original.

Languages frequently permit the sort of abbreviated prose we see in the Hebrew here, particularly in high-context settings. An English example might come from commuter reports on the radio during rush hour. When a radio announcer declares, "Mass transit's on or close," frequent listeners understand, "Mass transit is running on or close to schedule."

[4] *"Teaches"* This time, the Hebrew text contains the word "teaches." Above, we added the word to help the English reader understand the translation.

[4] *"Plant himself there"* Or maybe just "to stay there."

[5] *"They"* "They" are Joseph's brothers.

[5] *"Your servants'"* That is, "our." The quotation is from the Joseph narrative, in which characters frequently use the formal "your servants" to mean "us."

[5] *"Sir"* Hebrew, *na*, probably a sign of formality. We might also like "your highness" here. Obviously, we have no modern-English standardized form of address for ancient Egyptian officials.

[5] *"Stay"* In the sense of "stay overnight" at a hotel, not "remain."

[6] *"People"* Others, wrongly, "souls." In the Bible, *nefesh* referred to the physical aspect of life. For more, see *My People's Prayer Book*, Volume 1, *The Sh'ma and Its Blessings*, pp. 100, 102.

[6] *"Your"* Presumably, the people of Israel. The Hebrew (from Deut. 10:22) is actually singular, but we do find singular language in the Bible even when a group is being addressed.

[6] *"Made"* Literally, "placed."

[6] *"Populous"* The word is not exactly the same as the word for "populous" in verse 2, but it is clearly related. Above we saw an adjective; here we have the corresponding noun.

[7] *"Became a nation"* For reasons of English grammar, our translation has "became a [...] nation," with the adjectives before the noun. Hebrew, by contrast, puts adjectives after nouns, in this case, "became a nation large, mighty, and populous." The line-by-line midrash in Hebrew cannot match up perfectly with our English translation.

[7] *"Israel was"* We have two possible intents here, but both end up the same in American English. One is that the nation of Israel was distinct; for example, the entire nation lived separately. (In British English this would be "Israel were ....") Alternatively, the members of Israel could have been distinct, perhaps because they wore different

clothes, perhaps because they spoke a different language. (In British English, this would be "Israel were....")

⁷ *"Distinct"* Or perhaps, "singled out" or "noted."

⁸ *"Multiplied"* Or, "teeming" or "swarming." The Hebrew is the same verb used in Genesis regarding the living creatures that teem in the water and that swarm across the land. But "teeming" and certainly "swarming" have negative connotations that do not match the positive import of the passage. We would like something that suggests large hoards, but all of our English words (even "overran," "crowded," etc.) are inappropriately negative—even the word "hoard" seems oddly incompatible with a large group of good people.

⁸ *"Became very, very populous"* We would prefer an action verb here, instead of the weak "became…," but we need to repeat "populous," to capture the parallelisms in the Hebrew.

⁹ *"Your"* Jerusalem, symbolically representing Israel. In this case (from Ezekiel 16), Jerusalem is an unfaithful bride.

⁹ *"Population"* We choose "population" here because the word is related to, but slightly different from, the word for "populous," above.

⁹ *"Wildflowers"* Literally, field-plants. "Weeds" comes to mind, in terms of the degree of expansion, but because of the negative connotation of weeds, we choose "wildflowers" instead. (It is interesting to note that we cannot use the imagery of *how* these grow without also incorporating the imagery of *what* they are.) The point of this passage is that all sorts of good things happened to Jerusalem, yet she does not reciprocate. A few verses later in Ezekiel (in a passage that the Haggadah does not cite), Jerusalem will be called a harlot.

⁹ *"Grew into a woman"* The Hebrew here is enigmatic. "Grew into a woman" is one guess, consistent with the context. The Hebrew may literally mean, "you came into ornamental ornaments" (similar to the King James translation: "thou art come to excellent ornaments"), perhaps because grown women wear jewelry that girls do not. Interestingly, while our version of the Bible has two words with the Hebrew letter *dalet* in them *(ayin-dalet-yod* followed by *ayin-dalet-yod-yod-mem)*, the Septuagint seems to think both words have a *resh* in them and therefore translates the passage as though it involves cities, not ornaments or womanhood; the nineteenth-century English translation of the Greek reads, "[you did] enter into great cities."

⁹ *"Breasts grew"* Literally, "set" or "became firm." We would prefer a more poetic word, but nothing appropriate presents itself. *JPS*'s "became firm" loses the poetic impact by using two words, as does the King James "[were] fashioned." This image and the next refer to maturation.

⁹ *"Naked and bare"* Literally, "nakedness and bareness."

¹⁰ *"Passed by you"* From the Hebrew *avar*, which is unrelated to the Hebrew *pasach*, "pass over."

[10] *"Wallowing"* Others, "polluted" or "downtrodden." While we don't know exactly what the verb means, we can make a good guess from the verb form and from context.

[10] *"Blood"* Literally, "bloods." We obviously use the singular in English, here and below ("live in your blood"), but some midrashic material (see Arnow, *My People's Passover Haggadah*, Volume 2, p. 10) relies on the plural nature of the word.

[10] *"Live in your blood"* Frequently emended along the lines of *JPS*: "live in spite of your blood." Again (see immediately above), the word for "blood" is plural in Hebrew.

[12] *"Were evil toward us"* Or "treated us evilly."

[12] *"Them"* Literally, "it," that is, the "nation of the people of Israel." Languages differ in how they treat singular nouns that refer to groups of people. For example, in American English, a group "is," while in British English, the group "are." Exodus 1 (which we have here) refers both to "it" (here and below) and to "them," presumably the members of "it."

[12] *"In the event of a war"* Literally, either "if a war will take place" or "when a war will take place." We don't know if the original text assumes or merely hypothesizes a war.

[12] *"Having waged war, leave this land"* *JPS*: "[join our enemies] in fighting against us and rise from the ground." That is, *JPS* thinks that the phrase means "join in battle," while we think it refers to winning the war. It's not clear what *JPS*'s literal "rise from the ground" might mean. (A footnote there suggests: "perhaps from their wretched condition.") *NSRV* gives us the more likely "escape from the land." We, too, assume it means "leave the land," deliberately juxtaposing the literal "rise [from the land]" with the phrase "descend [to the land]" that describes how the Israelites arrived. The Septuagint agrees.

[13] *"Over them"* Literally, "over it," which contrasts with "their suffering." It is not clear if this transition from singular to plural mid-sentence has any significance.

[13] *"Afflict them"* Again, literally, "afflict it."

[13] *"They built"* Literally, "it" again.

[13] *"Garrison cities"* In keeping with *JPS*. "Fortified" is another possibility.

[14] *"With severity"* Below ("under duress," *My People's Passover Haggadah*, Volume 2, p. 82), for reasons of English grammar, we will translate the identical Hebrew as "under duress." Other translations include "ruthlessly." We do not know the exact nuances of the Hebrew.

[15] *"Misery"* Or "poverty."

[16] *"King"* Not "Pharaoh." Although there is a Hebrew word for "pharaoh," the text does not use it here.

[16] *"Sighed"* The English suggests a mild sound, which may be the point. Or we may have misunderstood the Hebrew.

[16] *"Because of"* Literally, "from," which in Hebrew can imply "because of."

[16] *"Because of"* Again, literally, "from." We repeat "because of" to make clear the connection between this line and the next, but in so doing, we remove an ambiguity from the Hebrew. While the Hebrew probably means what we have translated, another possibility is that the plea actually rose "from the work."

[17] *"Groaning"* Again, we have a Hebrew word whose exact connotations we do not know.

[18] *"Separation from worldly ways"* Hebrew, *derech erets*, that is, "the way of the land." Here it is a euphemism for sex, though now we use *derech erets* to mean "common courtesy."

[18] *"Knew"* The Hebrew "know" is frequently a euphemism for sex.

[19] *"This is"* Literally, "these are," but the plural "these" is merely a consequence of Hebrew grammar. Singular pronouns are usually used for a single referent, and plural for more than one, but sometimes the structure of language forces an exception. For example, in English, a customer requesting ten copies of a single piece of paper will generally refer to the single piece of paper but still ask for "ten of these," not "ten of this."

[19] *"Boys"* Or "sons."

———◆———

L. HOFFMAN (HISTORY)

1. "Begin with [Israel's initial] degradation *(mat'chil big'nut)*
2. Then conclude with praise [of God] *(m'sayem b'shevach)*
3. And seal [the whole thing] with [reference to Israel's] redemption *(v'chotem big'ulah)*"

At first, the way those instructions were carried out was left to each individual Seder leader. By the end of the second century, however, when the Mishnah was promulgated, more detailed instructions had been provided: the leader was to give a midrashic interpretation of Deuteronomy 26:5–8, a summary statement of Israel's sacred history, which was already well known, because in Temple times it had been recited (albeit without midrashic embellishment) by pilgrims bringing produce to Jerusalem.

How old is this midrash?

For many years, the predominant theory dated it to the third century BCE, when the Ptolemies in Egypt and the Seleucids in Babylonia (Iraq) vied for rule over Palestine. During the third century BCE, the Ptolemies were in control. Since the midrash identifies "Laban the Aramean" as worse than Pharaoh, and since biblical Aram corresponded to Seleucid territory, the midrash was explained as a political move to pacify the ruling Egyptian authorities. We can call this the "polemical approach" to understanding midrash.

Much as the argument sounds appealing, it is almost certainly wrong. Among other things, it dates our particular midrash far before any other instance of the midrash genre and even before the Rabbis who created it.

So a second school of thought, which we can call "textual," arose. It assumed that in order to date a particular midrash, we would need to find evidence of it in parallel literature and then adjust our dating to no earlier than whenever that parallel literature came into being. Now, in fact, the tannaitic (prior to 200 CE) composition *Sifre on Deuteronomy* does contain parallels to some of the lessons in the Haggadah midrash; but other parts are not found at all, except in our Haggadah, which was not written down until the geonic age (c. 750–1034). It followed that the midrash as we have it came into being no earlier than then. It included some second-century lessons plus later ones that had become attached over time. Most scholars agree with this solution.

Here we encounter another school of thought: the "ritual approach." The Haggadah midrash was not composed as literature to read and pour over—like the Talmud, say, or philosophy, or modern novels. It came about as part of a ritualized script of prayer called the Haggadah, which circulated orally for centuries. There is, therefore, no reason to expect early confirmatory evidence from external texts. Even if it was finally written down only in the geonic period, much—or even all—of it may have circulated orally well before that.

It is not unusual for early midrash to display polemical intent; tannaitic midrash frequently does so. We should, therefore, at least entertain the possibility that its salient lessons are polemical in nature and fit the period between 70 and 200 CE.

Midrash is an art, so it follows certain technical rules that make it what it is, the way a Shakespearean play has five acts, or a sonnet fourteen lines—for no other reason than convention. So we should ignore the purely technical aspects of the midrash and concentrate on the content of those parts that cannot be thus explained—especially if that content surprises us because it surpasses, and even contradicts, the biblical account. If we do that, we can see some polemic applicable to the period after the destruction of the Temple in 70 CE.

There are three such lessons:

1. That Laban the Aramean was even worse than Pharaoh—an odd claim for a holiday ritual designed specifically to recall freedom from Pharaoh.
2. That Jacob "descended to Egypt" only when forced to do so "by the word of God [*al pi hadibur*]" (v. 3), and that, even compelled as he was, he agreed only to stay there temporarily, not to settle in permanently. This too contradicts the biblical story, which has Jacob settling in Egypt without complaint, ecstatic over finding Joseph and receiving rich arable land on which to build a future.
3. That the Israelites who went there became *m'tsuyanim*, "distinct" (v. 7). While not contradicting the biblical account, it is at least interesting that the midrash, gratuitously, as it were, emphasizes this claim.

All this fits the circumstances immediately post–70 CE.

On the way to routing the Jews, the Romans destroyed the rich farmland of the Galil (Galilee), causing a famine. Many Jews fled, especially to Egypt, which became the chief diasporan community in the first and second centuries CE. Palestinian leaders, most notably Rabban Gamaliel II, who served as the Patriarch around 90 CE, fought to retain the centrality of the Land of Israel, despite the growing exodus.

Our midrash uses Jacob as the model—but only by twisting the tale. Jacob too moved to Egypt when faced with famine, where, indeed, he became "distinct"—but he must have been compelled to leave by God; and even then, he intended to return as soon as possible. The lesson for latter-day Jacobs in devastated Palestine was obvious. Without a mandate from God (an impossibility), they should stay and rebuild, not leave for Egypt, where conditions might allow even a poor immigrant to become rich and "distinct." And if they had already left, they might consider the model of staying briefly but never settling in.

In addition, the Hebrew *arami* (Aramean) can be read midrashically as *romi* (Roman), and *oved* (wandering) can become *ibed*, implying "tried to destroy," giving us the lesson that an *arami* who tried to destroy us was worse than Pharaoh. The entire issue of famine and forced emigration came about only because the *romi* (the Romans) did indeed outdo Pharaoh by trying to eradicate everyone.

[2] *"A wandering Aramean"* Above, we saw degradation defined as physical ("We were slaves," *My People's Passover Haggadah*, Volume 1, p. 161) and spiritual ("At first, our ancestors engaged in false service," Volume 1, p. 213). We now come to a biblical verse that suggests a third kind of degradation: social.

The Israelites are "wandering Jews," which is to say, belonging nowhere. Social degradation may not seem as serious as the other two. But social exclusion is insidious. It creates the illusion that the despised people are either superior (and therefore dangerous) or inferior (a lower order of humanity). Since they are dangerous, they should be enslaved or even eradicated; since they are less than human, it becomes morally excusable to do either. The midrash then creatively misreads the verse to demonstrate how truthful that is. It transforms the biblical account of wandering into the midrashic tale of slavery, the ultimate consequence of social degradation.

We know this lesson best from the Nazis, who painted Jews as Germany's most brilliant enemy, but also with the physiognomy of apes rather than of fully evolved human beings. That dual portrayal had its origins in nineteenth-century anti-Semitism, a racial doctrine that ensured the inability of Jews to be anything but outsiders.

The racist German intellectual Heinrich von Treitschke (1834–1896) published a tract explaining why Jews should be denied civil rights. Jewish philosopher Hermann Cohen (1842–1918) argued just the opposite on the grounds that more than anyone, Jews know the demeaning experience of marginality—ever being "a stranger in a strange land." Our history has outfitted us uniquely to appreciate the messianic vision of a time when a single God of the world is proclaimed the sole true ruler over all, so that no one ever again need suffer the social degradation that inevitably provides an excuse for "justified" enslavement.

[9] *"You attained to womanhood"* The two proof-text verses (vv. 16:7 and 6) come from a remarkable section of the book of Ezekiel. But here they are reversed. In Ezekiel, the prophet compares Israel to an unwanted baby left to die. God comes along, sees the baby wallowing in her birth-blood, rescues her and raises her to womanhood.

Verse 7 (the first verse here, but the second in the Bible) was chosen as a proof text because its first word *r'vavah* sounds like the last word of the midrash, *rav*. In addition, the content demonstrates how Israel (the metaphoric woman) grows even in harsh circumstances. No wonder Israel (the People) became many (*rav*).

But why was verse 6 added? It has nothing to do with the midrash.

It seems to be a late addition, often attributed to Isaac Luria of Tsfat (the *Ari*). Whether by Luria or not, what suggested the passage was probably a midrash connected with it, on the theme of blood. Our verse says, "I said to you, live in spite of your blood. Yea, I said to you, live in spite of your blood." Already in the second century, the verse was being creatively mistranslated, as "Live *by means of* your blood. Since that phrase appears twice in the verse, the Rabbis presumed it referred to two kinds of blood whereby Israel will be saved: the blood of circumcision (*brit milah*) and the blood of the paschal offering (*pesach*). Reference to the latter suggested its inclusion here.

In its original locus, the midrash polemicized against the Christian claim that we are saved by faith, not by works. (See, for example, Arnow, *My People's Passover Haggadah*, Volume 2, p. 10, "Naked and bare.") The larger midrash therefore begins with yet another verse from Ezekiel, the one following the two we have here, where God says, "You were naked and bare," interpreting it as implying that Israel was "naked of mitzvot," without good works by which they might be saved. So God supplied two commandments, circumcision and the Passover offering, thereby providing enough works to be saved.

Verse 6 (regarding the blood that saves) is said also as part of the liturgy for *brit milah*.

The idea that blood saves came from the story of the Exodus, where blood of the paschal lamb was smeared on the doorways of the Israelite houses, protecting Israelite firstborn from death during the final plague. The sacrificial cult too (which saved) called for blood, and in Christian lore, Jesus (the second paschal lamb) saves by shedding his blood on the cross.

Interestingly, Christianity did away with circumcision, and emphasized instead the blood of Jesus, its paschal lamb. Jews eventually played down the value of the lamb's blood (which, in any event, was no longer being offered after the Temple's fall), but emphasized the blood of circumcision. The Talmud maintains that were it not for the *blood* of circumcision, heaven and earth would topple. A boy born circumcised has to have a drop of *blood* drawn.

Jewish ritual still retains these references to circumcision blood, but modern Jews who recite the passages in question no longer associate them with the ancient and medieval belief that once underlay them.

———◆———

ZIERLER (FEMINIST VOICES)

barren, to arrogate control of the bodies of his kin to himself. When Jacob arrives in Haran, Laban declares Jacob his own flesh and blood, a figurative term that Laban makes literal. First he barters his daughters' bodies in exchange for Jacob's work. And once they are married, he treats them all like foreign slaves, as Rachel and Leah complain in Genesis 31:15, "Are we not considered strangers to him, for he sold us."

[9] *"'Populous'—as it says, I made your population like wildflowers"* This midrash on the fecundity of the people refers to Ezekiel 16, which includes a whole array of disturbing feminine personifications of the people of Israel and equally disturbing images of God. The prophesy begins with a description of the people as an abandoned female infant, wallowing in the blood of afterbirth. God passes by, sees the infant wallowing in her birth blood, and says, "In your blood live, in your blood live." God thus becomes like a father to this baby girl, caring for her and causing her to flourish; when she matures He discerns her budding womanhood and enters (incestuously) into a marital covenant with the girl, until she begins to whore with others and God casts her out again. At best, the feminized Israel is a helpless infant and a kept woman; at worst, she is humanity reduced to her most vulnerable and execrable state.

The verse that is cited at the end of this midrash, "I said to you, live in your blood," is recited as part of the *b'rit milah* liturgy; remarkably, the Rabbis transform a verse spoken to a bloody female infant, symbolic of the Jewish People, into a liturgical phrase celebrating the introduction of a male baby into a male-only blood covenant.

One way to make this set of midrashim more palatable for feminists is to move away from the treatment of female sexuality and fecundity as an allegory for the people of Israel. Instead, the word *varav*, "populous," can become an opportunity to discuss the heroism of the midwives Shifra and Puah, who saved the male infants and helped the Israelites live rather than die by the blood of childbirth. Likewise, it can become an opportunity to applaud the heroism of those men and women in ancient Egypt, as well as in later historical periods, who defied the persecution of their ages and persisted in having families despite visible dangers.

[19] *"'And our work'—this is the boys, as it says, 'You shall throw every boy who is born into the Nile'"* This midrash on the word *amalenu* understands the word as connoting the loss of sons due to Pharaoh's decree against the Israelite sons. The underlying logic of this midrash is an equation of sons with a labor force, resulting in a devaluation of woman's ability to work and contribute. It is lamentable that the Rabbis adopt this tack, since it mimics Pharaoh's thinking about the irrelevance of women in Exodus 1–2.

◆ ◆ ◆

10. THE ROLE OF GOD

A. God Brought Us Out of Egypt—Not by an Angel …"

[1]"Adonai brought us out of Egypt with a strong hand and with an outstretched arm and with great awe and with signs and with wonders."

[2]"Adonai brought us out of Egypt"—not by an angel and not by a seraph and not by a messenger, but rather the Holy One of Blessing Himself. As it says, [3]"I will pass through the Land of Egypt this very night and slay every first-born male in the Land of Egypt, from human to beast, and I will bring judgment upon all the gods of Egypt, I, Adonai."

[4]"I will pass through the Land of Egypt"—I and not an angel. "And slay every first-born male"—I and not a seraph. "I will bring judgment upon all the gods of Egypt"—I and not the messenger. "I, Adonai"—I am He, and none other.

[5]"With a strong hand"—this is the blight, as it says, "The hand of Adonai is upon livestock in your field and upon your horses, upon your donkeys, upon your camels, upon your cattle, and upon your sheep, a very severe blight."

[6]"And with an outstretched arm"—this is the sword, as it says, "His sword drawn in his outstretched hand against Jerusalem."

[7]"And with great awe"—this is the revelation of the *Shekhinah*, as it says, "Or has any god tried to come and take for himself a nation from among another nation with trials, with signs, with wonders, with war, and with a strong hand and with an outstretched arm and with great awe as Adonai your God did with you in Egypt before your very eyes."

וַיּוֹצִאֵנוּ יְיָ מִמִּצְרַיִם בְּיָד חֲזָקָה [1]
וּבִזְרֹעַ נְטוּיָה וּבְמֹרָא גָּדֹל וּבְאֹתוֹת
וּבְמֹפְתִים: [2]וַיּוֹצִאֵנוּ יְיָ מִמִּצְרַיִם. לֹא
עַל יְדֵי מַלְאָךְ. וְלֹא עַל יְדֵי שָׂרָף. וְלֹא
עַל יְדֵי שָׁלִיחַ. אֶלָּא הַקָּדוֹשׁ בָּרוּךְ הוּא
בִּכְבוֹדוֹ וּבְעַצְמוֹ. שֶׁנֶּאֱמַר: [3]וְעָבַרְתִּי
בְאֶרֶץ מִצְרַיִם בַּלַּיְלָה הַזֶּה וְהִכֵּיתִי
כָל־בְּכוֹר בְּאֶרֶץ מִצְרַיִם מֵאָדָם וְעַד
בְּהֵמָה וּבְכָל־אֱלֹהֵי מִצְרַיִם אֶעֱשֶׂה
שְׁפָטִים אֲנִי יְיָ: [4]וְעָבַרְתִּי בְאֶרֶץ
מִצְרַיִם. אֲנִי וְלֹא מַלְאָךְ. וְהִכֵּיתִי כָל־
בְּכוֹר. אֲנִי וְלֹא שָׂרָף. וּבְכָל־אֱלֹהֵי
מִצְרַיִם אֶעֱשֶׂה שְׁפָטִים. אֲנִי וְלֹא
הַשָּׁלִיחַ. אֲנִי יְיָ. אֲנִי הוּא וְלֹא אַחֵר:
[5]בְּיָד חֲזָקָה. זוֹ הַדֶּבֶר. כְּמָה שֶׁנֶּאֱמַר:
הִנֵּה יַד יְיָ הוֹיָה בְּמִקְנְךָ אֲשֶׁר בַּשָּׂדֶה
בַּסּוּסִים בַּחֲמֹרִים בַּגְּמַלִּים בַּבָּקָר
וּבַצֹּאן דֶּבֶר כָּבֵד מְאֹד: [6]וּבִזְרֹעַ נְטוּיָה.
זוֹ הַחֶרֶב. כְּמָה שֶׁנֶּאֱמַר: וְחַרְבּוֹ שְׁלוּפָה
בְּיָדוֹ נְטוּיָה עַל יְרוּשָׁלָיִם: [7]וּבְמֹרָא
גָּדֹל. זֶה גִּלּוּי שְׁכִינָה. כְּמָה שֶׁנֶּאֱמַר:
אוֹ הֲנִסָּה אֱלֹהִים לָבוֹא לָקַחַת לוֹ גוֹי
מִקֶּרֶב גּוֹי בְּמַסֹּת בְּאֹתֹת וּבְמוֹפְתִים
וּבְמִלְחָמָה וּבְיָד חֲזָקָה וּבִזְרוֹעַ נְטוּיָה
וּבְמוֹרָאִים גְּדֹלִים כְּכֹל אֲשֶׁר עָשָׂה
לָכֶם יְיָ אֱלֹהֵיכֶם בְּמִצְרַיִם לְעֵינֶיךָ:

[8]"And with signs"—this is the staff, as it says, "Take this staff in your hand that you might use it for signs."

[9]"And with wonders"—this is the blood, as it says, "I will put wonders in the sky and upon the earth …"

‏וּבְאֹתוֹת. זֶה הַמַּטֶּה. כְּמָה שֶׁנֶּאֱמַר: וְאֶת־הַמַּטֶּה הַזֶּה תִּקַּח בְּיָדֶךָ אֲשֶׁר תַּעֲשֶׂה־בּוֹ אֶת־הָאֹתֹת: ‎[9]וּבְמֹפְתִים. זֶה הַדָּם. כְּמָה שֶׁנֶּאֱמַר: וְנָתַתִּי מוֹפְתִים בַּשָּׁמַיִם וּבָאָרֶץ …[8]

B. God's Punishing Might: The Plagues in Egypt and at the Sea

Spill a drop of wine from the cups as each of the following is mentioned: "blood," "fire," and "pillars."

[10]"… blood and fire and pillars of smoke." [11]Also: "with a strong hand"—this is two; "with an outstretched arm"—this is two; "with great awe"—this is two; "with signs"—this is two; "with wonders"—this is two.

[12]These are the ten plagues that the Holy One of Blessing brought upon the Egyptians in Egypt. [13]And these are the plagues:

‏דָּם וָאֵשׁ וְתִימְרוֹת עָשָׁן: ‎[11]דָּבָר אַחֵר. בְּיָד חֲזָקָה שְׁתַּיִם. וּבִזְרֹעַ נְטוּיָה שְׁתַּיִם. וּבְמֹרָא גָּדֹל שְׁתַּיִם. וּבְאֹתוֹת שְׁתַּיִם. וּבְמֹפְתִים שְׁתַּיִם. ‎[12]אֵלּוּ עֶשֶׂר מַכּוֹת שֶׁהֵבִיא הַקָּדוֹשׁ בָּרוּךְ הוּא עַל הַמִּצְרִים בְּמִצְרָיִם. ‎[13]וְאֵלּוּ הֵן:[10]

Spill a drop of wine from the cups as each of the ten plagues is named.

[14]Blood	דָּם[14]
[15]Frogs	צְפַרְדֵּעַ[15]
[16]Lice	כִּנִּים[16]
[17]Swarms	עָרוֹב[17]
[18]Blight	דֶּבֶר[18]
[19]Boils	שְׁחִין[19]
[20]Hail	בָּרָד[20]
[21]Locusts	אַרְבֶּה[21]
[22]Darkness	חֹשֶׁךְ[22]
[23]Slaying of the first-born	מַכַּת בְּכוֹרוֹת:[23]

Spill one more drop of wine from the cups with the mention of each word in the following mnemonic.

24Rabbi Judah would make them into a mnemonic: *D'tsakh Adash B'achav.*

רַבִּי יְהוּדָה הָיָה נוֹתֵן בָּהֶם סִמָּנִים.
דְּצַ"ךְ עַדַ"שׁ בְּאַחַ"ב:

25Rabbi Yosei the Galilean says, "How do we know that the Egyptians suffered ten plagues in Egypt, and fifty plagues by the sea? 26In Egypt—what does it say? 'The magicians told Pharaoh: This is the finger of God.' 27By the sea—what does it say? 'Israel saw the great hand that God wielded against Egypt, and the nation feared Adonai and believed in Adonai and in Moses His servant.' 28If the Egyptians suffered ten plagues by God's finger in Egypt, they suffered fifty plagues by God's hand by the sea."

רַבִּי יוֹסֵי הַגְּלִילִי אוֹמֵר. מִנַּיִן אַתָּה אוֹמֵר שֶׁלָּקוּ הַמִּצְרִים בְּמִצְרַיִם עֶשֶׂר מַכּוֹת וְעַל הַיָּם לָקוּ חֲמִשִּׁים מַכּוֹת? 26בְּמִצְרַיִם מָה הוּא אוֹמֵר: וַיֹּאמְרוּ הַחַרְטֻמִּם אֶל פַּרְעֹה אֶצְבַּע אֱלֹהִים הוּא: 27וְעַל הַיָּם מָה הוּא אוֹמֵר: וַיַּרְא יִשְׂרָאֵל אֶת־הַיָּד הַגְּדֹלָה אֲשֶׁר עָשָׂה יְיָ בְּמִצְרַיִם וַיִּירְאוּ הָעָם אֶת־יְיָ וַיַּאֲמִינוּ בַּיְיָ וּבְמֹשֶׁה עַבְדּוֹ: 28כַּמָּה לָקוּ בְאֶצְבַּע עֶשֶׂר מַכּוֹת. אֱמוֹר מֵעַתָּה בְּמִצְרַיִם לָקוּ עֶשֶׂר מַכּוֹת וְעַל הַיָּם לָקוּ חֲמִשִּׁים מַכּוֹת:

29Rabbi Eliezer says, "How do we know that each and every plague that the Holy One of Blessing brought upon the Egyptians in Egypt was really four plagues? 30It says, 'He sent them His fierce fury, anger, wrath, sorrow, and a contingent of evil angels.' 31'Anger' is one, 'wrath' is two, 'sorrow' is three, and 'a contingent of evil angels' is four. 32So in Egypt they suffered forty plagues, and by the sea they suffered two hundred plagues."

רַבִּי אֱלִיעֶזֶר אוֹמֵר. מִנַּיִן שֶׁכָּל־מַכָּה וּמַכָּה שֶׁהֵבִיא הַקָּדוֹשׁ בָּרוּךְ הוּא עַל הַמִּצְרִים בְּמִצְרַיִם הָיְתָה שֶׁל אַרְבַּע מַכּוֹת? 30שֶׁנֶּאֱמַר: יְשַׁלַּח־בָּם חֲרוֹן אַפּוֹ עֶבְרָה וָזַעַם וְצָרָה מִשְׁלַחַת מַלְאֲכֵי רָעִים: 31עֶבְרָה אַחַת. וָזַעַם שְׁתַּיִם. וְצָרָה שָׁלֹשׁ. מִשְׁלַחַת מַלְאֲכֵי רָעִים אַרְבַּע. 32אֱמוֹר מֵעַתָּה בְּמִצְרַיִם לָקוּ אַרְבָּעִים מַכּוֹת. וְעַל הַיָּם לָקוּ מָאתַיִם מַכּוֹת:

[33]Rabbi Akiva says, "How do we know that each and every plague that the Holy One of Blessing brought upon the Egyptians in Egypt was really five plagues? [34]It says, 'He sent them His fierce fury, anger, wrath, sorrow, and a contingent of evil angels.' [35]'His fierce fury' is one, 'anger' is two, 'wrath' is three, 'sorrow' is four, and 'contingent of evil angels' is five. [36]So in Egypt they suffered fifty plagues, and by the sea they suffered two hundred fifty plagues."

c. God's Saving Might: *Dayyenu*

[37]How many degrees of goodness has God bestowed upon us!

[38]If He had brought us out of Egypt and not brought judgment upon them … Enough!

[39]If He had brought judgment upon them and not upon their gods … Enough!

[40]If He had brought judgment upon their gods and not killed their first-born … Enough!

[41]If He had killed their first-born and not given us their wealth … Enough!

[42]If He had given us their wealth and not split the sea for us … Enough!

[33]רַבִּי עֲקִיבָא אוֹמֵר. מִנַּיִן שֶׁכָּל־מַכָּה וּמַכָּה שֶׁהֵבִיא הַקָּדוֹשׁ בָּרוּךְ הוּא עַל הַמִּצְרִים בְּמִצְרַיִם הָיְתָה שֶׁל חָמֵשׁ מַכּוֹת? [34]שֶׁנֶּאֱמַר: יְשַׁלַּח־בָּם חֲרוֹן אַפּוֹ עֶבְרָה וָזַעַם וְצָרָה מִשְׁלַחַת מַלְאֲכֵי רָעִים: [35]חֲרוֹן אַפּוֹ אַחַת. עֶבְרָה שְׁתַּיִם. וָזַעַם שָׁלֹשׁ. וְצָרָה אַרְבַּע. מִשְׁלַחַת מַלְאֲכֵי רָעִים חָמֵשׁ. [36]אֱמוֹר מֵעַתָּה בְּמִצְרַיִם לָקוּ חֲמִשִּׁים מַכּוֹת. וְעַל הַיָּם לָקוּ חֲמִשִּׁים וּמָאתַיִם מַכּוֹת:

דַּיֵּנוּ

[37]כַּמָּה מַעֲלוֹת טוֹבוֹת לַמָּקוֹם עָלֵינוּ:

[38]אִלּוּ הוֹצִיאָנוּ מִמִּצְרַיִם.
וְלֹא עָשָׂה בָהֶם שְׁפָטִים   דַּיֵּנוּ:

[39]אִלּוּ עָשָׂה בָהֶם שְׁפָטִים.
וְלֹא עָשָׂה בֵאלֹהֵיהֶם   דַּיֵּנוּ:

[40]אִלּוּ עָשָׂה בֵאלֹהֵיהֶם.
וְלֹא הָרַג בְּכוֹרֵיהֶם   דַּיֵּנוּ:

[41]אִלּוּ הָרַג בְּכוֹרֵיהֶם.
וְלֹא נָתַן לָנוּ אֶת־מָמוֹנָם   דַּיֵּנוּ:

[42]אִלּוּ נָתַן לָנוּ אֶת־מָמוֹנָם.
וְלֹא קָרַע לָנוּ אֶת־הַיָּם   דַּיֵּנוּ:

43If He had split the sea for us and not brought us through it on dry land ... Enough!

43אִלּוּ קָרַע לָנוּ אֶת־הַיָּם.
וְלֹא הֶעֱבִירָנוּ בְּתוֹכוֹ בֶּחָרָבָה   דַּיֵּנוּ:

44If He had brought us through it on dry land and not plunged our enemies into it ... Enough!

44אִלּוּ הֶעֱבִירָנוּ בְּתוֹכוֹ בֶּחָרָבָה.
וְלֹא שִׁקַּע צָרֵינוּ בְּתוֹכוֹ   דַּיֵּנוּ:

45If He had plunged our enemies into it and not provided for our needs in the desert for forty years ... Enough!

45אִלּוּ שִׁקַּע צָרֵינוּ בְּתוֹכוֹ.
וְלֹא סִפֵּק צָרְכֵּנוּ
בַּמִּדְבָּר אַרְבָּעִים שָׁנָה   דַּיֵּנוּ:

46If He had provided for our needs in the desert for forty years and not fed us with manna ... Enough!

46אִלּוּ סִפֵּק צָרְכֵּנוּ
בַּמִּדְבָּר אַרְבָּעִים שָׁנָה
וְלֹא הֶאֱכִילָנוּ אֶת־הַמָּן   דַּיֵּנוּ:

47If He had fed us with manna and not given us Shabbat ... Enough!

47אִלּוּ הֶאֱכִילָנוּ אֶת־הַמָּן.
וְלֹא נָתַן לָנוּ אֶת־הַשַּׁבָּת   דַּיֵּנוּ:

48If He had given us Shabbat and not brought us together before Mount Sinai ... Enough!

48אִלּוּ נָתַן לָנוּ אֶת־הַשַּׁבָּת.
וְלֹא קֵרְבָנוּ לִפְנֵי הַר סִינַי   דַּיֵּנוּ:

49If He had brought us together before Mount Sinai and not given us the Torah ... Enough!

49אִלּוּ קֵרְבָנוּ לִפְנֵי הַר סִינַי.
וְלֹא נָתַן לָנוּ אֶת־הַתּוֹרָה   דַּיֵּנוּ:

50If He had given us the Torah and not brought us into the Land of Israel ... Enough!

50אִלּוּ נָתַן לָנוּ אֶת־הַתּוֹרָה.
וְלֹא הִכְנִיסָנוּ לְאֶרֶץ יִשְׂרָאֵל   דַּיֵּנוּ:

51If He had brought us into the Land of Israel and not built us the Temple ... Enough!

51אִלּוּ הִכְנִיסָנוּ לְאֶרֶץ יִשְׂרָאֵל.
וְלֹא בָנָה לָנוּ אֶת־בֵּית הַבְּחִירָה   דַּיֵּנוּ:

[52]How much more goodness, multiple and multiplied, has God bestowed upon us, [53]for He: brought us out of Egypt; [54]and brought judgment upon them; [55]and brought judgment upon their gods; [56]and killed their first-born; [57]and gave us their wealth; [58]and split the sea for us; [59]and brought us through it on dry land; [60]and plunged our enemies into it; [61]and provided for our needs in the desert for forty years; [62]and fed us with manna; [63]and gave us Shabbat; [64]and brought us together before Mount Sinai; [65]and gave us the Torah; [66]and brought us into the Land of Israel; [67]and built us the Temple to atone for our transgressions.

[52]עַל אַחַת כַּמָּה וְכַמָּה טוֹבָה כְפוּלָה וּמְכֻפֶּלֶת לַמָּקוֹם עָלֵינוּ. [53]שֶׁהוֹצִיאָנוּ מִמִּצְרַיִם. [54]וְעָשָׂה בָהֶם שְׁפָטִים. [55]וְעָשָׂה בֵאלֹהֵיהֶם. [56]וְהָרַג אֶת־בְּכוֹרֵיהֶם. [57]וְנָתַן לָנוּ אֶת־מָמוֹנָם. [58]וְקָרַע לָנוּ אֶת־הַיָּם. [59]וְהֶעֱבִירָנוּ בְתוֹכוֹ בֶּחָרָבָה. [60]וְשִׁקַּע צָרֵינוּ בְּתוֹכוֹ. [61]וְסִפֵּק צָרְכֵּנוּ בַּמִּדְבָּר אַרְבָּעִים שָׁנָה. [62]וְהֶאֱכִילָנוּ אֶת־הַמָּן. [63]וְנָתַן לָנוּ אֶת־הַשַּׁבָּת. [64]וְקֵרְבָנוּ לִפְנֵי הַר סִינַי. [65]וְנָתַן לָנוּ אֶת־הַתּוֹרָה. [66]וְהִכְנִיסָנוּ לְאֶרֶץ יִשְׂרָאֵל. [67]וּבָנָה לָנוּ אֶת־בֵּית הַבְּחִירָה לְכַפֵּר עַל כָּל־עֲוֹנוֹתֵינוּ:

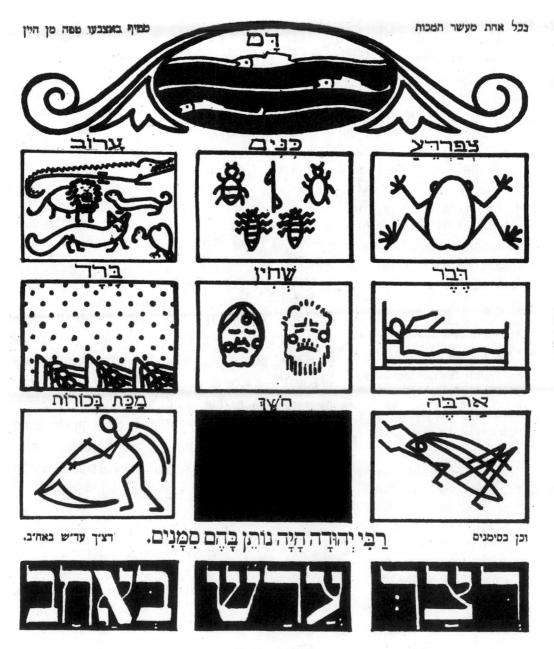

The Ten Plagues
Haggadah Shel Pesach, Berlin, 1927
Otto Geismar, illustrator

ARNOW (THE WORLD OF MIDRASH)

[1] *"Adonai brought us out of Egypt"* As a result of witnessing the Exodus, God wants humanity to know that "I am Adonai" (e.g., Exod. 6:7, 6:29, 7:5). The *Sifre on Deuteronomy* (346) offers a surprising perspective on this: "When you are My witnesses, I am God, but when you are not My witnesses, I am not God, as it were." (Heschel called this one of the most powerful statements in all of rabbinic literature.)[1] God saves us, but acknowledgment of God provides redemption for God as well. *Exodus Rabbah* (15:12) expresses it this way: "The redemption will be Mine and yours; as if to say: 'I will be redeemed with you....'"

(p. 43)

BALIN (MODERN HAGGADOT)

[12] *"Ten Plagues"* In 1984, the New Jewish Agenda published *Seder of the Children of Abraham*,[1] rephrasing the plagues with Israeli-Palestinian history in mind.

> "When, my friends, have we last seen peace?" the [Israeli] poet Chayim Guri exclaimed in a short prose piece. "This soil is insatiable," he wrote bitterly. "How many more graves, how many more coffins are *(p. 50)*

BRETTLER (OUR BIBLICAL HERITAGE)

[1] *"Great awe and with signs and with wonders"* Deuteronomy 26:8. The verse ends with several phrases that are typical of Deuteronomy, which together reflect the great power of God, especially in reference to bringing plagues. Rather than seeing them as coalescing into a single broad idea, *(p. 51)*

GILLMAN (THEOLOGICALLY SPEAKING)

[1] *"With a strong hand"* This reference to God's "hand" and, in the next paragraph, God's "outstretched arm" raises the issue of the many references, throughout our text, of anthropomorphic descriptions of God. God, of course, does not really have an arm, nor does God have a hand, nor, for that matter, does God speak and hear, stand or sit. Maimonides is particularly concerned with debunking the notion that God has a body. All of these references, he insists, are to be understood as metaphors. *(p. 55)*

[For prayer instructions, see page 30.]

10. THE ROLE OF GOD

A. "Adonai Brought Us Out of Egypt—Not by an Angel ..."

[1] "Adonai brought us out of Egypt with a strong hand and with an outstretched arm and with great awe and with signs and with wonders." [2] "Adonai brought us out of Egypt"—not by an angel and not by a seraph and not by a messenger, but rather the Holy One of Blessing Himself. As it says, [3] "I will pass through the Land of Egypt this very night and slay every first-born male in the Land of Egypt, from human to beast, and I will bring judgment upon all the gods of Egypt, I, Adonai."

GRAY (MEDIEVAL COMMENTATORS)

[2] *"Not by an angel and not by a seraph and not by a messenger"* **Ritba** points out that this text shows that the "angel" *(malakh)* and "seraph" are two different kinds of angels. Seraphs are actually made of fire; they are located underneath God's throne and immerse themselves each day in the mysterious river of fire that flows before the divine throne. Isaiah saw this type of angel in his inaugural vision: "Seraphs stood in attendance on Him" (Isa. 6:2). *(p. 57)*

GREEN (PERSONAL SPIRITUALITY)

[7] *"This is the revelation of the Shekhinah"* Liberation itself is a sacred moment, a time when God is "seen" in a special way. Much in our tradition makes a different claim: that the Exodus was only a first step, a preparation for the journey to Sinai, where God was to be revealed. We count the fifty days of the Omer in anticipation of that great event. The Torah itself says, "I am Y-H-W-H your God who brought you out of the Land of Egypt to be your God," and we often interpret this to mean that liberation was *(p. 61)*

וַיּוֹצִאֵנוּ יְיָ מִמִּצְרַיִם בְּיָד חֲזָקָה וּבִזְרֹעַ נְטוּיָה [1] וּבְמֹרָא גָּדֹל וּבְאֹתוֹת וּבְמֹפְתִים: וַיּוֹצִאֵנוּ יְיָ [2] מִמִּצְרַיִם. לֹא עַל יְדֵי מַלְאָךְ. וְלֹא עַל יְדֵי שָׂרָף. וְלֹא עַל יְדֵי שָׁלִיחַ. אֶלָּא הַקָּדוֹשׁ בָּרוּךְ הוּא בִּכְבוֹדוֹ וּבְעַצְמוֹ. שֶׁנֶּאֱמַר: וְעָבַרְתִּי בְאֶרֶץ מִצְרַיִם בַּלַּיְלָה [3] הַזֶּה וְהִכֵּיתִי כָל־בְּכוֹר בְּאֶרֶץ מִצְרַיִם מֵאָדָם וְעַד בְּהֵמָה וּבְכָל־אֱלֹהֵי מִצְרַיִם אֶעֱשֶׂה שְׁפָטִים אֲנִי יְיָ:

J. HOFFMAN (TRANSLATION)

[2] *"Seraph"* A six-winged angelic creature. The word also refers to "serpent."

[2] *"Himself"* The Hebrew has two words that both mean "himself." Our only other option in English is "in person," but the literal meaning of "person" conflicts too strongly with the notion of "God." So we use just one word here. (The literal meaning of "himself" also conflicts with many modern readers' notions of *(p. 61)*

SIGNPOST: THE ROLE OF GOD

GOD IS BEHIND EVERYTHING IN OUR FREEDOM STORY: BOTH THE PLAGUES AGAINST PHARAOH AND THE BENEFICENCE SHOWN TO ISRAEL. BEFORE LISTING THE PLAGUES, WE CONCLUDE THE MIDRASH FROM THE PRIOR SECTION, ASSURING US EXPRESSLY THAT GOD, AND GOD ALONE, BORE THE RESPONSIBILITY FOR *(p. 65)*

L. HOFFMAN (HISTORY)

[2] *"Not by a messenger"* This is almost certainly a polemic against Christianity. Origen of Alexandria (185– c. 254), the Church's first truly philosophic theologian, engaged in controversy with Rabbi Yochanan, the most significant Rabbi in the Palestinian Talmud, on precisely this *(p. 65)*

LANDES (HALAKHAH)

"Dayyenu" Through the verses of *Dayyenu*, we express detailed appreciation for the good that God has wrought for us in history. This public "recognition of the good" *(hakarat hatov)* is expressed in the uninhibited happiness of song. *(p. 68)*

ZIERLER (FEMINIST VOICES)

[7] *"'And with great awe'—this is the revelation of the Shekhinah"* In recent years, in an effort to counter the overwhelmingly masculine nature of our liturgy and theology, Jewish feminist theologians have increasingly embraced the idea of *Shekhinah* as a feminine aspect or *(p. 69)*

4"I will pass through the Land of Egypt"—I and not an angel. "And slay every first-born male"—I and not a seraph. "I will bring judgment upon all the gods of Egypt"—I and not the messenger. "I, Adonai"—I am He, and none other.

5"With a strong hand"—this is the blight, as it says, "The hand of Adonai is upon livestock in your field and upon your horses, upon your donkeys, upon your camels, upon your cattle, and upon your sheep, a very severe blight."

6"And with an outstretched arm"—this is the sword, as it says, "His sword drawn in his outstretched hand against Jerusalem."

7"And with great awe"—this is the revelation of the *Shekhinah*, as it says, "Or has any god tried to come and take for himself a nation from among another nation with trials, with signs, with wonders, with war, and with a strong hand and with an outstretched arm and with great awe as Adonai your God did with you in Egypt before your very eyes."

8"And with signs"—this is the staff, as it says, "Take this staff in your hand that you might use it for signs."

9"And with wonders"—this is the blood, as it says, "I will put wonders in the sky and upon the earth...."

⁴וְעָבַרְתִּי בְאֶרֶץ מִצְרַיִם. אֲנִי וְלֹא מַלְאָךְ. וְהִכֵּיתִי כָל־בְּכוֹר. אֲנִי וְלֹא שָׂרָף. וּבְכָל־אֱלֹהֵי מִצְרַיִם אֶעֱשֶׂה שְׁפָטִים. אֲנִי וְלֹא הַשָּׁלִיחַ. אֲנִי יְיָ. אֲנִי הוּא וְלֹא אַחֵר:

⁵בְּיָד חֲזָקָה. זוֹ הַדֶּבֶר. כְּמָה שֶׁנֶּאֱמַר: הִנֵּה יַד יְיָ הוֹיָה בְּמִקְנְךָ אֲשֶׁר בַּשָּׂדֶה בַּסּוּסִים בַּחֲמֹרִים בַּגְּמַלִּים בַּבָּקָר וּבַצֹּאן דֶּבֶר כָּבֵד מְאֹד:

⁶וּבִזְרֹעַ נְטוּיָה. זוֹ הַחֶרֶב. כְּמָה שֶׁנֶּאֱמַר: וְחַרְבּוֹ שְׁלוּפָה בְּיָדוֹ נְטוּיָה עַל יְרוּשָׁלָיִם:

⁷וּבְמֹרָא גָּדֹל. זֶה גִּלּוּי שְׁכִינָה. כְּמָה שֶׁנֶּאֱמַר: אוֹ הֲנִסָּה אֱלֹהִים לָבוֹא לָקַחַת לוֹ גוֹי מִקֶּרֶב גּוֹי בְּמַסֹּת בְּאֹתֹת וּבְמוֹפְתִים וּבְמִלְחָמָה וּבְיָד חֲזָקָה וּבִזְרֹעַ נְטוּיָה וּבְמוֹרָאִים גְּדֹלִים כְּכֹל אֲשֶׁר עָשָׂה לָכֶם יְיָ אֱלֹהֵיכֶם בְּמִצְרַיִם לְעֵינֶיךָ:

⁸וּבְאֹתוֹת. זֶה הַמַּטֶּה. כְּמָה שֶׁנֶּאֱמַר: וְאֶת־הַמַּטֶּה הַזֶּה תִּקַּח בְּיָדֶךָ אֲשֶׁר תַּעֲשֶׂה־בּוֹ אֶת־הָאֹתֹת:

⁹וּבְמֹפְתִים. זֶה הַדָּם. כְּמָה שֶׁנֶּאֱמַר: וְנָתַתִּי מוֹפְתִים בַּשָּׁמַיִם וּבָאָרֶץ . . .

B. God's Punishing Might: The
   Plagues in Egypt and at the Sea

10"... blood and fire and pillars of smoke." 11Also: "with a strong hand"—this is two; "with an outstretched arm"—this is two; "with great awe"—this is two; "with signs"—this is two; "with wonders"—this is two.

12These are the ten plagues that the Holy One of Blessing brought upon the Egyptians in Egypt. 13And these are the plagues:

14Blood

15Frogs

16Lice

17Swarms

18Blight

19Boils

20Hail

21Locusts

22Darkness

23Slaying of the first-born

24Rabbi Judah would make them into a mnemonic: *D'tsakh Adash B'achav.*

25Rabbi Yosei the Galilean says, "How do we know that the Egyptians suffered ten plagues in Egypt, and fifty plagues by the sea? 26In Egypt—what does it say? 'The magicians told Pharaoh: This is the finger of God.' 27By the sea—what does it say? 'Israel

10 דָּם וָאֵשׁ וְתִימְרוֹת עָשָׁן: 11דָּבָר אַחֵר. בְּיָד חֲזָקָה שְׁתַּיִם. וּבִזְרֹעַ נְטוּיָה שְׁתַּיִם. וּבְמֹרָא גָּדֹל שְׁתַּיִם. וּבְאֹתוֹת שְׁתַּיִם. וּבְמֹפְתִים שְׁתַּיִם. 12אֵלּוּ עֶשֶׂר מַכּוֹת שֶׁהֵבִיא הַקָּדוֹשׁ בָּרוּךְ הוּא עַל הַמִּצְרִים בְּמִצְרַיִם. 13וְאֵלּוּ הֵן:

14דָּם

15צְפַרְדֵּעַ

16כִּנִּים

17עָרוֹב

18דֶּבֶר

19שְׁחִין

20בָּרָד

21אַרְבֶּה

22חֹשֶׁךְ

23מַכַּת בְּכוֹרוֹת:

24רַבִּי יְהוּדָה הָיָה נוֹתֵן בָּהֶם סִמָּנִים. דְּצַ"ךְ עֲדַ"שׁ בְּאַחַ"ב:

25רַבִּי יוֹסֵי הַגְּלִילִי אוֹמֵר. מִנַּיִן אַתָּה אוֹמֵר שֶׁלָּקוּ הַמִּצְרִים בְּמִצְרַיִם עֶשֶׂר מַכּוֹת וְעַל הַיָּם לָקוּ חֲמִשִּׁים מַכּוֹת? 26בְּמִצְרַיִם מָה הוּא אוֹמֵר: וַיֹּאמְרוּ הַחַרְטֻמִּם אֶל פַּרְעֹה אֶצְבַּע אֱלֹהִים הוּא:

saw the great hand that God wielded against Egypt, and the nation feared Adonai and believed in Adonai and in Moses His servant.' [28]If the Egyptians suffered ten plagues by God's finger in Egypt, they suffered fifty plagues by God's hand by the sea."

[29]Rabbi Eliezer says, "How do we know that each and every plague that the Holy One of Blessing brought upon the Egyptians in Egypt was really four plagues? [30]It says, 'He sent them His fierce fury, anger, wrath, sorrow, and a contingent of evil angels.' [31]'Anger' is one, 'wrath' is two, 'sorrow' is three, and 'a contingent of evil angels' is four. [32]So in Egypt they suffered forty plagues, and by the sea they suffered two hundred plagues."

[33]Rabbi Akiva says, "How do we know that each and every plague that the Holy One of Blessing brought upon the Egyptians in Egypt was really five plagues? [34]It says, 'He sent them His fierce fury, anger, wrath, sorrow, and a contingent of evil angels.' [35]'His fierce fury' is one, 'anger' is two, 'wrath' is three, 'sorrow' is four, and 'contingent of evil angels' is five. [36]So in Egypt they suffered fifty plagues, and by the sea they suffered two hundred fifty plagues."

[27]וְעַל הַיָּם מָה הוּא אוֹמֵר: וַיַּרְא יִשְׂרָאֵל אֶת־הַיָּד הַגְּדֹלָה אֲשֶׁר עָשָׂה יְיָ בְּמִצְרַיִם וַיִּירְאוּ הָעָם אֶת־יְיָ וַיַּאֲמִינוּ בַּיְיָ וּבְמֹשֶׁה עַבְדּוֹ: [28]כַּמָּה לָקוּ בָאֶצְבַּע עֶשֶׂר מַכּוֹת. אֱמֹר מֵעַתָּה בְּמִצְרַיִם לָקוּ עֶשֶׂר מַכּוֹת וְעַל הַיָּם לָקוּ חֲמִשִּׁים מַכּוֹת:

[29]רַבִּי אֱלִיעֶזֶר אוֹמֵר. מִנַּיִן שֶׁכָּל־מַכָּה וּמַכָּה שֶׁהֵבִיא הַקָּדוֹשׁ בָּרוּךְ הוּא עַל הַמִּצְרִים בְּמִצְרַיִם הָיְתָה שֶׁל אַרְבַּע מַכּוֹת? [30]שֶׁנֶּאֱמַר: יְשַׁלַּח־בָּם חֲרוֹן אַפּוֹ עֶבְרָה וָזַעַם וְצָרָה מִשְׁלַחַת מַלְאֲכֵי רָעִים: [31]עֶבְרָה אַחַת. וָזַעַם שְׁתַּיִם. וְצָרָה שָׁלֹשׁ. מִשְׁלַחַת מַלְאֲכֵי רָעִים אַרְבַּע. [32]אֱמֹר מֵעַתָּה בְּמִצְרַיִם לָקוּ אַרְבָּעִים מַכּוֹת. וְעַל הַיָּם לָקוּ מָאתַיִם מַכּוֹת:

[33]רַבִּי עֲקִיבָא אוֹמֵר. מִנַּיִן שֶׁכָּל־מַכָּה וּמַכָּה שֶׁהֵבִיא הַקָּדוֹשׁ בָּרוּךְ הוּא עַל הַמִּצְרִים בְּמִצְרַיִם הָיְתָה שֶׁל חָמֵשׁ מַכּוֹת? [34]שֶׁנֶּאֱמַר: יְשַׁלַּח־בָּם חֲרוֹן אַפּוֹ עֶבְרָה וָזַעַם וְצָרָה מִשְׁלַחַת מַלְאֲכֵי רָעִים: [35]חֲרוֹן אַפּוֹ אַחַת. עֶבְרָה שְׁתַּיִם. וָזַעַם שָׁלֹשׁ. וְצָרָה אַרְבַּע. מִשְׁלַחַת מַלְאֲכֵי רָעִים חָמֵשׁ. [36]אֱמֹר מֵעַתָּה בְּמִצְרַיִם לָקוּ חֲמִשִּׁים מַכּוֹת. וְעַל הַיָּם לָקוּ חֲמִשִּׁים וּמָאתַיִם מַכּוֹת:

C. God's Saving Might: *Dayyenu*

[37]How many degrees of goodness has God bestowed upon us!

[38]If He had brought us out of Egypt and not brought judgment upon them ... Enough!

[39]If He had brought judgment upon them and not upon their gods ... Enough!

[40]If He had brought judgment upon their gods and not killed their first-born ... Enough!

[41]If He had killed their first-born and not given us their wealth ... Enough!

[42]If He had given us their wealth and not split the sea for us ... Enough!

[43]If He had split the sea for us and not brought us through it on dry land ... Enough!

[44]If He had brought us through it on dry land and not plunged our enemies into it ... Enough!

[45]If He had plunged our enemies into it and not provided for our needs in the desert for forty years ... Enough!

דַּיֵּנוּ

[37]כַּמָּה מַעֲלוֹת טוֹבוֹת לַמָּקוֹם עָלֵינוּ:

[38]אִלּוּ הוֹצִיאָנוּ מִמִּצְרַיִם.
וְלֹא עָשָׂה בָהֶם שְׁפָטִים דַּיֵּנוּ:

[39]אִלּוּ עָשָׂה בָהֶם שְׁפָטִים.
וְלֹא עָשָׂה בֵאלֹהֵיהֶם דַּיֵּנוּ:

[40]אִלּוּ עָשָׂה בֵאלֹהֵיהֶם.
וְלֹא הָרַג בְּכוֹרֵיהֶם דַּיֵּנוּ:

[41]אִלּוּ הָרַג בְּכוֹרֵיהֶם.
וְלֹא נָתַן לָנוּ אֶת־מָמוֹנָם דַּיֵּנוּ:

[42]אִלּוּ נָתַן לָנוּ אֶת־מָמוֹנָם.
וְלֹא קָרַע לָנוּ אֶת־הַיָּם דַּיֵּנוּ:

[43]אִלּוּ קָרַע לָנוּ אֶת־הַיָּם.
וְלֹא הֶעֱבִירָנוּ בְתוֹכוֹ בֶּחָרָבָה דַּיֵּנוּ:

[44]אִלּוּ הֶעֱבִירָנוּ בְתוֹכוֹ בֶּחָרָבָה.
וְלֹא שִׁקַּע צָרֵינוּ בְּתוֹכוֹ דַּיֵּנוּ:

[45]אִלּוּ שִׁקַּע צָרֵינוּ בְּתוֹכוֹ.
וְלֹא סִפֵּק צָרְכֵּנוּ
בַּמִּדְבָּר אַרְבָּעִים שָׁנָה דַּיֵּנוּ:

⁴⁶If He had provided for our needs in the desert for forty years and not fed us with manna … Enough!

אֵלוּ סִפֵּק צָרְכֵּנוּ ⁴⁶
בַּמִּדְבָּר אַרְבָּעִים שָׁנָה.
וְלֹא הֶאֱכִילָנוּ אֶת־הַמָּן
דַּיֵּנוּ:

⁴⁷If He had fed us with manna and not given us Shabbat … Enough!

אֵלוּ הֶאֱכִילָנוּ אֶת־הַמָּן. ⁴⁷
וְלֹא נָתַן לָנוּ אֶת־הַשַּׁבָּת
דַּיֵּנוּ:

⁴⁸If He had given us Shabbat and not brought us together before Mount Sinai … Enough!

אֵלוּ נָתַן לָנוּ אֶת־הַשַּׁבָּת. ⁴⁸
וְלֹא קֵרְבָנוּ לִפְנֵי הַר סִינַי
דַּיֵּנוּ:

⁴⁹If He had brought us together before Mount Sinai and not given us the Torah … Enough!

אֵלוּ קֵרְבָנוּ לִפְנֵי הַר סִינַי. ⁴⁹
וְלֹא נָתַן לָנוּ אֶת־הַתּוֹרָה
דַּיֵּנוּ:

⁵⁰If He had given us the Torah and not brought us into the Land of Israel … Enough!

אֵלוּ נָתַן לָנוּ אֶת־הַתּוֹרָה. ⁵⁰
וְלֹא הִכְנִיסָנוּ לְאֶרֶץ יִשְׂרָאֵל
דַּיֵּנוּ:

⁵¹If He had brought us into the Land of Israel and not built us the Temple … Enough!

אֵלוּ הִכְנִיסָנוּ לְאֶרֶץ יִשְׂרָאֵל. ⁵¹
וְלֹא בָנָה לָנוּ אֶת־בֵּית הַבְּחִירָה דַּיֵּנוּ:

⁵²How much more goodness, multiple and multiplied, has God bestowed upon us, ⁵³for He: brought us out of Egypt; ⁵⁴and brought judgment upon them; ⁵⁵and brought judgment upon their gods; ⁵⁶and killed their first-born; ⁵⁷and gave us their wealth; ⁵⁸and split the sea for us; ⁵⁹and brought us through it on dry land; ⁶⁰and plunged our enemies into it;

עַל אַחַת כַּמָּה וְכַמָּה טוֹבָה כְּפוּלָה ⁵²
וּמְכֻפֶּלֶת לַמָּקוֹם עָלֵינוּ. ⁵³שֶׁהוֹצִיאָנוּ
מִמִּצְרַיִם. ⁵⁴וְעָשָׂה בָהֶם שְׁפָטִים.
⁵⁵וְעָשָׂה בֵאלֹהֵיהֶם. ⁵⁶וְהָרַג אֶת־
בְּכוֹרֵיהֶם. ⁵⁷וְנָתַן לָנוּ אֶת־מָמוֹנָם.
⁵⁸וְקָרַע לָנוּ אֶת־הַיָּם. ⁵⁹וְהֶעֱבִירָנוּ
בְתוֹכוֹ בֶּחָרָבָה. ⁶⁰וְשִׁקַע צָרֵינוּ
בְּתוֹכוֹ.

⁶¹and provided for our needs in the desert for forty years; ⁶²and fed us with manna; ⁶³and gave us Shabbat; ⁶⁴and brought us together before Mount Sinai; ⁶⁵and gave us the Torah; ⁶⁶and brought us into the Land of Israel; ⁶⁷and built us the Temple to atone for our transgressions.

⁶¹וְסִפֵּק צָרְכֵּנוּ בַּמִּדְבָּר אַרְבָּעִים שָׁנָה. ⁶²וְהֶאֱכִילָנוּ אֶת־הַמָּן. ⁶³וְנָתַן לָנוּ אֶת־הַשַּׁבָּת. ⁶⁴וְקֵרְבָנוּ לִפְנֵי הַר סִינַי. ⁶⁵וְנָתַן לָנוּ אֶת־הַתּוֹרָה. ⁶⁶וְהִכְנִיסָנוּ לְאֶרֶץ יִשְׂרָאֵל. ⁶⁷וּבָנָה לָנוּ אֶת־בֵּית הַבְּחִירָה לְכַפֵּר עַל כָּל־עֲוֹנוֹתֵינוּ:

ARNOW (THE WORLD OF MIDRASH)

[4] *"Not an angel ... I am He, and none other"* The Haggadah's shift from historical narrative to theological polemic likely comes as a response to beliefs within and beyond Judaism that recognized the existence of more than one supernatural actor carrying out pivotal events in Jewish history such as the Exodus.[2] Such claims produced the Two Powers Heresy, a polemic spanning much of the first millennium. The *Mekhilta*, one of the Haggadah's prime midrashic sources, includes two important examples, both of which may have influenced the Haggadah's tone and language. On Exodus 12:12, "And slay every first-born male," the midrash states: "I might understand this to mean through an angel [*malakh*] or through a messenger [*shaliach*]. But Scripture says: 'Adonai slew all the first-born' (Exod 12:29)—not through an angel nor through a messenger."[3] The following comment—on "I am Adonai your God who brought you out of the Land of Egypt," *anokhi Adonai elohekha* ... (Exod. 20:2)—explicitly addresses claims that different divine figures had intervened in Egypt, at the Red Sea and Sinai: "Scripture, therefore, would not let the nations of the world have an excuse for saying that there are two powers, but declares: '*I am Adonai your God*. I am He [*ani hu*] who was in Egypt and I am He who was at the sea. I am He who was at Sinai.... As it is said, *See, then, that I, I am He; there is no god beside Me. I deal death and give life...*' (Deut. 32:39)."[4]

[5-6] *"With a strong hand ... the sword"* The passage in the Haggadah derives from a parallel midrashic tale concerning the Jewish community exiled in Babylonia following the destruction of the First Temple (*Sifre on Numbers, Piska* 115). Having fallen under foreign rule, the community felt that God had abandoned them and they were free to worship other gods. They were like slaves sold to a new master. Outraged, God told Ezekiel, a prophet living with them in Babylonia, "I will reign over you with a strong hand and with an outstretched arm ... (Ezek. 20:32–34). 'With a strong hand.' This is the blight [*dever*].[5] 'And with an outstretched arm.' This is the sword."[6] The midrash elaborates on these phrases exactly as in the Haggadah.

The midrash thus reinforces a central biblical axiom: Israel's faltering loyalty to God explains its history among the nations. "To Me the Israelites are servants [*avadim*, literally 'slaves']! 'If you ... refuse to obey Me ... I will bring a sword against you ... I will send pestilence [*dever*] among you, and you shall be delivered into enemy hands'" (Lev. 26:21, 26:25).

[7] *"This is the revelation of the Shekhinah"* The Rabbis envisioned the Exodus as a moment of direct encounter with God. "In Egypt the Israelites saw God in the open [i.e., in public]," says *Song of Songs Rabbah* (3:19). A most amazing claim from the *Mekhilta* asserts that "a maidservant saw ... what all the prophets together never saw."[7] To see is to believe; to believe is to see. Encounter affects both sides, however, so the *Shekhinah*, God's immanent presence suffered alongside Israel. "Whenever Israel is enslaved, the *Shekhinah* is enslaved with them. God shares the affliction of the community ... but also of the individual, for Scripture promises, 'When he calls on Me I will answer him; I will be with him in distress [*b'tsarah*, from the same root as *mitsrayim*, "Egypt"] and I will rescue him ...'" (Ps. 91:15).[8] The experience of God's presence remains available to each of us.

[7] *"Take ... a nation from among another"* Who bears responsibility for redemption? The *Mekhilta* provides a vivid simile. In redeeming the Israelites from Egypt—taking one nation from among another—God is likened to a shepherd who reaches in and helps deliver a kid unable to emerge from its mother's womb.[9] Here, responsibility for the Exodus belongs to God alone. Other passages, however, assign a role to both God and the Israelites. "Rabbi Judah the Prince says: Through alertness/strength [*biz'rizut*] of God, Israel left Egypt." But the same midrash holds also, "Through their own alertness/strength [*b'zrizut*]" they were redeemed.[10] Redemption hinges, then, on both Divine and human action. Another midrash takes this idea further. "God said to Israel, 'The time of *My* redemption is in your hand, and the time of *your* redemption is in My hand" (*Pesikta D'rav Kahana* 17:5). In a broken world God and humanity suffer and redeem one another.

[8] *"Take this staff in your hand"* These are God's final words to Moses at the burning bush. Moses' staff—which turned into a serpent and later helped bring on the plagues—is surrounded by legend. It was one of the final ten items that God created just before the first Shabbat (M. Avot 5:6). As Adam left Eden, God gave him the staff, and it was passed down over the generations from one righteous person to another until it reached Moses *(Pirkei D'rabbi Eliezer)*.[11] The sapphire staff was said to bear various inscriptions: the Tetragrammaton (*Deut. Rabbah* 3:8); the seventy names of God (*Pesikta D'rav Kahana* 3c); names of the three patriarchs and six matriarchs (*Targum Yonaton*, an Aramaic translation of the Bible, on Exod. 14:21); and the abbreviation of the ten plagues, *D'tsach Adash B'achav*, that we find in the Haggadah. According to the Talmud (Sot. 37a), at the Red Sea God chided Moses when he prayed excessively for divine intervention. Moses answered, "'What should I be doing?' God replied, "Lift up your rod and hold out your arm over the sea and split it ...'" (Exod. 14:16). Whatever

the staff's special qualities, it took the hand of Moses to carry it to Pharaoh and part the sea. We each possess gifts that can help redeem the world; but like Moses, we sometimes hesitate to use them.

[10] *"Blood and fire"* The Sages believed that what befell Egypt would likewise bring the downfall of subsequent oppressors of the Jewish people. An eleventh-century midrash, *Vayosha*, speaks of the "blood, fire, and pillars of smoke" (Joel 3:3) that would accompany the Holy Roman Empire's destruction. This midrash proves its point by noting that Joel prophesied desolation for both Egypt and Edom, the latter, in rabbinic parlance, equated with Rome. The vision of God's apocalyptic return to history—"the great and terrible day of Adonai" (Joel 3:3)—nourished hope in dark times and sated an understandable yen for vengeance.

"Spill a drop of wine for each of the plagues" It is commonly said that we spill wine from our cups to diminish our joy because our liberation came at the cost of much Egyptian suffering: "If your enemy falls, do not exult" (Prov. 24:17).[12] But according to the earliest explanations—from the fourteenth and fifteenth centuries—the wine taken from our cups represents the suffering we were spared and that we hope will befall those who hate us![13]

It is true, however, that Jewish sources reflect ambivalence regarding the defeat of our foes. When discussing the drowning of the Egyptians at the Red Sea, the Talmud questions whether *God* rejoices in the downfall of the wicked. "The ministering angels wanted to chant songs of praise, but the Holy One ... said, 'The work of My hands is being drowned in the sea, and you sing songs of praise?'" The discussion concludes that God doesn't rejoice, but causes others to do so (Meg. 10b). But even with respect to God, we find that "God takes pleasure when those who provoke Him perish" (*Num. Rab.* 3:4).[14]

[12] *"The ten plagues"* Surely, God could have delivered Israel with just one plague (*Exod. Rabbah* 15:10). So why were there ten? That question spawned a vast body of midrashic literature (see comments on individual plagues that follow), much of it attempting to justify God's relentless destruction of Egypt or venting vengeful feelings toward subsequent enemies of the Jewish people.

[14] *"Blood"* Promise and fulfillment: With the very first plague, God began to fulfill the promise that Abraham's descendants would leave Egypt with great wealth (Gen. 15:14; see *My People's Passover Haggadah*, Volume 1, p. 221). "If an Egyptian and an Israelite were in one house where there was a barrel full of water, and the two of them filled pitchers from it, the Egyptian would discover that it contained blood, but the Israelite's pitcher would still be full of water. If the Israelite gave the Egyptian his pitcher, it still became blood. Even if he said to him, 'Let us both drink from one vessel,' the Israelite would drink water, but the Egyptian blood. It was only when he had bought it from the Israelite for money [*b'damim*] that he was able to drink water, and this is how the Israelites became rich" (*Exod. Rab.* 9:10). The midrash achieves a certain sharpness because of the intriguing fact that in Hebrew, *damim* can mean "blood" or "money." As the Talmudic aphorism states, *damim tartei mashma*, "*damim* means two things" (Meg. 14b).

[15] *"Frogs"* God versus god: The plagues can be viewed as a contest of sorts between God and Pharaoh, who claimed divinity. God unleashes the powers of creation to destroy (to "de-create") Egypt in order to demonstrate the emptiness of Pharaoh's conceit. *Exodus Rabbah* (10:22) provides an excellent illustration: "God said to Pharaoh, 'You have said, *The Nile is mine, and I made it* (Ezek. 29:9). Well, I will show you whose it is. I will decree that it bring forth frogs, just as in the beginning I decreed: *Let the waters swarm with living creatures* (Gen. 1:20). As those waters fulfilled My command, so too will the Nile.'"[15]

[16] *"Lice"* Never too late to repent: One midrashic tradition compares the plagues to the military tactics a warrior king employs to quell a state revolt. "First he smashes their aqueducts (the Nile turning to blood). If they repent, well and good. If not, he brings war cries against them (the loud croaking of frogs). If they repent, well and good. If not, he shoots them with arrows (lice)" (*Tanchuma* on Exod. 10:21).[16]

[17] *"Swarms"* Ten plagues and Ten Commandments: An early rabbinic dictum sums up the relationship between the Exodus and divine commandment: "All who acknowledge the yoke of commandments acknowledge the Exodus, and all who deny the yoke of commandments deny the Exodus" (*Sifra, Shemini*, on Lev. 10:12). The Sages could therefore hardly refrain from discovering/creating correspondences between the Ten Commandments and the plagues. The midrash pairs the fourth plague, *arov*, "swarms," with the commandment to "remember the Sabbath day" (Exod. 20:8). "The Holy One, said: 'Do not mix up [*lo ta'arov*] weekday and Sabbath, nor treat them as though they were the same'" (*Pesikta Rabbati* 21:20). The midrash seems to rely on a play on words: *arov* (עָרֹב), "swarms," can also be read *arav* (עָרַב) "to mix."[17]

[18] *"Blight"* Measure for measure: Why blight? "Because when the Egyptians enslaved the Israelites' children they said, 'since they have no work to do let them tend our livestock.' So God brought the pestilence against their livestock" (*Midrash Hagadol* on Exod. 9:1).

[19] *"Boils"* Pharaoh's hardened heart: For the first five plagues Pharaoh hardens his own heart, but with the sixth, boils, God begins to do so. "Rabbi Yochanan worried lest that provide heretics with grounds for arguing that he had no means of repenting, to which Rabbi Shimon ben Lakish replied: 'When God warns a man once, twice, and even a third time, and he still does not repent, only then does God close his heart against repentance so that He should exact vengeance from him for his sins'" (*Exod. Rabbah* 13:3). "When God perceived that he did not relent after the first five plagues, He decided that even if Pharaoh now wished to repent, He would harden his heart in order to exact the whole punishment from him" (*Exod. Rab.* 11:6). Discomfort with God's hardening of Pharaoh's heart doubtless helps explain the complete absence of this motif from the Haggadah.

[20] *"Hail"* Overcoming indifference: The warning preceding the plague of hail differs from all others in two respects: God sends this plague upon Pharaoh's person, literally

"into your heart" (Exod. 9:14), and Moses tells the Egyptians to bring their cattle under shelter lest they perish. The midrash notes that until then the king remained indifferent because the plagues had not touched Pharaoh himself. "But as soon as his own body was smitten, he began to feel the pain and to cry 'I stand guilty this time'" (*Exod. Rab.* 15:10). *Tanchuma* (Exod. 9:18) explains Pharaoh's response somewhat differently: "When someone wants to fight with his companion and overcome him, he comes upon him by surprise. But God said to Pharaoh, 'Order your livestock ... under shelter.' It was then that Pharaoh said, 'Adonai is in the right'" (Exod. 9:27).

[21] *"Locusts"* Comic relief: "When the locusts first came, the Egyptians [apparently great fans of pickled locusts] tried to collect them. So God 'caused a shift to a very strong west wind, which lifted the locusts and hurled them into the Red Sea ...' (Exod. 10:19). What is the meaning of 'not a single locust remained in all the territory of Egypt' (Exod. 10:19)? Even those that had been pickled in their pots and barrels took wing and fled!" (*Exod. Rabbah* 12:5). The reference to pickled locusts is not as strange as it sounds. Leviticus 11:22 declares certain species of locusts fit for eating, and the Mishnah discusses the brine of various pickled locusts in detail (M. Ter. 10:9). The Talmud (Shab. 110b) recommends the brine of locusts to cure jaundice!

[22] *"Darkness"* In the dark: Why darkness? "God brought darkness upon the Egyptians for three days, so that the Israelites should bury their dead without their enemies seeing them...." Which Israelites died? God smote "transgressors in Israel who had Egyptian patrons and lived in affluence and honor, and were unwilling to leave" (*Exod. Rab.* 14:3). Leaving Egypt is not always as appealing as it may seem. Another tradition holds that the Egyptians could indeed see the Israelites. "They would see the Israelites eating and drinking and rejoicing, and they would see and worry. For all who are in the dark see those who are in the light."[18]

[23] *"Slaying the first-born"* Searching for explanations: Even first-borns who had been imprisoned and presumably had little direct role in oppressing the Israelites were slain (Exod. 12:29). The *Mekhilta* explains: "They rejoiced over each and every one of Pharaoh's cruel decrees against the Israelites. And, as Scripture says, 'He who rejoices over another's misfortune will not go unpunished' (Prov. 17:5)...."[19] But is death the proper punishment? In a horrific tale, *Pesikta D'rav Kahana* (7:6/9) ascribes responsibility for much of the carnage during the last plague to the Egyptians themselves rather than God. Their fate hanging in the balance, Egypt's first-born pleaded with their fathers to persuade Pharaoh to let the Israelites go. Their fathers replied, "Each one of us has ten sons; let one of them die, just so long as the Hebrews not be permitted to leave Egypt." The first-born took their case directly to Pharaoh. He had them beaten. In a final desperate act to placate God and save themselves, "the first-born went out and slew six hundred thousand of their fathers [corresponding to the number of Israelite males in Egypt]. Of this it is written, 'to Him that smote Egypt *with* [by means of, i.e., with the participation of] their first-born' (Ps. 136:10; see *My People's Passover Haggadah*, Volume 2, p. 170).[20]

[24] *"Rabbi Judah … a mnemonic"* Rabbi Judah, the great second-century sage, created what has surely become rabbinic literature's most widely known *siman*, or mnemonic. It first appears in *Sifre on Deuteronomy* (*Piska* 301), a tannaitic (pre-200 CE) source. A medieval text asserts that Rabbi Judah declared that this *siman* was inscribed on Moses' staff: "God said, 'In this order you shall bring the plagues upon [Pharaoh]'" (*Exod. Rab.* 8:3). Just as this mnemonic is a memory aid for us, so it was for Moses. In any case, Rabbi Judah did not look kindly upon errors—which may explain his fondness for mnemonics. In the Mishnah (Avot 4:13) he warns, "Be careful in study, for an error amounts to an intentional sin." He also created a *siman* to memorize the proper dimensions of sacrificial meal offerings—"lest you should err" (M. Men. 11:4).

[27] *"Moses His servant"* The Haggadah's only mention of Moses' name. The Haggadah likely downplayed Moses' role in the Exodus to help combat tendencies—well documented in Jewish sources—to deify him. *Deuteronomy Rabbah* (11:4) interprets the phrase *Moshe ish ha'elohim*, usually rendered "Moses, the man of God," as "Moses—man, the god" (Deut. 33:1). "When [Moses] was cast into [the Nile] he was a man; but when the river was turned into blood [by Moses] he was God…. When he fled from before Pharaoh he was a man, but when he drowned [Pharaoh in the sea] he was God…What is the meaning of 'man,' 'the God'? Rabbi Avin said: 'His lower half was man, but his upper half was God.'" The *Sifre on Deuteronomy* (*Piska* 42) comments on the phrase from the second paragraph of the *Sh'ma*: "'I will grant the rain for your land in season …' (Deut. 11:14). Since Moses is speaking, the text should read '*He* will grant.'" The midrash thus argues against the notion that a *supernatural* Moses would grant the rains: "I will grant" means "I [God]—not by means of an angel or messenger."

[28] *"By the sea"* Although these passages blithely proliferate the blows that struck the Egyptians at the Red Sea, a medieval midrash describes God's decision to drown them as a close call. Uzza, angel of the Egyptians, argued that there was no evidence that any of these individuals had personally killed an Israelite. And besides, the Israelites had been well compensated for their labor when they despoiled the Egyptians of their gold and silver prior to the Exodus. Uzza's final plea—"have mercy on the work of Your hands"—nearly convinced God. The angel Gabriel then appeared with a brick into which the body of an Israelite child had been molded. Rising from the throne of mercy, God sat upon the throne of justice and resolved to destroy the Egyptians at the sea (*Yalkut Shimoni, Beshalach* 241).

[36] *"Two hundred and fifty plagues"* The midrash found in the Haggadah did not exhaust the penchant for multiplying the punishments that would befall Israel's enemies. An early twelfth-century source—one that elsewhere alludes to the suffering of European Jewish communities during the First Crusade—expands the plagues visited upon the Egyptians to 410. When Pharaoh disavows any knowledge of God, God instructs Moses to tell Pharaoh, "By this [בְּזֹאת] shall you know that I am Adonai (Exod. 7:17)." The numerical value in the letters in בְּזֹאת equals 410, which equates to the 400 years that the Israelites were enslaved plus the ten plagues (*Lekach Tov* on Exod. 7:17).

[37] *"Dayyenu"* The Sages were familiar with the expression *dayyenu* and used it in contexts quite apart from the Exodus. God's promise to shower the people of Israel with blessings (Malachi 3:10), for instance, is said to mean: "Until you wear your lips out by saying, '*dayyenu*'" (*Lev. Rabbah* 35:12).[21] (The comment refers just to the word *dayyenu*, not to the song.) The *Sifre on Deuteronomy* (*Piska'ot* 337 and 339) may be one of the sources that shaped the song. Here the Israelites express anxiety lest they become separated from Moses, "the man who brought us out of Egypt [*hotsianu mi'mitsrayim*], split the sea for us, brought down manna for us, supplied us with quail [in the desert], and performed miracles and wonders for us...." By putting the focus on God rather than Moses, and extending the narrative beyond the Exodus, *Dayyenu* reminds us that leaving Egypt was only a beginning, a prerequisite for building an enduring relationship with the ultimate One of Being.

[38] *"Brought judgment upon them"* After sending the Israelites out of Egypt, "Pharaoh and his courtiers had a change of heart ..." (Exod. 14:5). To explain the reversal that would ultimately lead the Egyptian army to perish in the sea, the *Mekhilta* presents an Egyptian *Dayyenu* of sorts. "They said, 'If we had been plagued without letting them go, it would have been enough [*k'da'i hu*]. Or if we had been plagued and let them go without our money being taken, it would have been enough. But we were plagued, let them go, and our money was taken.'"[22] This litany of humiliations fuels the pursuit of what ends up being only self-destructive. Too many nations and individuals do the same thing.

[41] *"Given us their wealth"* According to the Bible, Pharaoh pursues the Israelites because God hardened the king's heart (Exod. 14:4, 14:8). Perhaps to draw our attention away from the moral ambiguities of God's actions, the *Mekhilta* concentrates on how Pharaoh persuaded his people to follow him. This midrash contains possibly the earliest appearance in rabbinic literature of the word *dayyenu*. Ironically, it comes from the lips of Pharaoh! "It would not be worth our while, *lo dayyenu*," says Pharaoh, "to pursue the Israelites [to get *them* back], but for the sake of the silver and gold they have taken from us it is worthwhile [*k'da'i hu*]. The Egyptians who had lost little money protested. "For the sake of a trifle shall we run after the Israelites?"[23] To awaken their love of wealth, Pharaoh then showered gold and jewels from his own personal treasury upon them. Proverbs (1:19) warns that "greed of gain takes away the life of its owner."[24]

[44] *"Plunged our enemies into it"* In contrast to the Bible, which highlights Pharaoh's unyielding stubbornness, the *Mekhilta* notes his capacity to change. "The mouth that had said, '... nor will I let Israel go' (Exod. 5:2), that same mouth said, 'I *will* let you go ...' (Exod. 8:24). What was the reward for this? 'You shall not abhor an Egyptian ...'" (Deut. 23:8).[25] *Pirkei D'rabbi Eliezer* holds that of all the Egyptians who entered the sea, only one emerged: Pharaoh. According to this source, just before his death the king acknowledged God. God then resurrected him and installed him as the king of Nineveh in the Jonah story, the prototypical ruler who leads his people in repentance.[26]

[67] *"The Temple to atone"* Following the Temple's destruction, when animal sacrifice was no longer possible, the Sages offered substitutes to provide atonement. (Indeed, the

early Passover Seder can well be understood as such a surrogate.) *Avot D'rabbi Natan* (version B, chap. 8) offers a classic example, citing Hosea 6:6, "I desire goodness, not sacrifice…." Elsewhere the Sages conclude that "he who leaves gleanings for the poor and does not reap the corners of the field is counted as if the Temple stood and he had offered his sacrifices in it" (*Sifra, Emor*, on Lev. 23:22).

———◆———

BALIN (MODERN HAGGADOT)

needed until it will cry out—enough, enough!"

We remove ten drops of wine from our full cup of joy in commemoration of ten places infamous in both … [the] histories of [Israelis and Palestinians] for the suffering which took place there. Each drop of wine we pour symbolizes our hope and prayer that these will be the last such bloody encounters between our two peoples, that beginning today we will both resolve to cast out killing and learn a new way to be together. Let us join in saying these names:

HEBRON	MAALOT
DEIR YASSIN	TEL AVIV ROAD
GUSH ETZION	NAHARIYA
KFAR KASSEM	NABLUS
BEIT NUBA	SABRA AND CHATILLA[2]

[37] *"Dayyenu"* In the *Seder of the Children of Abraham*, the traditional *Dayyenu*—where a long list of God's glorious deeds are typically recounted—is replaced with a litany of past failures and then specific hopes for reconciliation vis-à-vis the divisive modern-day children of Abraham.

If only there had not been mistrust	*OyLanu*
If only there had not been a holocaust	*OyLanu*
If only there had not been so many soldiers killed	*OyLanu*
If only there had not been so many made homeless	*OyLanu*
If only there had not been so many massacres	*OyLanu*
If only there had not been so many terrorist attacks	*OyLanu*
If only there had not been so many bombings	*OyLanu*
If only so many children had not died	*OyLanu*
If only both peoples would renounce violence	*Dayyenu*
If only both peoples would talk to one another	*Dayyenu*
If only both peoples would recognize each other's rights	*Dayyenu*
If only they would appreciate each other's cultures	*Dayyenu*
If only they would recognize their common origin and destiny	*Dayyenu*
If only the descendants of Isaac and Ishmael could live face to face	*Dayyenu*
If only they could beat their swords into plowshares	*Dayyenu*
If only both peoples could share the land	*Dayyenu*[3]

[46] *"And not fed us with manna"* To enliven the singing of *Dayyenu*, while adding some spice to the Seder, Noam Zion and David Dishon (*A Different Night*, Jerusalem, 1997) suggest the following Afghani Jewish custom:

> Distribute green onions. "Beginning with the ninth stanza: 'Even if You had supplied our needs in the desert for 40 years, but not fed us manna from heaven,' the participants hit each other (gently?) with the green onion stalks, every time they sing the refrain, 'Dayyenu.'" The editors suggest that this custom is linked to the biblical account of Israelites who complained about the manna God had given them and recalled with longing the onions in Egypt, "We remember the fish that we used to eat free in Egypt, the cucumbers, the melons, the leeks, the onions, and the garlic. Now our gullets are shriveled. There is nothing at all! Nothing but this manna to look to!" (Exod. 11:5–6). According to this interpretation, by participants' beating each other with onions, they admonish themselves not to yearn for the fleshpots of Egypt and not to forget Egyptian bondage.[4]

———◆———

BRETTLER (OUR BIBLICAL HERITAGE)

the midrash will insist that each has a particular meaning and will connect each to a particular text.

[2] *"Not by an angel ... not by a messenger"* The biblical story of the plagues and the Exodus is composed from several originally separate stories or sources. This was not recognized by the rabbis, who (1) solved this problem by giving one text a greater voice than others, or interpreting one to mean the same as the others; and (2) reinterpreting the biblical text so that it would fit rabbinic theology. This particular section is a polemic against what is clearly stated in Exodus 12:23: "and Adonai will protect [*JPS*: pass over] the door and not let the Destroyer enter and smite your home." The Destroyer here is *malakh*, often translated as "angel," but meaning a messenger—indeed, this is the meaning of the Greek word *angelos*, which has entered English as "angel." It is often unclear in the Bible if such a *malakh* is a semi-divine being separate from Adonai, as in this case, or if the *malakh* is a manifestation of Adonai. The polemical nature of this midrashic text is obvious from the repetition "not by ... and not by ... and not by ... but rather...."

[3] *"I will pass through"* Quoting Exodus 12:12, in which Adonai rather than an emissary Destroyer is active. Thus, this section highlights Exodus 12:12 over 12:23, since the author of this section did not believe in a divine being called "the Destroyer."

[4] *"I and not the messenger ... I am He, and none other"* The text of Exodus 12:12 is further explicated, highlighting the fact that the verbs are in the masculine singular, and thus Adonai alone must be the agent. Again, the repetitions have a polemical purpose, intended to make the reader "forget" or reinterpret what is explicitly said in Exodus

12:23 concerning the Destroyer.

[5] *"The hand"* Exodus 9:3; both this text and Deuteronomy 26:8 use the noun *yad*, "hand." On this basis, they are understood as referring to the same entity.

[6] *"His sword"* From the middle of 1 Chronicles 21:16, thus bringing in a reference from *K'tuvim* (Writings), the third part of the biblical canon, reinforcing the idea that all parts of the canon are Bible and are mutually enlightening. Both texts share the word "outstretched," showing by analogy that the word "outstretched" in Deuteronomy may refer to a sword. The quote from Chronicles is unusually short; the author has omitted the beginning that notes that an angel of Adonai is holding this sword, since that idea would contradict the previous emphasis on Adonai acting alone.

[7] *"Great awe"* Deuteronomy 4:34. The word *mora* ("awe") connects both passages. Most likely, it means "frightful acts," from the root *y-r-ʿ*, but it is understood here as from the root *r-ʿ-h/y*, which means "to see," and thus may refer to "the Revelation of the Divine Presence." In the ancient Greek and Aramaic Bible translations as well, *mora* was understood in connection to *y-r-ʿ*, "seeing," rather than *r-ʿ-h/y*, "fear."

[8] *"Take this staff ... for signs"* Exodus 4:17, which like the passage from Deuteronomy, uses the word "signs." A careful reading of the text in Exodus, focusing on the staff, indicates that the plague tradition is a mixture of several traditions. For example, in Exodus 7:17, Moses says, "See, I shall strike the water in the Nile with the rod that is in my hand, and it will be turned into blood," while two verses later, Adonai tells Moses to say to Aaron, "Take your rod and hold out your arm over the waters of Egypt...." In one tradition, which the Haggadah emphasizes here, the staff belongs to Moses, who uses it to strike, while in the other main tradition, Aaron has a staff, but he uses his arm to bring about the plagues.

[9] *"Wonders ... blood"* Joel 3:3 is cited to prove that "wonders," *moftim*, can include blood. Again, the author moves outside of the Exodus story in Exodus, citing a verse from *N'vi'im* (Prophets), again emphasizing the unity of the tripartite Scripture.

[11] *"Also"* This is a crucial rabbinic term that distinguishes between different, often mutually exclusive interpretations of the Bible, though typically none of the different interpretations is privileged. This highlights the crucial rabbinic theological principle that the Bible should not be interpreted in a univocal fashion but is fundamentally open to multiple interpretations. In contrast to rabbinic literature, which typically distinguishes between different opinions by using formulae like "another interpretation" or "Rabbi X says ...; Rabbi Y says," the Bible often places different traditions adjacent to one another without any clear formula that divides one from the other, blending them together. Modern biblical scholars must therefore use careful stylistic analysis and other tools to recover these originally separate voices.

[12] *"Ten plagues"* Although the number ten is never used in relation to the plagues in the Bible, most agree that Exodus narrates ten plagues. The different accounts in Psalms

78 and 105, however, suggest that in ancient Israel there was no standard order for these plagues and that not all traditions agreed that there were ten plagues. In Psalm 78, the seven plagues are blood, swarms of frogs, locusts, hail killing agriculture, hail killing beasts, pestilence, and death of the first-born; in Psalm 105, they are darkness, blood causing the death of fish, frogs, swarms of lice, hail, locusts, and death of the first-born. In fact, the number ten may be the result of two or three varying plague traditions, each of which had fewer than ten plagues—only when they were redacted together did ten plagues result.

[14-23] *"Blood ... Slaying of the first-born"* Ten is a stereotypical number in the Bible, and it is not surprising that the redactor combined earlier sources to equal ten plagues. In Exodus, they progress from nuisance plagues to more serious ones, and to those that cannot be repeated by the Egyptian magicians. They are structured as three triads, with, for example, each initial plague of the triad (plagues 1, 4, 7) noting that Moses must "station himself" before Pharaoh "in the morning." A climactic tenth plague, the slaying of the first-born, follows the three triads.

[24] *"D'tsakh Adash B'achav"* This mnemonic helped to reinforce the idea that there are ten plagues and that the order of Exodus, rather than Psalms, is canonical. It is unclear when the use of acronyms (abbreviations composed from the first letters of successive words) developed in Hebrew; some plausible, but not entirely convincing examples for this phenomenon have been suggested already for the Bible.

[25] *"Rabbi Yosei"* This playfulness is typical of religious literature, including the Bible. Religious literature can convey its message by being playful and humorous. At least in its completed form, this entire section plays upon "And everyone who really discusses the Exodus from Egypt is praised" (see *My People's Passover Haggadah*, Volume 1, p. 169), where the word *marbeh*, translated there as "really," may also be understood as "multiply." Thus, this section offers different numbers by which the ten plagues may be multiplied, as the rabbis vie with each other to show the greater and greater extents of the greatness of Adonai.

[26] *"The finger of God"* The first half of Exodus 8:15; this mentions a single finger.

[27] *"The great hand"* Exodus 14:31, immediately preceding the Song of the Sea; this mentions a hand, which contains five fingers, and thus, according to Rabbi Yosei, the miracle was five times greater (5 x 10 = 50).

[30] *"He sent them"* Psalm 78:49. This psalm describes the plagues in vv. 44–51, generally describing one plague per verse. Verse 49, which stands between *barad*, hail killing animals (v. 48), and *dever*, pestilence (v. 50), however, does not describe any specific plague known from Exodus. Rabbi Eliezer thus understands it as a general description for all of the plagues, where "fury," understood as a general designation for each plague, is composed of the four elements "anger, wrath, sorrow, and a contingent of evil angels," and thus each plague may be multiplied by four. A careful reading of Psalm 78 suggests that it does not contain all ten plagues found in Exodus (see above, "Ten plagues"); by using Psalm 78:49 to explicate the Exodus tradition, this discrepancy

is ignored as the Exodus tradition in the Torah is given priority over different traditions found in Psalms.

[35] *"His fierce fury' is one"* Rabbi Akiva uses the same verse as Rabbi Eliezer, immediately above, but understands each of the five elements of the verse "He sent them His fierce fury, anger, wrath, sorrow, and a contingent of evil angels" as describing each plague, rather than assuming that the last four elements modify the first.

[37] *"How many degrees"* This introduces a reprise of Israel's history, from the Exodus through the building of the First Temple. Like all such summaries, it is selective. In terms of content, it does not follow the model of any of the biblical historical summaries (e.g., Deut. 26:5–9; Josh. 24:3–13; 1 Sam. 12:8–12; Pss. 78, 105, 106: Neh. 9).

[38] *"Brought judgment"* Exodus 6:6, 7:4.

[40] *"Judgment upon their gods"* Literally, "do against their gods," which makes little sense. The direct object, "judgments," is meant to be supplied from the previous line, and these lines are thus a paraphrase of Exodus 12:12, "and I will *bring judgment* (*e'eseh sh'fatim*—literally "do punishments") upon all *the gods* of Egypt, I, Adonai."

[41] *"Their wealth"* As noted in Genesis 15:14, "But I will judge the nation they serve, and then they will leave with great wealth," and Exodus 12:36, "And Adonai had disposed the Egyptians favorably toward the people, and they let them have their request; thus they stripped the Egyptians." The word *mamon*, "wealth," is a post-biblical borrowing from Aramaic to Hebrew, further indicating that this poem is not a pastiche of biblical verses, but a new composition, selecting and rephrasing various biblical episodes.

[45] *"Our needs"* Tsorkenu, from *tsorekh*, a late biblical-Hebrew word found only in 2 Chronicles 2:15, in a context that has no connection to the Exodus and wandering traditions.

[47] *"Shabbat"* Shabbat is first legislated in Exodus 16 (several chapters before the Decalogue of Exodus 20), within the chapter describing the manna. The Israelites "discover" Shabbat when a double portion of the manna falls on Friday and none falls on Shabbat.

[49] *"Given us the Torah"* Following the rabbinic understanding of revelation on Sinai, the entire Torah was given there, although this is nowhere explicitly stated in the Torah. The late biblical Nehemiah 9:13, "You came down on Mount Sinai and spoke to them from heaven; You gave them right rules and true teachings, good laws and commandments," may share a similar understanding.

[50] *"The Land of Israel"* This is a wonderful illustration of the selectivity of this historical reprise—all of the post-Sinai, pre-conquest traditions narrated in the Torah are omitted. Some, such as the sin of the golden calf, are left out since they are thematically inappropriate, for they do not illustrate God's greatness; others, such as the

conquest of Sihon and Og to the east of the Jordan, are simply not narrated.

[51] *"Built us the Temple"* Although the term used for Temple is post-biblical, the idea that the construction of the Temple, rather than the conquest, is the climax of Israel's history is likely also found in the Song of the Sea, Exodus 15:17, "You will bring them and plant them in Your own mountain, / The place You made to dwell in, O Adonai, / The sanctuary, O Adonai, which Your hands established."

[67] *"To atone"* Note the conclusion to the ritual of cleansing the Tabernacle, the precursor to the Temple, in Leviticus 16:34, "This shall be to you a law for all time: to make atonement for the Israelites for all their sins once a year. And Moses did as Adonai had commanded him." Both sacrifices and prayers may lead to atonement. The function of the Temple as a conduit for Israel's penitential prayers is emphasized in one of Solomon's prayers where he dedicates the Temple (1 Kings 8:22–53); see, for example, 1 Kings 8:30: "And when You hear the supplications which Your servant and Your people Israel offer toward this place, give heed in Your heavenly abode—give heed and pardon."

———◆———

GILLMAN (THEOLOGICALLY SPEAKING)

The only way we humans can speak of God is by using metaphors because, Maimonides claims, most people have a clear perception only of bodies. "The Torah speaks in the language of men" (*Mishneh Torah*, bk. 1, 1:9).

It is worth noting that Maimonides here is quoting a statement by the talmudic sage Rabbi Ishmael. In its original context, this is not at all what Ishmael intended by this principle. Ishmael here was disagreeing with Rabbi Akiva, who used every single word or letter in the biblical text to produce a new ruling or interpretation. Ishmael disagreed. "The Torah speaks in the language of men," that is, human language has its own idiosyncratic structure, which it is compelled to use (e.g., see Sanh. 64b). Maimonides reinterpreted this comment and used it as a guiding philosophical principle.

By and large, Ishmael's original intent is ignored. The statement is now widely used as Maimonides uses it. But of course, God is not "really" male or female, in the heavens or in our hearts, in space or in time, happy or sad. To speak of God is to resort to the language of metaphor.

[14–23] *"Blood ... Slaying of the first-born"* We don't simply run through the list of the ten plagues. We recite each one slowly, aloud, dipping our fingers in our wine cup, and dripping one droplet of wine onto our plates for each plague. This historical recollection of the ten plagues is a source of discomfort to many. The image of a vengeful God who inflicts terrible suffering on the Egyptian people, even as retribution for the suffering Egypt inflicted on our ancestors, is troubling. We like to think of God as compassionate and nurturing, the "good guy" God who is always nice. But even if we eliminate the retribution issue, this is far from the only instance where the Bible portrays God in less than favorable terms.

Consider, for example, the image of God in the first two chapters of the Book of Job. This God allows the adversary (later to become Satan) to bring terrible suffering on an innocent man, simply to win a bet. Or consider the God of Psalm 44:24, who sleeps while Israel is destroyed by its enemies. Or the God who strips away Saul's kingship because he disobeyed God by not killing the Amalekite king and the Amalekite animals (1 Sam. 15).

Sometimes God is portrayed as nurturing, and sometimes not. Sometimes God is viewed as vindictive. We must remember, first, that all of these portraits of God are crafted by human beings. None of us knows what God really is like, precisely because God is God and we are human beings. Invariably, these portraits reflect the personal experience of the authors of our biblical texts. More radically, they may reflect the self-perception of these authors, who knew very well that all of us are capable of being charitable in some instances and cruel in others.

Second, our ancestors were committed to the notion that God is active in human history. If we believe that God does direct the course of human events, then on some occasions, God must act in ways that are injurious. In this instance, the plagues are evidence of God's love for and determination to redeem Israel through a display of divine power. In the wake of the Holocaust, some Jews understand quite well why God would act to destroy Israel's enemies.

Much more troubling, however, is the image of God in Job. Here, God is portrayed as acting in a cruel and capricious way in the face of Satan's challenge. Why is this image of God included in our Bible? Here are two possible answers: One, the main message of Job is to celebrate a man whose faith in God was unshaken despite his sufferings; the image of God in this book is incidental to that central purpose. Two, since no one really knows why God permits innocent people to suffer, here is one more explanation to be added to the repertoire. But how do we feel about worshiping this God?

Our own discomfort at God's punishment of the Egyptians is anticipated by a talmudic legend. When the Egyptians were drowning in the Red Sea, the ministering angels wished to utter a song before Adonai. But God rebuked them saying, "The works of My hands are drowning in the sea, and you would sing in My presence!" (Sanh. 39b). To this day, we recall God's sadness through the ritual of dripping wine from our cups. The drops of wine are said to represent God's tears. Apparently even God was ambivalent about the divine need to punish.

[23] *"Slaying of the first-born"* From the sixth plague on, the Torah refers to God's hardening Pharaoh's heart (Exod. 9:12) so that he would not free the Israelites. This seems to pose a moral/theological dilemma: if God is responsible for limiting the king's freedom, why then should Pharaoh be punished for refusing to free the slaves? The conventional response to this apparent dilemma is that God simply reinforced what was apparently Pharaoh's natural inclination.

But if our theological approach permits us to say that it is the human community who constructs the narrative of God's activity in history, then this reading of the story reflects our ancestors' wish to view God as aggressively manifesting divine power in redeeming Israel. Our judgment here applies not to God but to our ancestors, who, in this reading at least, felt little compunction about sparing Pharaoh.

---◆---

GRAY (MEDIEVAL COMMENTATORS)

"Angels" rank lower than "seraphs" in the heavenly hierarchy. They are created anew every day. The "messenger" is the highest angel of all: Metatron, who protects Israel, and who was the commander of God's host that appeared to Joshua (Josh. 5:14). The Talmud (Sanh. 38b) identifies Metatron as the "messenger" whom God said He would send before Israel to protect them (Exod. 23:23). In identifying Metatron as the "messenger," *Ritba* follows in the footsteps of *Ramban*, who explains Exod. 12:12 ("I will mete out punishments to all the gods of Egypt") as meaning that God Himself will carry out judgments against the gods of Egypt, not act through Metatron, as He ordinarily would do.

Machzor Vitry includes a fascinating midrash that was apparently recited as part of the Haggadah in the "provinces," but excluded in the Land of Israel. *Machzor Vitry* explains the exclusion partly on theological grounds (the midrash, as we'll see, implies that God actually needs physical protection) and partly on literary/thematic grounds (the midrash interrupts the flow of the Haggadah narrative). According to the midrash, when God descended to liberate Israel from Egypt, He descended with tens of thousands of legions of angels—among them angels of fire, of hail, and of destruction. These angels asked God to let them do God's will (i.e., liberate Israel), but God said that He would do "the will of My children" Himself. The angels then tried to argue that just as a human king goes out to battle surrounded by servants so as to stay safe from bodily harm, how much more so should they perform this protective service for the Holy Blessed One. Yet God still refused, saying that His mind (as it were) would not be at rest until He descended personally to wreak vengeance on Egypt (*Hilkhot Pesach*, p. 293).

6 *"And with an outstretched arm'—This is the sword"* Rashbetz observes that there is no reference to a sword in the Torah's account of the deliverance from Egypt. Abudarham explains that the answer may lie in a proper understanding of Psalm 136:10, which states that God smote Egypt *bivkhoreihem*, which literally means "*by means of* their first-born." Abudarham alludes to a midrash that explains that in an effort to save themselves, the Egyptian first-born actually slew their parents. (See Arnow, *My People's Passover Haggadah*, Volume 2, pp. 47–48, "slaying the first-born.")

7 *"'And with great awe'—this is the revelation of the Shekhinah"* Abudarham reads *uv'mora* ("and with great awe") with an added letter *heh* at the end as *b'mar'eh* ("and with a great appearance"). That is, the divine presence revealed itself fully in Egypt to fulfill

God's promise to the patriarchs in a spectacular way, despite the fact that Egypt was filled with idolatry that ordinarily would repel the divine presence.

[11] *"Also"* Abudarham points out the connection between this material and what has preceded it. "With a strong hand," "and with an outstretched arm," "and with great awe," "and with signs," "and with wonders" are five items. The Haggadah now goes on to explain that the ten plagues God inflicted on the Egyptians were actually all subsumed within these five categories—two plagues per category. This makes sense because the Hebrew phrase *b'yad chazakah* ("with a strong hand") consists of two words, as do the phrases *uv'mora gadol* ("and with great awe") and *uvizro'a n'tuyah* ("with an outstretched arm"). The plural words "signs" *(otot)* and "wonders" *(moftim)* yield two plagues each, because the minimum plural number is two. This having been established, the Haggadah is now ready to move into the enumeration of the plagues themselves.

"Spill a drop of wine.... Spill a drop of wine.... Spill one more drop of wine" There are different customs for spilling the wine: spilling one drop for each of the ten plagues (yielding a total of ten drops); or spilling three drops for "blood, fire, and pillars of smoke," ten for the plagues, and another three for Rabbi Judah's abbreviations of them (yielding a total of sixteen drops).

The contemporary scholar Rabbi Ephraim Kanarfogel has shown that R. Eliezer Hagadol (Germany, c. 990–1060) seems to be the source of the practice to remove sixteen drops of wine from the cups. The practice was transmitted from R. Eliezer Hagadol to other German scholars and is noted in the pietistic work *Sefer Rokeach* (R. Eleazar of Worms, Germany, twelfth century).[1] *Maharil* (R. Jacob Moellin, Germany, c. 1360–1427) later points to *Sefer Rokeach* and *Ravyah* as sources for two forms of the practice of removing sixteen drops of wine from one's cup in connection with the plagues: either removing wine with the finger or actually pouring some out of the cup. *Maharil* himself explains the practice as symbolizing our wish that these plagues come upon our enemies rather than ourselves.[2] *R'ma* (R. Moses Isserles, Poland, 1520–1572) says that one must toss wine out of the cup with one's finger. This is symbolic of God's sword, which was called *Yohakh*, the name given by kabbalists to an angel appointed over divine vengeance.[3] Kanarfogel points out that this association between the tossing of the wine and God's avenging sword goes back to the tenth or eleventh century, the tossing of the wine perhaps being understood as a way to magically conjure this avenging sword.[4] Moreover, the early German scholars understood this sword to be sixteen-sided, an understanding that may go back to the late antique mystical work *Sefer Heikhalot*.[5] The sword's sixteen sides are alluded to in the name for it provided by *R'ma*: the numerical value of *Yo* (Heb.: *yod vav*), the first part of the sword's name *(Yohakh)*, is sixteen.

The use of the finger to remove the wine is reminiscent of Exodus 8:15 ("This is the finger of God"), the Egyptian magicians' acknowledgment of God's punishing power.

R'ma's explanations of the link between spilling the wine sixteen times and the divine sword were reiterated later by *Magen Avraham* (R. Abraham Gumbiner, Poland, seventeenth century)[6] and *Be'er Heiteiv* (R. Judah Ashkenazi, Poland, eighteenth century).[7]

Some have claimed that Don Isaac Abarbanel (Spain and Italy, 1437–1508) explained the practice in his *Zevach Pesach* Haggadah commentary by reference to Proverbs 24:17 ("If your enemy falls, do not exult"), but the text of his commentary does not include such an explanation. However, as we will see, a related view has been used to explain why we recite only a partial *Hallel* during most of Passover (see Gray, *My People's Passover Haggadah*, Volume 2, p. 164, "*Hallel*").

[12] *"These are the ten plagues ... brought upon the Egyptians in Egypt"* Ramban emphasizes that the plagues struck the Egyptians alone in his comments to Exodus 8:18. There, he asks why God said, "I will set apart the region of Goshen" (Exod. 8:18) and "I will make a distinction between My people and your people" (Exod. 8:19) in connection with the fourth plague. Weren't those distinctions made with the first three plagues? His answer is that, indeed, only the Egyptians suffered the effects of the plagues. Yet the fourth plague was different; once swarms (as *Ramban* and our Haggadah interpret *arov*) begin to move throughout the land, there is no stopping them. Without God's active intervention to distinguish between the two communities, the swarms would have injured Israelites and Egyptians alike. Based on a plain reading of the text in Exodus, R. Abraham ibn Ezra (Spain and various countries, 1089–1164), interestingly, claims that the first three plagues struck the Israelites as well as the Egyptians. This view casts the plagues in a rather different light (Ibn Ezra to Exod. 7:24, 7:29).

[24] *"Rabbi Judah would make them into a mnemonic"* Rashbetz points out that Rabbi Judah is already known in the Talmud for assigning acronyms to laws so that students would be able to remember them well (Men. 96a). Both *Rashbetz* and, earlier, Abudarham point out that Rabbi Judah's acronym is meant to assure us that the plagues happened in the order they are recounted in the Torah, and not according to the order presented in Psalms 78 (blood, wild beasts, frogs, locusts, hail, pestilence, slaying of the first-born) and 105 (darkness, blood, frogs, wild beasts, lice, hail, locusts, slaying of the first-born).

[37] *"How many degrees of goodness has God bestowed upon us"* Ritba and Abudarham ponder why this poem contains fifteen stanzas (fourteen stanzas expressing the notion that it would have been enough had God done only X and not Y, and then the last, a straightforward recitation of what God in fact did). *Ritba* points out, among other things, that the Book of Psalms contains fifteen psalms (Pss. 120–134) called "Psalms of Degrees" (*ma'alot*, meaning "degrees," is the same word that appears in the Haggadah). Also, the Mishnah (Middot 2:5) describes fifteen steps by which pilgrims would ascend from the Women's Court in the Jerusalem Temple to the Court of the Israelites. The Mishnaic reference to the fifteen steps in the Temple is especially interesting since *Dayyenu* moves in chronological order from the Exodus to the building of the Temple. Thus *Dayyenu* recapitulates an aspect of the Temple's architecture, and this aspect of the Temple's architecture represents in brick and mortar the progress of Jewish history up until the Temple was built.

[38] *"If He had brought us out of Egypt"* Abudarham pursues a fairly consistent line of interpretation according to which we are not saying literally that it would have been enough had God—*without doing more*—redeemed us from Egypt or done any of the other thirteen listed favors. Each favor was part of a divine promise that God was bound to keep. Rather, he explains, the point is that God could have fulfilled all of his promises by using means that fell short of the spectacular means He in fact used. For example, God could have taken us out of Egypt and executed judgment on only *some* of the Egyptians—yet He judged all. He could have judged all of the Egyptians, but not their gods—and yet He judged their gods as well. He could have only given us the possessions of the Egyptians located in Egypt—but He did more, and even gave us the possessions of the Egyptians who left Egypt to pursue the Israelites and were killed at the Red Sea.

[49] *"If He had brought us together before Mount Sinai and not given us the Torah"* Abudarham interprets this to mean that had God not given us the Ten Commandments Himself, but through Moses, or had He given us only some, but not all, of the 613 commandments, that would have been sufficient. *Orchot Chayim* (R. Aharon b. R. Jacob Hakohen of Lunel, France and Spain, thirteenth to fourteenth century) offers another interpretation. The Talmud states that when the serpent beguiled Eve, he actually seduced her and had sexual intercourse with her.[8] By means of this intercourse, he conveyed to her what the Talmud calls *zohama*, or "filth." The Talmud implies that this "filth" was some sort of physical substance passed on by humans forevermore—a sort of talmudic version of "original sin." The Talmud says that the people of Israel were able to rid themselves of this "filth" when they stood on Mount Sinai. *Orchot Chayim* turns this "filth" into a metaphor, explaining that it was not physical, but spiritual: doubt about God's unity.[9] Such doubt entered Eve when she disobeyed God and listened to the serpent instead (thus making him a sort of deity for herself), and this doubt was overcome by Israel when they stood at Mount Sinai and witnessed divine revelation.

[51] *"And not built us the Temple"* Ritba points out that the Temple is called the *bet hab'chirah* (literally, the "chosen house") because it is on the site that God chose, per Deuteronomy 12:5 ("look only to the site that Adonai your God will choose …"). *Rashbetz* notes that the building of the Temple is a fitting end to this list of divine favors, because, in contemporary parlance, the Temple was a "favor that kept on giving" through its status as a venue in which people could continually atone for their sins through the sacrificial system.

——◆——

GREEN (PERSONAL SPIRITUALITY)

only for the sake of the covenant that was to follow. But here the Haggadah speaks differently, reminding us that we can see God in the moment we become free. "A handmaiden at the Sea saw more than the greatest prophet," we are taught. There she was, dancing for freedom, seeing God. Liberation itself is a moment in which God's face is revealed.

[49] *"And not given us the Torah"* This verse of *Dayyenu*, says Rabbi Levi Yitzchak of Berdichev, makes no sense. What would be the purpose of coming to Sinai if there was to be no Torah, no revelation? The answer, he says, lies in what happened to Israel in the three days of preparation for the great event. Each one who was present, he says (and of course all of us were present at Sinai!), so sincerely and deeply opened themselves to Torah, casting aside all material concerns in order to hear only God's word, that they were able to discover the entire Torah already implanted within their own hearts. Each of us contains Torah within us; it is only our preoccupation with trivial and superficial pursuits that keeps us from turning inward to find it. The *promise* of revelation was enough, he says, to evoke this discovery/revelation from within.

Avraham Avinu, Abraham our Father, the Talmud tells us, fulfilled the entire Torah, even down to the last detail. (He even fed the angels milk *before* meat, just as the law permits!) But how did he know Torah, living hundreds of years before it was given? Abraham was able to look within. Having left his homeland and his father's house, following God faithfully across the desert, Abraham was stripped of all but the most basic physical needs. There was no wall left that separated him from his own innermost self, where he was able to discover all the secrets of the Torah.

This teaching is as fresh for us as it was for the Chasidic ears that first heard it two hundred years ago. We too understand its eternal truths: the sacred journey into the heart, the need for letting go, and the discovery that all we need to know is already inscribed within us. Nothing in our Jewish journey contradicts this.

———◆———

J. HOFFMAN (TRANSLATION)

God, because it is exclusively masculine, but our translation does not try to capture modernity. Rather, the translation strives to convey as nearly as possible what the Hebrew would have meant to those who compiled and composed it.)

[3] *"First-born"* Usually, "first-born" in English refers only to people, but here (as in the Bible) we use it to mean people and animals alike.

[3] *"I, Adonai"* Or "I am Adonai." Probably the latter was intended in the original Torah text, while our translation accords with the midrashic meaning in the Haggadah.

61

[4] *"I and not an angel"* More colloquially and a little more accurately, "not an angel but Me." In English, it is difficult to emphasize the word "I."

[4] *"The messenger"* So reads the Hebrew, instead of the expected "a messenger."

[4] *"I am He"* Or "I am the one." But we avoid this translation because it would resonate with the creed that "God is one," in a way that the Hebrew does not.

[5] *"Blight"* One possible translation for the Hebrew *dever*. See "Blight" below.

[5] *"Your horses"* Literally, "the horses." Hebrew frequently omits possessives where English requires them. The situation is not unlike the colloquial English, "I'll get the car," which frequently means "I'll get my car."

[6] *"Against"* Literally, "upon."

[7] *"With trials"* The Hebrew *b'* ("with," here) is more general than anything we have in English. Here we would prefer "by," but this is the same preposition that we translate as "with" above. While it is not always necessary to use the same English word for a Hebrew word, in this case we want to preserve the direct connection between these two passages.

[7] *"Awe"* Literally, "awes," the plural of the word at the beginning of verse 7. Probably the word means "awe-inspiring deed(s)."

[11] *"Also"* Hebrew, *davar acher*, frequently used to introduce a second midrashic interpretation of a text. It is a technical term for which we have no English equivalent. It literally means "another thing." (It is tempting but wrong to translate "and another thing!" here.)

[12] *"These are the ten plagues"* Or, perhaps, "there are ten plagues."

[13] *"These are the plagues"* Literally, depending on dialect, "these are they" or "they are these."

[15] *"Frogs"* Literally, "frog." It is not uncommon for languages to use a singular animal noun to refer to more than one animal. We see an example in English with "the bald eagle is returning to the East Coast," which refers, of course, not to one bald eagle but to many of them. Curiously, in the original biblical source in Exodus we find the plural noun "frogs."

[17] *"Swarms"* Although the word is singular (here and in Exodus), it takes a plural verb, so we assume that it is best translated as "swarms." Other translations include the common "wild beasts" and the King James "swarms of flies." We do not know the exact meaning of the word.

[18] *"Blight"* Others, "pestilence" *(JPS)*, "mortality" (Brenton English translation of the Septuagint), "murrain" (King James). ("Murrain" used to be a general term for plagues affecting animals. Now it refers more specifically to contagious diseases of cattle

such as anthrax.) We do not know the exact meaning of the Hebrew word.

[19] *"Boils"* Once again, we do not know the exact meaning of the word. According to the text, it is a skin ailment that afflicts man and beast alike, but we do not know, for example, if the appearance of "boils" on the animals is extraordinary or common. More generally, the common approach of trying to match up historically plausible diseases with the ten plagues suffers from the fundamental flaw that even in the text, the plagues are described as unlikely occurrences. We cannot look at likely historical possibilities to understand specifically unlikely events.

[20] *"Hail"* Even in English, we find this word and similar ones used with some imprecision. What some people call "hail" others call "sleet," for example. This common pattern of multiple meanings for a single word highlights the difficulty we have in translating ancient technical terms accurately.

[21] *"Locusts"* Again, the Hebrew is singular. The word may mean "grasshopper."

[23] *"First-born"* As above, we are faced with a dilemma. In English "first-born" generally refers only to people, but we have no better phrase. ("Firstling," to the extent that it still means anything at all, refers only to animals.)

[24] *"Mnemonic"* Literally, "signs." The mnemonic in Hebrew consists of the first letter of each plague, using "first-born" (instead of "death of ...") for the last plague. In Hebrew, words always begin with consonants, so the acrostic ends up with ten consonants. Vowels are added to make the words pronounceable.

[25] *"How do we know"* More literally, "why do you say." In more colloquial English, we might translate "why do they say ..." or "how do you know...."

[25] *"By"* Literally, "on." Another possibility is "in."

[26] *"Magicians"* Literally, "engravers," or perhaps more generally, "writers." The word is always used in the Bible in the derogatory sense of Egyptian or Babylonian false diviners, as here, in Genesis (also of Egyptians), and in the Book of Daniel (of Babylonians).

[27] *"Hand"* Translated literally. *JPS* prefers "power." Although the literal "hand" may refer to "power" here, we prefer to translate literally to preserve the word play with "finger/hand."

[27] *"Wielded"* Following *JPS*.

[27] *"Feared"* The word for "feared," *yir'u*, sounds like the word for "saw," *yar*, just before, perhaps on purpose. Curiously, "feared" is plural, while "saw" is singular, even though both have a group as their subject (Israel/nation).

[28] *"If the Egyptians suffered ten plagues"* We paraphrase the somewhat confusing Hebrew here, to make the point clearer. Literally, it reads something like: "How many did they suffer from God's finger? Ten plagues. Say then in Egypt they suffered ten

plagues. And by the sea, they suffered fifty plagues."

[29] *"Really"* We add this word. Another possibility is "could be considered as...." In the end, the point is the same.

[30] *"Fierce fury"* Literally, "fury of his nose," a common idiom in the Bible.

[30] *"Sorrow"* Others, "trouble." Neither English word works all that well in context.

[30] *"Evil angels"* As in King James, *JPS* prefers "deadly messengers," probably to avoid the theologically difficult notion of evil angels of God. Perhaps they are "angels of evil," not "evil angels."

[32] *"So"* Again, we paraphrase. The Hebrew here is similar to the Hebrew above.

[36] *"Two hundred fifty"* Literally, in Hebrew, "fifty and two hundred." That word order is common in Hebrew. (Languages differ in the preferred order for compound numbers. German, for example, prefers "three and thirty" over "thirty-three"; we have remnants of that Germanic word order in the song lyrics "four and twenty blackbirds.") We generally ignore such minor linguistic differences. Here, however, the transition from "fifty" to "fifty and two hundred" is more powerful than from "fifty" to "two hundred fifty," a subtlety we cannot capture in (modern) English.

[37] *"Bestowed"* Literally, "are on us." But the Hebrew syntax is poetic. We are unable to replicate the poetic syntax, so we use poetic vocabulary instead.

[38] *"Them"* That is, the Egyptians, as in Exodus 12:12.

[38] *"Enough"* Commonly, "it would have been enough for us." Hebrew grammar makes it possible to express "enough for us" in one succinct word. We prefer to retain the brevity of expression in English even at the expense of overtly indicating "us," particularly because the Hebrew is tenseless and moodless. It is not necessarily past, nor is it necessarily conditional.

[38] *"Brought judgment"* Literally, "brought it" or, even more literally, just "brought." (In Hebrew, "it" is frequently omitted.) "Done it to their gods" is a tempting translation, but that phrase has the wrong connotations.

[41] *"Wealth"* Or "stuff," but "stuff" is too colloquial. "Material goods" is the right idea but sounds too stiff for this poetic setting. Regarding the "giving" of the Egyptian wealth, a story in the Talmud (in San. 91a) recounts a lawsuit in the court of Alexander the Great. The Egyptians sue the Jews and demand their wealth back. The Jews countersue, demanding back wages for six hundred thousand slaves working for 430 years. The case is adjourned and never reconvened.

[42] *"For us"* The word "for us" in Hebrew, *lanu*, is the same as the word for "to us," used in the first part of the sentence ("If he had given *lanu* their wealth ...."), creating a parallel structure we cannot capture in English.

[49] *"Brought us together"* Literally, "brought us near." See "brought us," Volume 1, p. 218.

[51] *"Temple"* Hebrew, *bet hab'chirah* (literally, "house of the choice"), not the more common *bet hamikdash* ("house of the holy [place]" or "house of the sanctuary"). But we have only the one English phrase for "Temple."

[65] *"Gave"* The Hebrew here matches the language in *Dayyenu* exactly. English grammar forces us to make minor changes, such as from "given" to "gave."

———◆———

SIGNPOST: THE ROLE OF GOD

SLAYING THE EGYPTIAN FIRST-BORN, WHICH FINALLY PERSUADED PHARAOH TO LET US GO. ONLY THEN DO WE RECITE THE PLAGUES. THE COMPILERS OF THE HAGGADAH LEFT US WITH ANOTHER ANCIENT MIDRASH THAT ACTUALLY EXTENDS THE NUMBER OF PLAGUES! AFTER SAYING IT TOO, WE CELEBRATE GOD'S SAVING MIGHT IN DAYYENU.

———◆———

L. HOFFMAN (HISTORY)

point. Origen claimed that the Christian "second" covenant through Jesus surpassed the Jewish "original" one through Moses, because Jesus was the Christ, a part of God, whereas Moses was merely a human agent or messenger. Deliverance from Egypt was therefore secondary to salvation through Christ.

[14] *"Blood"* Since the fourteenth century, it has been common practice to dip a finger in the wine cup and accompany each plague by spattering drops of wine on the table, floor, or (nowadays) a plate. Some communities spill the wine directly from the cup, but originally, using one's finger was the norm. This practice is often explained nowadays according to the commonly cited midrash where God chastises Israel for rejoicing at the death of the Egyptian soldiers, who are also God's creatures. Each drop commemorates the tragedy of spilled blood.

But the practice emerged among German Jews trying to come to terms with rampant persecution, so it was probably intended as the reverse—a reminder that God would indeed spill the blood of our enemies. Using one's finger probably anticipates the following midrash which uses the image of a finger to compute the number of plagues God sent the Egyptians at the Red Sea (vv. 25–28, and "How do we know that the Egyptians suffered ten plagues," L. Hoffman, *My People's Passover Haggadah*, Volume 2, p. 66).

[24] *"D'tsakh ... "* [*the Mnemonic*] The midrash ends with a listing of the plagues, after which we hear of Rabbi Judah's mnemonic for them. Elsewhere, we find the mnemonic without the plagues (*Sifre on Deuteronomy*, c. second century). But why use a

mnemonic in the first place? In an era of oral communication, the Rabbis memorized huge chunks of Torah. Didn't Rabbi Judah know the plagues by heart?

There is no easy solution to this conundrum. Tradition notes that his mnemonic divides the plagues into three groups and suggests that the point was not recalling each plague, but indicating the qualitative distinctiveness of each group. Alternatively, the mnemonic was said to have been written on Moses' staff.

The attempt to divide the plagues into groups has a long history. Even Philo, for example, the first-century Jewish philosopher in Alexandria, and hardly a rabbinic Jew, "knew" that the first three plagues came about by Aaron; the next three by Aaron, Moses, or neither of them; then three more came about by Moses alone; and the final one (killing of the first-born) happened solely by the hand of God. Ibn Ezra reports that philosopher and poet Judah Halevi divided the plagues into pairs, according to provenance (from the water, airborne, weather related, and so on), the point being that the last two were supernatural and, therefore, demonstrations of God's absolute "otherness."

None of these explanations is very convincing, so other interpretations point to the fact that the Bible carries more than one list of plagues! Psalm 78 lists them as blood, flies, frogs, swarms, hail, plague, and slaying of the first-born (only seven, not ten). Psalm 105 lists darkness, blood, frogs, flies, lice, hail, swarms, slaying of the first-born (eight, in all). Presumably, Rabbi Judah was reminding people to use the listing in Exodus, not the parallel accounts in Psalms.

[25] *"How do we know that the Egyptians suffered ten plagues"* An early midrash, carried in two tannaitic collections (prior to 200), both called *Mekhilta*. But the first Haggadah usage is in *Seder Rav Amram* (c. 860) and in some (but not many) Genizah fragments from Eretz Yisrael. Saadiah Gaon (c. 920) calls it just "an option," presumably because, as part of the Haggadah, it was only a relatively recent addition.

It was added here to elaborate on God's vengeance upon Egypt. *Dayyenu*, which follows, is a parallel account describing the opposite: God's grace toward Israel (see below, *Dayyenu*). The two expansions were originally considered a single piece.

Modern editors have viewed them separately. "How do we know ..." seems bloodthirsty. Except for a line or two, *Dayyenu* praises God's merciful goodness. Modern theology would like to imagine a God who saves the poor and oppressed (*Dayyenu*), but without mass destruction of the oppressors ("How do we know"). So "How do we know" is usually dropped, while *Dayyenu* is featured.

[37] *"Dayyenu"* Liturgically, *Dayyenu* is a litany (from the Greek, *litaneia*), a technical term for a set of short (usually one- or two-line) petitions with parallel poetic structure. We use the word for *any* liturgy—not just petitions—structured that way. (Another well-known litany—which is petitional—is *Avinu Malkenu*, a poem for the High Holy Days.)

One of the first studies of *Dayyenu* emerged through the study of Jewish and Christian liturgical parallels. A homily had been composed by Bishop Melito (died c. 180) of Sardis (Turkey); it denounced Jews for killing Christ (for detail, see *My*

People's Passover Haggadah, Volume 1, p. 33). So *Dayyenu* was identified as an ancient Jewish response to Melito, a litany-like expression of Israel's appreciation for, rather than its contempt of, God. Others, noting that the number of verses in *Dayyenu* (fifteen) equals the number of steps in the Temple of old, assume that *Dayyenu* may even predate Melito, so that Melito's diatribe is actually a sarcastic response to the prior Jewish claim.

In all probability, neither view is correct. The first mention of *Dayyenu* is in *Siddur Saadiah* (c. 920 CE), which calls *Dayyenu* one of two Haggadah "options," the other being the parallel midrash extending the number of plagues (see above "How do we know ..."). Characterizing them as "options" suggests that they are recent innovations, hardly ancient staples. Fortunately, Saadiah's *Siddur* has an introduction. The purpose of the *Siddur*, Saadiah tells us there, is to weed out liturgical innovations that are theologically or otylistically improper, while indicating also where such novel prayers are acceptable. *Dayyenu* is one of the recent alternatives that Saadiah permits—only as an option, however, because it is indeed just a relatively recent creation, certainly post-talmudic.

In all probability, both the ancient poem by Melito and our medieval *Dayyenu* are midrashic commentaries on Psalm 78, a litany-like listing of all that God did for Israel, followed by the charge that Israel "defiantly tested God ... fell away, disloyal ... and incensed Him with their idols" (Ps. 78:56–58). Self-deprecating poetry is common to the psalms. Melito drew on it to chastise the Jews of his day. *Dayyenu* transformed it into words of praise.

[51] *"The Temple"* Medieval Rabbis shaped history to fit theology. They divided history into three eras: the time of the Temple, when sacrifices were possible; the era we live in now; and a messianic time to come when the Temple will be restored. In the interim, our task is to do God's will, so as to merit the Temple's restoration.

The Temple's purpose is its sacrifices, which atone for our sins. So until it is rebuilt, we need especially to concentrate on secondary means of atonement, like "repentance, prayer, and charity" *(t'shuvah, t'fillah, ts'dakah)*, a triad of concerns that we stress during the High Holy Day period.

On Yom Kippur, the pinnacle of the High Holy Days, we add a lengthy liturgical composition called the *Avodah*, a description of the Yom Kippur offerings that were made by the high priest to achieve divine pardon. Ancient and medieval poets wrote introductions for it, describing sacred history from Adam and Eve to the destruction of the Temple. These poems, like *Dayyenu*, end at the same point in historical time: the end of the sacrificial system. Since all we do in this interim period is wait for the messiah, nothing after that matters.

Most Jews today would disagree. We are a people almost obsessed with our history. Author Isaac Bashevis Singer is reputed to have said, "We Jews have many flaws; amnesia is not among them." So some Haggadot have made use of the litany nature of *Dayyenu* to compose new verses, bringing sacred history up to date. A good example is Classical Reform Judaism, which omitted reference to the Temple, but added stanzas thanking God for sending the prophets and for dispatching us on "the mission of Israel," the duty to spread the prophetic message around the world. My own family Haggadah adds praise for "renewing our Land [of Israel]."

———◆———

LANDES (HALAKHAH)

[49] *"And not given us the Torah"* Rabbi Yosef Shalom Eliashiv (contemporary halakhic authority for Ashkenazi Charedi Orthodoxy in Israel) cites a question and answer from his grandfather, the author of the influential *Leshem Sh'vo Va'achlamah* (Rabbi Shlomoh Eliashiv, early twentieth century, Lithuania and Jerusalem): How could a rabbinic Jew ever say that the Sinai experience would have been "enough" without the actual giving of the Torah? The answer depends on emphasizing "and not given *us* the Torah." He reminds us of the talmudic debate regarding the purity of the oven of Achnai (B.M. 59a). Rabbi Eliezer points to miracles that occur in support of his opinion—a tree changes places and a river flows upstream, at his command. Everyone else holds fast in opposition. Finally, a *bat kol* ("heavenly voice") exclaims, "What is it with you, that you oppose Rabbi Eliezer, even though the Halakhah follows him in every case!" A senior figure, Rabbi Joshua, stands up and insists, "'It [a halakhic decision] is not in heaven [*lo bashamayim hi*] [Deut. 30:12]. We therefore pay no attention to a *bat kol.*" Rabbi Eliezer remained defeated, despite divine attestation to his authority.

According to Rabbi Eliashiv, even if God "had not given us the Torah," means that even if we "had not been given the power of halakhic decision making [*p'sak*]." The point is that even so, we would still have had access to Torah decisions via direct divine instruction (the *bat kol*), and that would suffice. It would be *Dayyenu*, for we would know what to do. Now, however, that we have been given the power to decide halakhic matters, then "how much more so is this [gift] a most increased blessing that God has given us!"

This answer contains a compelling understanding of the Halakhah. "If He had brought us together before Mount Sinai," we would have the Torah and its way of life. And certainly we could say, *Dayyenu*, "Enough," for we would know how to act morally and spiritually. But now that the Torah has been given to us—that is, we have the power to decide Halakhah according to a set of articulated rules—we have both the authenticity of Sinai and the creativity of our own participation in the halakhic process. Alone, Sinai would grant us a top-down Torah, true but authoritarian. Alone, the ability to decide Halakhah would have created a process whereby "Man is the measure of all things," and Halakhah becomes whatever we decide it to be. The "divine rub" providing warmth and light is the tension between Torah in its "purity" before it is given, and the Torah as interpreted and applied by humans afterward. *Dayyenu* gives thanks for both, as it builds each verse upon the one before, adding one truth on top of another. Each successive gift from God is added to, but does not negate, the earlier. These two gifts of

Halakhah (pure revelation and interpretive capacity) infuse each other in dialectical tension.

———◆———

ZIERLER (FEMINIST VOICES)

manifestation of divine presence. Accordingly, many feminist Haggadot incorporate *Shekhinah* as God's name in alternative feminist *b'rachot*. In this regard, it is worth noting the association here of *gilui Shekhinah* (revelation of the *Shekhinah*) with "great awe," for it points out the variegated nature of our *Shekhinah* tradition. As Sharon Koren notes, the *Shekhinah*, though grammatically feminine, "remains male or at the very least androgynous in early rabbinic literature."[1] Kabbalistic literature develops the notion of the *Shekhinah* as a female aspect of God, but the result is rarely palatable for feminists, as the kabbalistic *Shekhinah*—contrary to this Haggadah passage, which celebrates God's awesome deliverance of the people from the midst of another nation—is typically passive, dependent, and vulnerable to the demonic *sitra achra* (other side). However, some *Shekhinah* traditions have proved more "usable" for feminists. In both rabbinic and kabbalistic thought, "mother-*Shekhinah*" is said to follow the Jews into exile. Like the weeping Rachel at Ramah (Jer. 31:15), "[s]he cannot forsake them in their time of trouble, and she tries to bear the burden of defeat and subjection with them, in order to strengthen them and protect them, and to hasten their final redemption."[2] According to Lynn Gottlieb, Jewish sources on the *Shekhinah* offer a broad array of feminine images through which one can encounter the divine: "Waxing and waning moon, evening and morning star, mirror, well of waters, primordial sea, rose amid the thorns, lily of the valley, Mother of Wisdom, the oral tradition of Torah, Womb of Emanations, gateway and door, house and sacred shrine, doe, dove, mother eagle, serpent, the soul of women ancestors, the community of Israel, the Sabbath Queen and Bride, the Tree of Life, the menorah, and the earth itself."[3]

[13] *"And these are the plagues"* Margaret Moers Wenig has written a modern midrash in which she imagines Miriam quarreling with Moses about his willingness to acquiesce to God's plans for the plagues against the Egyptians. "When God threatened to destroy all of Sodom, Abraham argued with him. Will you destroy the righteous along with the wicked? Surely you will not allow the innocent to die?!" In this midrash, Miriam becomes a frustrated advocate of nonviolent protest. Wenig's answer to this midrash as to why in Exodus 15 Miriam only sings a faint echo of Moses' longer song is that the destruction of Egypt was not what she wanted, rather what she had tried to avert.[4]

Many women's Seders use the framework of the ten plagues as a forum to discuss societal wrongdoings against women. The *San Diego Women's Haggadah* (and many subsequent privately printed women's Haggadot) included the following "Plagues of Jewish Women":

1. The consistently male image of God.
2. The lack of recognition of women rabbis, cantors, scholars and decision makers who could serve as models for all of us.
3. The biblical stories traditionally selected for commentary, which neglect the role of women.
4. The sexist language of most prayers and blessings.
5. The repressive divorce laws, and the exclusion of women as witnesses in a Jewish court.
6. The education of our young women not being taken as seriously as that of our young men.
7. The lack of equality in salary and promotional opportunities for women in Jewish education and community service.
8. The devaluation of Jewish womanhood after childbearing years are over.
9. The denial by omission of single women, childless women, battered women, lesbians, the elderly, the poor and disabled, from among the central concerns of organized Judaism.
10. The prison created by rigid traditional views of men and women.[5]

[25] *"Rabbi Yosei the Galilean says"* In 1981, Arnold M. Rothstein published an article in the *Journal of Reform Judaism* expressing theological opposition to a 1979 Haggadah produced by the Union of American Hebrew Congregations and the Task Force on Equality of Women in Judaism. The Haggadah in question, like many previous and subsequent feminist Haggadot, included discussion of the deeds of the women of Exodus: Shifra, Puah, Yocheved, and Miriam. Rothstein's based his opposition on the idea that the Haggadah is meant to emphasize God's singular role in taking the people of Israel out of Egypt: "'Adonai brought us out of Egypt'—not by an angel and not by a seraph and not by a messenger, but rather the Holy One of Blessing Himself" (v. 1).

Rothstein supported his argument against including the women of the Exodus story by noting that Moses himself is mentioned only once in the Haggadah, specifically in this midrash quoted in the name of Rabbi Yosei the Galilean.[6] What Rothstein ignores, however, is that this one mention of Moses, *vaya'aminu b'Adonai uv'Moshe avdo*, "and [Israel] believed in Adonai and in Moses His servant" (v. 27), is taken from Exodus 14:31, the overture verse before the Song of the Sea, a celebratory moment in which Miriam plays a significant part. Even if one agrees with Rothstein's reading of the theology of the Haggadah, it seems very appropriate to include Miriam here, alongside Moses. Indeed, based on the fact that Miriam's answer to the people in Exodus 15:21 is said *lahem* ("to them," masculine) and not *lahen* ("to them," feminine), it is fair to assume that Miriam sang not merely for the women, but for the entire people, and so this great moment by the sea was one that she shared equally with her brother.

[37] *"Dayyenu"* The gratitude expressed in *Dayyenu* in no way typifies the attitude of the Israelites in the desert. In the Bible, the people express little satisfaction. They miss Egypt, with its cucumbers and melons; they lack water to drink and meat to eat; they abhor the idea of dying in the wilderness. Certainly, from the viewpoint of Moses and God, these complaints are intolerable; and yet, complaints can also be understood as a

healthy expression of autonomy, especially for a group that formerly had no avenues for protest.

Feminist Haggadot have in large measure adopted a *lo dayyenu* mode, insisting on the need to supplement tradition, rather than to be complacent with that which was done or said in the past. E. M. Broner and Naomi Nimrod's *The Women's Haggadah* includes a lengthy list of *lo dayyenu*s that begins with a dissatisfaction with the Bible's depiction of Eve as helpmeet rather than as equal partner, made in the image of God, and culminates with more contemporary complaints about the conflict between a desire to advance at work and the "need to perform housewifely duties as well."[7]

◆ ◆ ◆

Moses and the Israelites Crossing the Red Sea;
and a Pioneer (Chaluts) Working the Land
The Haggadah of Passover, New York, 1944
Nota Koslowsky, illustrator
Collection of Stephen P. Durchslag

11. SUMMING IT ALL UP …

A. Symbols of the Night: Passover, Matzah, Bitter Herbs

[1]Rabban Gamaliel used to say, "Anyone who doesn't explain these three things on Passover has not fulfilled his obligation: Passover, matzah, and bitter herbs."

רַבָּן גַּמְלִיאֵל הָיָה אוֹמֵר. כָּל־שֶׁלֹּא אָמַר שְׁלֹשָׁה דְבָרִים אֵלּוּ בַּפֶּסַח לֹא יָצָא יְדֵי חוֹבָתוֹ. וְאֵלּוּ הֵן: פֶּסַח. מַצָּה. וּמָרוֹר:

Without pointing to or lifting the shank bone, recite:

[2]The Passover that our ancestors ate when the Temple still stood: What is it for? [3]It is for the Holy One of Blessing's passing over the houses of our ancestors in Egypt, as it says, "You shall say the Passover sacrifice is for Adonai, who passed over the houses of the children of Israel in Egypt when He struck the Egyptians but saved our houses. The people then bowed down low."

פֶּסַח שֶׁהָיוּ אֲבוֹתֵינוּ אוֹכְלִים בִּזְמַן שֶׁבֵּית הַמִּקְדָּשׁ קַיָּם. עַל שׁוּם מָה? עַל שׁוּם שֶׁפָּסַח הַקָּדוֹשׁ בָּרוּךְ הוּא עַל בָּתֵּי אֲבוֹתֵינוּ בְּמִצְרָיִם. שֶׁנֶּאֱמַר: וַאֲמַרְתֶּם זֶבַח פֶּסַח הוּא לַיָי אֲשֶׁר פָּסַח עַל בָּתֵּי בְנֵי יִשְׂרָאֵל בְּמִצְרַיִם בְּנָגְפּוֹ אֶת־מִצְרַיִם וְאֶת־בָּתֵּינוּ הִצִּיל וַיִּקֹּד הָעָם וַיִּשְׁתַּחֲווּ:

Point to or lift the matzah and recite:

[4]The matzah that we eat: What is it for? [5]It is for our ancestors' dough not sufficing to leaven by the time the king over the kings of kings, the Holy One of Blessing, was revealed to them and redeemed them, as it says, "They baked the dough that they brought out of Egypt into cakes of matzah, because it had not leavened, because they were evicted from Egypt and they could not delay, and they hadn't prepared any provisions."

מַצָּה זוֹ שֶׁאָנוּ אוֹכְלִים עַל שׁוּם מָה? עַל שׁוּם שֶׁלֹּא הִסְפִּיק בְּצֵקָם שֶׁל אֲבוֹתֵינוּ לְהַחֲמִיץ עַד שֶׁנִּגְלָה עֲלֵיהֶם מֶלֶךְ מַלְכֵי הַמְּלָכִים הַקָּדוֹשׁ בָּרוּךְ הוּא וּגְאָלָם. שֶׁנֶּאֱמַר: וַיֹּאפוּ אֶת־הַבָּצֵק אֲשֶׁר הוֹצִיאוּ מִמִּצְרַיִם עֻגֹת מַצּוֹת כִּי לֹא חָמֵץ כִּי גֹרְשׁוּ מִמִּצְרַיִם וְלֹא יָכְלוּ לְהִתְמַהְמֵהַּ וְגַם צֵדָה לֹא עָשׂוּ לָהֶם:

Point to or lift the bitter herbs and recite:

[6]The bitter herbs that we eat: What are they for? [7]They are for the Egyptians embittering the lives of our ancestors in Egypt, as it says, "They embittered their lives with hard work with mortar

מָרוֹר זֶה שֶׁאָנוּ אוֹכְלִים עַל שׁוּם מָה? עַל שׁוּם שֶׁמֵּרְרוּ הַמִּצְרִים אֶת־חַיֵּי אֲבוֹתֵינוּ בְּמִצְרָיִם. שֶׁנֶּאֱמַר: וַיְמָרְרוּ אֶת־חַיֵּיהֶם בַּעֲבֹדָה קָשָׁה בְּחֹמֶר

and brick, and with all manner of work in the field; they did all of their work under duress."

B. The Essence of the Night: "In Each and Every Generation …"

[8]In each and every generation people must regard themselves as though they personally left Egypt, as it says, "Tell your child on that very day: 'This is what Adonai did for me when I left Egypt.'" [9]The Holy One of Blessing did not redeem only our ancestors, but He even redeemed us with them, as it says, "He brought us out of there in order to bring us to and give us the land that He swore to our ancestors."

וּבִלְבֵנִים וּבְכָל־עֲבֹדָה בַּשָּׂדֶה אֵת כָּל־עֲבֹדָתָם אֲשֶׁר עָבְדוּ בָהֶם בְּפָרֶךְ:

[8]בְּכָל־דּוֹר וָדוֹר חַיָּב אָדָם לִרְאוֹת אֶת־עַצְמוֹ כְּאִלּוּ הוּא יָצָא מִמִּצְרָיִם. שֶׁנֶּאֱמַר: וְהִגַּדְתָּ לְבִנְךָ בַּיּוֹם הַהוּא לֵאמֹר בַּעֲבוּר זֶה עָשָׂה יְיָ לִי בְּצֵאתִי מִמִּצְרָיִם: [9]לֹא אֶת־אֲבוֹתֵינוּ בִּלְבָד גָּאַל הַקָּדוֹשׁ בָּרוּךְ הוּא. אֶלָּא אַף אוֹתָנוּ גָּאַל עִמָּהֶם. שֶׁנֶּאֱמַר: וְאוֹתָנוּ הוֹצִיא מִשָּׁם לְמַעַן הָבִיא אֹתָנוּ לָתֶת לָנוּ אֶת־הָאָרֶץ אֲשֶׁר נִשְׁבַּע לַאֲבֹתֵינוּ:

Pointing Fingers: Husband and Wife Blame Each Other for Embittering Their Lives
Germany, second half of the fifteenth century, Bibliothèque nationale de France (Ms. Hebr. 1333, 19 verso)
Note: The motif of the husband pointing to his wife as a source of bitterness appears in a number
of medieval Haggadot. This one is unusual because here the wife dishes it right back to her husband.
Of special note is the fact that the Hebrew citations over their heads depict both husband and
wife as learned enough to use word-plays rooted in the language of Talmudic debate.

ARNOW (THE WORLD OF MIDRASH)

[3] *"He struck the Egyptians but saved our houses"* The *Mekhilta D'rabbi Shimon bar Yochai* poses an interesting hypothetical regarding the death of the first-born. What if an Egyptian were visiting an Israelite and even lying in the same bed? The Egyptian alone would die, because Scripture says, "I will pass over *you*" (Exod. 12:13).[1] More than five hundred years later, *Exodus Rabbah* (18:2) developed the same case to teach a profound lesson. "When the Egyptians heard that God would strike down their first-born, some of them brought their first-born to an Israelite and said: *(p. 77)*

BRETTLER (OUR BIBLICAL HERITAGE)

[1] *"Passover, matzah, and bitter herbs"* These three items are connected only in the following two verses, which legislate how the pascal lamb should be consumed: Exodus 12:8, "They shall eat the flesh that same night; they shall eat it roasted over the fire, with unleavened bread and with bitter herbs," and Numbers 9:11, "they shall offer it in the second month, *(p. 78)*

GILLMAN (THEOLOGICALLY SPEAKING)

[8] *"As though they personally left Egypt"* This is the most explicit statement of the theme that the Exodus was not simply a historical event that happened once upon a time, way back when. Rather, it inhabits an eternal present; it is contemporaneous, it is happening today, to us.

Two qualifications: First, *(p. 79)*

GRAY (MEDIEVAL COMMENTATORS)

[1] *"Rabban Gamaliel used to say '… has not fulfilled his obligation'"* Rabban Gamaliel's directive is found in Mishnah Pesachim 10:5 (also in Pes. 116a–b). Abudarham, among other commentators, explains Rabban Gamaliel to mean that even if one ate the Passover sacrifice, matzah, and *maror*, one would not have fulfilled his obligation as to those *mitzvot* unless he also explained their meaning, since the Torah is very particular about the need to recite and discuss matters relating to *(p. 80)*

[For prayer instructions, see page 72.]

11. SUMMING IT ALL UP …

A. Symbols of the Night: Passover, Matzah, Bitter Herbs

[1] Rabban Gamaliel used to say, "Anyone who doesn't explain these three things on Passover has not fulfilled his obligation: Passover, matzah, and bitter herbs." [2] The Passover that our ancestors ate when the Temple still stood: What is it for? [3] It is for the Holy One of Blessing's passing over the houses of our ancestors in Egypt, as it says, "You shall say the Passover sacrifice is for Adonai, who passed over the houses of the children of Israel in Egypt when He struck

GREEN (PERSONAL SPIRITUALITY)

[4] *"The matzah"* The Haggadah offers us two explanations for the eating of matzah. One is taken directly from the Torah: matzah represents the unleavened bread that the Israelites carried on their shoulders as they departed in haste; it was baked only by the hot desert sun. This interpretation means that in matzah we are to taste the moment of liberation, the rush out of Egypt and into freedom that has forever transformed our lives. But we are also told, earlier in the Seder, "This is the *(p. 81)*

J. HOFFMAN (TRANSLATION)

[1] *"Explain"* Literally, "say." The next word can mean "things" or "words," so one logical possibility is that the requirement is only to mention the three words that follow. But we assume that the point is to explain the things, not merely say the words. Another possibility is "discuss."

[1] *"Passover"* That is, *pesach*, which refers to the holiday and to the sacrifice associated with it.

[2] *"Passover"* That is, the Passover offering. *(p. 82)*

רַבָּן גַּמְלִיאֵל הָיָה אוֹמֵר. כָּל־שֶׁלֹּא אָמַר שְׁלֹשָׁה [1] דְּבָרִים אֵלּוּ בַּפֶּסַח לֹא יָצָא יְדֵי חוֹבָתוֹ. וְאֵלּוּ הֵן: פֶּסַח. מַצָּה. וּמָרוֹר: [2] פֶּסַח שֶׁהָיוּ אֲבוֹתֵינוּ אוֹכְלִים בִּזְמַן שֶׁבֵּית הַמִּקְדָּשׁ קַיָּם. עַל שׁוּם מָה? [3] עַל שׁוּם שֶׁפָּסַח הַקָּדוֹשׁ בָּרוּךְ הוּא עַל בָּתֵּי אֲבוֹתֵינוּ בְּמִצְרָיִם. שֶׁנֶּאֱמַר: וַאֲמַרְתֶּם זֶבַח פֶּסַח הוּא לַיְיָ אֲשֶׁר פָּסַח עַל בָּתֵּי בְנֵי יִשְׂרָאֵל בְּמִצְרַיִם בְּנָגְפּוֹ

L. HOFFMAN (HISTORY)

[1] *"Rabban Gamaliel used to say"* This is a remarkable passage, since nowhere else does our liturgy insist that we explain *mitzvot* in addition to actually doing them. Some scholars see in this anomaly a polemic against Christians, who were defining their own "separatist" Christian identity precisely when Gamaliel II (the patriarch in about 90 CE) was determining the shape of post–70 CE Judaism. Christians did so by composing the Gospels, which included the description of Jesus' last supper as a Seder. *(p. 83)*

SIGNPOST: SUMMING IT ALL UP

OUR STORY HAS BEEN TOLD, BEGINNING WITH TWO SHORT CONSIDERATIONS OF THE NATURE OF ENSLAVEMENT (SEE MY PEOPLE'S PASSOVER HAGGADAH, VOLUME 1, P. 161, 213) AND CONTINUING WITH A LONGER MIDRASHIC ACCOUNT OF HOW WE WERE SAVED FROM IT. THE RABBIS INSISTED THAT WE (1) START WITH ENSLAVEMENT, THEN (2) *(p. 84)*

KUSHNER AND POLEN (CHASIDIC VOICES)

[1] *"Rabban Gamaliel ... [must explain] Passover"* Rabbi Levi Yitzchak of Berditchev (*Kedushat Levi, Parashat Bo,* vol. 1, p. 146) notes that the Torah refers to Passover as *chag hamatzot,* "the festival of unleavened bread." But Jews throughout history have *(p. 84)*

LANDES (HALAKHAH)

[2] *"Passover"* This refers specifically to the *korban pesach,* the Passover (sometimes called "paschal") sacrifice. This is the core ritual of Passover. The Rabbis distinguish *pesach mitsrayim,* the "Passover offering of Egypt," from *pesach dorot,* "Passover *(p. 85)*

ZIERLER (FEMINIST VOICES)

[3] *"Passover sacrifice"* An interesting story of female religious zeal is told in Nedarim 36a. The father in this story challenges his children to a race, saying, "I will sacrifice the Passover offering with whichever of you goes up first to Jerusalem." As it turned out, *(p. 92)*

the Egyptians but saved our houses. The people then bowed down low."

אֶת־מִצְרַיִם וְאֶת־בָּתֵּינוּ הִצִּיל וַיִּקֹּד הָעָם וַיִּשְׁתַּחֲווּ:

⁴The matzah that we eat: What is it for? ⁵It is for our ancestors' dough not sufficing to leaven by the time the king over the kings of kings, the Holy One of Blessing, was revealed to them and redeemed them, as it says, "They baked the dough that they brought out of Egypt into cakes of matzah, because it had not leavened, because they were evicted from Egypt and they could not delay, and they hadn't prepared any provisions."

⁴מַצָּה זוֹ שֶׁאָנוּ אוֹכְלִים עַל שׁוּם מָה? ⁵עַל שׁוּם שֶׁלֹּא הִסְפִּיק בְּצֵקָם שֶׁל אֲבוֹתֵינוּ לְהַחֲמִיץ עַד שֶׁנִּגְלָה עֲלֵיהֶם מֶלֶךְ מַלְכֵי הַמְּלָכִים הַקָּדוֹשׁ בָּרוּךְ הוּא וּגְאָלָם. שֶׁנֶּאֱמַר: וַיֹּאפוּ אֶת־הַבָּצֵק אֲשֶׁר הוֹצִיאוּ מִמִּצְרַיִם עֻגֹת מַצּוֹת כִּי לֹא חָמֵץ כִּי גֹרְשׁוּ מִמִּצְרַיִם וְלֹא יָכְלוּ לְהִתְמַהְמֵהַּ וְגַם צֵדָה לֹא עָשׂוּ לָהֶם:

⁶The bitter herbs that we eat: What are they for? ⁷They are for the Egyptians embittering the lives of our ancestors in Egypt, as it says, "They embittered their lives with hard work with mortar and brick, and with all manner of work in the field; they did all of their work under duress."

⁶מָרוֹר זֶה שֶׁאָנוּ אוֹכְלִים עַל שׁוּם מָה? ⁷עַל שׁוּם שֶׁמֵּרְרוּ הַמִּצְרִים אֶת־חַיֵּי אֲבוֹתֵינוּ בְּמִצְרַיִם. שֶׁנֶּאֱמַר: וַיְמָרְרוּ אֶת־חַיֵּיהֶם בַּעֲבֹדָה קָשָׁה בְּחֹמֶר וּבִלְבֵנִים וּבְכָל־עֲבֹדָה בַּשָּׂדֶה אֵת כָּל־עֲבֹדָתָם אֲשֶׁר עָבְדוּ בָהֶם בְּפָרֶךְ:

B. The Essence of the Night: "In Each and Every Generation …"

⁸In each and every generation people must regard themselves as though they personally left Egypt, as it says, "Tell your child on that very day: 'This is what Adonai did for me when I left Egypt.'" ⁹The Holy One of Blessing did not redeem only our ancestors, but He even redeemed us with them, as it says, "He brought us out of there

⁸בְּכָל־דּוֹר וָדוֹר חַיָּב אָדָם לִרְאוֹת אֶת־עַצְמוֹ כְּאִלּוּ הוּא יָצָא מִמִּצְרַיִם. שֶׁנֶּאֱמַר: וְהִגַּדְתָּ לְבִנְךָ בַּיּוֹם הַהוּא לֵאמֹר בַּעֲבוּר זֶה עָשָׂה יְיָ לִי בְּצֵאתִי מִמִּצְרָיִם: ⁹לֹא אֶת־אֲבוֹתֵינוּ בִּלְבַד גָּאַל הַקָּדוֹשׁ בָּרוּךְ הוּא. אֶלָּא אַף אוֹתָנוּ גָּאַל עִמָּהֶם. שֶׁנֶּאֱמַר: וְאוֹתָנוּ הוֹצִיא מִשָּׁם

in order to bring us to and give us the land that He swore to our ancestors."

לְמַעַן הָבִיא אֹתָנוּ לָתֶת לָנוּ אֶת־ הָאָרֶץ אֲשֶׁר נִשְׁבַּע לַאֲבֹתֵינוּ:

ARNOW (THE WORLD OF MIDRASH)

'Please let him pass the night with you.' [The Israelites granted the Egyptians asylum] but when they awoke at midnight, they found the Egyptians dead." They had tried to save the Egyptians, but discovered they could not alter God's plan. Notwithstanding *God's* actions, however, *we* remain bound by the imperative to save life.

[5] *"They were evicted"* The Bible uses the same root (*g.r.sh*) to describe God's expulsion of Adam and Eve from Eden and Pharaoh's ejection of Israel from Egypt. *Exodus Rabbah* (18:6) extends the Eden-Egypt parallel by elaborating on a phrase from Genesis 13:10, "like the garden of Adonai, like the Land of Egypt." To reward Egypt for welcoming Joseph and his family, God called Egypt "Eden." Despite slavery, the Israelites found leaving it difficult. Given that Pharaoh had to evict (i.e., expel) the Israelites from Egypt, their subsequent yearning to return also comes as no surprise.

[5] *"Hadn't prepared any provisions"* The *Mekhilta D'rabbi Shimon bar Yochai* asserts that when the Israelites left they had such faith in God that they took no provisions for the journey, not even snacks for their children.[2] The *Mekhilta D'rabbi Yishmael* valorizes Israel's faith—in Moses rather than God.[3] They were willing to follow him anywhere. But just a few days later they excoriate Moses: "Was it for want of graves in Egypt that you brought us to die in the wilderness?" (Exod. 14:11). Despite all the mighty deeds of God and Moses, the Israelites' faith proved shallow. Perhaps it takes something more intimate to nurture enduring faith.

[7] *"Embittered"* "God raised up a deliverer for them—Miriam, whose name intimates the bitterness, *mirur* [*mirur* and *Miri*am], of slavery" (*Exod. Rab.* 26:1).

[8] *"In each and every generation"* This passage expresses the ultimate goal of the Seder. The *Mekhilta* comments on the words "doing wonders" (Exod. 15:11), a phrase the Israelites sing after crossing the Red Sea. "God *did* wonders for us and *does* them for us in each and every generation."[4] Our ancestors experienced redemption. So can we.

[9] *"The land that He swore to our ancestors"* A medieval midrash asserts that when the dead are resurrected even the generation that died in the wilderness will enter the land God "swore to our ancestors" (*Midrash Lekach Tov, Ekev*, 15a). If there was hope for the generation that worshiped the golden calf, faithful Jews who endured subsequent exiles could surely have hope.

◆———

on the fourteenth day of the month, at twilight. They shall eat it with matzah and bitter herbs."

[3] *"Passing over"* The root *p-s-ch*, usually translated as "pass over," may be homonymic in biblical Hebrew and may also mean "protect." This is almost certainly its meaning in Isaiah 31:5, "Like the birds that fly, even so will Adonai of hosts shield Jerusalem, shielding and saving, protecting [*paso'ach*] and rescuing." To the extent that various texts and traditions recall the idea that God protected Israelite houses from a Destroyer who killed the first-born (see "Not by an angel … not by a messenger," *My People's Passover Haggadah*, Volume 2, p. 29), the translation "protect" may be more appropriate than "pass over" here.

[3] *"The Passover sacrifice … Adonai, who passed over"* From Exodus 12:27, the only place where the noun *pesach* and the verb *pasach* are used together in a single verse.

[4] *"Matzah"* Matzah was a regular food item in ancient Israel, eaten and served to guests (e.g., Gen. 19:3), and often accompanying sacrifices, according to the legislation of Leviticus. Etymologically, it may be connected to a root meaning "flat" or to an Arabic word meaning "tasteless." Though unleavened, it should not be imagined like contemporary hard flat matzah; indeed, the matzah that the Samaritans use today for their Passover celebration is more like pita than contemporary Jewish matzah.

[5] *"King over the kings of kings"* Never found in Hebrew in the Bible, the Aramaic equivalent of this term is found only in Daniel 2:37, where it is used for King Nebuchadnezzar; it became a common term for God in post-biblical literature. A similar term is used in Akkadian for Mesopotamian kings; it was borrowed into Aramaic, and then into Hebrew, where it was applied to God.

[5] *"Because it had not leavened, because they were evicted from Egypt"* Quoting Exodus 12:39 in terms of the origin of the custom of eating matzah, rather than the tradition of Deuteronomy 16:3 that it is poor man's bread and thus reminds us of the Israelite's enslavement (see *My People's Passover Haggadah*, Volume 1, p. 123).

[6] *"Bitter herbs"* Most likely the biblical word *maror* was a generic word for something bitter, rather than a designation for a particular plant. In Lamentations 3:15 it is used together with wormwood.

[7] *"They embittered"* Exodus 1:14.

[8] *"As though they personally left Egypt"* This radical idea of reliving the Exodus experience is never found explicitly in the Bible. Although it is not cited as a proof text, this idea may also be based on Deuteronomy 29:1, "Moses summoned all Israel and said to them: You have seen all that Adonai did before your very eyes in the Land of Egypt, to Pharaoh and to all his courtiers and to his whole country"; after all, the generation of the Exodus had died out by the end of the wandering and did not literally see God's

wonders in Egypt. Thus, this might be imagined as meaning that this generation must see itself *as if* it has seen these things, and all generations must follow this practice.

[8] *"Tell your child"* Quoting Exodus 13:8, which, according to 13:5, applies "when Adonai has brought you into the land of the Canaanites." The generation that entered the land, however, is not the same as the generation that might literally say, "This is what Adonai did for me when I left Egypt." This suggests that all post-Exodus generations must imagine that they participated in the Exodus.

[9] *"He brought us out"* From Deuteronomy 6:23, which also suggests that the very same generation that was delivered from Egypt entered the land, ignoring the traditions concerning the death of that generation as a result of the sin of the spies (Num. 14:23).

———◆———

GILLMAN (THEOLOGICALLY SPEAKING)

note that the text does not say that "every Jew" must see him- or herself as having come out of Egypt, but rather "every one" or "every individual." The Hebrew word is *adam*, which is, first, gender neutral and, second, means simply a person, a human being. The liberation from Egypt has universal significance that extends way beyond Jewish history. That is why the exodus theme has been taken up by oppressed peoples everywhere on earth. That explains why there are Haggadot that tell the story of other communities' liberation from their own oppression—black Haggadot, feminist Haggadot, secular Israeli Haggadot, and the rest

Second, note the Hebrew word *k'ilu*, "as though." Every person must see him- or herself "as though" having personally come out of Egypt. The "as though" here implies the author's awareness that there is a touch of hyperbole in the claim. Taken literally, I was not *really* in Egypt. But first, I might have been—an accident of birth located me where I am now in space and time, but I could have been born in another time and in another place. And second, more important, I must learn to see myself "as though" I was there by virtue of my communal memory. Memory is what knits together the generations; memory creates the possibility of continuity and history. Memory creates community. If you would doubt all of this, consider those we know who have lost the ability to remember; nothing is more devastating than this sense of total isolation that this victim must feel.

So in a somewhat less than literal sense, it is important that we feel "as though" we were in Egypt, and at Sinai, and the rest. What we do at the Seder table is reenact the Exodus by telling the story and performing the rituals that bring the original events back into our lives.

———◆———

GRAY (MEDIEVAL COMMENTATORS)

the Exodus. Abudarham leaves us with a question: What exactly is left unfulfilled if these three *mitzvot* are not explained? Other scholars, notably *Ran* (Rabbenu Nissim Gerondi, Spain, fourteenth century) are also ambiguous on this point; *Ran* merely says that if one fails to explain these three *mitzvot*, one has still fulfilled them, albeit not in the proper manner.[1] One possibility is that by not explaining these *mitzvot*, one has not properly fulfilled the obligation to eat them (*M'yuchas L'Rashbam*, a commentary attributed to *Rashbam*).[2] Another possibility is that by not explaining these *mitzvot*, one has not properly fulfilled the Torah's requirement of telling the Exodus story properly to one's children (*Rashbetz*, on the basis of Exod. 12:26–27, 13:8; Deut. 6:20–25). *Rashbetz's* interpretation makes a lot of sense. Exodus 12:26 mentions the child's question about the Passover sacrifice, which is followed by the parent's explanation of it (a la Rabban Gamaliel) in verse 27. Clearly the Torah seems to connect the parent's duty to explain the Passover offering to his child to his duty to explain the Exodus overall.

But hadn't these three *mitzvot* already been discussed in the questions asked at the beginning of the Seder? (Remember that the Mishnah's original three questions dealt with the same issues as Gamaliel's threefold injunction.) *Rashbetz* explains that the earlier mention of these *mitzvot* was only done in order to point out the differences between Pesach night and all other nights. Only now, at this stage of the Seder, are these *mitzvot* being discussed fully on their own terms.

"Without pointing to or lifting the shankbone .... Point to or lift the matzah.... Point to or lift the bitter herbs" On Pesachim 116b, Rava says that one must actually lift up the matzah and *maror* when one is speaking of them. On the other hand, one need not (and should not) lift up the shankbone (representative of the Passover offering), because it then appears as if one is engaging in sacrificial service outside of the Temple, which is prohibited. *Rashbam* explains that we must lift up the matzah and *maror* in order to make these *mitzvot* "beloved" to the Seder participants.[3] Lifting up the items while speaking of them focuses the Seder participants' attention on them; in turn, their ardor for these *mitzvot* may well increase.

2–3 *"The Passover that our ancestors ate ... passing over the houses"* Mishnah Pesachim 10:5 explains the significance of the Passover offering in light of Exodus 12:27: The offering is a "Passover" offering because God "passed over" the houses of the Israelites. *Rashbetz* nuances the mishnah's interpretation: God skipped from Egyptian house to Egyptian house, avoiding any Israelite houses that may have been among them. *Rashbetz* clearly notes that it was God who skipped from house to house, citing Exodus 12:27 in this connection ("He passed over the houses of the Israelites"). Nevertheless, *Rashbam* makes the point in his Torah commentary that it was an angel who jumped over the Israelite houses to smite the Egyptian first-born (*Rashbam* to Exodus 12:11). Martin Lockshin, the contemporary translator and annotator of *Rashbam*'s Torah commentary, notes the contradiction between *Rashbam*'s comment and the Haggadah's firm affirmation that God alone passed through Egypt ("I and not an angel" [see *My*

People's Passover Haggadah, Volume 2, p. 29]). He suggests that *Rashbam*'s reference to an angel makes the most sense of the biblical references to this "passing over," especially considering Exodus 12:23, which refers to the "passing over" of both God and the "Destroyer," who is presumably an angel ("Adonai will pass over the door and not let the Destroyer enter and smite your home").[4]

[5] *"And they hadn't prepared any provisions"* This language comes from Exodus 12:39. *Ritba* quotes the *Mekhilta D'rabbi Yishmael*, which interprets the Torah's recollection as praise of Israel. The Israelites trusted in God to such an extent that they eagerly prepared to leave Egypt, without even preparing food or asking where their food was going to come from.[5]

[6] *"The bitter herbs that we eat: What are they for"* On Pesachim 120a, Rava says that the commandment to eat matzah in this post-Temple period (when there is no Passover sacrifice) is still biblical in status, but the commandment to eat *maror* is only rabbinic (still quite important, but not equal in status to a biblical commandment). This difference between matzah and *maror* is derived from a careful reading of verses. Numbers 9:11 and Exodus 12:8 say that the Passover sacrifice must be eaten with *matzah* and bitter herbs, thus linking both matzah and *maror* to the Passover sacrifice. Nevertheless, the Torah also commands the eating of matzah separately, without linking it to the sacrifice (e.g., Exod. 12:18). This indicates that matzah is a biblical commandment even absent a Passover sacrifice. By contrast, the Torah never commands *maror* by itself, implying that *maror* is only biblically commanded when there is a Passover sacrifice, but not otherwise. Hence, because nowadays we only eat *maror* *without* the paschal offering, doing so fulfills a rabbinic requirement.

Maharil (R. Jacob Moellin, Germany, fifteenth century) asks why *Rambam* discusses lifting up and discussing the *maror* prior to the matzah, whereas our practice is the opposite (Laws of *Chamets* and Matzah 8:4). He answers that *Rambam* is describing how these *mitzvot* would have been performed in Temple times. When there was a Passover offering, the *maror* was biblically linked to it and thus was discussed right after it. But now, when there is no Passover offering, we proceed to matzah first, followed by *maror*.[6]

———◆———

GREEN (PERSONAL SPIRITUALITY)

bread of affliction our ancestors ate in the Land of Egypt." Here matzah is about the memory of poverty and suffering, rather than of liberation and joy. Matzah is both of these. If one explanation is not what you need to hear this Pesach, turn the matzah over and try the other.

———◆———

J. HOFFMAN (TRANSLATION)

[2] *"Stood"* Literally, "existed."

[3] *"You shall say"* From Exodus 12:27. Exodus 12:26 sets the stage: "When your children ask: Why do you perform this service…."

[3] *"Struck"* Commonly, "smote," a word no longer part of most people's English dialect.

[5] *"King over the kings of kings"* Literally, "king of the kings of kings." We reword slightly to make the English a little more readable. The Babylonians called their gods the "kings of kings." The Rabbis called their God the "king over the kings of kings."

[5] *"Was revealed"* Elsewhere, the passive voice is frequently employed in modern translations to avoid the use of "He …" In this translation, we attempt to capture the Hebrew as closely as possible. Even though the passive is rare in Hebrew, in this case we find a passive verb and translate as a passive English verb.

[5] *"Provisions"* Hebrew, *tseidah*, apparently a technical word used for the food one prepared for a journey. "Hadn't packed lunch" is close to what the phrase could mean. The importance of the line is that not only didn't their bread have time to rise, but they didn't take any of the previous day's bread with them either.

[7] *"Mortar"* Or, perhaps, "clay" or "mud."

[7] *"Under duress"* Frequently, "ruthlessly," which requires rewording the sentence, as in *JPS*: "Ruthlessly they made life bitter for them with harsh labor at mortar and bricks and with all sorts of tasks in the field." Above ("with severity," *My People's Passover Haggadah*, Volume 2, p. 23), we translated this as "with severity."

[8] *"People must regard themselves"* Literally, "man" must regard "himself," but the Hebrew refers to men and woman. We have no convenient way of indicating this inclusivity in English with singular nouns and pronouns, so we resort to the plural. Other, less convenient options include "one must see oneself…," "one must see him/herself…," etc.

[9] *"To bring us to and give us"* Literally, "to bring us to, to give us." The asyndeton is too awkward in English, so we reword the sentence. (Asyndeton is the literary device of omitting conjunctions. Probably the most famous example is, "I came, I saw, I conquered.")

———◆———

L. HOFFMAN (HISTORY)

Only after the Council of Nicea (325) did Easter get indelibly set so that it could not coincide with Passover. Before that, Palestinian Christians kept Easter (still called *Pascha*, the Aramaic word for *Pesach*), on the fourteenth of Nisan—it was their Passover. At their Seder, the biblically mandated foods would have received Christological interpretation. The Gospels themselves (as well as the prior letters of Paul) identified bread (in this case, matzah), as Jesus' body; and Jesus' body as the new sacrificial paschal lamb *(pesach)* that saves. (For details, see *My People's Passover Haggadah*, Volume 1, "This Bread: Christianity and the Seder," pp. 21–36). The Christian approach to *maror* (bitter herbs) would have to be imagined as, perhaps, the bitter vinegar that the Romans gave Jesus to slake his thirst while he was dying on the cross (e.g., Matt. 27:48).

This theory is buttressed by the fact that the Talmud cites Rabban Gamaliel as the force behind the blessing against *minim* ("heretics") found in the *Amidah* (see *My People's Prayer Book*, Volume 2, *The Amidah*, pp. 132–134), the early Palestinian versions of which condemn Jewish Christians *(notsrim* or *natsrim)* specifically. Clearly, Gamaliel was active in defining Judaism against the alternative Jewish-Christian identity.

But however likely such an interpretation may appear, other than symbolizing Jesus' body, we have no evidence of the symbols being used this way at a Christian Seder. Until we do, the theory remains interesting, even intriguing, but still just a hypothesis.

[6] *"Bitter herbs"* As today, regardless of how serious the Seder is, it was not unusual, even in the Middle Ages, for Jews to have fun as well. Illustrations from some Haggadot of the time show the leader of the Seder announcing *maror zeh* ("this bitter herb") while holding aloft the *maror*, but also pointing to his *wife*. In one illustration, she is pointing back at him.

[8] *"As though* [k'ilu] *they personally left Egypt"* The English "as though" is misleading, since it might imply the subjunctive mood—only "as though," but "not really." The Hebrew is intended as just the opposite. We are really to experience leaving Egypt ourselves. At issue is the nature of liturgical memory.

Steeped in history as we are, we can only imagine things "as though" we were alive "back then." But the Rabbis lacked historical consciousness. When they spoke of memory *(zikaron* or *zekher)*, they meant the Hellenistic concept of *anamnesis*, meaning the collapse of time so that past and present merge into one. Thinking of ourselves "as though" we are leaving Egypt connotes an existential consciousness of truly "being there," because what happened "there" and "then" is replicated "here" and "now." (For theological detail, see "Remembering [*zekher*] the Temple according to Hillel," *My People's Passover Haggadah*, Volume 2, pp. 127–129.)

SIGNPOST: SUMMING IT ALL UP

PRAISE GOD FOR SAVING US, AND (3) AFFIRM OUR NEWFOUND STATUS OF REDEMPTION. OF THE THREE TOPICS (IDENTIFICATION OF ENSLAVEMENT, PRAISE OF GOD, AND AFFIRMATION OF REDEMPTION), WE HAVE FINISHED THE FIRST. PRAISE AND REDEMPTION FOLLOW. BUT FIRST WE SUM UP THE SYMBOLS AND MESSAGE OF THE SEDER. FOLLOWING RABBINIC MANDATE, WE ACTUALLY STOP TO IDENTIFY PESACH, MATZAH, AND MAROR (THE THREE FOODS THAT THE BIBLE ASSOCIATES WITH THE EXODUS); AND WE RELATE THE MIRACLE IN EGYPT TO OURSELVES. WE ARE TO SEE OURSELVES AS IF WE HAD PERSONALLY LEFT EGYPT.

———◆———

KUSHNER AND POLEN (CHASIDIC VOICES)

called the festival Pesach. *Why is this so?* He then cites Song of Songs 6:3, "I am my beloved's and my beloved is mine." The love relationship is reciprocal. In the same way, we, too, normally sing God's praises and God sings ours.

Now, according to Berakhot 6a, both Jews and God wear *t'fillin*. In our *t'fillin* are the words of the *Sh'ma*, "… Adonai is our God, Adonai is One," and in God's *t'fillin* are the words "Who is like My people Israel, unique [= one] on the earth?!" Wearing *t'fillin* means being conscious of your lover, so if you are singing God's praises, you are wearing human *t'fillin*. Whereas, when you sing the praises of Israel, you are wearing God's *t'fillin*.

And the reason the Torah refers to Pesach as *chag hamatzot*, "the festival of unleavened bread," is that when we left Egypt, we were willing to follow this old-new God into the wilderness with no real bread other than matzah. The Berditchever then cites Jeremiah 2:2, "I remember the love of your youth and the affection of your betrothal when you went after Me in the wilderness.…" Thus we may conclude that when God's Torah calls it *chag hamatzot*, God must be wearing God's *t'fillin*—emphasizing Israel's act of faithful love. And, in the same way, when we call it Pesach, we are recalling God's act of mercy in "passing-over," sparing, the first-born of the children of Israel (Exod. 12:27). By calling the festival Pesach, we are wearing our *t'fillin*. Each partner's preferred name for the festival highlights the other partner's devotion. In this way, both God and Israel reenact Song of Songs 6:3, "I am my beloved's and my beloved is mine."

[6] *"Bitter herbs"* Yehuda Aryeh Leib of Ger in his *S'fat Emet* (*Pesach*, 1873) cites his grandfather, Rabbi Yitzchak Meir of Ger, who poses a rhetorical question, "Why do we eat bitter herbs?" The answer, he suggests, is that feeling pain (bitterness) is actually a sign of redemption. Just feeling the bitterness was itself the first glimmer of freedom. Indeed, the worst slavery is when we grow so accustomed to it that we accommodate ourselves to it.

[8] *"In each and every generation"* Rabbi Levi Yitzchak of Berditchev (*K'dushat Levi*, Jerusalem, vocalized ed., vol. 1, [Jerusalem], p. 239), puns on the word *Pesach* (peh-

sach), noting that its two syllables can be read literally as two discrete words: "[a] speaking mouth."

Indeed, he suggests, the purpose of all the miracles surrounding our going out from Egypt is to help us reaffirm our belief that God is not merely the One who spoke creation into being at the beginning, but who remains an ever-speaking mouth, *creating* the world continuously! In the words of the *Yotser* blessing in the morning liturgy (see *My People's Prayer Book*, Volume 1, *The Sh'ma and Its Blessings*, p. 45), God is the One who *m'chadesh b'khol yom tamid ma'aseh v'reishit*, the One who "forever renews daily the work of creation."

Consider this, he says, as analogous to the decrees of an earthly king. As long as his ministers remain in conversation with him, they can influence and even alter the king's decree. But once he leaves the conversation and the room, then the royal edict is frozen. It cannot be changed and must be implemented. God, however, is different. The "holy ones," the *tsadikim*, are capable of continuing the dialogue with God. They have it in their power to actually turn a divine decree of strict and even punitive justice into a decree of loving and lenient mercy.

Indeed, as we learn in Yoma 86b, through *t'shuvah* ("returning to God")—and the eternal conversation that goes with it—not only can premeditated sins be transformed into merits, but even that which was once a source of shame can be transformed into a source of praise. According to kabbalistic tradition, the letters of the divine decree can themselves be rearranged so as to make whole new words and new decrees, for through the *tsadikim*, God remains in continuous conversation with each and every one of us: God is always a *peh-sach*, "a speaking mouth."

———◆———

LANDES (HALAKHAH)

through the generations," including the later Passover offerings in the desert *mishkan* ("tabernacle") and the *bet hamikdash* ("the Temple")—which reiterate but can hardly repeat the utterly unique historic event of Egypt. Our rabbinic Seder also is a vicarious reenacting of the *pesach dorot*.

Consequently, there are concentric circles of Pesach consciousness: the original Passover sacrifice at the core *(pesach mitsrayim)*; then, built upon it, the Passover sacrifice at the Temple *(pesach dorot)*; and, finally, the rabbinic evocation of the Passover sacrifice during the Seder within which we find the Haggadah.

The sacrificial system is commonly derided. I have heard the scorn heaped on this so-called brutal and wasteful cultic rite—often at banqueting halls or fine restaurants where mounds of flesh are consumed by ravenous crowds and even greater mounds are discarded afterward. How different was the sacrifice, a *KoRBaN* in Hebrew (from Hebrew *k.r.v/b*), meaning "to draw us near," and intended to bring us closer *(l'KaReV)* to God. The *korban* is an expression of life's finitude, an encounter with mortality, a forced admission of how fleeting life really is. The priests of old would lay hands upon the sacrifice, then (in some cases) say a *vidui* (pronounced vee-DOO-ee—"a confession"), and then sprinkle or dash the blood on the altar, as if to say, "There but for the grace of God go I."

But even as sacrifice allows us to encounter human finitude, it also draws us near to infinity. The *korban* allows for transformation: the offering and the lifting up of the merely material into the spiritual. From the most base and mundane parts of existence, one brings a gift that finds its way to God.

It also connects us to another form of life. Judaism clearly embraces a hierarchy of life—it places animal existence below the human plane. But it demands a reverence for that life, as expressed by the laws of ritual slaughter. First, *sh'chitah* requires a blessing; second, it demands skill in using a specially sharpened blade that limits suffering because the animal dies instantly, without so much as an unnecessary nick in the neck.

Finally, pedagogically speaking, sacrifice enhances the sacrificer's dedication to others. Sacrifice is counter-egocentric—one offers up and gives. Eventually, one is supposed to be able to give willingly in a wider and deeper sense. Sacrifice becomes a template for how life is to be lived. With these lessons in mind, we can describe the Passover sacrifice.

The sacrifice consisted of an unblemished male lamb or goat under a year old (Exod. 12:5) offered up on the latter part of the fourteenth day of Nisan, the seventh month (by our count, but because of its significance, considered in Torah as also the first month [Exod. 12:2]). It was to be offered "only at the place which Adonai your God will choose to establish His name" (Deut. 16:5–6).

The Mishnah describes the sacrificial system as it existed during the Second Temple. Every afternoon a communal sacrifice called the *tamid* (the "regular" or "perpetual" offering) was the rule; in addition, on the afternoon prior to the Seder (*Erev Pesach*) a representative of each *chavurah*, each set of family groups planning on eating together that night, brought its Passover lamb to be sacrificed. During the rest of the year, the *tamid* was offered late in the day: slaughtered at 8½ halakhic hours (daylight being divided into twelve halakhic hours) and offered up at 9½ hours (the twelfth hour being nightfall). But the *pesach* (the Passover offering) had to be offered after the *tamid*, and the number of people coming to sacrifice it was so enormous that the *tamid* was moved up by an hour to allow more time afterward (M. Pes. 5:1). The Passover pilgrims were divided into three lines that moved simultaneously toward the altar so that three people at a time could make their sacrifice. When *Erev Pesach* fell on Friday (*Erev Shabbat*), the *tamid* was moved up yet another hour, to make sure everyone's *pesach* offerings were completed in plenty of time for Shabbat.

When the Temple courtyard was filled, the gates were locked. Priests sounded a straight blast of the trumpets, then a trembling broken blast, then once again a straight blast (*t'ki'ah, t'ru'ah, t'ki'ah*). As the blasts were sounded, the designated person from each *chavurah* severed the esophagus and windpipe of their lamb with a razor-sharp blade with no nicks, while another member of the *chavurah* held the body and feet of the lamb. A priest crouched next to each lamb, ready to collect the spurting blood into a long, oval receptacle, rounded at the bottom so that it could not be set down and allow the blood to coagulate. Each row of priests held either silver or gold pitchers (M. Pes. 5:5), each with a handle. The receptacles were quickly passed from one priest to the other up the rows until the last priest gently splashed the blood on the wall of the altar so that it dripped down to its foundation (Obadiah Bertinoro [Italy, fifteenth to sixteenth century] to M. Pes. 5:2, 6).

As the filled receptacles were passed forward, the empty ones were passed back. All during this ritual, *Hallel* was recited, either by the participants (Obadiah Bertinoro to M. Pes. 5:7) or by the Levite choir (Tosafot, Maimonides) while onlookers repeated a psalmic refrain. If *Hallel* was completed, they would start again. The ritual was performed so quickly that they never finished a complete third recitation.

Each individual lamb was hung on a specially prepared wooden pillar with hooks, or from hooked poles, and stripped of its hide. The carcass was split open, the forbidden fat was removed along with the kidneys, the excess portion of the liver, and the fat tail—all of which were offered on the altar (Lev. 9:10). Stripping the hide and gathering the portions offered up on the altar were performed by certain designates, freeing the priests for the other part of this time-pressured divine service (Pes. 84b, and Meiri comment there [Menachem ben Solomon, 1249–1316, Provence, France]). If it was Shabbat, members of the three groups waited in the greater Temple area until dark and then went to roast their *pesach*. If it wasn't Shabbat, they would leave immediately.

The four essential elements of the *avodah* (the sacrificial service)—slaughtering, receiving the blood in the receptacles, bringing the receptacles forward, and the splashing of the blood—all demanded special intent *(lishmah)*. An extraneous thought by the designate or the priests would invalidate the sacrifice; the same was true for a misdirected intent as to whose benefit this *avodah* served (M. Pes. 5:2, Talmud and Meiri thereto).

The principle of *t'umah d'chuyah b'tsibbur* ("Ritual/spiritual impurity is set aside if the majority of a community is impure") allowed the Passover ritual to be performed without caution lest people were inadvertently impure. But there were cases of individuals knowing they were impure; others were away on a distant journey; others still had suffered some accident or just mistakenly did not offer the sacrifice when it was due. Such people were allowed to bring a lamb a month later (fourteenth of Iyar), at twilight—an occasion known as *Pesach Sheni* ("second Passover"), and a holiday in its own right (Maimonides, Laws of the Pesach Offering 5:21). The slaughtering of this second *pesach* is an independent commandment and even takes precedence over the Shabbat laws if the fourteenth of Iyar falls on Saturday.

Based on the Torah instructions (Exod. 12:43), "No foreigner may eat of it" *(kol ben nekhar lo yokhal bo)*, it became an absolute requirement for the *pesach* offering that the participants be fully Jewish (Maimonides, Laws of the Pesach Offering 5:5, 9:8,9).

The *pesach* was fully roasted, a necessity derived from Exodus 12:9, "You shall not eat it partially roasted or cooked in water, only roasted over fire—its head and legs with its innards." The Mishnah (Pes. 7) demands the roasting be done directly on the fire with no "cooking" involved. The lower thigh and the innards were detached from the lamb and put on the first part of a pomegranate wood skewer next to the head of the lamb, which was skewered by the rod from its mouth to its end. A specific etiquette of consumption was followed. First of all, the lamb was eaten without breaking any bones (Exod. 12:46) and *al hasova* ("when feeling full"). To satisfy the latter requirement, the *pesach* was consumed only after eating another sacrifice, the *shalmei todah* ("the peace offerings part of the thanksgiving sacrifices"). When people felt full, they could eat the *pesach*; even *k'zayit* (a minimally required amount—taken to be the size of an olive) of the *pesach* sufficed (Pes. 70a). Following biblical instructions, "They shall eat it with matzah and bitter herbs" (Num. 9:11), the *pesach* was accompanied by matzah and *maror*. However, the key *mitzvah* was the *pesach*. Maimonides is clear: "The [lack of] matzah and *maror* do not prevent [the observance of the *pesach*]: if matzah and *maror* are not available, the *mitzvah* is fulfilled by eating the meat of the *pesach* alone. But *maror* without the *pesach* is not a *mitzvah*" (Laws of the Pesach Offering 8:1). While the *pesach* was eaten, *Hallel* was sung (M. Pes. 9:3).

The Torah demands, "You shall not leave any of it over until morning; if any of it is left until morning you shall burn it" (Exod. 12:10). As a precaution against any of it being left over, the Rabbis ordained that nothing could be eaten after the middle of the night.

In this way, the original *pesach mitsrayim* ("*pesach* offering made in Egypt") was relived by the ritual of *pesach dorot* ("*pesach* offering for generations") thereafter. Critical was the institution of the eating fellowship, the *chavurah*, an intentional micro-community within which the *pesach* could be offered and consumed. This was a covenantal experience, in that everyone who consumed the *pesach* was fully a Jew. As the Torah puts it, "The whole community of Israel shall offer it" (Exod. 12:47); so just eating it together underscored membership in the community. The *pesach* both reflected and created identity.

The transformational aspect of this ritual deserves mention. Imagine the scene: Sacred food is eaten by people approaching satiation, to the accompaniment of joyous song. It is eaten roasted, reminiscent of the miracle of leaving Egypt in haste. There are no leftovers; even though, care is taken not to break any bones to search for meat. This all occurs in one defined, bonded group. The group's attention is fixed only on the moment and the people present, rather than searching for another group or meal to attend. And all are free people (indeed, like royalty) who eat without worry or concern, but with trust, hope, and joy (*Sefer Hachinukh*, Aaron Halevi of Barcelona, thirteenth century, *Bo*, Negative Commandments 13, 14, 20).

[4] *"Matzah"* A key *mitzvah* of Seder night is to display the matzah during the telling of the story and to consume at least *k'zayit* (the minimum amount to fulfill the *mitzvah*—literally, the size of an olive, taken nowadays to be less than an ounce).

The *mitzvah* demands *matzah shmurah* (colloquially, *shmurah matzah*). *Matzah shmurah* means "guarded matzah." There are two different forms of guarding it. The first refers to the intentionality to bake matzah for the express purpose of eating it at the Seder *(l'shem matzot mitzvah)*. The second guarding is from any contact with water that would produce a leavening effect.

The Torah provides clear guidelines for other considerations: "Seven days you shall eat unleavened bread" (Exod. 12:15)—we might understand this to mean unleavened bread of any kind; therefore Torah adds, "You shall eat nothing leavened with it" (Deut. 16:3). The law then applies only to such grains as could be leavened as well as unleavened, what we call the "five species [of grain that grow in the Land of Israel]": wheat, barley, spelt, oats, and rye. Further, we have the parallel instruction in Deuteronomy 16:4, "No leavened bread be found with you in all your territory." The Midrash (*Mekhilta*, Lauterbach, pp. 144, 148) explains: "This compares leaven to leavened bread and leavened bread to leaven ... just as the one, leavened bread, is forbidden [on Passover] only when it is made of one of the five species, so also is the other, leaven, forbidden [on Passover] only when it comes from the five species."

Matzah and *chamets* are reciprocally defining categories. Matzah is made specifically from the five species, which can just as easily become *chamets*. The preparation of matzah, therefore, is a risky and potentially dangerous ritual undertaking. One must use grain that could become *chamets* in the process of grinding, kneading, and baking. Worse still, if subjected to water prior to the baking process, the grain might undergo undetected leavening. The very storage of grain and preparation of matzah are customarily prohibited on Passover itself, out of fear of its becoming *chamets*. We guard the matzah at every stage of its manufacture, to prevent first the grain, then the dough, and finally the finished matzah from becoming *chamets*.

The two types of guarding function together, as *Rashi* (1040–1107) explains: "Intending and guarding [i.e., both types, are practiced] so that there be properly prepared matzah to fulfill the commandment *(matzot mitzvah)*" (Pes. 28b). For the nonobligatory matzah used not to fulfill the commandment, but just to "fill one's belly" (as the Rabbis put it), only the second kind of guarding is needed (Pes. 40a; see classical commentaries there). While a distinct precaution in and of itself, the guarding of intent "always requires the practical guarding from *chamets*" (*Ritba*, Yomtov ben Abraham Hasevilli, 1250–1330, Seville, Spain).

The halakhic development of both guardings exhibits a wide degree of elasticity. Guarding from *chamets* is a matter of assessing fact: that this bread in preparation is, and remains, unleavened. On this basis, Rav Huna, in an accepted statement in the Talmud, claims even the kneaded dough of a gentile can be considered fit for Passover consumption as long as one can ascertain by a sight test that it is *chamets* free (*Rashi*; Rosh on M. Pes. 2:26; *T'shuvot Harosh* 14:4 [Asher ben Yechiel, 1250–1327, Toledo, Spain]). Later authorities, however, required an actual guarding by a commanded individual (i.e., a Jew), sensitive to and bound by the prohibition of *chamets* (*Rif* [Isaac ben Jacob Alfasi, 1013–1103, Fez, Morocco]; Nissim ben Reuven of Gerona, 1320–1380, Barcelona, Spain). This activist approach contributes a conservative turn to matzah preparation, implying that everything possible be done to prevent leavening.

We find a parallel expansion for guarding of intent. The Talmud mandates this guarding only during the kneading process (Pes. 40a), but it was subsequently extended, by many, back to the time of grinding (*Hagahot Maimuniyot*, Laws of *Chamets* and Matzah 5, n. 8) and even, by others, to the harvest itself (*Rif* following Rabbah).

All this informs the debate regarding the introduction of machine matzah in the nineteenth century (see Rabbi David Ellenson's translation of responsum by Rabbi Solomon Kluger [1763–1869, Brody], *Moda'ah L'vet Yisrael*, Breslau, 1859, No. 1 in *Jewish Legal Interpretation: Literary, Scriptural, Social and Ethical Perspectives* and my own response, "Law, Ethics and Ritual in Jewish Decision Making," in *Semeia* 34, 1985). Opponents worried about two matters: that machines might retain some of the dough and therefore render the next batch leavened; and how to ensure that the intent of making *matzot mitzvah* be performed in a mechanical process. The third and decisive problem for Kluger was that the matzah-baking was a monopoly of the poor, who undertook this arduous work in order to maintain themselves for the holidays. He feared that the machine matzot with their lower price would render their situation dire.

Later authorities debated the pros and cons. Decisively, in the early twentieth century, Rabbi Zvi Pesach Frank (rabbinic head of the religious court of Jerusalem for over forty years) decided to allow machine matzot. By this time, the machinery was sophisticated enough that, with a good protocol for cleaning, there would be no fear of leaven left behind, and the machines had the advantage over human labor in that there was no problem with perspiration (a liquid, obviously, and therefore potentially a leavening agent).

Also, greater familiarity with industrial machinery has allowed us to use it with intent, by declaring *l'shem matzot mitzvah* at the beginning of the process. Finally, by the time of Rabbi Frank, the radically cheaper price of machine *shmurah matzah* benefited the wide segment of those in need, more than a continued monopoly helped the small group of manufacturers. On the Saturday night prior to Passover and accompanied by the great rabbis of Jerusalem, Rabbi Frank would go to the factory to clean the machinery and bake his own matzah there. And so we, his family, continue to do so.

Shmura matzah, whether hand or machine made, should be used for the ritual parts of the Seder. This means that the matzah has been "guarded" from *chamets* from the time of its harvest.

The laws of eating matzah *l'shem mitzvah* (for the sake of the *mitzvah*) are as follows:

1. During *Hamotsi*, grasp the three matzot (the top whole one, the middle broken one, and the bottom whole one).
2. Lay down the bottom matzah. Pick up the top whole one and the middle broken piece, having in mind also the *afikoman* (according to some, it is the central *mitzvah* of matzah). Recite the blessing, "… *al achilat matzah*."
3. Eat while reclining.
4. Take, if possible, *k'zayit* of the top and *k'zayit* of the middle, and eat them together. If this is too hard, take separately, first from the top and then from the middle.
5. If even that is too difficult, eat only *k'zayit*, from the top or from the middle.
6. If there is not enough to go around to all participants and they do not have their own matzot, make sure they have at least a little from these matzot, and other *shmurah matzot* can be added for their *k'zayit*.

7. Eat steadily without interruption in order to finish promptly.

8. Those with wheat allergy should note that with forethought and research, spelt and oat *shmurah matzah* can be found.

⁶*"Bitter herbs"* Matzah and *maror* (bitter herbs) are adjunct; we saw above that the sacrificial requirement of Pesach can be fulfilled without them, if need be. Nonetheless, there remains a separate, independent *mitzvah* of matzah. Exodus declares, "In the evening you shall eat matzot" (Exod. 12:18), and does not mention any connection with *pesach*.

But *maror* has no independent status. Thus: "Raba said: matzah in our day [after the destruction of the Temple and the end of the sacrificial rites] is *mid'ora'ita* [it has a Torah warrant for its observance], while *maror* is *mid'rabbanan* [it is only commanded rabbinically].... It also states, 'On matzot and on *maror* shall you eat it' (Num. 9:11), [meaning] when there is the *pesach*, there is [the Torah command for] *maror*, and when there is no *pesach*, there is no [Torah command for] *maror*" (Pes. 120a).

⁸⁻⁹*"In each and every generation ... regard* [lirot] *themselves ... our ancestors"* The paragraphs at the end of the *Maggid* are held tightly together by a literary halakhic logic.

We have told of our liberation from Egypt and from idolatry. At this point we can state that we see ourselves as having gone up from Egypt. The term *lirot* is given by Maimonides as *l'harot*, "to show," so that the statement reads: "In every generation people must *show* themselves as if they personally left Egypt." Now we are able to say that God "did not redeem only our ancestors ... but we ourselves along with them."

This realization places a responsibility upon us:

> The House of Israel is obliged to thank and praise heaven when a miracle occurs, as it says, 'Praise Adonai all you nations, for He has overwhelmed us [*gavar alenu*] with His mercy' (Ps. 117:1–2). How much more so do we [the Jewish People] need to offer praise for it was *us* that His mercy overwhelmed (*Sh'eltot* 26, Rab Achai of Shabcha, eighth century).

The *N'tziv* (Naftali Tzvi Judah Berlin, 1816–1893, Lithuania) comments that this obligation to praise devolves only upon those who have experienced the event, not those who merely remember it. Applied to the liturgical dramatic context of the *Maggid*, the halakhic logic must be that we ourselves at this point are those who are leaving Egypt! Therefore, we lift the glass to indicate the equivalent of a blessing over *Hallel*. The only formal blessing connected to *Hallel* is its very final blessing found at the end of the Great *Hallel* section (see *My People's Passover Haggadah*, Volume 2, pp. 159–162; see also L. Hoffman, "[They] will praise You," Volume 2, p. 183). Consider the rush of words, all of them synonyms for "praise," that mark the beginning of this section: "We must therefore thank, praise, honor, glorify, exalt, magnify, bless, elevate and celebrate...." The excessive use of synonyms for *Hallel* emphasizes the miracle taking place and the resulting responsibility (and desire) to offer praise.

That is why we are moved to sing, in the words of many versions of the Haggadah, a "new song"—this is a new miraculous moment in which we have been set free. After two hopefully vitally sung psalms of the deliverance from Egypt, a concluding blessing—as there is a concluding blessing to the regular *Hallel*—is recited, capped by the blessing of the wine. Thus, the *Maggid* has dissolved from telling into being and then into song and thanksgiving.

---◆---

ZIERLER (FEMINIST VOICES)

his daughters arrived before his sons. "The daughters [thus] showed themselves zealous, and the sons indolent."

⁵ *"It is for our ancestor's dough not sufficing to leaven by the time the king over the kings of kings, the Holy One of Blessing, was revealed to them and redeemed them"* Historically, Jewish women baked bread for the family; for this reason, *hafrashat challah* (the separation of dough as a donation to the Temple priests) is designated by the Rabbis as a woman's mitzvah. With regard to the baking of matzah, the Mishnah refers to women's kneading of the matzah (M. Pes. 3:4). Pesachim 116a, however, in providing several exegeses of the expression *lechem oni* (bread of poverty), offers a poignant picture of husband and wife working together urgently to bake bread: "Bread of poverty—just as a poor man fires [the oven] and his wife bakes [without delay so as not to use excessive fuel], so here too [in the case of matzah baking], he heats and she bakes." Matzah is "bread of poverty," then, because regardless of our financial status, we are required in baking it to work together speedily and to avoid waste. The following gender-inclusive account of matzah baking from the memoirs of Pauline Wengeroff offers an interesting portrait of men and women in a family working together to bake matzah:

> The baking took almost two whole days. My mother made tireless rounds to inspect the rolling pins of the women and scrape off the dough, which was considered to have become leavened and must not come in contact with the unleavened dough of the *matzehs*. My brother and brothers-in-law helped her with this work, using bits of broken glass. The young men also helped prick the *matzeh*; it occurred to no one that this might not be "men's work." Anything to do with *Pesach*, especially with *matzeh*, is sacred work.¹

⁸ *"In each and every generation"* This passage of the Haggadah enjoins each one of us to personalize the *y'tsi'at mitsrayim* story and infuse it with contemporary relevance. Feminism, with its insistence that the personal is political, has provided many avenues for creative and personal reinterpretation of this narrative. Many feminist Haggadot note that the word *mitsrayim* connotes narrowness. To go out of Egypt is to leave a realm of limitation and constraint and emerge into a world of options and possibilities.

---◆ ◆---

C. ...To Praise and Redemption

12. "Praise"—*Hallel*, Part One, Psalms 113–114

A. An Introduction to *Hallel*

Lift the cups of wine and recite:

[1] We must therefore thank, praise, honor, glorify, exalt, magnify, bless, elevate, and celebrate the One who did all these miracles for us and for our ancestors, and who brought us from slavery to freedom, from sorrow to happiness, from mourning to celebration, and from darkness to great light, and from enslavement to redemption. [2] So let us sing (a new song) before Him: "Halleluyah!"

לְפִיכָךְ אֲנַחְנוּ חַיָּבִים לְהוֹדוֹת לְהַלֵּל לְשַׁבֵּחַ לְפָאֵר לְרוֹמֵם לְהַדֵּר לְבָרֵךְ לְעַלֵּה וּלְקַלֵּס לְמִי שֶׁעָשָׂה לַאֲבוֹתֵינוּ וְלָנוּ אֶת־כָּל־הַנִּסִּים הָאֵלּוּ. וְהוֹצִיאָנוּ מֵעַבְדוּת לְחֵרוּת מִיָּגוֹן לְשִׂמְחָה מֵאֵבֶל לְיוֹם טוֹב וּמֵאֲפֵלָה לְאוֹר גָּדוֹל וּמִשִּׁעְבּוּד לִגְאֻלָּה. [2] וְנֹאמַר לְפָנָיו (שִׁירָה חֲדָשָׁה) הַלְלוּיָהּ׃

Replace the cups of wine.

B. Psalm 113

[3] Halleluyah. Praise His name you servants of Adonai, praise Adonai's name. [4] May God's name be blessed from now and ever more. [5] From the sun's rising to its setting Adonai's name is praised. [6] Adonai is exalted above every nation, and His glory above the heavens. [7] Who is like Adonai our God, enthroned up high, [8] and seeing down below, in the heavens and on earth! [9] He lifts up the poor from dust, raises the needy from filth [10] to let them sit with princes, with the princes of His nation. [11] He lets the barren woman sit as a mother rejoicing with her children. Halleluyah!

[3] הַלְלוּ יָהּ הַלְלוּ עַבְדֵי יְיָ הַלְלוּ אֶת־שֵׁם יְיָ׃ [4] יְהִי שֵׁם יְיָ מְבֹרָךְ מֵעַתָּה וְעַד עוֹלָם׃ [5] מִמִּזְרַח־שֶׁמֶשׁ עַד מְבוֹאוֹ מְהֻלָּל שֵׁם יְיָ׃ [6] רָם עַל כָּל־גּוֹיִם יְיָ עַל הַשָּׁמַיִם כְּבוֹדוֹ׃ [7] מִי כַּייָ אֱלֹהֵינוּ הַמַּגְבִּיהִי לָשָׁבֶת׃ [8] הַמַּשְׁפִּילִי לִרְאוֹת בַּשָּׁמַיִם וּבָאָרֶץ׃ [9] מְקִימִי מֵעָפָר דָּל מֵאַשְׁפֹּת יָרִים אֶבְיוֹן׃ [10] לְהוֹשִׁיבִי עִם נְדִיבִים עִם נְדִיבֵי עַמּוֹ׃ [11] מוֹשִׁיבִי עֲקֶרֶת הַבַּיִת אֵם הַבָּנִים שְׂמֵחָה. הַלְלוּ־יָהּ׃

c. Psalm 114

[12]When Israel went forth from Egypt, the house of Jacob from a foreign nation, [13]Judah became holy to Him, Israel ruled by Him. [14]The sea saw and withdrew, the Jordan turned back. [15]The mountains danced like rams, the hills like lambs. [16]Why did you withdraw, sea; turn back, Jordan; [17]dance like rams, mountains; like lambs, hills? [18]Before Adonai tremble, earth, before the God of Jacob, [19]who turns rocks into pools of water, stones into springs of water.

בְּצֵאת יִשְׂרָאֵל מִמִּצְרָיִם בֵּית יַעֲקֹב [12]
מֵעַם לֹעֵז: הָיְתָה יְהוּדָה לְקָדְשׁוֹ [13]
יִשְׂרָאֵל מַמְשְׁלוֹתָיו: הַיָּם רָאָה וַיָּנֹס [14]
הַיַּרְדֵּן יִסֹּב לְאָחוֹר: הֶהָרִים רָקְדוּ [15]
כְאֵילִים גְּבָעוֹת כִּבְנֵי־צֹאן: מַה־לְּךָ [16]
הַיָּם כִּי תָנוּס הַיַּרְדֵּן תִּסֹּב לְאָחוֹר:
הֶהָרִים תִּרְקְדוּ כְאֵילִים גְּבָעוֹת [17]
כִּבְנֵי־צֹאן: מִלִּפְנֵי אָדוֹן חוּלִי אָרֶץ [18]
מִלִּפְנֵי אֱלוֹהַּ יַעֲקֹב: הַהֹפְכִי הַצּוּר [19]
אֲגַם־מָיִם חַלָּמִישׁ לְמַעְיְנוֹ־מָיִם:

Hallel continues after dinner.

בן - בנימין

לְפִיכָך אֲנַחְנוּ חַיָּבִים ...

"We Must Therefore ..."
A Survivor's Haggadah, Munich, 1946
Printed by the U.S. Army of Occupation
American Jewish Historical Society, Newton Center, Massachusetts and New York, New York
Hebrew (top): "Go forth ... to the land" (Gen. 12:1)
Hebrew (bottom): From the Haggadah's introduction to the Hallel
(see My People's Passover Haggadah, Volume 2, p. 93). The absence
of the next word in the text—"thank"—seems intended.

ARNOW (THE WORLD OF MIDRASH)

[1] "*Thank, praise, honor, glorify*" The Talmud expresses concern about overpraising God, as if we can ever truly convey the magnitude of God's greatness. "One's words should always be few in addressing the Holy One, as Scripture says 'Let not your throat be quick to bring forth speech before God. For God is in heaven and you are on earth; that is why your words should be few' (Eccl. 5:1)" (Ber. 61a). Even tenfold praise of God is as if "an earthly king had a million gold coins and someone praised him for silver ones" (Ber. 33b). The *Midrash on Psalms* (89:1) comments *(p. 99)*

BRETTLER (OUR BIBLICAL HERITAGE)

[1] "*We must therefore*" This follows directly from the previous idea—since we were liberated, it is *our* duty. This idea is emphasized in the continuation, where the miracles were performed "for us and for our ancestors."

[1] "*Thank ... celebrate*" This chain of nine infinitives has no biblical parallel in *(p. 100)*

GILLMAN (THEOLOGICALLY SPEAKING)

[1] "*We must therefore thank*" Note the repeated transitions that are being marked on this night: "from slavery to freedom, from sorrow to happiness, from mourning to celebration, and from darkness to great light, and from enslavement to redemption." Transitions of this kind are called *(p. 101)*

GRAY (MEDIEVAL COMMENTATORS)

[1] "*We must therefore thank, praise*" *Rashbetz* explains that this transition to *Hallel* is in keeping with the talmudic requirement that we "begin with disgrace and end with praise" (Pes. 116a). It is inappropriate for us to seem ungrateful to God, who did all these miracles for us, and thus we must praise Him.

Abudarham says that according to earlier commentators, each Seder participant must at this point lift up the cup of wine, since we are moving from the narrative recitation of the Haggadah to *(p. 102)*

[For prayer instructions, see pages 93–94.]

12. "PRAISE"—*HALLEL*, PART ONE, PSALMS 113–114

A. An Introduction to *Hallel*

[1]We must therefore thank, praise, honor, glorify, exalt, magnify, bless, elevate, and celebrate the One who did all these miracles for us and for our ancestors, and who brought us from slavery to freedom, from sorrow to happiness, from mourning to celebration, and from darkness to great light, and from enslavement to redemption. [2]So let us sing (a new song) before Him: "Halleluyah!"

J. HOFFMAN (TRANSLATION)

[1] "*Thank*" Elsewhere, we translate this word as "gratefully acknowledge." The point here is not the meaning of each word, but rather the stream of near-synonyms. So we try to find nine English words that roughly capture the meanings of the nine Hebrew ones. In so doing, we convey the overall impact of the stream of words, as well its rhythm.

[1] "*Celebrate*" The Hebrew is from the root *k.l.s*, which in the Bible always has a negative connotation *(p. 104)*

L. HOFFMAN (HISTORY)

"Hallel" Popular practice nowadays is to use the word *Hallel* (meaning "praise") to refer specifically to Psalms 113–118, recited in synagogue on Passover, Shavuot, Sukkot, Chanukah, and Rosh Chodesh and at home as part of the Seder. More precisely, this set of psalms is called *Hallel Hamitsri* ("The Egyptian *Hallel*"), because of the verse that begins Psalm 114 (see below, "When Israel went forth from Egypt"). Our current liturgy knows two other *Hallels* as well: the Daily *Hallel* (Pss. 145–150), recited as

(p. 106)

SIGNPOST: "PRAISE"—HALLEL, PART ONE, PSALMS 113–114

RELIVING THE JOURNEY FROM ENSLAVE-MENT TO FREEDOM LEADS NATURALLY TO PRAISE OF GOD, WHO FREED US. THAT PRAISE COMES IN THE FORM OF A HALLEL, A SET OF PSALMS. BUT THE PSALMS ARE DIVIDED. BEFORE DINNER, WE SAY TWO OF THEM, CULMINATING IN PSALM 114, WHICH RECOLLECTS LEAVING EGYPT (V. 1). AFTER DINNER, WE WILL ENCOUNTER MORE PSALMS, AS THE HALLEL CONTINUES.

———◆———

¹לְפִיכָךְ אֲנַחְנוּ חַיָּבִים לְהוֹדוֹת לְהַלֵּל לְשַׁבֵּחַ לְפָאֵר לְרוֹמֵם לְהַדֵּר לְבָרֵךְ לְעַלֵּה וּלְקַלֵּס לְמִי שֶׁעָשָׂה לַאֲבוֹתֵינוּ וְלָנוּ אֶת־כָּל־הַנִּסִּים הָאֵלּוּ. וְהוֹצִיאָנוּ מֵעַבְדוּת לְחֵרוּת מִיָּגוֹן לְשִׂמְחָה מֵאֵבֶל לְיוֹם טוֹב וּמֵאֲפֵלָה לְאוֹר גָּדוֹל וּמִשִּׁעְבּוּד לִגְאֻלָּה. ²וְנֹאמַר לְפָנָיו (שִׁירָה חֲדָשָׁה) הַלְלוּיָהּ:

LANDES (HALAKHAH)

"Hallel" The night of the Seder enjoys special sanctity. Joseph Caro (1488–1575, Safed) demonstrates this status by noting the uniqueness of saying *Hallel* not just at the Seder, but during the evening synagogue service prior to it (*Shulchan Arukh*, O. Ch. 487:4): "The first Passover night we recite the *Hallel* communally [*batsibbur*] with pleasant singing and a blessing at its start and finish. So also for the second day in the diaspora."

The *R'ma* (Moses Isserles, *(p. 108)*

ZIERLER (FEMINIST VOICES)

²*"So let us sing (a new song) before Him: 'Halleluyah!'"* In *Song of Songs Rabbah* 1:3, Rabbi Berekiah in the name of Shmuel bar Nachman presents a very different understanding of the expression *shirah chadashah.*

"Israel," he says, "is compared to a female. Just as a female [unmarried] child takes a tenth of the property of her father and departs, so Israel inherited the land of the seven nations, which is a tenth of that of the seventy nations [comprising all of the nations of the world].

"And because Israel inherited like a female, the song they uttered is called in the feminine form, *shirah*, as it says, 'Thus sang Moses and the children of Israel this *shirah* song unto Adonai.' But in the days to come the people *(p. 108)*

B. Psalm 113

³Halleluyah. Praise His name you servants of Adonai, praise Adonai's name. ⁴May God's name be blessed from now and ever more. ⁵From the sun's rising to its setting Adonai's name is praised. ⁶Adonai is exalted above every nation, and His glory above the heavens. ⁷Who is like Adonai our God, enthroned up high, ⁸and seeing down below, in the heavens and on earth! ⁹He lifts up the poor from dust, raises the needy from filth ¹⁰to let them sit with princes, with the princes of His nation. ¹¹He lets the barren woman sit as a mother rejoicing with her children. Halleluyah!

C. Psalm 114

¹²When Israel went forth from Egypt, the house of Jacob from a foreign nation, ¹³Judah became holy to Him, Israel ruled by Him. ¹⁴The sea saw and withdrew, the Jordan turned back. ¹⁵The mountains danced like rams, the hills like lambs. ¹⁶Why did you withdraw, sea; turn back, Jordan; ¹⁷dance like rams, mountains; like lambs, hills? ¹⁸Before Adonai tremble, earth, before the God of Jacob, ¹⁹who turns rocks into pools of water, stones into springs of water.

³הַלְלוּ יָהּ הַלְלוּ עַבְדֵי יְיָ הַלְלוּ אֶת־שֵׁם יְיָ: ⁴יְהִי שֵׁם יְיָ מְבֹרָךְ מֵעַתָּה וְעַד עוֹלָם: ⁵מִמִּזְרַח־שֶׁמֶשׁ עַד מְבוֹאוֹ מְהֻלָּל שֵׁם יְיָ: ⁶רָם עַל כָּל־גּוֹיִם יְיָ עַל הַשָּׁמַיִם כְּבוֹדוֹ: ⁷מִי כַּייָ אֱלֹהֵינוּ הַמַּגְבִּיהִי לָשָׁבֶת: ⁸הַמַּשְׁפִּילִי לִרְאוֹת בַּשָּׁמַיִם וּבָאָרֶץ: ⁹מְקִימִי מֵעָפָר דָּל מֵאַשְׁפֹּת יָרִים אֶבְיוֹן: ¹⁰לְהוֹשִׁיבִי עִם נְדִיבִים עִם נְדִיבֵי עַמּוֹ: ¹¹מוֹשִׁיבִי עֲקֶרֶת הַבַּיִת אֵם הַבָּנִים שְׂמֵחָה. הַלְלוּ־יָהּ:

¹²בְּצֵאת יִשְׂרָאֵל מִמִּצְרָיִם בֵּית יַעֲקֹב מֵעַם לֹעֵז: ¹³הָיְתָה יְהוּדָה לְקָדְשׁוֹ יִשְׂרָאֵל מַמְשְׁלוֹתָיו: ¹⁴הַיָּם רָאָה וַיָּנֹס הַיַּרְדֵּן יִסֹּב לְאָחוֹר: ¹⁵הֶהָרִים רָקְדוּ כְאֵילִים גְּבָעוֹת כִּבְנֵי־צֹאן: ¹⁶מַה־לְּךָ הַיָּם כִּי תָנוּס הַיַּרְדֵּן תִּסֹּב לְאָחוֹר: ¹⁷הֶהָרִים תִּרְקְדוּ כְאֵילִים גְּבָעוֹת כִּבְנֵי־צֹאן: ¹⁸מִלִּפְנֵי אָדוֹן חוּלִי אָרֶץ מִלִּפְנֵי אֱלוֹהַּ יַעֲקֹב: ¹⁹הַהֹפְכִי הַצּוּר אֲגַם־מָיִם חַלָּמִישׁ לְמַעְיְנוֹ־מָיִם:

ARNOW (THE WORLD OF MIDRASH)

on a verse from Jeremiah (9:23): "'For I Adonai act with kindness, justice and equity in the world....' God says, '... Anyone who would praise Me must praise Me only with these things.'"

[1] *"The One who did all these miracles"* The Rabbis disapproved of praising God in general terms, like "the One who" provides a bountiful meal. Listeners might think we had the dinner host in mind. But we *do* say, "the One who did all these miracles."[1] The Talmud (Ber. 50a) explains that there the meaning is obvious, for who other than God performs miracles?

[1] *"From slavery to freedom ... from darkness to great light"* The Bible calls the month in which Passover falls the first month of the year (Exod. 12:2). In a parable that uses language reminiscent of the Haggadah, *Exodus Rabbah* (11:15) pictures a king (God) whose son (Israel) has gone free from prison. The ruler commands, "Celebrate for all time the day on which my son went forth from darkness to light, from an iron yoke to life, from slavery to freedom, and from bondage to redemption."

[1] *"From sorrow to happiness, from mourning to celebration"* The phrase comes from the Book of Esther (9:22). Although that book omits any reference to Passover, its references to specific dates in Nisan indicate that much of the Purim story unfolds during Passover. The midrash makes the Passover/Purim connection explicit. Before launching her plan to destroy Haman, Esther declares a three-day fast. *Esther Rabbah* 8:7 has Mordecai objecting to Esther's declaration of this fast because it includes the beginning of Passover. "She replied, 'Elder of Israel, why is there a Passover?' [i.e., what good is Passover if all the Jews are killed?].' Mordecai thereupon acceded to her request...."

Because the Book of Esther fails to mention God, it is said to highlight the human role in redemption. In admitting a reference reminiscent of Purim into the Haggadah— at the very moment when we celebrate God's strong hand—perhaps the compilers of the Haggadah are quietly reminding us that the Exodus from Egypt required a human hand as well.

[2] *"A new song"* The word for "song" may be masculine *(shir)* or feminine *(shirah)*. The Sages explained the use of the feminine here by comparing the cycle of Israel's travails— burdened, freed, burdened, freed—to bearing children. Deliverance from Egypt was followed by subsequent experiences of pain and suffering. But the final deliverance— from this world into the world-to-come— will be not be followed by pain. Then we will utter a song *(shir)* in the masculine form *(Song of Songs Rabbah* 1:36).

[2] *"Halleluyah"* "The Psalms include ten synonyms of praise.... The greatest of all is 'halleluyah,' because it embraces God's name [Yah] and praise [*Hallel*] simultaneously" (Pes. 117a).

[3] *"Halleluyah. Praise His name you servants of Adonai"* The first verse of *Hallel* refers

to "servants" of God, using the same word the Bible regularly employs to denote servants or slaves of Pharaoh. *Midrash Hallel*, a medieval composition, explains: On the night of the last plague, Moses exclaims, "Last night we were servants to Pharaoh, and now we are servants to God." He and Aaron then praise God, "who brought us from slavery to freedom," and say, 'So let us exclaim: "Halleluyah!"'[2] The purpose of the Exodus is not freedom for its own sake, but freedom to direct our lives toward the ultimate One of Being.

[12] *"When Israel went forth from Egypt"* In this psalm Israel rejoices over having left Egypt. But the *Midrash on Psalms* (114:1) thinks, "'*Egypt* rejoiced when they [the Israelites] left' (Ps. 105:38). Rabbi Berechiah pictures a heavy man riding a donkey, and wondering, 'When can I get off?' The donkey wonders similarly, 'When will he get off me?' When the time comes for rider to dismount, it is hard to say which one is more relieved!"[3]

[13] *"Judah became holy to Him"* Why was the Temple built upon land belonging to the tribe of Judah? The *Mekhilta* explains that when the Israelites stood at the Red Sea, the various tribes deliberated with one another as to which should have the honor of entering the Sea first. As they debated, "Nachshon, son of Amminadav [from the tribe of Judah], led the way and jumped in. As a reward, 'Judah became holy to him' [i.e., the Temple was built in Judah]" (Ps. 114:2).[4] Other versions of the same incident are less flattering to the other tribes. One holds that none of them had the courage to take the plunge. Another suggests that the tribes were in such competition to be first that they threw stones at whoever dared take the lead.[5] Dissension among Jews is nothing new. "Why," asks the *Mekhilta*, "was the Torah not given in the Land of Israel? To avoid causing dissension among the tribes."[6]

◆

BRETTLER (OUR BIBLICAL HERITAGE)

style; in the Bible, no more than three successive infinitives are used (see, e.g., Esther 3:13, "to destroy, massacre, and exterminate"). The extensive repetition is meant to express the great extent of gratitude we owe.

[1] *"Miracles"* Only in post-biblical Hebrew does *nes* mean a wonder or miracle; in biblical Hebrew it means a flag or standard, as in Isaiah 11:12, "He will hold up a *nes* to the nations / And assemble the banished of Israel, / And gather the dispersed of Judah / From the four corners of the earth."

[1] *"From slavery to freedom, from sorrow to happiness, from mourning to celebration, and from darkness to great light, and from enslavement to redemption"* These five "from ... to" phrases extend Esther 9:22, "... the same month which had been transformed for them from one of grief and mourning to one of festive joy," which is included as the second and third phrase.

[2] *"A new song"* Although the phrase "a new song" appears several times in the Bible (though always as the masculine *shir chadash* rather than this feminine *shirah chadashah*), it never refers to Psalms 113–114, which follow. It is unclear why these psalms should be called "a new song."

"Psalm 113" The function of Psalm 113, most likely from the post-exilic period, is not clear. (The use of the suffix –i throughout this psalm in words such as *hamagbihi* and *hamashpili* is archaistic—that is, improperly mimicking an ancient usage—rather than being truly archaic; this is one indication of the late date of composition of this psalm.) It likely quotes sections of Hannah's prayer in 1 Samuel 2 (this is another indication of its late date of composition) and might be understood as a psalm of thanksgiving recited by a formerly barren woman after she has given birth.

"Psalm 114" The function of the post-exilic Psalm 114 is likewise unclear, though perhaps it can be read as a wish for a new Exodus, that is, a new restoration of Israel to its land. Its personifications and mythological language are very striking. Although it is often read in tandem with the preceding psalm, style and context suggest that it is a separate composition.

———◆———

GILLMAN (THEOLOGICALLY SPEAKING)

"liminal moments," where the term "liminal" signifies thresholds or "in-betweens," moments when we leave one structure or identity behind and enter into a new one. Rites of passage (e.g., marriage) are all liminal moments, as are sunset and sunrise, a new month, a new year, and the beginning and the end of the Sabbath. So is Passover, because it marks our transition from an enslaved people to a free people. It is, in fact, our birthday as a people. Liminal moments are typically marked by rituals, as all of the instances listed above exemplify. In the course of the Passover Seder, we celebrate that transition by telling the story and performing rituals that mark what it means to be slaves and what it means to be free. During the Seder itself, we are all "in between."

[1] *"Who did all these miracles"* What was miraculous about the Exodus? Some of the plagues, yes, and certainly the splitting of the sea. But our text continues, "who brought us from slavery to freedom...." But that act, in and of itself, was not intrinsically miraculous unless we insist, as our tradition does, that it was God who engineered the Exodus, that it was not simply a concatenation of natural events. The Maccabean victory and the redemption in the time of Esther are identified liturgically as miracles, but there is no explicit reference to God as having brought either of them about. In fact, the Maccabean events are all post-biblical. That they are viewed as divine interventions is the work of the talmudic rabbis.

This might indicate to us that there are two dimensions to every so-called miracle. One is God's intervention, and the other, our human perception of God's intervention. Both are indispensable, but we would not be aware of the first unless the second is also present. Our liturgy (in every *Amidah*) refers to the "miracles that are with us daily"—and that phrase refers not to extraordinary events, but to the daily "miracles" involved in the normal course of nature and of our human existence. I am very much aware that the simple fact of my body's natural functioning is as obvious a miracle as anything I read about in Torah.

———◆———

GRAY (MEDIEVAL COMMENTATORS)

song *(shir)*, and the Talmud says that song *(shirah)* is only recited over wine (Ber. 35a). Abudarham's references to *shir* and Berakhot 35a are interesting; the Talmud there is not referring to Pesach or to *Hallel* at all, but to songs sung over Temple rituals, which were also accompanied by wine libations. Abudarham may be using Berakhot 35a in an attempt to draw a link between those ancient wine libations and the custom of lifting up the wine cups for *Hallel* at the Seder, for which he otherwise had no clear support. Perhaps the lack of textual support for this practice accounts for his observation that in "these lands" people do not lift up their cups until the Blessing of Redemption (see *My People's Passover Haggadah*, Volume 2, p. 112).

[1] *"Who redeemed us"* A related issue requiring attention is the identification of *shirah* with *Hallel*. The contemporary Israeli scholar Joseph Tabory elaborates on *Ramban's* (Nachmanides, Spain and Land of Israel, 1194–1270) fundamental insight that *Hallel* became the liturgical means by which we praise God in the Seder only after an incremental process of liturgical development. The geonic-era code, *Halakhot G'dolot* (R. Shimon Kayyara, Iraq, ninth century), includes the recitation of *Hallel* at its proper times among its listing of the 613 commandments received at Sinai. *Rambam* (Maimonides, Spain and Egypt, 1135/8–1204) objected to the inclusion of *Hallel* on this list, on the sensible grounds that *Hallel* consists of psalms authored (as tradition has it) by King David, who lived well after Moses and Sinai. *Ramban* defended the geonic idea through a fascinating "historical" reconstruction. As *Ramban* explains, Moses originally commanded Israel to recite praises to God on their festivals in recognition of the God who saved them from Egypt, split the Red Sea for them, and singled them out for His service.[1] To *Ramban*, Moses' "command" that Israel recite *Hallel* at appropriate times renders that requirement "Sinaitic." Yet, continued *Ramban*, Moses did not fix the text they were to recite in praise. Only after Psalms was redacted as a book (which *Ramban*, in keeping with rabbinic tradition, believed was done by King David) were Psalms 113–118 fixed as *Hallel*. Thus, the unspecific requirement to recite *shirah* and praise to God on the Seder night eventually came to be understood as a requirement to recite *Hallel*. Tabory supplements *Ramban's* insight that *Hallel* entered the Seder after a time with a more nuanced consideration of the stages of development of *Hallel* itself. Did the placement of the two textual pieces we know as *Hallel* in the Seder result in the crystallization in other liturgical contexts of the full *Hallel* we know, or did the Seder originally include only the *Hallel* passages we recite prior to the meal, with other *Hallel* passages added later after *Birkat Hamazon* because they had come to be included in the *Hallel* recited in other contexts? There is no definitive answer.[2]

Apropos, one reason R. Hai Gaon (Baghdad, d. 1038) gave for not reciting a blessing over the *Hallel* at the Seder is that we do not recite it qua *Hallel*, but as a *shirah*, and so the *Hallel* blessing is not appropriate (*Responsa Sha'arei T'shuvah, siman* 102). Another issue relevant to whether or not a blessing should be recited over the Seder *Hallel* is that of the effect, if any, the Seder *Hallel*'s division into two parts has on the blessing. *Sefer Ha-Agur* (R. Jacob b. R. Judah Landa, Germany, fifteenth century) points out that some earlier scholars held that we should recite blessings over both parts of the *Hallel*, but others—notably including the *Rosh*—held that no blessing at all should be recited over this *Hallel*, since it is separated into two parts. Our practice, he points out, follows the *Rosh* (*Hilkhot Leil Pesach, siman* 805).

[1] *"Thank, praise, honor, glorify, exalt, magnify, bless, elevate, and celebrate"* The Hebrew text of the Haggadah includes a number of different expressions of praise. Different versions of the Haggadah had differing lists, and commentators provided explanations for their own versions. Abudarham says that there are seven expressions of praise (*l'hodot, l'hallel, l'shabe'ach, l'fa'er, l'romem, l'hader, l'kales*), which correspond to the seven heavens.[3] Tosafot are more prescriptive on this point than Abudarham and quote "those who say" that no more than seven expressions of praise should be uttered, in order to correspond to the seven heavens.[4] Don Isaac Abarbanel adds that the seven expressions correspond to the seven "shepherds" of Israel: Abraham, Isaac, Jacob, Aaron, Moses, David, and Solomon (*Zevach Pesach*). *Rashbetz*'s Haggadah also included the expression *l'aleih*, for a total of eight. He explained that these eight expressions of praise correspond to the four divine miracles mentioned in this paragraph: God took us from slavery to freedom, from sorrow to happiness, from mourning to celebration, and from darkness to great light. Just as these miracles were so spectacular that they were, in effect, *doubled*, so should we recite four times two, or eight, expressions of praise. In our Haggadah, we have the additional expression *l'varekh* ("to bless"), for a total of nine.

Rav Amram Gaon and, later, *Ritba* both say that we should not include *"l'kales,"* which is a negative expression found in Psalm 79:4 (*keles*, the root of which is the same as *l'kales*, means "derision"). *Rambam* as well does not include this expression in his Haggadah. *Rashbetz* quotes their views but argues that there are a number of places in the Bible and rabbinic literature where the word is used to mean "praise." His examples are not all compelling. For example, *Rashi* and Ibn Ezra (R. Abraham ibn Ezra, Spain, then various countries, 1089–1164), two authoritative biblical commentators, had earlier pointed out that one of the examples *Rashbetz* was later to present (*yitkalas*, again of the root *k.l.s*, from Hab. 1:10) was more accurately understood as "derision." In another case (A. Z. 49b–50a), *Rashbetz* argued (rather fancifully) that *l'kales* should mean "praise" based on how ancient idolaters might have interpreted a word that was not even in Hebrew! Yet, although *Rashbetz*'s arguments for the inclusion of *l'kales* were not entirely compelling, the term is nevertheless present in our Haggadah.

[1] *"From slavery to freedom ... and from enslavement to redemption"* *Rashbetz* comments on a Sefardi version of the Haggadah, which apparently lacked the concluding phrase— "from enslavement to redemption"—that we have in the Ashkenazi Haggadah. He

explains that "from slavery to freedom" is the main miracle. Once we were redeemed, we naturally moved from "sorrow to happiness," because slaves are characteristically sad and only attain happiness upon being freed. Similarly, he continues, a slave is like a person in mourning, because the difficult and dangerous conditions of his or her life do not permit joy. Just as the Jews in the story of Esther (9:22) were said to have moved *mei'eivel l'yom tov* ("from mourning to celebration") when the danger to their lives was removed, so do slaves, when they are freed and the danger is gone, move *mei'eivel l'yom tov*, as the Haggadah states. Finally, slaves wander about as if in darkness, perhaps from keeping their heads perpetually bowed low. Yet, when they are freed, they walk in God's light (Isa. 60:2).

Rambam, also a Sefardi, includes the phrase "from enslavement to redemption," but—apparently following Natronai Gaon (ninth century)—places it immediately after "from slavery to freedom" in his Haggadah. Thus his list ends, like that of *Rashbetz*, with "from darkness to great light." Don Isaac Abarbanel's list is identical to that of *Rambam*. It appears that one clear issue in the transmission of this text was with which phrase to end it: with "from darkness to great light" or "from enslavement to redemption," as our Haggadah does. One advantage of ending with "from enslavement to redemption," as we do, is that this ending nicely epitomizes the theme of the Haggadah and the holiday.

—◆—

J. HOFFMAN (TRANSLATION)

and is generally translated "mock." It is not clear how the verb came to mean something positive, but one possibility is that it is like "laugh": one can laugh in derision or in celebration. While some words appear in almost all of these lists of words meaning "praise," this word is not always included. Some Geonim even objected to "Halleluyah," but in inclusion of "(a new song)" forces us to translate "sing." (One doesn't exclaim a song in English.)

2 *"Halleluyah"* That is, "praise God."

3 *"Praise His name"* Literally, just "praise." In Hebrew, the verb can take an implied object, whereas in English we have to spell it out. *JPS*'s "give praise" is another option. If it were grammatical in English, we would prefer "Praise! Praise Adonai's name!"

3 *"You servants"* Others, "O servants."

5 *"From the sun's rising to its setting"* *JPS*'s "from east to west" assumes that this line is spatial; we assume that it is temporal and that "from the rising to the setting" is a poetic way of saying "all day," not "everywhere."

6 *"Heavens"* Or, perhaps, just "sky."

7 *"Enthroned"* Literally, "sitting." While God "sits" here, in a few verses He will let the

poor "sit" with princes. Our translation does not reflect the progression in the imagery.

[7] *"Up high"* While the point of the Hebrew word is clear, its particular grammatical form is not. The *yod* at the end is surprising. We assume that it is a poetic form that doesn't alter the word's meaning. The same form, with different verbs, is repeated in the next several verses. We use "up high" here instead of "on high" so that we can use "down below," immediately following, using "up/down" in English where the Hebrew has these unusual verb forms. Our translation thus maintains some sense of the parallelism of the original.

[9] *"Lifts up"* This is another verb with the peculiar *yod* ending. We continue the pattern of using particles ("up," "down," etc.) for each such verb. (See "up high," immediately above.)

[9] *"Filth"* Others, the more specific "dunghill," which may have been the literal meaning of the word.

[10] *"Let them sit"* Or, perhaps, even "enthrone them with…." See above, "enthroned."

[11] *"Barren woman"* Literally, "barren women of the house." It's not clear what purpose "of the house" has. One possibility is that this psalm was originally sung and more syllables were needed for metrical reasons. The English "barren women" is already more awkward than the Hebrew, and we don't want to make it worse with "barren women of the house."

[11] *"Sit as"* This is one possible understanding of the Hebrew. The other is that the "barren woman" actually becomes a happy mother, not just like a happy mother. (King James gives us, "He maketh the barren woman to keep house, and to be a joyful mother of children."

[12] *"Went forth from"* We would prefer simply "left," but then we would have no way of completing the line, because "when Israel left Egypt, the house of Jacob from a foreign nation …" doesn't make sense in English, and we want to maintain the apocopated grammar here and below.

[12] *"Foreign"* Hebrew, *loez*, usually reserved for "foreign language." *JPS* translates, "people of a strange speech," reflecting King James, "people of strange language."

[13] *"Holy to Him"* Literally, "His holiness," often emended to "His holy one" or "His sanctuary."

[13] *"Ruled by Him"* Literally, "His dominions." Although the pair "holy to Him/ruled by Him" is not quite as pat as the Hebrew pair "His holiness/His dominion," it is pretty close and seems to make much more sense in English.

[15] *"Danced"* Others, "skipped."

[15] *"Lambs"* Literally, "children of the flock," or maybe "members of the flock," so either sheep or lambs. While animals are common in the Bible, this particular expression is rare.

[16]*"Why"* Literally, "what to you." The "to you" is technically known as a benefactive dative, a slightly misleading term that refers to a dative (e.g., "to you") that indicates who is affected (positively or negatively) by a certain action. In English, we use "on" similarly, as in "Who took the apple on me?"—that is, "Who took the apple? And, incidentally, I was affected by the apple-taking." The translation "what it is to you" is clearly wrong. *JPS*'s "what alarmed" may be right, but that translation incorrectly introduces the overt concept of "alarm" in English where it does not exist in the original.

[18]*"Adonai"* Literally, "before a lord." We assume that the Hebrew *adon* here is a poetic abbreviation of *adonai*.

[19]*"Turns rocks"* Others, "turned the rock."

[19]*"Stones"* The literal "flint," though perhaps accurate, misses the point in English. We want two words that roughly mean the same thing: "rock."

L. HOFFMAN (HISTORY)

part of the early morning service (*P'sukei D'zimrah*; see *My People's Prayer Book*, Volume 3, *P'sukei D'zimrah* [*Morning Psalms*]); and the Great *Hallel* (*Hallel Hagadol*) (Ps. 136), which forms part of the Seder (see "Give thanks to Adonai," *My People's Passover Haggadah*, Volume 2, pp. 157–158). All three—Egyptian *Hallel*, Daily *Hallel*, and Great *Hallel*—are mentioned in tannaitic (pre-200 CE) sources.

Psalms 113–118 are said to have been recited in Temple times, during the sacrifice of the Passover offerings. But the original practice at the Seder was to eat, then recite the Haggadah, and end with Psalms 113 and 114, as the culmination of the evening. Eventually, the meal was put off until after the Haggadah was recited, and it seemed advisable to end the night with more praise, not just food (see below, "When Israel went forth from Egypt"). That would be when Psalms 115–118 were added, as an after-dinner continuation of the *Hallel*.

Originally, the choice and number of *Hallel* psalms varied. Until the Crusades, for example, Palestinian Jews said up to thirty psalms for the Daily *Hallel* or even a seemingly random mélange of verses taken from a variety of psalms (hence the term for that part of the service, *P'sukei D'zimrah*, literally, "Verses [!] of Song").

As long as people had choices for what counted as a *Hallel*, it would have been possible for most homes to include some psalm or other at their Seder. Even in the time of Bet Shammai and Bet Hillel (c. 1–70 CE), when that *Hallel* was designated as Psalm 113 or 114, average Seder leaders might memorize the necessary biblical lines. But after the meal was moved and an additional set of psalms was added, it became hard for householders to master the necessary biblical material.

The Tosefta (a companion compendium to the Mishnah) may reflect this later situation, when it discusses the custom of households taking time out from their Seder to go to the synagogue to hear the *Hallel* read. "People who do not have someone to read the *Hallel* for them go to the synagogue and read the first part, then go home to eat and drink, and then return to finish it off. If that proves impossible, they finish the whole thing [in a single trip to the synagogue, prior to eating]."

(For the choice specifically of Psalms 115–118 after dinner, see "Not for us, Adonai, not for us," *My People's Passover Haggadah*, Volume 2, pp. 164–165. For discussion of the reason we say no opening blessing, see "The breath of every living being," Volume 2, p. 184.)

[1] *"The One who did all these miracles for us and for our ancestors"* When passing a place where miracles occurred for our ancestors, the Mishnah mandates a blessing thanking God, "who wrought miracles for our ancestors in this place." That duty was later generalized to saying such a blessing for other times as well. On Purim and Chanukah, therefore, we say, "Blessed ... who wrought miracles for our ancestors in those days and at this time." Medieval rabbis wondered why we do not say this at Passover too. The general answer given is that we already thank God for the miracle of Passover—here, when we acknowledge "the One who did all these miracles for us and for our ancestors." Others found that answer insufficient, so added the understanding that the purpose of the biblical foods for Passover (matzah and *maror*) is to constitute the recollection and acknowledgment of God's Passover miracle. An extra blessing would be redundant.

[2] *"A new song [shirah chadashah]"* This introduction to the *Hallel* had puzzled commentators. How we can say we will sing "a new song"? Surely, the psalms that follow are hardly new! They go back centuries.

In fact, the two Hebrew words in question seem to be a late interpolation. They are missing from geonic records, for example, and also from Maimonides, and the Sefardi rite. By the twelfth century, however, some Ashkenazi authorities mention it, asking whether they should say *shirah chadashah* (the feminine) or *shir chadash* (the masculine)—both of which mean the same thing, "a new song." The masculine form *(shir chadash)* actually occurs just after the *Hallel* as part of the Blessing of Redemption (see "A new song" [*shir chadash*], *My People's Passover Haggadah*, Volume 2, p. 126). The parallel expression (in the feminine) here may be tied to the later instance, which does seem to be ancient in origin; it was added through the process of "verbal leakage"—the influence of one passage on another, an easy thing to happen in an oral culture, where no printed books exist to define proper usage.

Later commentators seize on the fact that the later instance is masculine, and this one feminine, explaining that the Blessing of Redemption represents a final song of deliverance, whereas this one simply echoes stages of God's salvation along history's way. Each of the latter has turned out to be temporary, eventually giving birth (as it were) to eras of persecution. The concept of birth suggests the reason for the feminine here—an allusion to the expectation of more trials being born even after our singing of the *Hallel*. The masculine (without suggestion of giving birth) is said to be reserved for the later "new song," the one we promise to sing when ultimate and eternal deliverance dawns.

At any rate, "new song" here is known to be of questionable origin, and that is why it occurs in most Haggadah texts (as here) in parentheses.

[12] *"When Israel went forth from Egypt"* This, the first verse of Psalm 114, is what recommends it for a Passover-eve *Hallel*. Psalm 113 precedes it, perhaps because in

general, *Hallel* seems to have implied more than a single psalm. The exception to the rule is the Great *Hallel*, which is now Psalm 136 (see "Give thanks to Adonai," *My People's Passover Haggadah*, Volume 2, pp. 157–159). But the identification of Psalm 136 as the Great *Hallel* is just one of several provided by the later authorities of the Talmud (Amoraim) who inherited the term from their tannaitic predecessors (Pes. 118a) but were unsure of what psalm(s) it was meant to designate.

At the time of Bet Hillel and Bet Shammai, the Seder probably ended with these two psalms. (The Haggadah came after, not before, dinner then). The two schools debate how much of these two psalms to say. Bet Hillel prescribes them both; Bet Shammai would stop at the end of Psalm 113, just before Psalm 114:1, "When Israel went forth from Egypt."

The Tosefta (Pes. 10:9) implies that the debate hinges on the question of exactly when Israel left Egypt. Ideally, "When Israel went forth from Egypt" (Ps. 114:1) would be recited at the very moment when Israel did, in fact, leave. Bet Shammai thought that the Exodus occurred at midnight, so Psalm 113 could be recited whenever the Seder ended, and Psalm 114 might be put off until then. Bet Hillel argued that the Exodus did not take place until the next day, later than it would seem reasonable to postpone Psalm 114. So it might as well be said along with Psalm 113 to end the Seder.

LANDES (HALAKHAH)

1530–1575, Poland), however, reflecting Ashkenazi custom, says, "We do not do any of this. We do not say *Hallel* at night in the synagogue at all." Reb Chayim of Brisk (Lithuania, early twentieth century) explains the two recitations by saying that there are two separate obligations of *Hallel*. The major one in the Seder is attached to the telling of the Exodus story and the *pesach* offering. The other (in the synagogue) is a holiday recitation. The Talmud (Arakh. 10b) interprets Isaiah 30:29, "There shall be singing, as on a night when a festival is hallowed," as referring to Passover night, making it equivalent to any holy day when *Hallel* is said. As a night that demands song, it requires the recitations of *Hallel* in the synagogue.

ZIERLER (FEMINIST VOICES)

of Israel will inherit fully like a male who inherits all of his father's property, saying, 'sing unto the Lord a new song' (Ps. 96:1): it is not written *shirah chadashah*, but *shir hadash*."

According to this midrash, there is a feminine mode of song and a masculine mode. Exile is the feminine mode. Redemption is the masculine mode. Significantly, the Haggadah does not make this discrimination. In anticipating the final redemption, the Haggadah imagines us singing a *shirah chadashah*, recalling the *shirah* sung by Moses and Miriam by the sea.

13. Redemption: Blessing and Meal

A. The Blessing of Redemption and the Second Cup

Blessing of Redemption

Lift the second cup of wine and recite:

On Saturday night, substitute the words in parentheses for the preceding phrase.

[1]Blessed are You, Adonai our God, ruler of the world, who redeemed us and redeemed our ancestors from Egypt, and brought us to this night on which to eat matzah and bitter herbs. [2]So too, Adonai our God and our ancestors' God, bring us to other holidays and festivals that are approaching in peace, that we might be happy as we rebuild Your city, and joyful as we serve You. [3]There we will eat from the *zevachs* and the *pesachs* (from the *pesachs* and the *zevachs*), the blood from which will reach the wall of Your altar and please You. [4]And we will thankfully acknowledge You with a new song for our redemption and for the ransoming of our lives. [5]Blessed are You, Adonai, redeemer of Israel.

בָּ[1]רוּךְ אַתָּה יְיָ אֱלֹהֵינוּ מֶלֶךְ הָעוֹלָם אֲשֶׁר גְּאָלָנוּ וְגָאַל אֶת־אֲבוֹתֵינוּ מִמִּצְרַיִם. וְהִגִּיעָנוּ לַלַּיְלָה הַזֶּה לֶאֱכָל־בּוֹ מַצָּה וּמָרוֹר: [2]כֵּן יְיָ אֱלֹהֵינוּ וֵאלֹהֵי אֲבוֹתֵינוּ הַגִּיעֵנוּ לְמוֹעֲדִים וְלִרְגָלִים אֲחֵרִים הַבָּאִים לִקְרָאתֵנוּ לְשָׁלוֹם שְׂמֵחִים בְּבִנְיַן עִירֶךָ וְשָׂשִׂים בַּעֲבוֹדָתֶךָ. [3]וְנֹאכַל שָׁם מִן הַזְּבָחִים וּמִן הַפְּסָחִים (בְּמוֹצָאֵי שַׁבָּת מִן הַפְּסָחִים וּמִן הַזְּבָחִים) אֲשֶׁר יַגִּיעַ דָּמָם עַל קִיר מִזְבַּחֲךָ לְרָצוֹן. [4]וְנוֹדֶה לְךָ שִׁיר חָדָשׁ עַל גְּאֻלָּתֵנוּ וְעַל פְּדוּת נַפְשֵׁנוּ: [5]בָּרוּךְ אַתָּה יְיָ גָּאַל יִשְׂרָאֵל:

Second Cup of Wine

כּוֹס שֵׁנִי

[6]Blessed are You, Adonai our God, ruler of the world, who creates the fruit of the vine.

בָּרוּךְ[6] אַתָּה יְיָ אֱלֹהֵינוּ מֶלֶךְ הָעוֹלָם בּוֹרֵא פְּרִי הַגָּפֶן:

Drink the wine while reclining ceremoniously to the left.

B. Blessings over the Meal: The
   Second Washing *(Rochtsah),*
   Motsi, Matzah, *Maror,* and Hillel's
   Sandwich *(Korekh)*

ROCHTSAH: *Washing with a Blessing*

רָחְצָה

Participants wash hands and recite:

[7]Blessed are You, Adonai our God, ruler of the world, who sanctified us with His commandments and commanded us about washing our hands.

בָּרוּךְ אַתָּה יְיָ אֱלֹהֵינוּ מֶלֶךְ הָעוֹלָם [7]
אֲשֶׁר קִדְּשָׁנוּ בְּמִצְוֹתָיו וְצִוָּנוּ עַל
נְטִילַת יָדָיִם:

MOTSI: *The Blessing over Bread in General (Leavened or Unleavened)*

מוֹצִיא

The Seder leader lifts the remaining two and one-half pieces of matzah; then all recite the following:

[8]Blessed are You, Adonai our God, ruler of the world, who brings bread out of the earth.

בָּרוּךְ אַתָּה יְיָ אֱלֹהֵינוּ מֶלֶךְ הָעוֹלָם [8]
הַמּוֹצִיא לֶחֶם מִן הָאָרֶץ:

MATZAH: The Seder Blessing over Unleavened Bread Specifically

מַצָּה

While the Seder leader holds only the half piece of matzah, all recite the following:

[9]Blessed are You, Adonai our God, ruler of the world, who sanctified us with His commandments and commanded us about eating matzah.

בָּרוּךְ אַתָּה יְיָ אֱלֹהֵינוּ מֶלֶךְ הָעוֹלָם [9]
אֲשֶׁר קִדְּשָׁנוּ בְּמִצְוֹתָיו וְצִוָּנוּ עַל
אֲכִילַת מַצָּה:

Eat the matzah while reclining ceremoniously to the left.

MAROR: *The Seder Blessing over Bitter Herbs*

מָרוֹר

Dip some bitter herbs into charoset; then all recite:

[10]Blessed are You, Adonai our God, ruler of the world, who sanctified us with His commandments and commanded us about eating bitter herbs.

בָּרוּךְ אַתָּה יְיָ אֱלֹהֵינוּ מֶלֶךְ הָעוֹלָם [10]
אֲשֶׁר קִדְּשָׁנוּ בְּמִצְוֹתָיו וְצִוָּנוּ עַל
אֲכִילַת מָרוֹר:

Eat the bitter herbs without reclining.

KOREKH: *The "Hillel Sandwich"*

כּוֹרֵךְ

Using pieces from the bottom matzah, make a sandwich of bitter herbs (some include charoset as well); then all recite:

[11]Remembering the Temple according to Hillel: This is what Hillel would do when the Temple still existed. [12]He would make a sandwich of (the Passover sacrifice), the matzah, and the bitter herbs, eating them together, in order to fulfill that which is said, [13]"They shall eat it with matzah and bitter herbs."

[11]זֵכֶר לַמִּקְדָּשׁ כְּהִלֵּל: כֵּן עָשָׂה הִלֵּל בִּזְמַן שֶׁבֵּית הַמִּקְדָּשׁ קַיָּם. [12]הָיָה כּוֹרֵךְ (פֶּסַח) מַצָּה וּמָרוֹר וְאוֹכֵל בְּיַחַד. לְקַיֵּם מַה שֶׁנֶּאֱמַר: [13]עַל מַצּוֹת וּמְרֹרִים יֹאכְלֻהוּ:

Eat the sandwich while reclining ceremoniously to the left.

C. **The Meal**

SHULCHAN OREKH: *Dinner Is Served!*

שֻׁלְחָן עוֹרֵךְ

After eating, continue as follows:

D. **Coda to the Meal: The "Hidden" Afikoman (Tsafun), Grace after Meals (Barekh), and the Third Cup**

TSAFUN: *Finding the* Afikoman

צָפוּן

Ransom the afikoman (see My People's Passover Haggadah, Volume 1, p. 113) and distribute a piece of it to each participant. Eat while ceremoniously reclining to the left.

BAREKH: *Grace after Meals*

בָּרֵךְ

The Birkat Hamazon (Grace after Meals) is recited (found in any standard prayer book).

Third Cup of Wine

כּוֹס שְׁלִישִׁי

Immediately after concluding Birkat Hamazon, lift the third cup of wine and recite:

[14]Blessed are You, Adonai our God, ruler of the world, who creates the fruit of the vine.

[14]בָּרוּךְ אַתָּה יְיָ אֱלֹהֵינוּ מֶלֶךְ הָעוֹלָם בּוֹרֵא פְּרִי הַגָּפֶן:

Drink the wine while reclining ceremoniously to the left.

ARNOW (THE WORLD OF MIDRASH)

[2] *"Joyful as we serve you"* Longing for the sacrificial service that had been performed in the Temple eventually gave rise to notions that the Temple had not been destroyed, but only relocated from earth to heaven. An early collection of stories known as the *Midrash of the Ten Commandments* describes the heavenly Temple in which the angel Michael serves as high priest. Instead of serving God by sacrificing animals, he offers up the *(p. 116)*

BALIN (MODERN HAGGADOT)

[8] *"Brings forth bread out of the earth"* Two modern Karaite Haggadot—separated in time by nearly a century and in space by an ocean[1]—share exclusive reliance on biblical scripture to tell the story of the Exodus. In that spirit, in contrast to the *(p. 119)*

BRETTLER (OUR BIBLICAL HERITAGE)

[1] *"Who redeemed us and redeemed our ancestors"* See "As though they personally left Egypt" and "Tell your child," *My People's Passover Haggadah*, Volume 2, p. 73, concerning the obligation for all individuals to imagine that they were redeemed from Egypt. *(p. 120)*

GILLMAN (THEOLOGICALLY SPEAKING)

[1] *"Who redeemed us and redeemed our ancestors"* Our story began with the disgrace—three versions of what that disgrace might be—and it ends now with the glory. On what constitutes the glory, there is not the slightest hint of *(p. 121)*

GRAY (MEDIEVAL COMMENTATORS)

[1] *"Blessed are You ... redeemer of Israel"* Here the Haggadah uses the past tense with regard to God's having redeemed us from Egypt. In Mishnah Pesachim 10:6 (found also in Pes. 116b), the anonymous sage says that "one closes with redemption," meaning that one closes this first part of the Haggadah (ending with Ps. 114), with a blessing for redemption. Rabbi Tarfon and Rabbi Akiva disagree about the text of the blessing. Rabbi Tarfon held that the blessing should read simply *(p. 121)*

[For prayer instructions, see pages 109–111.]

13. REDEMPTION: BLESSING AND MEAL

A. The Blessing of Redemption and the Second Cup

Blessing of Redemption

[1] Blessed are You, Adonai our God, ruler of the world, who redeemed us and redeemed our ancestors from Egypt, and brought us to this night on which to eat matzah and bitter herbs. [2] So too, Adonai our God and our ancestors' God, bring us to other holidays and festivals that are approaching in peace, that we might be happy as we rebuild Your city, and joyful as we serve You.

GREEN (PERSONAL SPIRITUALITY)

[5] *"Redeemer of Israel"* "How dare we recite such a blessing," asks Rabbi Levi Yitzchak, "while we are still in exile? Aren't we afraid that saying an untrue blessing would be a profanation of God's name?

"A child wants to eat a cookie," the master said. "He cries out 'Daddy, may I have a cookie?' The father says no. But if the child *really* wants to eat that cookie, what will he do? He'll loudly call out the blessing *borei* *(p. 123)*

J. HOFFMAN (TRANSLATION)

[2] *"Other holidays"* Curiously, the Hebrew does not read, "the other holidays."

[3] *"That we might be happy"* Literally, just "happy" (*smechim*), which is plural in Hebrew. Because it is plural, it naturally connects with the word "we." In English, we must repeat "we" to make the sentence as clear as it is in Hebrew.

[2] *"As we rebuild"* Literally, "in the building of." Hebrew has no prefix "re-," expressing both "building" and "rebuilding" with the same *(p. 123)*

בָּרוּךְ אַתָּה יְיָ אֱלֹהֵינוּ מֶלֶךְ הָעוֹלָם אֲשֶׁר גְּאָלָנוּ וְגָאַל אֶת־אֲבוֹתֵינוּ מִמִּצְרָיִם. וְהִגִּיעָנוּ לַלַּיְלָה הַזֶּה לֶאֱכָל־בּוֹ מַצָּה וּמָרוֹר: [2] כֵּן יְיָ אֱלֹהֵינוּ וֵאלֹהֵי אֲבוֹתֵינוּ הַגִּיעֵנוּ לְמוֹעֲדִים וְלִרְגָלִים אֲחֵרִים הַבָּאִים לִקְרָאתֵנוּ לְשָׁלוֹם שְׂמֵחִים בְּבִנְיַן עִירְךָ וְשָׂשִׂים בַּעֲבוֹדָתֶךָ.[1]

L. HOFFMAN (HISTORY)

[5] *"Redeemer of Israel"* A blessing on the theme of redemption once virtually ended the entire Haggadah. The meal followed, after which a few psalms capped off the night.

The idea of such a blessing arose from the third requirement in the outline of the Seder as given in the Mishnah:

1. "Begin with [Israel's initial] degradation *(mat'chil big'nut)*,

(p. 125)

SIGNPOST: REDEMPTION—BLESSING AND MEAL

WE NOW COME TO THE THIRD CONCEPT THAT THE RABBIS LAID DOWN FOR THE NIGHT'S PROCEEDINGS. BEYOND (1) ACKNOWLEDGMENT OF OUR ENSLAVEMENT AND (2) PRAISE FOR OUR FREEDOM, WE (3) AFFIRM OUR ACTUAL REDEMPTION! AFTER RECITING A BLESSING OF REDEMPTION, WE EAT THE MEAL OF REDEMPTION, WHICH BEGINS WITH VARIOUS FOODS THAT SYMBOLIZE ASPECTS OF OUR DELIVERANCE. WE EAT THE MEAL ITSELF WITH THE AWARENESS THAT ONLY BECAUSE WE ARE FREE CAN WE EAT IT IN THE FIRST PLACE. *(p. 129)*

KUSHNER AND POLEN (CHASIDIC VOICES)

"Charoset" Rabbi Mordecai Yosef Leiner of Izbica (*Sefer Hazmanim, Haggadah shel Pesach,* Ya'akov Leiner, Lublin, 1903, p. 54) offers an answer to the question in Pesachim 116a, "Why *charoset*?" Apples are the main ingredient for *charoset*, so more than symbolizing the "mortar for bricks," he says, *charoset* should remind *(p. 129)*

LANDES (HALAKHAH)

"Rochtsah" The rules of *rochtsah* are as follows:

1. One's hands should be clean and dry before washing.
2. Using the left hand, one pours a cup of clean water over the right. One then places the cup in the right hand and pours over the left. Repeat. Alternatively, pour twice over the right hand and then over the left. *(p. 130)*

³There we will eat from the *zevach*s and the *pesach*s (from the *pesach*s and the *zevach*s), the blood from which will reach the wall of Your altar and please You. ⁴And we will thankfully acknowledge You with a new song for our redemption and for the ransoming of our lives. ⁵Blessed are You, Adonai, redeemer of Israel.

Second Cup of Wine

⁶Blessed are You, Adonai our God, ruler of the world, who creates the fruit of the vine.

B. Blessings Over the Meal: The Second Washing *(Rochtsah)*, *Motsi*, **Matzah,** **Maror, and Hillel's Sandwich** *(Korekh)*

ROCHTSAH: *Washing with a Blessing*

⁷Blessed are You, Adonai our God, ruler of the world, who sanctified us with His commandments and commanded us about washing our hands.

MOTSI: *The Blessing over Bread in General (Leavened or Unleavened)*

⁸Blessed are You, Adonai our God, ruler of the world, who brings bread out of the earth.

MATZAH: *The Seder Blessing over Unleavened Bread Specifically*

⁹Blessed are You, Adonai our God, ruler of the world, who sanctified us with His commandments and commanded us about eating matzah.

³וְנֹאכַל שָׁם מִן הַזְּבָחִים וּמִן הַפְּסָחִים (בְּמוֹצָאֵי שַׁבָּת מִן הַפְּסָחִים וּמִן הַזְּבָחִים) אֲשֶׁר יַגִּיעַ דָּמָם עַל קִיר מִזְבַּחֲךָ לְרָצוֹן. ⁴וְנוֹדֶה לְךָ שִׁיר חָדָשׁ עַל גְּאֻלָּתֵנוּ וְעַל פְּדוּת נַפְשֵׁנוּ: ⁵בָּרוּךְ אַתָּה יְיָ גָּאַל יִשְׂרָאֵל:

כּוֹס שֵׁנִי

⁶בָּרוּךְ אַתָּה יְיָ אֱלֹהֵינוּ מֶלֶךְ הָעוֹלָם בּוֹרֵא פְּרִי הַגָּפֶן:

רָחְצָה

⁷בָּרוּךְ אַתָּה יְיָ אֱלֹהֵינוּ מֶלֶךְ הָעוֹלָם אֲשֶׁר קִדְּשָׁנוּ בְּמִצְוֹתָיו וְצִוָּנוּ עַל נְטִילַת יָדָיִם:

מוֹצִיא

⁸בָּרוּךְ אַתָּה יְיָ אֱלֹהֵינוּ מֶלֶךְ הָעוֹלָם הַמּוֹצִיא לֶחֶם מִן הָאָרֶץ:

מַצָּה

⁹בָּרוּךְ אַתָּה יְיָ אֱלֹהֵינוּ מֶלֶךְ הָעוֹלָם אֲשֶׁר קִדְּשָׁנוּ בְּמִצְוֹתָיו וְצִוָּנוּ עַל אֲכִילַת מַצָּה:

MAROR: *The Seder Blessing over Bitter Herbs*

מָרוֹר

[10]Blessed are You, Adonai our God, ruler of the world, who sanctified us with His commandments and commanded us about eating bitter herbs.

בָּרוּךְ אַתָּה יְיָ אֱלֹהֵינוּ מֶלֶךְ הָעוֹלָם [10] אֲשֶׁר קִדְּשָׁנוּ בְּמִצְוֹתָיו וְצִוָּנוּ עַל אֲכִילַת מָרוֹר:

KOREKH: *The "Hillel Sandwich"*

כּוֹרֵךְ

[11]Remembering the Temple according to Hillel: This is what Hillel would do when the Temple still existed. [12]He would make a sandwich of (the Passover sacrifice), the matzah, and the bitter herbs, eating them together, in order to fulfill that which is said, [13]"They shall eat it with matzah and bitter herbs."

[11]זֵכֶר לַמִּקְדָּשׁ כְּהִלֵּל: כֵּן עָשָׂה הִלֵּל בִּזְמַן שֶׁבֵּית הַמִּקְדָּשׁ קַיָם. [12]הָיָה כּוֹרֵךְ (פֶּסַח) מַצָּה וּמָרוֹר וְאוֹכֵל בְּיַחַד. לְקַיֵם מַה שֶׁנֶּאֱמַר: [13]עַל מַצּוֹת וּמְרֹרִים יֹאכְלֻהוּ:

c. **The Meal**

SHULCHAN OREKH: *Dinner Is Served!*

שֻׁלְחָן עוֹרֵךְ

d. **Coda to the Meal: The "Hidden" *Afikoman (Tsafun)*, Grace after Meals *(Barekh)*, and the Third Cup**

TSAFUN: *Finding the* Afikoman

צָפוּן

BAREKH: *Grace after Meals (found in any standard prayer book)*

בָּרֵךְ

Third Cup of Wine

כּוֹס שְׁלִישִׁי

[14]Blessed are You, Adonai our God, ruler of the world, who creates the fruit of the vine.

בָּרוּךְ אַתָּה יְיָ אֱלֹהֵינוּ מֶלֶךְ הָעוֹלָם [14] בּוֹרֵא פְּרִי הַגָּפֶן:

---

souls of the righteous—until messianic times, when the Temple will return to Jerusalem.[1]

The Sages also developed more tangible ways of filling the void. One of them was especially well suited to the Seder. "If three have eaten at the same table but spoken no Torah, it is as if they have eaten from altars of the dead [i.e., idols].... But if three have eaten at the same table and spoken Torah, it is as if they have eaten from the table [i.e., the altar] of the Omnipresent ..." (M. Avot 3:4).[2]

[5] *"Redeemer of Israel"* The Haggadah speaks of God as redeemer of Israel using the past tense. A parallel blessing in the daily *Amidah* uses the same expression but in the present tense. Several ancient Haggadot also use the present tense in this blessing. Written in times of great Jewish suffering, the midrash could not help but wonder how we could praise God for a redemption that hasn't been brought about! God acknowledges that actually, the children of Israel were only redeemed for a while and then enslaved again. But because they did not lose faith, God will someday redeem them permanently (*Midrash on Psalms* 31:8). At the core of Judaism lies an unshakable hope that the present does not represent the final reality, that a brighter future— radically so—lies ahead. The Exodus provides but a taste of the potential for change.

[6] *"Fruit of the vine"* The Jerusalem Talmud (Pesachim 68b, 69b, 10:37a) offers five explanations as to why we drink four cups of wine.

1. They correspond to four divine acts of redemption mentioned in Exodus 6:6–7: "I will free you ... and deliver you ... I will redeem you ... and I will take you to be My people."
2. They relate to four cups of wine mentioned in connection with Pharaoh in the Joseph story. The Sages saw Joseph's release from prison as a prefiguration of the Exodus.
3. They refer to the downfall of Babylonia, Persia, Greece, and Rome, traditionally viewed as the four kingdoms that have oppressed Israel.
4. They correspond to the "four cups of retribution that God will give the nations to drink."
5. Finally the four cups at the Seder relate to four biblical allusions to the cup of consolation that God will bestow upon Israel in the messianic future.[3]

[7] *"Washing our hands"* The Sages recount dire stories in which the failure to wash— both before and after the meal, as was customary in ancient times—sets in motion an ill-fated chain of events. Hence the ominous warning at the end of one such tale: "The omission to wash before the meal caused one to eat the flesh of swine and the omission to wash after the meal caused a murder" (Chul. 106a). A medieval teaching further underscores the gravity of overlooking what might otherwise seem trifling. "Washing hands ... is included among the things that are most elevated above the world [i.e., it involves a basic religious principle]. All who make light of this practice are condemned by

heaven and, all the more so, have no place in the world-to-come. When you wash your hands, raise your fingers upward and bless your creator. Do not utter this blessing until your hands are washed, because it is forbidden to mention His holy name with dirty hands, and do not let someone else whose hands are unwashed pour water for you."[4]

[8] *"Who brings bread out of the earth"* Several sages wonder whether this blessing points to the Edenic past, to the messianic future, or to a sense of the fulsome present. All agreed "that *motsi* means 'who brought forth' [in the past tense], since it is written, 'God who brought them forth [*motsiam*] from Egypt' (Num. 23:22)." The disagreement arose over *hamotsi*, written with the definite article *ha*. One sage thought it connoted the present. To prove his point, he cited a verse from Exodus: "I am Adonai your God who brings you forth [*hamotsi*] from under the burdens of Egypt" (6:7).[5] Awareness of the Exodus so suffused the rabbinic mind that it was impossible to say the blessing over an ordinary piece of bread without thinking of that wondrous event.

[9] *"Eating matzah"* Beyond its connection with the Exodus, Philo viewed Passover as a season of spiritual purification, an allegorical remembrance of creation and simpler times. "When unleavened, [bread] is a gift of nature. When leavened, it is a work of art.... Children of the earth in its first or second generation must have used the gifts of the universe in its unperverted state [unleavened bread, that is], before pleasure had ... [gotten the upper hand. Therefore God] ordained for use on this occasion [of Passover] the food most fully in accordance with the season [i.e., unleavened bread]. He wished every year to rekindle the embers of the serious and ascetic mode of [eating], and to employ the leisure of a festal assembly to confer admiration and honor on the old-time life of frugality and economy, and as far as possible to assimilate our present-day life to that of the distant past."[6]

How to savor matzah? It is said that Rabbi Judah the Prince, compiler of the Mishnah, avoided eating during the day preceding the Seder in order to sharpen his appetite for that first taste of matzah (PT 68b, 10:37:b).

[10] *"Bitter herbs"* "In four things there is said to be bitterness. The inability to conceive children ... bereavement over children ... a broken heart ... and terrible illness. And when the Egyptians enslaved Israel, they caused all of these" (*Midrash Hagadol* on Exod. 1:14).

"Charoset" The Talmud (Pes. 116a) describes two qualities of *charoset*. First, it must be thick like the clay from which the Israelites made bricks. The second involves a story told by Rabbi Akiva (Sot. 11b), who said, "Israel was redeemed from Egypt because of the righteous women of that generation." How so? To prevent the Israelites from multiplying, Pharaoh decreed the "separation from worldly ways, separating husbands and wives" (see *My People's Passover Haggadah*, Volume 2, p. 2). Husbands were sent to work in the fields and prevented from returning home. How then did the Israelite population continue to grow? The Israelite women stole out into the fields and met their husbands secretly for a romantic interlude under the apple trees and then returned there nine months later to give birth. That, says Rabbi Akiva, is what Song of Songs 8:5 alludes to: "Under the apple tree I roused you; it was

there your mother conceived you, there she bore you." Hence, the Talmud's second prescription for *charoset*: "It must be tart, to commemorate the apple trees!"[7]

[11] *"Remembering the Temple"* "What is the basis," asks the Talmud, "for doing things in remembrance of the Temple?" (R.H. 30a). The justification lies in scriptural personifications of the Temple as a wounded and forgotten outcast about whom only God bothered to inquire (Jer. 30:17). Because God remembered the Temple, so should we. But even without ritualized acts of remembrance, forgetting the Temple was unlikely, given how its fate touched upon the very heart of Israel's complex relationship with God. *Lamentations Rabbah* (Prologue 24) portrays God's reaction to the destruction: "The Holy One, blessed be He, wept and said, 'Woe is Me! What have I done?… Woe is Me for my house! My children, where are you? My priests, where are you? My lovers, where are you?… I am now like a man who had an only son, for whom he prepared a marriage canopy, but he died under it.'" The unspoken protest—"You, God, bear responsibility for Your own loss"—could not ring more loudly.

[11] *"Hillel"* Of the ten sages mentioned in the Haggadah, Hillel appears last, although he was the only one to have lived out his days while the Temple still stood. According to talmudic legend, Hillel was appointed leader of the community in Israel after demonstrating his ability to answer a question pertaining to the halakhah that permits slaughtering the paschal lamb on Shabbat (Pes. 66a).

Rabbinic tradition views Hillel as the founder of the rabbinic dynasty of leaders lasting over four centuries. Indeed, the *Sifre on Deuteronomy* (*Piska* 357) compared him to Moses. Both lived to the age of 120. "Moses was in Egypt for forty years and in Midian for forty years. Hillel … came up from Babylonia when he was forty years old, served the Sages for forty years, and led Israel for forty years." Of his many teachings, this one seems especially apt for a night when we celebrate our redemption from slavery: "What is hateful to you, do not to your neighbor. That is the whole Torah, while all the rest is commentary. Now go and learn it!" (Shab. 31a).

"Dinner is served [Shulchan Orekh]" The language denoting the Passover feast, *shulchan orekh*, literally "the table is set" (or "spread"), is rich in overtones of redemption. One midrash cites Psalm 23:5, "You spread a table for me in full view of my enemies": "When they left Egypt the nations jeered, 'They'll die for sure in the desert. Can God spread a table in the desert?' (Ps. 78:19). So God had [the Israelites] recline beneath the clouds of glory and fed them manna, quails, and water from Miriam's well. Similarly in the messianic age, God will establish peace for them, and they will recline and eat in the Garden of Eden …" (*Exodus Rab.* 25:7). The Seder plate recalls Egypt; the meal evokes Eden regained.

"Tsafun" The various meanings of *tsafun*—not only "hidden" or "laid away," but "treasured away"—deepens the mystery surrounding the Seder's last morsel of matzah. In one sense, this matzah represents the absent Passover sacrifice, which in ancient times had also been eaten at the meal's conclusion. It may also represent a taste of *s'udat hatsadikim*, the feast that God prepares for the righteous in the world-to-come.[8] Rabbi

Joshua taught that one who serves God fully will be "satisfied with the bread of the future world" (*Gen. Rabbah* 82:8). Also speaking in a messianic context, the *Midrash on Proverbs* (chap. 2) comments: "'Treasure up [*titspon*] My commandments' (Prov. 2:1)— if you succeed in storing away [*litspon*] words of Torah [in your hearts], I will sate you with the stored-up [*hatsafun*] goodness which I have laid away [*tsafanti*] for the future, as it is said, 'How abundant is the goodness that you have in store [*tsafanta*] for those who fear You'" (Ps. 31:20).

———◆———

BALIN (MODERN HAGGADOT)

traditional first of two blessings recited over matzah (i.e., *hamotsi lechem min ha'arets*), the Karaites say:

> *Barukh atah adonai elohenu melekh h'aolam asher kidshanu b'mitzvotav v'tzivanu le'ekhol matzah shivat yamim v'hamotzi lechem oni min ha'aretz.* ("Blessed are you Adonai our God, King of the universe, who has sanctified us with commandments and commanded us to eat unleavened bread for seven days, and who brings forth bread of affliction from the earth".)

"Matzah" Across Europe, even in the darkest days of World War II, enlisted men observed Passover and attended Seders. In many ways, the themes of Passover resonated with servicemen of all types, Jew and non-Jew alike. Lieutenant General Mark W. Clark, Commander of the United States Fifth Army, addressed Jewish soldiers attending a Seder in Naples, Italy, in April of 1944 with the following message drawn from the festival's "bread of affliction":

> Tonight you are eating unleavened bread just as your forebears ate unleavened bread. Because the Exodus came so quickly the dough had no time to rise. There was a time of unleavened bread in this war. The time when it looked as though we might not have time to rise—time to raise an army and equip it, time to stop the onrush of a Germany that has already risen. But the bread has begun to rise. It started at Alamein [a battle fought in the deserts of North Africa, seen as one of the decisive victories of the war]. It was rising higher when the Fifth Army invaded Italy. It is reaching the top of the pan and soon the time will come when it will spread out and into a finished product.[2]

"Maror" Reform rabbi David Einhorn (Baltimore, Philadelphia, New York, 1809–1879) imbued the bitter herbs with new significance:

> And what was the meaning of the bitter herbs?
> ... The bitter herbs again were destined to warn those marching out in arms towards Canaan that they were selected by God to carry on a severe and *bitter* struggle among the nations, to found a realm of priests, and to propagate the doctrine of the Only-One among all the peoples.... And God's promise has been fulfilled in a course of thousands of years.[3]

Sometimes Jews gave no new symbolic meaning to food, but substituted unique substances for the symbolic food they did not have. During the Civil War, a group of Jewish Union soldiers made a Seder in the wilderness of West Virginia. With none of the ingredients available to make *charoset*, they put a brick in its place on the Seder plate.[4]

"Korekh" In keeping with the antireligious campaign under way in the 1920s, members of the Yevsektsiia—the Jewish section of the Commissariat of Nationalities of the Communist Party—were charged with the task of directing the cultural fate of Soviet Jewry. Its Haggadah of 1927 reads, "Put together the Second International and the League of Nations. Between them place Zionism, and say—'Let them be eaten.' May they be eaten up by the world revolutionary uprising of the proletariat"[5] (*Hagodeh far gloiber un apikorsim* [Haggadah for Believers and Atheists], Moscow, 1927). See *My People's Passover Haggadah*, Volume 1, Balin, *urchats*, p. 120.

———◆———

BRETTLER (OUR BIBLICAL HERITAGE)

[2] *"Happy as we rebuild Your city, and joyful as we serve You"* A biblical-style poetic couplet, where "joyful as we serve You" repeats and extends the idea of the previous phrase, "happy as we rebuild Your city."

[3] *"From the zevachs and the pesachs"* The first term refers to offerings in general, while the second refers to the Passover offering in particular.

[3] *"The blood"* In ancient Israel, the blood of sacrificial offerings functioned as a "ritual detergent" that cleansed the altar of various types of impurities. Such rituals played a very important part in ensuring that God would dwell in the Temple; if it became seriously impure, the divine presence would leave and no longer protect Israel.

[4] *"A new song"* New songs are connected to God's redemption in several biblical contexts (e.g., Isa. 42:10; Ps. 98:1).

[10] *"Eating bitter herbs"* This follows the injunctions of Exodus 12:8 and Numbers 9:11 that the paschal lamb should be eaten with matzot and bitter herbs. These are eaten even in the absence of paschal lamb and are consumed in the order noted in both of these verses: first matzot and then *maror*. Also, in both of these verses the word "matzot" appears in the plural—this may explain why more than one matzah is eaten with the blessing.

[11] *"Remembering the Temple according to Hillel"* Citing the second half of Numbers 9:11, "They shall eat it with [*al*] matzah and bitter herbs," the sage Hillel is interpreting the broad preposition *al*, here rendered "with," as "upon." Contextually, this is a possible but not necessary reading of the sense of the biblical text.

———◆———

GILLMAN (THEOLOGICALLY SPEAKING)

disagreement. The glory is redemption: our redemption—because we too were slaves in Egypt—and that of our ancestors.

This *G'ulah* benediction (where *g'ulah* is Hebrew for "redemption") is a combination of two versions that appear sequentially in the Mishnah (Pes. 10:6), the first in the name of Rabbi Tarfon, and the second in the name of Rabbi Akiva. There is a significant difference between the two: the first refers only to the past, the redemption from Egypt; the second anticipates the redemption to come. Rabbis Akiva and Tarfon lived in the second century CE, when Israel was once again under the dominion of a foreign power, this time Rome. Rabbi Akiva, who is reputed to have embraced messianic strivings, extends the redemption blessing to a future redemption when Israel would once again be master of its own destiny in a rebuilt Jerusalem with a rebuilt Temple. To Rabbi Akiva, the earlier redemption was a guarantor of the later redemption; what God did once, God would do again.

Redemption is a deceptively familiar term. It can signify achieving political freedom—the freedom to determine one's own life experience. But in Judaism, every aspect of the life of the Jewish people has a religious dimension. It is God who is the ultimate redeemer, and the redemption is the fulfillment of God's covenantal promise to our ancestors. Apart from freedom from oppression, the Rabbis of the Talmud held that God's redemption would bring about the end of the exile, the rebuilding of Jerusalem and the Temple, and the restoration of the sacrificial cult. Visions of redemption also include a universal dimension with its visions of an ideal world, a world at peace, where all people will worship the God of Israel and enjoy the fruits of justice and compassion.

This broader universal dimension is missing from our text because the Haggadah deals specifically and exclusively with Israel's journey from slavery to freedom. Yet a third dimension of redemption, the personal dimension, redemption from death, will appear at the very end of the Haggadah.

———◆———

GRAY (MEDIEVAL COMMENTATORS)

"Blessed are You ... Who redeemed us and redeemed our ancestors from Egypt." Rabbi Akiva presumably accepted Rabbi Tarfon's version, but wished to add "So too ..." and close with "Blessed are You, Adonai, redeemer of Israel." Ultimately it is Rabbi Akiva's more expansive version of the blessing that we include in our Haggadah.[1]

Rava says that the redemption blessing immediately preceding the *Amidah* should read *ga'al yisra'el* ("who redeemed Israel") in the past tense, as should the conclusion of this redemption blessing at the Seder. The redemption blessing *within* the *Amidah*, however, should read *go'el yisra'el* in the present tense ("who redeems Israel") (Pes. 117b). The reason for this difference is that the blessing within the *Amidah* is a petition for divine mercy concerning the future messianic redemption (*Rashbetz*). But in the Seder, we thank God for the redemption from Egyptian slavery as well as the future messianic redemption, and our hearkening back to the past requires us to use the past tense.

"Rochtsah: Washing with a Blessing" Why is it necessary to wash the hands a second time? *Rambam* (Laws of *Chamets* and Matzah 8:6) explains that we diverted our attention away from a focus on our washed hands by our recitation of the Haggadah. Hence, as we prepare to fulfill the *mitzvah* of eating matzah, we must wash our hands again.

"Motsi and Matzah" Abudarham explains that we recite the blessing over bread before the blessing over matzah because it is proper first to thank God, who causes grain to grow from the earth, and only then to recite the specific *birkat mitzvah* over the matzah, which is made from that grain.

Unlike on Shabbat and other festivals, when we bless *hamotsi* over two complete loaves of bread, we make the blessing at the Seder over one complete matzah and one broken piece (which we break off toward the beginning of the Seder). Already in the Talmud, Rav Papa says that "all agree" that on Pesach we break bread over one complete and one broken matzah (Ber. 39b). Why does Pesach differ from other festivals in this respect? *Rambam* answered that the reason is because of the Torah's reference (Deut. 16:3) to *lechem oni*—just as a poor person must make do with a broken-off piece of bread, so do we make do here at the Seder with one broken-off piece of matzah (Laws of *Chamets* and Matzah 8:6).

"Maror" *Rambam* quotes the talmudic rationale (from Pes. 120a) according to which the eating of *maror* in the post-Temple period is a rabbinic, as opposed to a biblical obligation (Laws of *Chamets* and Matzah 7:12). This is because, as noted earlier (see "The bitter herbs [*maror*] that we eat …" *My People's Passover Haggadah*, Volume 2, p. 81), the Torah always connects the eating of *maror* to the eating of the Passover sacrifice, while it also mentions the eating of matzah separately, thus preserving the latter's status as a biblical obligation.

"Korekh: The Hillel Sandwich" The Talmud (Pes. 115a) notes that Hillel used to combine the Passover sacrifice, matzah, and *maror* and eat them together in fulfillment of Numbers 9:11 ("they shall eat it with unleavened bread and bitter herbs"). Hillel believed that eating these three items together was the only proper way to fulfill the *mitzvah* of eating them at all. The Talmud notes that the Sages in Hillel's day disagreed with him. They held that the *mitzvah* of eating those three items could be fulfilled even if they were eaten separately. The Talmud states that since the law is not stated definitively in accordance with either opinion, we compromise. First we bless and eat the matzah, then bless and eat the *maror*, and then combine the matzah and *maror* and eat them together without an additional blessing, but with the recitation "Remembering the Temple according to Hillel" (since the destruction of the Temple, the Passover sacrifice is, of course, missing). This talmudic compromise is exactly what we now find in our Haggadah.

"Afikoman" The changing definitions of *afikoman* are interesting and complex; we will only touch here on the identification that came to be made between the *afikoman*

and the matzah eaten at the very end of the meal, prior to *Birkat Hamazon*. The contemporary Israeli scholar of Jewish liturgy Joseph Tabory has suggested that the earliest identification of *afikoman* with matzah is found in a halakhic text collected by students of the school of *Rashi*.[2] According to this text,[3] *Rashi* had forgotten to eat the "matzah of *afikoman*" prior to reciting *Birkat Hamazon*. Tabory points out that from this point on, this understanding of *afikoman* became widespread. Interestingly, *Rambam* (twelfth century; a Sefardi, unlike *Rashi* and his school) discusses the requirement to eat matzah at the end of the meal in remembrance of the Passover sacrifice, but he does not designate this matzah as *afikoman* (Laws of *Chamets* and Matzah 8:9). Yet the Sefardi Abudarham, in the fourteenth century, said that "and last, he should eat an olive's worth of the piece of matza that is under the cloth as *afikoman* in remembrance of the Passover sacrifice that he would eat in [a state of] satiety." Thus, by the fourteenth century, *Rashi*'s understanding of *afikoman* is visible in a Sefardi context. Abudarham adds that we do not eat anything after the *afikoman* (and may only drink the required two final cups of wine) in order that the taste of matzah should remain in our mouths. Moreover, like the Passover sacrifice of old that it commemorates, the *afikoman* must be consumed no later than midnight.

---◆---

Green (Personal Spirituality)

minei m'zonot, thanking God for creating foods of grain, the blessing recited before eating a cookie. The father, hearing the child mention God's name, will not let it be in vain. He *has to* give the child his cookie. So we cry out, 'Blessed are You, Adonai, redeemer of Israel!' and God will *have to* redeem us."

---◆---

J. Hoffman (Translation)

word. In English we must choose one or the other. We change the noun to a verb to make it possible to translate this line and the next grammatically while still maintaining the parallel structure in English.

[2] *"Serve You"* Literally, "in Your service." See "As we rebuild," immediately above.

[3] *"Zevachs"* That is, sacrifices. We leave *zevach* untranslated here to maintain the parallel with *pesach*s, next. It is not entirely clear if *zevach* here is a sacrifice in general (yielding the confusing concept "sacrifices and *pesach* sacrifices") or a specific sacrifice.

[4] *"Ransoming"* Better would be "redeeming," but we have used that word for *ga'al* and we cannot also use it for *padah*. Unfortunately, "ransoming" has two meanings. Properly, it means to offer something of value to get something back; that is how we use

it here. But colloquially the word also means "to take captive (in order to get a ransom payment)." As chance would have it, both "ransom" and "redeem" come from the Latin *redemptio*. We get "redeem" directly, while "ransom" comes (via Middle English) from Old French, in which the /d/ sound became /s/. (We see a similar process in "mince," which also comes via Old French and Middle English from the Latin *minutia*, "small[ness].")

[4] *"Lives"* Others (wrongly), "souls." See *My People's Prayer Book*, Volume 1, *The Sh'ma and Its Blessings*, pp. 100, 102, for more on *nefesh*, the Hebrew word here.

[7] *"About"* Commanding "about" is a common rabbinic idiom. We retain it in English only so that we can distinguish between "commanding about" and "commanding to," though it is not clear what the exact difference is. (Halakhah distinguishes the two fomulae, but the distinction is not implicit in the language.)

[7] *"Washing"* The Hebrew comes from the verb *natal*, which means "to lift" or "to take." (It is the same verb usually translated as "to shake" in the blessing for the *lulav*.) It is not clear how it came to mean "to wash." There is a Greek word *antlion*, meaning "bucket," which may have influenced the creation of the Hebrew word *natlah*, the bowl for washing ones hands, but that connection seems dubious. Alternatively, *n'tilah* may mean "taking away of," and hence "cleansing" in a metaphoric sense.

[7] *"Our hands"* Literally, "the hands." See "your horses," *My People's Passover Haggadah*, Volume 2, p. 62.

[8] *"Blessing over bread"* Our English is necessarily verbose, and reflects the fact that the word here, *motzi*, is the name of the blessing over the bread. Because we have no name for that blessing in English, we are forced to spell out the concept. The word literally means, "brings out," and in addition to its appearance in the blessing ("... brings bread out of the earth ..."), it is the present tense of the verb used for "brought out" in the phrase, "brought us out of Egypt."

[8] *"Brings bread out of the earth"* We use this translation, rather than the more common "bring forth ..." because the Hebrew here matches the phrasing in, for example, *Dayyenu*: "brought us out of Egypt." Of course, bread doesn't come directly out of the ground. Originally, *lechem* ("bread") meant food more generally, and in some contexts the Hebrew word retains that meaning. This prayer probably reflects the importance of the societal advance of farming, which made it possible to get food from the ground, instead of killing it as it walked around. (In Arabic, too, the cognate *lachmu* originally meant "food." Now it generally means "meat.")

"Matzah" In some Haggadot, this word is appended to *motzi* (above, "Blessing over the bread"), in which case the phrase, taken together, might mean "blessing over the bread applied to matzah."

[10] *"Bitter herbs"* That is, *maror*.

[12] *"Sandwich"* Or "wrapping." The Hebrew, *korekh*, comes from the root that progressed in meaning from "to encircle," "to wind," "to wrap," etc., eventually

meaning "to bind [a book]." Our use of "sandwich" here is, in a sense, an anachronism, in that the original point may have been "eat the food wrapped like a non-food product," whereas "sandwich" refers only to food. This Hebrew phrase also suggests that matzah used to be flexible. (The English word "sandwich" is popularly derived from John Montagu [1718–1792], the 4th Earl of Sandwich, who stayed at a gaming table long enough to require that his food be brought to him in the form of sandwiches.)

¹³ *"They shall eat it"* The "it" (in Num. 9:11) is the *pesach*, the Passover sacrifice.

"Hidden" Hebrew, *tsafun*, which also means "pointed/headed northward." "North" in Hebrew is *tsafon*, apparently from the same root, perhaps because the north was once considered unknown territory.

———◆———

L. HOFFMAN (HISTORY)

2. then conclude with praise [of God] *(m'sayem b'shevach)*,
3. and seal [the whole thing] with [reference to Israel's] redemption *(v'chotem big'ulah)."*

It reflects a division of opinion between two second-century Tannaim, Rabbi Akiva and Rabbi Tarfon. To understand it, we need to know the difference between "long" and "short" blessings.

Short blessings are the one-liners that we say over such enjoyments as food, like *Barukh atah Adonai ... hamotsi lechem min ha'arets* ("Blessed are You Adonai ... who brings forth bread from the earth"); and over commandments, like *Barukh atah Adonai ... v'tsivanu l'hadlik ner shel shabbat* ("Blessed are You Adonai ... [who] commanded us to light a Shabbat candle"). Most of our liturgy consists of long blessings, however—whole paragraphs or more that amount to mini-essays on a given subject. Like the one-liners, these often (but not always) begin with *Barukh atah Adonai* ("Blessed are You ...") and then develop their topic. At the end, they revert to the standard blessing form, a summary statement of the blessing's theme. A familiar example is the *Kiddush*, which takes up a whole paragraph but eventually ends with *Barukh ... ham'kadesh yisra'el v'haz'manim*, "Blessed ... who sanctifies Israel and the times of year" (see *My People's Passover Haggadah*, Volume 1, p. 115).

Rabbi Tarfon provided a short blessing, verse 1, in our text. Rabbi Akiva converted it into a long blessing by adding the rest, including the summary line, "Blessed ... redeemer of Israel." Our Haggadah has the longer version preferred by Rabbi Akiva.

Some scholars see theological meaning behind the debate. Akiva is known for his support of the messianic revolt led by Bar Kokhba; but he is also remembered for his advocacy of the *Malkhuyot* ("kingship verses"), the part of the shofar service that celebrates God's *ultimate* messianic rule. Perhaps he elongated the blessing so as to emphasize the coming of a better time when the Temple would be rebuilt, and "we will eat from the *zevach*s [probably denoting sacrifices in general] and the *pesach*s [the Passover offering in particular]" (v. 3).

On the other hand, Rabbi Tarfon is associated with requiring the presence of a fifth cup of Seder wine, to be drunk if final redemption arrives that very night (see "Give thanks to Adonai," *My People's Passover Haggadah*, Volume 2, p. 183). Needless to say, it never had, but perhaps he refused to lengthen the blessing until it did, not uttering the final praise of God "redeemer of Israel" until God actually does the redeeming.

Historically, neither claim is demonstrable, but theologically, they reflect conflicting doctrines of messianism. Rabbi Akiva represents the standard Jewish position that refuses to press God to hasten redemption. Rabbi Tarfon is a precursor for the long Jewish tradition of arguing with God, in this case, going on strike (as it were), by refusing to finish the blessing (and, therefore, the Seder) until final redemption actually arrives.

[3] *"The zevachs [offerings] and the pesachs [Passover sacrifices]"* On Shabbat, the order is reversed. At stake is the identification of the "offerings" *(z'vachim)* mentioned here. The Torah mandates that every male visit Jerusalem on the three Pilgrimage Festivals (Passover, Shavuot, and Sukkot) and eat a celebratory meal there. The Rabbis required several sacrifices, including a *chagigah* ("festival offering") to fulfill the specific requirement "to celebrate a festival" *(tachog)* at the time of a pilgrim's appearance there (Exod. 23:14). It was a specific instance of the category of sacrifice called *sh'lamim*, sometimes translated as "peace offerings." Any edible animal would do. The priests were given their share (technically a gift to God), usually a thigh, a longtime practice borrowed from the Greeks (see *The Odyssey*, book 17, lines 264–65, for example). The pilgrim ate the rest.

On Passover, a paschal lamb *(pesach)* was also offered and then consumed by the people offering it. The Rabbis identified the *z'vachim* here as specifically the *chagigah*. So our prayer says "z'vachs ... p'sachs" (plural, putting the more frequently offered sacrifice, the *zevach*, first. On Shabbat, however, it was impossible to follow this order, since by rabbinic law, the *chagigah* (unlike the *pesach*) could not be offered then, while the *pesach* had to be. In that case, since eating the *chagigah* could occur any time before the end of the second day, sacrificing it would be postponed until Shabbat was over. So on Shabbat, the order is reversed.

[4] *"A new song"* A tannaitic (pre-200 CE) midrash elucidates nine songs that the Israelites sang at various times in their history when God delivered them. A tenth song, a "new song," is said to be reserved for the final deliverance of history—the deliverance that this blessing anticipates.

The Hebrew word for "song" can be spelled with or without a final *heh*—either the masculine *shir* or the feminine *shirah*. The midrash stipulates the masculine here but believes all the past songs should be referred to in the feminine. That is because in the past, every act of redemption gave birth to another round of oppression. The feminine reminds us of giving birth. The final redemption will really be *final*, without giving birth to more pain and sorrow, so is represented by the masculine *shir*.

[11] *"Remembering [zekher] the Temple according to Hillel"* How could Hillel have said that he was "remembering the Temple"? The Temple was still standing in his day. The answer lies partly in the fact that he didn't say it. The phrase occurs in the Talmud (after

the Temple's destruction, that is), but only as an explanatory remark of what later Rabbis thought Hillel had done.

But that solution is not altogether satisfying, because we are still left wondering how these later Rabbis could imagine Hillel doing it: they knew that Hillel had lived in Temple times; didn't they think it odd to say that Hillel had been "remembering [*zekher*] the Temple"? They might, therefore, have been saying that they, generations after Hillel, remembered the Temple, when they emulated Hillel's practice.

There is also a deeper understanding of the term *zekher*. Its root, *z.k(h).r*, does mean "remember," but when used ritually, the technical term *zekher* (like the cognate *zikaron*) means more than that. When the Rabbis of Hillel's day allude to remembering, they mean more than what we imply in such aphorisms as "Remember the Alamo" or "I remember Mama."

The deeper meaning of *zekher* comes to us from a repeated talmudic illustration of legal evidence. At times, no absolute proof can be found for a generally accepted, or even obvious, proposition. In such cases, the Talmud locates a biblical verse suggestive of the conclusion, ruling, "Though there is no proof for the proposition, there is a *zekher* to it." In this legal context, *zekher* can hardly have anything to do with "remembering." A better translation would be "pointer"—the idea being that since there is no proof, we are forced to rely on a biblical verse that "points to" the proper conclusion. Indeed, what we have is a genderization of language, since *zekher* (in the form *zakhar*) can also mean "male," an allusion to the male sexual organ, which "points." (In parallel fashion, *n'kevah*, "female," comes from *n.k.v*, meaning "to be hollowed out.")

As a "pointer," *zekher* can apply across many lines of thought: temporally, it is indeed "memory"; in arguments, it is an act of logic; spatially, it is like a road sign drawing our attention from one place to another. In all three cases, however, it "points" attention elsewhere. If Hillel was doing anything with regard to the Temple he was "pointing" to it across space. Later Rabbis could only point to it across time.

Christian liturgy is especially linked to this use of *zekher*. (For details, see "This Bread: Christianity and the Seder," *My People's Passover Haggadah*, Volume 1, pp. 30–31.)

"The Passover offering, the matzah, and the bitter herbs" The parentheses around the Hebrew word *pesach* reflect alternative traditional texts that go back to our most ancient rabbinic sources. The Tosefta (Pes. 2:14) cites the three foods in question and says clearly that Hillel combined "the three of them." But the idea of replicating his practice comes from the Babylonian Talmud (Pes. 115a), which recalls only that Hillel "combined them," without stipulating what "them" means. The chief commentator to the passage, Samuel ben Meir (the *Rashbam*, 1085–1174) supplies the information that "them" means all three. But later in the passage, in what became the directions for our practice, we are told to eat matzah first, then *maror*, and then "eat matzah and *maror* together remembering the Temple according to Hillel." Why doesn't this final sentence include the third food, the *pesach*?

In all probability, it is because in context, the sentence concludes a separate strand of the argument that concerns only the matzah and *maror*: namely, whether (technically speaking) eating the two together nullifies the force of one of them. That very narrow issue is concluded with the suggestion that the two of them get eaten separately, and then together. Nonetheless, the literal wording does omit the word *pesach*, and that is how Maimonides repeats it in his code, where he provides instructions to eat the matzah and *maror* (Laws of *Chamets* and Matzah, 8:8).

Practice differs, therefore. Some texts include reference to *pesach*, following what the Tosefta says Hillel actually did, a practice with which *Rashbam* concurs. Others omit the word, following the exact wording of the Talmud, and reinforced by their reading of Maimonides.

[12] *"Sandwich [korekh]"* Judaism has developed a high regard for human experience of the world. It forbids bundling together moments of joy *(simchah)* lest attention given to one mitigate appreciation of the others. Similarly, we do not customarily combine *mitzvot*, so that full attention may be paid to each and every commandment we are privileged to do. This latter concern ran counter to the oldest rabbinic account of eating the required Passover foods (*pesach* [the paschal lamb], matzah, and *maror* [bitter herbs]), namely, Hillel's practice of eating them all at once. The Tosefta (2:22) describes Hillel's practice, and a midrash from roughly the same time (before 200 CE) actually proclaims it a *mitzvah*.

Hillel got the idea from the Torah, which twice (Exod. 12:8 and Num. 9:11) prescribes these foods in such a way as to suggest they are supposed to be eaten that way. The verse in Numbers is clearest: "They shall eat it [the *pesach*] together with matzah and *m'rorim* [plural for *maror*]" (Num. 9:11). Hillel may just have been enjoying pleasant cookery, especially if matzah then was not the crackly wafer-like substance that we have today, but rather a kind of flat baked bread akin to pita, or even a crepe or wrap—in which case, Hillel was simply eating barbecued lamb with spices wrapped up in thin bread—like a Mexican burrito. Alternatively, he was reading the verse literally, since the word for "together" here is the Hebrew *al*, which usually means "on."

The later ban on mixing *mitzvot*, however, led talmudic authorities retroactively to wonder how the great Hillel could have done such a thing. The Bavli (Pes. 115a) therefore rules to the contrary, saying that "we recite a blessing over matzah, and eat it; then a blessing over *maror*, and eat it" (they could ignore the paschal lamb, which had ceased by then). We follow the Bavli. Out of deference to Hillel, however, we repeat the practice his way, but need not worry about mixing *mitzvot*, since the two foods have already been eaten (as *mitzvot*) separately. That is why there is no further blessing here. It is not a *mitzvah*. We just emulate Hillel as a historical recollection.

"Afikoman" The first we hear of *afikoman* is the talmudic warning not to serve fancy desserts or go partying. *Afikoman* was what you were *not* supposed to do—go from party to party carousing (see "It is forbidden to conclude the *afikoman* after the Passover offering," *My People's Passover Haggadah*, Volume 1, p. 200). Eventually, however, *afikoman* was just the reverse: a final piece of matzah that you *had to have*. Actually entitling that matzah *"afikoman,"* is medieval, but the use of matzah to finish off the meal goes back to the first and second centuries. Originally, a piece of sacrificed Passover lamb *(pesach)* was the last thing eaten. Eventually, matzah took the place of lamb. How that happened is a fascinating tale! (For details, see *My People's Passover Haggadah*, Volume 1, "This Bread:

Christianity and the Seder," pp. 21–36.) Sefardi Jews accompany the *afikoman* by saying expressly, "Remembering the paschal sacrifice, which was eaten while a person was full" (*zekher lapesach hane'ekhal al hasova*).

"Third cup" Each cup corresponds to a different aspect of the Seder. This one, the third, is the normal cup that once used to accompany *Birkat Hamazon* (Grace after Meals), which, to save space, we have omitted here, since it is not unique to Passover, but common to all Jewish meals.

———◆———

SIGNPOST: REDEMPTION—BLESSING AND MEAL

AS A CODA TO THE MEAL, WE EAT THE AFIKOMAN *IN PLACE OF THE PASCHAL LAMB, WHICH IN ANCIENT TIMES HAD BEEN OUR LAST TASTE OF FOOD FOR THE NIGHT. MATZAH IS THEREBY TRANSFORMED FROM THE BREAD OF AFFLICTION (WHEN WE BEGAN—SEE* MY PEOPLE'S PASSOVER HAGGADAH, *VOLUME 1, P. 113) TO THE BREAD OF REDEMPTION (HERE). AS WITH EVERY MEAL, GRACE AFTER MEALS (*BIRKAT HAMAZON*) FOLLOWS. AS FOR THE FOUR CUPS OF WINE, WE DRANK THE FIRST AT* KIDDUSH *(SEE* VOLUME 1, P. 111). *THE SECOND PRECEDED OUR MEAL (SEE* VOLUME 2, P. 109), *AND THE THIRD CONCLUDES IT. (FOR REASONS OF SPACE, WE OMIT THE LENGTHY TEXT OF* BIRKAT HAMAZON. *IT IS FOUND IN MOST STANDARD PRAYER BOOKS.)*

———◆———

KUSHNER AND POLEN (CHASIDIC VOICES)

us of an apple tree! He alludes to the midrash explaining that during our slavery in Egypt, the Hebrew women would come go out into the fields to nurture and offer their love to their husbands. And this, according to the midrash, happened beneath the shade of apple trees. *Charoset*, then stands for the act of love and commitment personified in the Jewish women of the time.

Moreover, according to a classical kabbalistic understanding of the Song of Songs, the apple additionally symbolizes—even in the bleakest situations—the desire for redemption. In Egypt, we were aroused from our own complacency and its inevitable inertia of tolerating things the way they were. (Even after the Exodus, we continued to remember all the "good food" we had in Egypt!) The beginning of redemption, in other words, springs from a spiritual dissatisfaction with one's present situation. Apples thus rouse us to yearn for redemption.

———◆———

LANDES (HALAKHAH)

3. The water need only be sufficient to cover the full hand.

4. It is customary to fill the cup for the next person.

5. With one's hand held upright, fingers facing upward so that the water drips toward one's wrists, one dries with a clean, dry cloth and recites, "... *al n'tilat yada'im.*"

6. One should not speak until the *Motsi* is said and the matzah is eaten. A *niggun* (wordless tune) may be sung at this point. The *niggun* could be that of *Kadesh urchats*—the same as is done with words *simanei haseder*, the "Signs of the Seder," *Kadesh, Urchats, Karpas* .... see *My People's Passover Haggadah*, Volume 1, p. 107. Done here wordlessly, it adds spirituality to the moment and intrigues the children.

7. With one's hands in a state of ritual purity, one should not touch one's hair, shoe soles, or anything dirty or greasy.

"Maror" The Talmud lists five types of bitter herbs (M. Pes. 2:6; Pes. 39a). Two are available to us today:

1. *Chazeret*, identified in Hebrew as *chasah* and known to us as *salat* (Hebrew) or lettuce (English). The best example is romaine lettuce, because its roots are bitter tasting. Other acceptable leaves (mentioned in M. Pes. 2:6) are endive and dandelion.

2. *Tanchah*, known today as *ch'rain* or horseradish.

Both present difficulties.

The problem with *chazeret* (*chasah* or lettuce) is that most of the types available today taste only faintly bitter. Indeed, the *Ridbaz* (Jacob David ben Ze'ev Wilovsky, Belarus, Israel, America, 1845–1913) finds it insufficient for the requirement. But most authorities accept it, for three reasons: (1) it is the herb first mentioned by the Mishnah (*Tur*, O. Ch. 473); (2) the term *chasah* also means "mercy," evoking God's mercy upon us; and (3) as Egyptian bondage began softly and then became harsh, so too salad begins with a sweet taste but, after a time, turns bitter (see *P'risha* on the *Tur* 473).

Tanchah (*ch'rain* or horseradish) presents the opposite problem: it is almost too bitter to eat. Therefore, the *Gra* (to *Shulchan Arukh* 475) decides that it must be broken up (or grated), for its full strength makes it *sam hamavet*—deadly (see *Mishnah B'rurah* there, no. 36).

The Chazon Ish (Abraham Isaiah Karelitz, Lithuania, Israel, 1878–1953) insists that there be some bitterness (commentaries on Pes. 39 and *Shulchan Arukh* 124). This can be accomplished by mixing some horseradish into the lettuce or romaine. This is a good practice, for there are two types of slavery: the bitterness of violent oppression—one must taste the horseradish and have one's palate, eyes, and nose immediately "attacked," to remember these events of our history; and the dull, undifferentiated, gray life imposed by totalitarian monolithic dictatorships—symbolized by the dull, monotonous, slightly bitter taste of the romaine.

"Charoset" Mishnah Pesachim 10:3 debates whether this sweet paste is itself a *mitzvah* or not. The anonymous opinion *(stam mishnah)* is that it is not, and the Talmud (Pes. 115a, 116a) explains that we dip the bitter herbs in it in order to overcome *kappa*—either some poison due to the extreme bitterness of the *maror* (*Rashi*) or a type of dangerous worm that the *charoset* kills or renders harmless (Tosafot). In either case, *charoset* is there to prevent harm.

Elazar ben Tzadok provides the Mishnah's minority opinion: it *is* a *mitzvah*. The Talmud explains its symbolism: *charoset* is evocative of the "apple" *(tapu'ach)*, the symbol of love in Song of Songs 8:5, "Under the apple tree I roused you." The Talmud adds also (from Sot. 116a) that the Israelite women gave birth in the field without crying out so as not to alert the Egyptian guards, who would snatch away their male children for death *(Rashbam)*. It is also reminiscent of the mortar that the Israelites used in their hard labor. *Charoset* must therefore be acidic (to remind us of the apples), and pounded into a paste (to remind us of the mortar). Maimonides only accepts the opinion that it commemorates the mortar and therefore doesn't include apples in his description of a thick paste (Laws of *Chamets* and Matzah 7:11). The *Shulchan Arukh* (473:5) provides a complete "recipe":

> *Charoset* is a *mitzvah*, and it commemorates the apple and the mortar. The custom is to thicken it like the mortar and to place within it sharply flavored items. It is customary to make the *charoset* from the kinds of fruit to which Israel is compared in the Prophets and the Song of Songs—like figs, apples, and dates. We also place within it *tavlin* [spices] such as cinnamon and ginger, commemorating the *teven* [straw]. And we add vinegar or red wine, commemorating the blood [of the Israelites that was spilled].

The rules of eating *charoset* are as follows:

1. Dip the *maror* in the *charoset*.
2. Brush most of it off before eating.

"Korekh" The unique practice of Hillel is presented in the Talmud:

> They said concerning Hillel that he would make a sandwich of them [*pesach*, matzah, and *maror*] together and eat them, as it says, "They shall eat it [the *pesach* offering] with matzah and bitter herbs" [Num. 9:11]. Rabbi Yochanan said: Hillel's colleagues disagreed with him, as we see from a *baraita* [a tannaitic teaching outside the Mishnah]: "Is it really possible that you *have* to sandwich them together and eat them as Hillel did? [No!] Scripture teaches, "They shall eat it with matzah and bitter herbs," meaning even this [*mitzvah*] alone and this [*mitzvah*] alone [that is, separately, in which case one has fulfilled the obligation equally well]. (Pes. 115a)

Hillel (Hillel the Elder, first century BCE) and his colleagues disagree on the meaning of Numbers 9:11, "Upon matzot and *maror* you shall eat it" *(al matzot um'rorim yochluhu)*. The *Ramban* (Moses ben Nachman, Nachmanides, 1194–1270, Gerona, Spain) explains that the disagreement is on the word *al*. Does it mean "with" or (taken literally) "upon"? Choosing the latter, Hillel decides to eat all three foods together. His dissenters choose the definition of "with," connoting temporal proximity but not "all at once."

The Talmud makes no decision in favor of one party or the other.

So we do them both. We begin with matzah, clearly an independent Torah commandment (d'oraita). We then eat the *maror*, a rabbinic requirement (d'rabbanan), which properly comes only after the *d'oraita* commandment but has its own independent status nonetheless. Even Hillel would agree with this practice, now that the Temple is gone, making matzah and *maror* independent commandments that stand on their own. But then we replicate Hillel's practice. There is no need for a further blessing here, however, because in making the sandwich, we are not fulfilling a *mitzvah* but only remembering a rite that could only be done during the Temple times, when matzah and *maror* had equal significance as Torah commandments (see Pes. 115a, Tosafot s.v. *Ella*; *Mishnah B'rurah* 475:14) and had equal billing with the *pesach*.

[11] *"Remembering the Temple according to Hillel"* The *Bi'ur Halakhah* (Israel Meir Hakohen Kagan's elaboration on his work *Mishnah B'rurah*, 1838–1933, Radun, Poland) believes that the recitation of this whole paragraph may pose a problem, for it interrupts the continuation between eating matzah and *maror* separately, and the practice of Hillel (which is halakhically part of the same thing). He seems to suggest that the explanatory paragraph should be said only *after* eating. In defense of the *Shulchan Arukh*, however (which is the first code to mandate it), one could argue (a) as said earlier, the eating of the sandwich is only a commemoration of the practice of Hillel during the Temple period and not a way of fulfilling the *mitzvah*; or (b) even if the sandwich is a fulfillment of the *mitzvah*, the *zekher* ("remembrance") then acts as a form of blessing, providing the intention for the action.

The laws of Hillel's "sandwich" are as follows:

1. Take *k'zayit* from the bottom matzah and *k'zayit* of *maror* to form a sandwich. Dip this in *charoset* (*Siddur Rashi*, Maimonides, Laws of *Chamets* and Matzah 5:8). Some oppose this dipping, whether because the Haggadah speaks only of two dippings, (i.e., the *karpas* and *maror*) (*Ravyah* on Pes. 525, p. 166) or because the matzah itself will neutralize any poison in the *maror* (Mordecai, Pes. 76A).
2. Recline, because matzah represents freedom.
3. The *Gryz* was careful to chew the *maror* and matzah at exactly the same time.

A note on the measurements. There is a dispute as to how much volume constitutes *k'zayit* (the volume of an olive) as well as how one measures matzah to obtain whatever figure we use for it: is it a whole piece, is it the piece crumbled and then measured, or is it multiple pieces ground and then measured? The *Shulchan Aruch* (O. Ch. 486) states that the measure of a *k'zayit* is one-half volume of an egg (*k'betsah*). The *Chazon Ish* concluded that our eggs are half the size of talmudic eggs and, therefore, *k'zayit* is the size of a contemporary egg; thus one should eat 1.69 ounces of matzah. *Shi'urim Shel Torah* (Rabbi Avraham Chaim Na'eh, early twentieth century, Israel) cites the measurement at 0.975 ounces. Rav Moshe Feinstein required *k'zayit* of matzah, measured as 6¼ x 7 inches, approximately the size of a square of machine-made matzah.

According to Rav Moshe, if one uses freshly grated horseradish, the quantity for *maror* is 1 fluid ounce (33 cc) and for *korekh* 1.1 fluid ounces (33 cc). If one uses the leafy part of romaine lettuce, the quantity is 8 x 10 inches each for *maror* and *korekh*. And if one uses the stalks of romaine lettuce, one should use enough to cover 3 x 5 inches for both eatings.

"*Shulchan Orekh*" According to the Mishnah (Pes. 4:4), "Now that there is no *pesach* [the sacrifice]: Wherever the custom is to eat roasted meat on Passover night, they may do so. Where the custom is not to eat it roasted, they may do so."

The Talmud (Pes. 53a–b) explains that the reference is to a fully roasted lamb, like the *pesach* lamb that was roasted and eaten in Jerusalem. The danger is that it may seem as if we are still offering a *pesach* sacrifice—which is forbidden. No *kodashim* ("holy" [sacrifices]) are permitted without a Temple in which to offer them. The Talmud extends the prohibition for any lamb which—even if not roasted whole—might give the wrong impression.

Maimonides retains the prohibitions of serving roasted *whole* lamb on Passover night, "for it looks as if one is eating *kodashim*." But he adds, "If it is sliced, or missing a limb, or if boiled with a still-connected limb, these cases are permitted in a place where they are accustomed [to eat roasted meat]" (Laws of *Chamets* and Matzah 8:11). Any slight difference from a completely roasted lamb signals that it is not a *pesach*. It has become the custom of the Yemenite community to serve roasted lamb on Passover night as a commemoration of the *pesach* but with clear distinctions showing that it is not actually the *pesach*.

The *Tur* (Jacob ben Asher, 1269–1343) adds prohibitions mentioned in the Yerushalmi (PT Pes. 4:4) that include *any* roasted meat. Anything that requires ritual slaughtering, "even a calf or fowl," is prohibited if it is roasted (O. Ch. 476).

By contrast, the *Shulchan Arukh* (O. Ch. 476) preserves the lenient version of Maimonides, in which any distinction that shows that it is not completely roasted is permitted in those places where roasted meat is customarily eaten. The *Magen Avraham* (Abraham Abli of Kalish, 1633–1683), however, approvingly quotes the *L'vush* (Mordecai Jaffe, Poland, 1530–1612), which says that in Ashkenaz meat that is roasted is not eaten even if the meat was first cooked and only then roasted.

The rules of eating are as follows:

1. Regardless of debates between Maimonides and the more stringent position of others, it is certainly forbidden to eat a fully roasted lamb, lest it be confused with the *pesach* offering.
2. It is customary for Ashkenazim not to eat any roasted meat. If it is roasted, cooked, and served with gravy, however, one may be lenient. The *z'ro'a* should not be eaten.
3. Fish, eggs, and vegetables may be roasted and eaten.
4. It is customary to eat a hard-boiled egg—including especially the roasted egg of the Seder plate—at the beginning of the meal, in commemoration of the *chagigah*, the holiday sacrifice, or in consolation for the destruction of the Temple (the ninth of Av—the day of mourning for the Temple occurs yearly on the same day

of the week, beginning at nightfall as the Seder). The egg is a traditional food of comfort, symbolizing rebirth and continuity.

5. It is customary not to eat extraneous "dips" during the meal. The only dips allowed would be *karpas* in salt water and *maror* in *charoset*.

6. Some follow the custom of reclining as free people while eating; others do not, for we find it difficult to eat this way.

7. The meal should be festive. People should eat and drink as desired, but must leave room for the *afikoman* and remain sober enough to conclude with the last two cups.

"Tsafun" The last course of the Seder meal is the broken-off, hidden *(tsafun)*, and especially guarded half-piece of matzah called *afikoman*. This *afikoman* is eagerly awaited as the necessary last bit of Seder food. Even though the term originally referred to just the opposite: what is to be avoided, not anticipated. We need to follow the legal history of the term.

The Mishnah and the Talmud create parallel legal maxims concerning *afikoman*. Mishnah Pesachim 10:8 says, *Ein ma: ftirin achar hapesach afikoman* ("One does not finish after the *pesach* [with the] *afikoman*"). The Talmud, quoting the third-century Amora Samuel, says (Pes. 119b), *Ein maftirin achar hamatzah afikoman* ("One does not finish after the matzah [with the] *afikoman*"). Thus, the two crucial Passover foods, *pesach* and matzah, are not to be followed with the *afikoman*.

This follows the translation/interpretation of *Rashi* and *Rashbam* (*Rashi*'s grandson, Samuel ben Meir, 1080–1160, Franco-Germany), who understood the word *maftirin* to come from the Hebrew root *p.t.r*, meaning "to end, complete, depart, or finish. "Obadiah Bertinoro (Italy, fifteenth to sixteenth century) translates *maftirin* as "to open"—thus, "one does not *commence* after the *pesach*/matzah with the *afikoman*." The legal implication is the same.

We also note that the dominant maxim is the Mishnah, which refers to the time of the Temple and the actual *pesach* offering. The talmudic maxim reflects the post-Temple reality, when matzah, but not *pesach* (as ritual food *d'ora'ita*—with Torah status) still remains.

As for *afikoman*, whatever its possible Greek origin, halakhically it is read as being from the Aramaic root *n.f.k*, "to go or to take out." (We will return to the last syllable of the word, *man*.) The Bavli contains two answers to the question "What is the *afikoman*?" Rav answers, "People should not *get up and leave* one *chavurah* for another." As *Rashbam* explains, Rav is concerned lest upon finishing the eating of the *pesach* as a member of one *chavurah*, a person leave to join another and eat at that one as well. As we have seen (see *My People's Passover Haggadah*, Volume 1, "This is the bread of affliction [*Ha lachma anya*]," p. 142), one must eat the *pesach* in just the one designated *chavurah* that he has joined prior to the slaughtering. As to the last syllable of *afikoman*, *man*, *Rashbam* translates it as *mina'icho* (in Hebrew, *k'leikhem*), "your utensils or clothes." The maxim then would be "Do not finish the eating of the *pesach* with a call to grab your coat and go out to another *pesach* feast!"

Rav's rabbinic debate partner, Samuel, is concerned with eating after the *pesach* "so as not to lose the taste." He translates *man* as standing for *minei m'tikah*, "sweet things such as his delight in mushrooms and truffles and Rav's delight in chicklings." This renders the maxim "Do not finish off after eating the *pesach* with consuming a dessert." A third tannaitic opinion (given in a *baraita*, a tannaitic statement outside the Mishnah, but quoted here in the Talmud) supports Samuel by identifying *afikoman* as such dainties as dates, parched grain, and nuts.

A major difference separates Rav from Samuel. Rav is only concerned with the eating of a second *pesach* with a second group; Samuel is concerned that no food be eaten that will disturb the lingering taste of the *pesach*. For the *Razah* (Zerachya Halevi, 1130–1186, Gerona), the lingering of the *pesach* taste inspires us to go on to the third cup of wine and then to the *Hallel* on the fourth. A Passover macaroon would evidently not provide the same impetus.

The *Razah*'s own debate partner, *Ramban*, posits the reason as being that the *pesach* must be eaten *al hasova*, "when one is getting full." Eating a real dessert, or even just some nuts, thereafter, would ipso facto prove that when a person ate the *pesach*, he had not felt full.

We can now understand the second maxim, "One does not finish after the matzah with the *afikoman*." As *Rashi* and *Rashbam* (on Pes. 199b) explain, the matzah here is what remains of the *pesach* ritual. It "stands in" for the *pesach* lamb. "We are therefore bidden to eat this *broken* matzah as *the* obligatory matzah [*chovat matzah*]." For the *Rishonim*, this final matzah is the *real* matzah. But they then have the problem of the matzah that we eat at the beginning of the meal: if it is not the *real* matzah that fulfills the *mitzvah*, it must be only *r'shut*, "discretionary" or "permissible." Then how is it that we make the blessing "... who has commanded us about eating matzah" over it? *Rashi* and *Rashbam*'s answer is the halakhic equivalent of an exasperated shrug, as if to say, "What can we do? We eat that matzah first and in quantity, so it naturally takes the blessing, but the real *mitzvah*-fulfilling matzah is the one we call the *afikoman*." The *Ramban*, however, maintains that we actually do fulfill the commandment with the first matzah; the *afikoman* is just *zekher l'pesach*—just "a commemoration of the *pesach*." In any event, all authorities agree that the taste of the *afikoman* becomes the taste of the *pesach*, allowed to linger (without any other food) so as to inspire us to praise God.

Maimonides writes: "At the end [of the Seder meal] a person eats from the meat of *pesach*.... And today, he eats *k'zayit* of matzah and nothing afterward, in order that there should be an end to his meal and the taste of the meat of the *pesach* or the matzah in his mouth—for eating them is the *mitzvah*" (Laws of *Chamets* and Matzah 8:9).

Rabbi Yerucham Fischel Perlow (Warsaw, Israel, early twentieth century) focuses on Maimonides' last phrase: "for eating them is the *mitzvah*." He compares it to Mishnah Rosh Hashanah 3:3: "The shofar of Rosh Hashanah [is sounded from the middle], while the two trumpets [are sounded] from both sides. The shofar extends [its sound], while the trumpets are shortened. For the *mitzvah* of the day is through the shofar."

Rabbi Perlow comments, "We learn that we conclude with the *mitzvah* of the day. And that is what our master [Maimonides] meant, that the eating of *pesach* and matzah is the *mitzvah* of Passover night, and with that, therefore, we conclude." The Seder, like Rosh Hashanah, builds to a final crescendo of intent, *mitzvah*, and meaning.

The rules of the *afikoman* are as follows:

1. The hiding, snatching, and ransoming of the *afikoman* by children is part of the *mitzvah* of education. The idea is to keep the children alert and excited.
2. The *afikoman* must be eaten at the proper time, generally in the middle of the night's proceedings (but certainly before midnight).
3. If possible, one should eat two *k'zayit* of matzah, one commemorating the *pesach*, the other commemorating the matzah (eaten originally with the *pesach*).
4. For some authorities, the *afikoman* is the essential performance of the *mitzvah* of matzah.
5. All present should eat the *afikoman*.
6. The *afikoman* should be eaten while reclining and all at once, without interruption. People who forget to recline or for whom reclining is too difficult are excused from doing so.
7. The *afikoman* should be eaten *al hasova*—while feeling full.
8. If one does not have enough *afikoman*, or if it is lost, other *shmurah matzah* may be substituted.
9. One may eat nothing after the *afikoman* other than the remaining two cups of wine, and water. Coffee and tea are counted as water.

Elijah Heralds the Messiah
Haggadah Shel Pesach,
Mantua, 1568
Klau Library, Cincinnati
Hebrew Union College–
Jewish Institute of Religion
The messiah rides on a donkey,
fulfilling the prediction of Zechariah
9:9—"A poor man riding on an ass."
Elijah follows, blowing a shofar, to
announce the messiah's coming.
Hebrew: "Pour out Your wrath …"
(see next page).

D. YEARNINGS AND HOPES

14. MEDIEVAL ADDITIONS

A. Welcoming Elijah

Fill the cup of Elijah.

Open the door.

In some homes it is customary to sing Eliyahu Hanavi *("Elijah the Prophet")
either before or after reciting "Pour Out Your Wrath" below.*

[1]Elijah the prophet, Elijah the Tishbite, Elijah the Giladite, quickly, in our day, let him come to us with the messiah, David's descendant.

אֵ֫לִיָּ֫הוּ הַנָּבִיא אֵלִיָּהוּ הַתִּשְׁבִּי
אֵלִיָּהוּ הַגִּלְעָדִי. בִּמְהֵרָה בְיָמֵינוּ
יָבוֹא אֵלֵינוּ עִם מָשִׁיחַ בֶּן־דָּוִד:

B. God's Triumph over Evil: "Pour Out Your Wrath …"

[2]Pour out Your wrath on the nations who do not know You and on the countries who do not call upon You. [3]For they have devoured Jacob and desolated his home. [4]Pour Your anger over them, and let Your fury overtake them. [5]Pursue them in fury and destroy them beneath Adonai's sky.

[2]שְׁפֹךְ חֲמָתְךָ אֶל הַגּוֹיִם אֲשֶׁר לֹא
יְדָעוּךָ וְעַל מַמְלָכוֹת אֲשֶׁר בְּשִׁמְךָ לֹא
קָרָאוּ: [3]כִּי אָכַל אֶת־יַעֲקֹב. וְאֶת־נָוֵהוּ
הֵשַׁמּוּ: [4]שְׁפָךְ־עֲלֵיהֶם זַעְמֶךָ וַחֲרוֹן
אַפְּךָ יַשִּׂיגֵם: [5]תִּרְדֹּף בְּאַף וְתַשְׁמִידֵם
מִתַּחַת שְׁמֵי יְיָ:

Close the door.

*Elijah Arrives by Train
Haggadah, Baghdad, 1908
Collection of Stephen P. Durchslag*

ARNOW (THE WORLD OF MIDRASH)

"Welcoming Elijah" By the third century, if not before, midrash linked the night of the Seder with messianic redemption: "In that night they were redeemed [from Egypt] and in that night they will be redeemed in the future."[1] But it wasn't until the early Middle Ages that sources explicitly connected this night with Elijah, applying an earlier midrash: "And on that night [interpreted now as Passover] the messiah and Elijah will be made great" (*Exod. Rab.* 18:12). The Rabbis of the Mishnah (Eduy. 8:7) differed as to just what Elijah, herald of the messiah, would do upon his return. Would he root out (push away) families of *(p. 140)*

BALIN (MODERN HAGGADOT)

[2] *"Pour out Your wrath"* Among the most controversial passages for editors of liberal-leaning Haggadot, *Sh'fokh chamatkha* instructs God to punish those who have killed Jews. It is customarily associated with opening the door for the prophet Elijah and is positioned after *Birkat Hamazon* and before *Hallel*.

Whereas Reformers have *(p. 140)*

BRETTLER (OUR BIBLICAL HERITAGE)

[2] *"Pour out Your wrath"* From Psalm 79:6–7, a psalm most likely written in response to the destruction of the First Temple, as indicated by its first verse: "O God, heathens have entered Your domain, defiled Your holy temple, and turned Jerusalem into ruins." (A similar verse is found in Jer. 10:25.) This sentiment is conditioned by *(p. 144)*

GILLMAN (THEOLOGICALLY SPEAKING)

[2] *"Pour out Your wrath"* Again, a disturbing passage that some versions of the Haggadah choose to omit. These four biblical verses, three from Psalms (79:6–7 and 69:25) and one from the Book of Lamentations (3:66)—the collection of dirges that mourn the destruction of Jerusalem and the exile of Israel to Babylonia. We recite this book liturgically on the fast of Tisha B'av, the ninth day of the month of Av, the anniversary of the destruction of the Temple, first by Babylonia in 586 BCE and later by Rome in 70 CE. *(p. 144)*

[For prayer instructions, see page 137.]

14. MEDIEVAL ADDITIONS

A. Welcoming Elijah

[1] Elijah the prophet, Elijah the Tishbite, Elijah the Giladite, quickly, in our day, let him come to us with the messiah, David's descendant.

B. God's Triumph over Evil: "Pour out Your wrath …"

[2] Pour out Your wrath on the nations who do not know You and on the countries who do not call upon You.

GRAY (MEDIEVAL COMMENTATORS)

"Fill the cup of Elijah" None of the medieval commentators mention the practice of pouring a cup of wine for Elijah at this time. As Elijah is seen to be a harbinger of the messianic era (Mal. 3:23), it makes sense that he would come to be associated with the recitation of "Pour out Your wrath" (see below), which as a unit expresses the hope that God will punish the persecutors of the Jewish people—presumably before the messianic era. But why then should a cup of wine be poured for Elijah? What is the significance of that fifth cup? *(p. 145)*

J. HOFFMAN (TRANSLATION)

[2] *"Nations"* Or "gentiles" or "non-Jews." The Hebrew here, *goy*, can mean either "nation" or "non-Jewish nation." But in light of the continuation ("… who do not know You") and the second part of the line (see below, "Countries"), "nations" seems appropriate. The point of the line, of course, is to refer to the non-Jews and, probably (given its history), to the Christian Crusaders in particular.

[2] *"Do not know You"* Or "did not know You." The line is taken from Psalm 79, and in the Bible, *(p. 148)*

(p. 148)

SIGNPOST: MEDIEVAL ADDITIONS

UNTIL THE CRUSADES, THE CLIMAX OF THE SEDER OCCURRED BEFORE DINNER WITH THE MIDRASH CELEBRATING OUR FREEDOM (MY PEOPLE'S PASSOVER HAGGADAH, VOLUME 2, P. 1), THEN PRAISE OF GOD (VOLUME 2, P. 93), AND AFFIRMATION OF REDEMPTION (VOLUME 2, P. 109). ONLY A FEW PSALMS WOULD BE LEFT TO SAY. BUT THE CRUSADES AND THE CENTURIES FOLLOWING BROUGHT DESTRUCTION AND DESPAIR, TO WHICH JEWS REACTED WITH YEARNING AND HOPE: (p. 151)

LANDES (HALAKHAH)

[2] *"Pour out Your wrath"* The doors are open, the fourth cup is poured, and we recite this while standing and while holding a wine cup, so as to fulfill the verses of *Kohelet* (Ecclesiastes), "A time is set for everything, a time for every experience under heaven … a time to love and a time to *(p. 151)*

(p. 151)

¹אֵלִיָּהוּ הַנָּבִיא אֵלִיָּהוּ הַתִּשְׁבִּי אֵלִיָּהוּ הַגִּלְעָדִי. בִּמְהֵרָה בְיָמֵינוּ יָבוֹא אֵלֵינוּ עִם מָשִׁיחַ בֶּן־דָּוִד:

²שְׁפֹךְ חֲמָתְךָ אֶל הַגּוֹיִם אֲשֶׁר לֹא יְדָעוּךָ וְעַל מַמְלָכוֹת אֲשֶׁר בְּשִׁמְךָ לֹא קָרָאוּ:

L. HOFFMAN (HISTORY)

"Elijah the prophet" The Bible calls the night Israel left Egypt *leil shimurim*, "a night of vigil," not just back in Egypt, but "for all the children of Israel throughout the ages" (Exod. 12:42). It seemed reasonable, then, to anticipate God's deliverance from other traumatic events on the very same night. *Piyyutim* (liturgical poems) were composed, checking off the various enemies whom God had visited with revenge, not just Pharaoh, but the Persian king Balshazzar (Dan. 5:30) and even Haman. Daniel was saved *(p. 149)*

(p. 149)

ZIERLER (FEMINIST VOICES)

"Fill the cup of Elijah" It has become a standard practice both at women's and family Seders to fill a cup or pitcher of water to pay tribute to *b'erah shel miriam*, the miraculous "well of Miriam" whose healing water followed the Israelites in their wanderings (Taan. 9a; Shab. 35a; B.M. 86b; *Num. Rab.* 18; *Tanchuma B'midbar, siman 2, Vay'daber*). While the cup of Elijah signifies our hope for future redemption, Miriam's cup represents the miraculous redemptions of everyday life. It also reminds us that so many of the miracles in the *(p. 152)*

(p. 152)

³For they have devoured Jacob and desolated his home. ⁴Pour Your anger over them, and let Your fury overtake them. ⁵Pursue them in fury and destroy them beneath Adonai's sky.

כִּי אָכַל אֶת־יַעֲקֹב. וְאֶת־נָוֵהוּ הֵשַׁמּוּ׃ ³
שְׁפָךְ־עֲלֵיהֶם זַעְמֶךָ וַחֲרוֹן אַפְּךָ ⁴
יַשִּׂיגֵם׃ תִּרְדֹּף בְּאַף וְתַשְׁמִידֵם מִתַּחַת ⁵
שְׁמֵי יְיָ׃

ARNOW (THE WORLD OF MIDRASH)

impure lineage, restore (bring near) families that had been wrongfully—and forcibly—banished over such matters, or more generally resolve disputes among the Sages? The dominant view held that Elijah would come "neither to push away nor to bring near, but to make peace in the world, as it says, 'Lo I will send the prophet Elijah to you before the coming of the awesome, fearful day of Adonai. He shall turn the heart of parents to the children and the heart of the children to their parents …' (Mal. 3:23–24)."[2] Peace in the world begins in the family.

[2] *"Pour out Your wrath"* Given Rome's apparent immunity from divine retribution for the suffering it inflicted upon Israel, it was not unreasonable for the Sages to seek—and find—evidence that God's fury had not been completely spent upon Egypt. The *Mekhilta* provides a good example and brings together most of the verses that almost a millennium later would find their way into this passage of the Haggadah.[3] The midrash initially focuses on a phrase from the song Israel chanted after crossing the Red Sea. What is usually rendered "You send forth Your fury" (Exod. 15:7) should be read as "You *will* send forth Your fury"—in the future. The midrash then cites three examples from Scripture that use similar imagery, but refer to the destruction of the First Temple and the ensuing exile in Babylon, many centuries after the Exodus: "Pour out Your wrath on them" (Ps. 69:25) and "Pour out Your wrath on the nations who do not know You …" (Jer. 10:25). Why, asks the midrash, should God vent divine fury on these nations? "For they have devoured Jacob" (Jer. 10:25).[4] The Babylonian Empire fell forty-eight years after the first Temple's destruction. If God avenged Israel's enemies then—centuries after the Exodus—there was hope that God would do so again.

——◆——

BALIN (MODERN HAGGADOT)

generally avoided burdening their Seders with the thorny implications of divine retribution occasioned by this prayer, in 1882, Rabbi Leopold Stein preserved it but re-wrote it as a "gentler and kindler" statement of universal reconciliation. Drawing loosely on Zephaniah 3:8–9, Stein replaced "Pour out Your anger on all flesh," to

> Pour out Your spirit [*sh'fokh ruchakha*] on all flesh
> So all peoples will come to serve You;
> With one accord and one language
> Will Adonai's name be Sovereign.

שְׁפֹךְ חֲמָתְךָ עַל הַגּוֹיִם, אֲשֶׁר לֹא יְדָעוּךָ וְעַל מַמְלָכוֹת אֲשֶׁר בְּשִׁמְךָ לֹא קָרָאוּ. כִּי אָכַל אֶת יַעֲקֹב וְאֶת נָוֵהוּ הֵשַׁמּוּ. שְׁפָךְ עֲלֵיהֶם זַעְמֶךָ וַחֲרוֹן אַפְּךָ יַשִּׂיגֵם. תִּרְדֹּף בְּאַף וְתַשְׁמִידֵם מִתַּחַת שְׁמֵי ה׳.

"Pour Out Your Wrath …" Haggadah, Benghazi, Libya, 1941, Battalion 403, Water Carriers from the Land of Israel. (Benghazi is a Libyan port and the site of an important Allied victory over Italian forces in February 1941.) Collection of Stephen P. Durchslag

In *The Union Haggadah* (Reform, 1907), *Sh'fokh* is absent, and Elijah is relegated to an explanatory appendix where he is described as a popular folk hero.[2] Its 1923 revision interrupts *Hallel* with the instruction "The door is opened for Elijah"; it remains open for the reading of Psalm 117, after which "The door is closed." While there is no commentary explaining the opening of the door for the prophet in this newer edition, the re-introduction of welcoming Elijah bespeaks his powerful hold on the popular imagination.[3] As to the placement, the editors probably needed something to be said while the door was open. Having dispensed with the usual *Sh'fokh*, they substituted the nearest thing, Psalm 117, which fits the occasion admirably, since it constitutes a call for the universal praise of God—precisely the condition Elijah's coming is supposed to introduce.

In 1943, the Reform Movement's rabbinic organization, the CCAR, provided an "experimental leaflet" to be inserted into *The Union Haggadah* entitled "Ceremonial for Opening the Door of Elijah." In response to a child's query, it provides a simplified explanation of Reform's notion of messianism:

> Child: Why does Elijah come?
> Reader: He comes in answer to Israel's prayer. Again and again has our lot seemed utterly without hope…. In this darkest night our fathers were comforted by the hope of the coming of the messiah. They believed that a better world would come with him, a world in which Israel will live in dignity and in peace.
> Child: When will this better world come?
> Reader: That is a mystery in the keeping of God. But when it comes Elijah will be its herald. Before the Messianic day comes, the spirit of Elijah must live in the hearts of men….
> (child opens door)
> Child: Has Elijah come? I do not see him.

> Reader: He cannot be seen. He comes as the goodness that is in the hearts of men. He is justice. He is brotherhood. He is peace. As his spirit prevails more and more in the deeds of men and nations, does mankind come nearer to the Messianic day.[4]

In *A Passover Haggadah: The New Union Haggadah* (Reform, 1974), not only is Elijah present, but he has his own section entitled "*Kos Eliyahu*: The Cup of Elijah" opened by three paragraphs of explanation. This is followed by Psalm 79:7, "They devoured Jacob…," the least offensive line of *Sh'fokh*, and contextualized as reflecting a time "when our doors were open to surveillance, when ignorant and hostile men forced our doors with terror!"[5]

In contrast, the Reform Movement's latest Haggadah, *The Open Door* (2002), includes the traditional passage of revenge in its entirety, but then offers an alternative message of conciliation and compassion:

> Other voices call for a different response to hatred and prejudice, for the Jewish spirit burns with a passion for peace. In every generation, courageous souls seek understanding with those who oppose us. Tonight, we begin a new tradition, asking God for guidance as we seek partners to shape a world of justice and peace.[6]

Sh'fokh does not appear in the Reconstructionist's *The New Haggadah for the Pesach Seder* (1941), but there is a section called "The Cup of Elijah" after *Birkat Hamazon*. As the door is opened, the reader announces that Elijah is the herald of the messiah, who will usher in an era when "all peoples throughout the world shall be free"[7]—a clear reflection of the universalizing tendency so central to the teaching of the movement's founder (and this Haggadah's chief author) Mordecai Kaplan.

Sixty years later, in *A Night of Questions: A Passover Haggadah* (2000), the Reconstructionists would couple the prophet Elijah with the prophet Miriam in a ceremony titled "The Cups of Miriam and Elijah, Drawing from the Present / Waiting for the Future." The accompanying text reads:

> While the return of Elijah is left to the future and all its potential, Miriam is present with us always. She is here to provide healing, inspiration, and wisdom. She and her waters sustain us as we await Elijah.
>
> There is still a long journey to freedom, a long while before Elijah can herald the messianic age. Miriam the Prophet calls us to work for—not wait for—that day.[8]

Interestingly enough, while liberals were removing *Sh'fokh* but recovering Elijah, traditional Haggadot retained *Sh'fokh* but had not yet firmly included Elijah. *Sh'fokh* was a standard part of the liturgy, while opening the door for Elijah was still a folk custom. References to Elijah are therefore absent from Birnbaum's *The Passover Haggadah* (1953 and 1976), while *Sh'fokh* appears with a faithful translation. In his commentary, however, Birnbaum makes a link between the open door (with Elijah), *Sh'fokh*, and the "night of vigil" mentioned in Exodus 12:42 ("That was …. a night of vigil to bring them out of the Land of Egypt; that same night is …. one of vigil for all the children of Israel throughout the ages"):

> This passage [*Sh'fokh*] is recited while the door is kept open so as to indicate that this night, denominated *night of vigils*, is protected against all harmful forces. The opening of the

door also symbolizes the awaited appearance of Elijah as the forerunner of the messiah....[9]

The Conservative Movement's *Feast of Freedom* (1982) contains *Sh'fokh* with a translation and commentary, which seeks to justify its presence. On behalf of those who cringe at *Sh'fokh*'s vindictiveness, the Haggadah commentator asks: "Why does this impassioned invocation of divine wrath belong in our celebration of freedom?" and he responds, "Because, by opting conveniently for chronic amnesia, the world compels us to remember freedom's foes."[10] Admitting to a paradoxical position, the commentator explains that while "we are forbidden to hate the Egyptians," we are also "enjoined to remember the crimes of the Amalekites."[11] Liturgist and critic Jakob Petuchowski criticized this commentary for being overly apologetic: "Can't the *Haggadah* simply tell us that, at this point in the Seder, our poor, persecuted ancestors used to give vent to their stifled outcries...?"[12]

A notable feature of *Feast of Freedom* is its six-page mini-anthology of texts devoted almost exclusively to the Holocaust and the founding of the State of Israel. This may have been modeled on *The Passover Haggadah* (1972) of Conservative rabbi Morris Silverman, which contains a lengthy section "Remembering the Holocaust," followed by a special ritual in which participants are instructed to drink a fifth cup of wine "in gratitude for the State of Israel."[13] Indeed, among the hundreds of Haggadot published since World War II, many evoke, in one way or another, these two monumental events of twentieth-century Jewish history.

According to the interpretation in *Feast of Freedom*, biblical Israel's servitude and deliverance created a repetitive Jewish paradigm throughout time. The Holocaust and the founding of the State of Israel are contemporary Jewry's subjection to this age-old cycle. This new section attempts to demonstrate that in each generation, Jews experience both persecution and redemption.[14]

The Sholem Aleichem Folk Institute, an educational organization founded in America by Jewish socialists who stressed Yiddish literature and Jewish history, published a Haggadah (1962) a year after the Adolf Eichmann trial in Jerusalem. The Haggadah contains the traditional text in Hebrew, Yiddish, and English, illuminated by etched drawings with a strong Holocaust resonance. So, for example, one illustration depicts an ancient Israelite slave flanked by an Egyptian pyramid enmeshed in barbed wire. The symbolism is unmistakable: the Holocaust, as represented by so many twisted strands, is but the last link in the chain of tragedies—commencing with their bondage in Egypt—that have befallen the Jewish people.

The centerpiece of this Haggadah is the "Seder Ritual of Remembrance," which includes several passages and songs recalling, "with reverence and love, the six million ... who perished at the hands of a tyrant more wicked than Pharaoh." Despite the sorrow, the supplemental ritual ends triumphantly, with the Warsaw Ghetto uprising of Passover 1943 described in near-messianic terms:

> On the first day of Passover the remnants in the Ghetto of Warsaw rose up against the adversary, even as in the days of Judah the Maccabee. They were lovely and pleasant in their lives, and in their death, they were not divided, and they brought redemption to the name of Israel.[15]

What provides the passage with particular poignancy is its echo of *Hazkarat nishmot hak'doshim* ("commemoration of the martyrs"), a liturgical addition to the Shabbat morning service, composed to reflect the tragedy of the First Crusade (see *My People's Prayer Book*, Volume 4, *Seder K'ri'at Hatorah [The Torah Service]*, pp. 177–182). Then, too, Jewry along the Rhine River was decimated, giving rise to this martyrological encomium to those who died and a call for vengeance on those who had killed them. The phrase "lovely and pleasant in their lives" is taken directly from that prayer. The hopeful words of Maimonides follow: "I believe with perfect faith in the coming of the messiah; and even though he may tarry, I will wait every day for his arrival."

——◆——

BRETTLER (OUR BIBLICAL HERITAGE)

the historical circumstances of the destruction of the First Temple. The notions of exclusivity and hate expressed here are sometimes found in prophetic rhetoric, which also contains more moderate voices. For example, Isaiah 2:1–4 imagines God and Jerusalem as supreme, but allows other nations to maintain their ethnic identity, and uses peaceful rather than violent imagery (v. 4 contains the famous "And they shall beat their swords into plowshares / And their spears into pruning hooks").

[4] *"Pour Your anger"* Psalm 69:25. In context, the verse refers to unnamed enemies, though v. 36, "For God will deliver Zion / and rebuild the cities of Judah; / they shall live there and inherit it," suggests that these as well might be the Babylonians, who destroyed the First Temple. This verse follows well from the previous one; they both begin with the imperative verb *sh'fokh*, "pour out."

[5] *"Pursue them"* Lamentations 3:66. This verse is likely chosen because it continues and extends the pursuing and overtaking image of the previous one and, like the two previous verses, is connected to the destruction of the First Temple. (Lamentations is composed of five poems commemorating that event.) This verse, in seeking God's angry destruction, ignores the common motif that the Temple was destroyed and Judah exiled for its sins, and that Babylon was being used as God's agent of destruction and thus not deserving of punishment.

——◆——

GILLMAN (THEOLOGICALLY SPEAKING)

These three verses express the Jewish people's collective sense of vindictiveness toward its enemies in all generations.

Some Jews prefer to view God as gentle and compassionate and find this prayer inappropriate. Other Jews who have personally experienced the hostility of other nations find no difficulty reciting it.

But if we put these words into their ritual context in the Seder itself, they acquire a different tone. It is customary for us to stand as these verses are recited, open the front door of our home, and pour a cup of wine to welcome Elijah into our homes. What does this complex ritual signify?

First, following a verse in the book of the prophet Malachi (3:23), Elijah's role in the Jewish tradition is to herald the coming of the messiah. More generally, Elijah is the personalization of redemption because he never really died. According to 2 Kings 2:11, Elijah was taken up to heaven in a fiery chariot. He is the ultimate liminal personality who has mastered the threshold between life and death. As such, he returns to earth at various liminal moments, at every circumcision ritual, for example, at the *Havdalah* ritual at the close of the Sabbath, and at this climax of the Passover Seder.

Elijah's "appearance" in our homes at this moment celebrates our achievement of redemption. But we understand, at the same time, that redemption is not complete; the world is not as yet redeemed. We remind ourselves of that unfinished work by opening our doors and looking out into the world at large.

Part of that unfinished work is the hostility of the nations toward the people of Israel. It is on these nations that we ask God to "Pour out Your wrath," not indiscriminately, but on those nations that have opposed Israel's redemptive vision of a just and charitable world.

———◆———

GRAY (MEDIEVAL COMMENTATORS)

The phantom fifth cup of wine has left an interesting trail of textual variation and halakhic complexity that can only be touched on here. On Pesachim 118a R. Tarfon is quoted as saying that we complete *Hallel* and recite the Great *Hallel* over the fourth cup of wine. *Rashi, Rashbam,* and Tosafot[1] all direct that the text of R. Tarfon's teaching should read "fourth cup," implying that they were aware of a different textual reading. Rabbenu Hananel (North Africa, eleventh century) indicates that the other reading may have been that we complete *Hallel* and then recite Great *Hallel* over a "fifth cup." *Rif* indeed codifies R. Tarfon as requiring a fifth cup. *Rabad* (R. Abraham b. David of Posquières, Provence, 1125–1198) comments on the Rif that just as the undisputed four cups were midrashically understood to have scriptural support from the four expressions of divine redemption in Exodus 6:6–7, the fifth cup finds its support in Exodus 6:8: "I will bring you into the land...." *Rambam,* who has a somewhat different order of the recitation of *Hallel* after the meal, provides that one should drink the fourth cup after concluding the "song blessing" ("Let Your name be forever praised" [see *My People's Passover Haggadah,* Volume 2, p. 161]), after which one should drink nothing but water all night. And yet, continues *Rambam,* one must pour a fifth cup over which the Great *Hallel* is to be recited, although this cup is not obligatory like the preceding

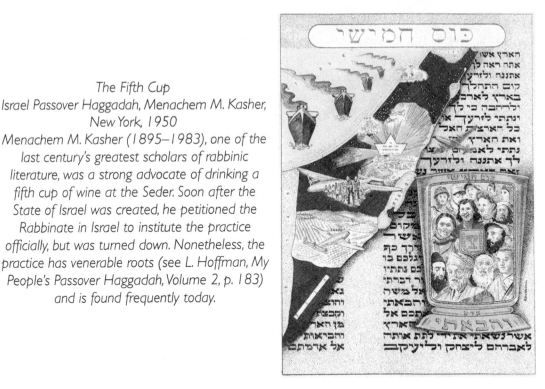

The Fifth Cup
Israel Passover Haggadah, Menachem M. Kasher, New York, 1950

Menachem M. Kasher (1895–1983), one of the last century's greatest scholars of rabbinic literature, was a strong advocate of drinking a fifth cup of wine at the Seder. Soon after the State of Israel was created, he petitioned the Rabbinate in Israel to institute the practice officially, but was turned down. Nonetheless, the practice has venerable roots (see L. Hoffman, *My People's Passover Haggadah*, Volume 2, p. 183) and is found frequently today.

four cups (Laws of *Chamets* and Matzah 8:10). *Rambam* implies that one does not actually drink the fifth cup, although *Hagahot Maimuniyot* (R. Meir Hakohen of Rothenburg, thirteenth to fourteenth century), commenting on *Rambam*, rules that one must only refrain from drinking it while at the table; one may drink it away from the table. *Hagahot Maimuniyot* also quotes earlier scholars who mention the possibility of a fifth cup. The Ashkenazi scholars R. Joseph Tov-Elem (France, mid-eleventh century) and *Ravyah*, and even earlier, the geonic *Seder Rav Amram* provide that if one is ill or otherwise in urgent need of more drink, one may pour a fifth cup of wine for oneself and assign it the liturgical role of accompanying the Great *Hallel*. Similarly, *Hagahot Maimuniyot* quotes Rav Sar Shalom Gaon (Baghdad, ninth century), who said that a fifth cup is optional; if one *wishes*, one can recite the Great *Hallel* over it. What we see is that the Gaon and *Rambam* see the fifth cup as optional for everyone, while *Seder Rav Amram* and the early Ashkenazi scholars see it only as an option for one who is ill or otherwise in particular need of additional refreshment. The *Rosh* sensibly observed that according to the version of the Talmud in which R. Tarfon spoke of a fifth cup, that fifth cup was meant to be obligatory, but the trend in the law was to make it optional. It seems the *Rosh* is implying that regardless of whether one's Talmud text records R. Tarfon as teaching about a "fourth" or a "fifth" cup, the trend in the law in any case was to render the fifth cup optional. The *Rosh* also points to a more practical reason for not indulging in the permission to drink a fifth cup: the concern that this fifth cup will lead to drunkenness, which will prevent us from being able to stay up late telling of the miracle of the Exodus. He invokes the story of the Rabbis of B'nai B'rak in this context, again indicating that our goal should be to emulate them (presumably even at the expense of a fifth cup) (*Rosh* to Pes. 10:33). Ultimately, R. Joseph Karo does not mention the fifth cup in the *Shulchan Arukh*, although *R'ma* did add a note, consistent with some of the earlier views we have seen, that "one who is delicate or extremely thirsty can drink a fifth cup and recite Great *Hallel* over it" (*R'ma's* glosses to *Shulchan Arukh*, O. Ch. 481:2).

It is possible that what we know as the "cup of Elijah" reflects another stage of legal compromise regarding the fifth cup. Since the fifth cup was not clearly established in law, and since there were differing views on whether or not it should be drunk, or even who should make use of it, Elijah's cup reflects a compromise: a cup that is poured but not drunk. But if it is not to be drunk, it cannot be the cup over which any part of *Hallel* is recited. Yet it cannot be left without any liturgical link whatsoever. Its link to "Pour out Your wrath" makes the fifth cup a sort of visual presentation of exactly what we are asking God there to "pour out" over the nations. The connection between "Pour out Your wrath," the fifth cup, and Elijah may stem from the ideational linkage of "Pour out Your wrath" to Malachi 3:23, "I will send the prophet Elijah to you before the coming of the awesome, fearful day of Adonai"—which will presumably include the "pouring out" of divine wrath and the reduction of "the arrogant all the doers of evil" to "straw" (Mal. 3:19).[2]

[2] *"Pour out Your wrath"* The recitation of "Pour out Your wrath" consists of Psalms 79:6–7 and 69:25 and Lamentations 3:66. The recitation of these verses as a unit in connection with the fourth cup of wine and prior to the second part of *Hallel* is not mentioned in either Talmud. The custom likely began to appear in France in the late twelfth century. The textual variations are of great interest but can only be touched upon here.[3] *Machzor Vitry* (twelfth century, *Hilkhot Pesach*, p. 296) includes those two verses and adds the third and fourth verses found in our Haggadah ("Pour Your anger" and "Pursue them in fury"). *Machzor Vitry* also interpolates other pointed, graphic, and angry material between the third and fourth verses directed at Israel's persecutors. *Sefer Or Zarua* (R. Isaac b. R. Moses of Vienna, Germany, thirteenth century) quotes the comment of an earlier scholar, R. Shmuel, that we recite "Pour out Your wrath" because we have mentioned the wicked, persecuting Egyptians a number of times in the course of the evening, and the wicked should be cursed when mentioned (*Hilkhot Pesachim*, end of *siman* 256). Interestingly, neither the *Rosh* (1250–1327) nor his son R. Jacob b. Asher (*Tur*, 1270–1340) mention "Pour out Your wrath." On the Sefardi side, neither *Rif* (1013–1103) nor *Rambam* (1135/8–1204) mentions it, although *Ran* (fourteenth century) refers to it in his commentary on the *Rif* to Pesachim (19a in the *Rif's* pages). Abudarham (fourteenth century) refers only to the recitation of "the verse 'Pour out Your wrath,'" which may imply that the recitation of the one verse was all he was aware of. *Rashbetz* (fourteenth century) and *Ritba* are also aware of "Pour out Your wrath"; *Ritba* (thirteenth to fourteenth century) explains that "Pour out Your wrath" is found just before filling the fourth cup because the four cups are said to symbolize, among other things, the "four cups of punishment" that

God will in the future give as drink to the nations that persecuted the Jewish people (PT Pes. 10:1, 73c). *Rashbetz* asks the logical question of why the Yerushalmi's interpretation requires that "Pour out Your wrath" be recited in connection with the fourth cup and not one of the earlier three. Abudarham provides a good answer: it is as if we are saying, "Look God, we fulfilled the *mitzvah* of the four cups; now You fulfill Your promise of pouring out the four cups of punishment on our persecutors."

R'ma (*Darkhei Moshe* to *Tur*, O. Ch. 480) says that the practice of opening the door for the recitation of "Pour out Your wrath" stems from *Or Zarua* (*Hilkhot Pesachim, siman* 234). *Or Zarua* quoted R. Nissim Gaon (Tunisia, 990–1062), who, in turn, quoted his father as saying that we should not lock our houses on the night of Pesach as a sign of faith in God's promises. As a reward for this faith, we will merit (ultimate) redemption. Presumably, then, by opening our doors and expressing our faith that God will mete out appropriate justice to our persecutors, we are also expressing our readiness for redemption.

———◆———

J. HOFFMAN (TRANSLATION)

the Hebrew "past" tense is used for the present as well as the past. (Even calling it the "past tense" is somewhat misleading, for reasons that are too complicated for this setting.) We also have a choice between "do not" and "don't." The former is more formal. While now we regard Scripture in its entirety as formal, we have no reason to believe that it was formal when it was written. "Don't" might therefore be better.

[2] *"Countries"* Or "kingdoms." The issue is that, technically, there were no countries in the Middle Ages, when the line was introduced into the Haggadah, or in the first millennium BCE, when the line was originally composed. Nonetheless, we frequently use "country" colloquially for older France, Germany, etc., and even for ancient Canaan, etc.

[2] *"You"* Literally, "Your name," a frequent biblical idiom.

[3] *"They"* Surprisingly, the Hebrew has "he" here. This is probably an error in the text. The Septuagint gives us the more sensible "they." Also, Jeremiah 10:25 contains almost the same line: "Pour out Your wrath on the nations who don't know You and upon the families who do not call upon You, for they have devoured Jacob...."

[3] *"Devoured"* Literally, "eaten." But while "devour," like the Hebrew *akhal*, functions nicely metaphorically, "eat" in English does not.

[4] *"Overtake"* "Overcome" might make a little more sense here, but the Haggadah juxtaposes this image with "pursuing," next, and "pursue/overtake" completes a nice poetic image, while "pursue/overcome" does not.

———◆———

L. HOFFMAN (HISTORY)

from the lion's den that night also (*Exod. Rab.* 8:12), and on that day too, Elijah will appear heralding the messiah.

It should come as no surprise, therefore, to see Jews standing vigil for Elijah on Seder eve. But that is a medieval development. Elijah does not make his appearance in Jewish liturgy until after the Crusades, at which time he seems to appear elsewhere also.

This development goes back to an eighth-century Palestinian work, *Pirkei D'rabbi Eliezer*, which combines two traditions. First, we have Elijah's repeated assertion that he is moved by *zeal* to fight the false prophets of Baal (1 Kings 19:10, 19:14). Second, we have a dual prediction by the prophet Malachi: he says that God will send "an angel [or messenger] of the covenant" *(malakh habrit)* to chastise Israel (Mal. 3:1) and also that Elijah will herald "the awesome, fearful day" of reckoning (Mal. 3:23). *Pirkei D'rabbi Eliezer* combines all of this to conclude that Elijah himself (Mal. 3:23) is the "messenger of the *covenant*" (Mal. 3:1) whose zeal (1 Kings 19:10, 19:14) will be rewarded by his being sent to watch over "the *covenant* of circumcision" throughout time. "The sages," he says, have therefore established a "seat of honor" for him there.

There is no evidence that such a chair became part of the ritual, however, until after the Crusades, when it eventually became known officially as *kisei eliyahu*, an empty "chair for Elijah," placed in every circumcision home to welcome the prophet. Similarly, Jews began expecting Elijah every Saturday night at *Havdalah*; he would never break Shabbat law by traveling on Shabbat day, but if Israel kept Shabbat well enough, perhaps he would come the minute Shabbat was over. A song was written for him: *Eliyahu Hanavi*, "Elijah the Prophet." And Elijah was expected also on Passover eve, the "night of vigil."

The practice of opening a door had earlier precedents, but unconnected to Elijah. During the geonic period (c. 750–1034), some Jews kept their doors open as a symbol of "the night of vigil." Among Christians too, the Passover night of vigil was observed. It is still part of the liturgy for Easter Saturday, the night prior to Jesus' resurrection. Both groups, then, cast an expectant eye on the messianic coming (a second time for Christians, just once for Jews)—with the good news of final salvation.

After the Crusades, the customs of opening the door and expecting Elijah merged. Illustrated medieval Haggadot display householders standing in the doorway, a cup of wine in hand. Since Zechariah 9:9 had predicted that the messianic "king" would arrive on "a donkey," we see such an animal off in the distance, carrying Elijah, who is blowing a shofar; sometimes it is the messiah himself on the donkey, and at times it is both Elijah and the messiah, merged into one person. Through the window, we sometimes see the usual four cups of wine, connected by tradition with four occasions when God had wrought salvation in Israel's past. The householder is holding a fifth cup, hoping that the messiah will appear this one final time—and he will drink it to welcome the fifth, last, and ultimate redemption.

That fifth cup, however, is not immediately known as Elijah's cup. The name *kos eliyahu* is first mentioned only in the fifteenth century. But the idea of having a fifth cup in waiting, just in case final redemption arrived, was old; it had survived from the second century (see "Give thanks to Adonai [Psalm 136]," *My People's Passover Haggadah*, Volume 2, p. 183). The *Gra* (the Vilna Gaon, Rabbi Elijah of Vilna, 1720–1797) connects the two cups halakhically, saying that the fifth cup was renamed Elijah's cup because when Elijah comes, he will resolve the question of whether to drink it or not. More likely, the connection is topical-historical. The name is a result of merging the older custom of holding a fifth cup in reserve for the final redemption, and the newer one of awaiting Elijah as harbinger of that redemption.

It became customary, then, to open the door, curse Israel's enemies ("Pour out Your wrath"), invite Elijah as the messianic herald, and prepare to drink the fifth (Elijah's) cup.

² *"Pour out Your wrath"* The German Jewish community came into being when Italian Jews traversed the Alps in the tenth century and founded settlements in the Rhineland. The tenth and eleventh centuries saw them flower, with talmudic academies that boasted such names as Rabbenu Gershom (called *M'or Hagolah,* "light to the diaspora," 960–1040) and Jacob ben Yakar (d. 1064). *Rashi,* the greatest medieval commentator of all, studied there before returning to France to establish his own school of thought.

This glorious chapter in Jewish history came to an end with the First Crusade, dispatched by Pope Urban II from Clermont, France, in 1095. At stake for Christian Europe was the reputation of the papacy, its claim to surpass the eastern Patriarch in Constantinople, enormous riches from the east, control of Palestine, and (back home) growing lawlessness that was making organized life impossible. A surge in population had produced too many young men for the available feudal land holdings to support, with the result that they became mercenaries for regular warfare among nobles, and outright highway robbers. These are the people to whom Urban appealed when he charged, "Let those who, for a long time, have been robbers, now become knights. Let those who have been fighting against their brothers and relatives now fight in a proper way against the barbarians. Let those who have been serving as mercenaries for small pay now obtain the eternal reward."

Jews in the path of official Crusaders the year later weathered the storm, largely protected by the nobles and churchmen in charge. But in the interim, a growing mob of people moved by word of the pope's promises set out for Jerusalem and bogged down in the Rhineland, where they decimated the Jewish community. It would rise anew, but in the interim, its remaining members expressed their grief, shock, and anger liturgically.

One such response was "Pour out Your wrath," a call to God for vengeance. It first appears in *Machzor Vitry*, a liturgical compendium from eleventh- to twelfth-century France. France had remained untouched by the devastation but must have reacted to news about it with this prayer for revenge. Our version comprises four biblical verses, but custom varies, from reciting as few as two verses to as many as seventeen. All versions, however, express hope for God to repay the violence of Israel's enemies.

Prior to the Crusades, the dramatic flow of the Seder would already have culminated, in the first set of *Hallel* psalms (Pss. 113–114; see *My People's Passover Haggadah*, Volume 2, pp. 93–94) and the Blessing of Redemption following (Volume 2,

p. 109). A few more after-dinner psalms (Psalms 115–118, Volume 2, pp. 154–157) would have remained, but the Seder climax would have passed. The post-Crusade period, however, launched a new chapter in Jewish history and a set of additions to the Haggadah to express it. "Pour out Your wrath" was one of them. Another was opening the door for Elijah (see above, "Elijah the prophet").

Modern liberal Haggadot make much of opening the door for Elijah but omit the call for revenge that once went with it. When artist Leonard Baskin was commissioned to prepare the artwork for the American Reform Haggadah of 1974, he painted a page to accompany "Pour out Your wrath." That prayer had already been omitted from the text, however, and, after some debate, it was decided to exclude the accompanying painting as well.

———◆———

SIGNPOST: MEDIEVAL ADDITIONS

PERHAPS GOD WOULD PUNISH THE CRUSADERS WHO HAD DEVASTATED JEWISH COMMUNITIES; EVEN ELIJAH AND THE MESSIAH MIGHT ARRIVE. WITH THE HOPE OF FINAL REDEMPTION IN MIND, JEWS OPENED THE DOOR FOR ELIJAH—AS WE DO NOW.

———◆———

LANDES (HALAKHAH)

hate" (3:1, 3:8). Hatred, even when justified, is of such power that it must be controlled and contextualized. It is controlled in that its sole home expression in Judaism is here, in the Seder, limited to only a few short, albeit vivid, lines; and the vengeance is turned over to God. It comes while we open our doors: this is *leil shimurim* ("the night of watching"), after all. On it we "own" the anger that we have repressed throughout the years during hostile times. At this point, having gone through slavery and freedom, we achieve the clarity to identify our enemies, who claim to believe in God but attempt to destroy His people.

The Menachem Tzion (Rabbi Menachem B. Sacks, Jerusalem, Chicago, twentieth-century Torah educational leader) comments that the beginning of the *Sh'fokh Chamatkha* talks of the *nations*, in the plural, but then switches to the singular when describing them as those who "devoured Jacob" *(achal et ya'akov)*. The Menachem Tzion's explanation: alone, they are separate, disparate, and at odds. True anti-Semites, however, are ready to unite as one when they confront the Jewish People (heard while still a child at his father's Seder table).

At the end, the joyous singing of *Eliyahu Hanavi* invokes a calm wish for the eventual reconciliation of mankind.

———◆———

ZIERLER (FEMINIST VOICES)

Exodus story take place in or around water. As we learn from the midrash (*Deut. Rab.* 3:8): "Come and see how all the miracles that God wrought for Israel occurred only through water. How? While the [Israelites] were still in Egypt He wrought miracles for them through the river [turning red].... At the well [of Miriam] He wrought miracles for them...."

There are many extant Miriam's-cup rituals, including different versions of the *Miryam Han'vi'ah* song included here. Its most common version refers to "Miriam dancing with us to repair the world" *(l'taken et ha'olam)*, rendering Miriam a liberal feminist heroine. I wrote this version to fit the standard melody, but also to remain true to the biblical/rabbinic sources on Miriam, rather than revert to an anachronistic rendering of what Miriam might have been in our time.[1]

Miryam han'vi'ah	מִרְיָם הַנְּבִיאָה
Im hatof b'yadah	עִם הַתּוֹף בְּיָדָהּ
Miryam liv'tah otanu b'shir Hallel al s'fat hayam.	מִרְיָם לִוְּתָה אוֹתָנוּ בְּשִׁיר הַלֵּל עַל שְׂפַת הַיָּם.
Miryam rak'dah itanu l'harbot et simchat ha'am.	מִרְיָם רָקְדָה אִתָּנוּ לְהַרְבּוֹת אֶת־שִׂמְחַת הָעָם.
Bimherah uviz'khutah	בִּמְהֵרָה וּבִזְכוּתָהּ
Nizkeh li'shuah:	נִזְכֶּה לִישׁוּעָה:
Mayyim chayyim mib'erah.	מַיִם חַיִּים מִבְּאֵרָהּ.
Mayyim chayyim mib'erah.	מַיִם חַיִּים מִבְּאֵרָהּ.

Miriam the prophet
With the timbrel in her hand,
Miriam led us in a song of praise by the sea shore.
Miriam danced with us to increase the people's joy.
Speedily and by her merit
Let us be worthy of salvation:
Living waters from her well,
Living waters from her well.

[2] *"Pour out Your wrath"* Many liberal and feminist Haggadot take issue with the wrathful, adversarial stance adopted in this section of the Haggadah. While we must continue to be vigilant with respect to those who seek to harm us as Jews, we must also be open to the possibilities of mutual understanding. In the Bible, Elijah the prophet, the figure whom we invite to our homes at this point in the Seder, represents an uncompromising, combative attitude with respect to those who reject monotheistic belief. In Malachi 3:24, however, it is Elijah who will reconcile *(v'heshiv)* estranged parents and children. But in the Talmud, Elijah is invoked as the figure who will answer

Miriam and Women of the Exodus
Center: Miriam leads women in dance after crossing the Red Sea.
The Moriah Haggadah, Israel, 2005
Avner Moriah, illuminator

(*meshiv*, a different form of same verb used in Malachi) open questions and resolve nagging legal controversies. When we welcome Elijah to the Seder, it helps to think of him not only as an emissary of rage and revenge, but as an ambassador of understanding and reconciliation, as a *meshiv kushyot*, "an answerer of questions," and a *meshiv lev avot al banim*, "a reconciler of parents and children."

◆ ◆ ◆

15. "PRAISE"—*HALLEL*, PART TWO, PSALMS 115–118, 136

A. Psalms 115–118 and Conclusion

הַלֵּל

Hallel, which began before dinner, continues:

Psalm 115

[1]Not for us, Adonai, not for us, but for Your name glorify Your love and truth. [2]Why should the nations say, Where is their God?—[3]while our God is in heaven, doing whatever He pleases. [4]Their idols are silver and gold, the work of human hands. [5]They have a mouth and cannot speak. They have eyes and cannot see. [6]They have ears and cannot hear. They have a nose and cannot smell. [7]Their hands, and they cannot touch. Their legs, and they cannot walk. They cannot vocalize in their throat. [8]Those who make them, all who trust in them, shall be like them. [9]Israel, trust in Adonai, who is their help and shield. [10]House of Aaron, trust in Adonai, who is their help and shield. [11]You who revere Adonai, trust in Adonai, who is their help and shield.

[12]Adonai who remembers us will bless us, bless us and bless the house of Israel. [13]He will bless the house of Aaron. He will bless those who revere Adonai, the small with the great. [14]Adonai will increase you, you and your children. [15]You are the blessed of Adonai, maker of heaven and earth. [16]Heaven is Adonai's heaven, and the earth He gave to people. [17]The dead cannot praise God, nor can anyone who descends into silence. [18]We will praise God from now and ever more: Halleluyah!

[1]לֹא לָנוּ יְיָ לֹא לָנוּ כִּי לְשִׁמְךָ תֵּן כָּבוֹד עַל חַסְדְּךָ עַל אֲמִתֶּךָ: [2]לָמָּה יֹאמְרוּ הַגּוֹיִם אַיֵּה־נָא אֱלֹהֵיהֶם: [3]וֵאלֹהֵינוּ בַשָּׁמָיִם כֹּל אֲשֶׁר חָפֵץ עָשָׂה: [4]עֲצַבֵּיהֶם כֶּסֶף וְזָהָב מַעֲשֵׂה יְדֵי אָדָם: [5]פֶּה לָהֶם וְלֹא יְדַבֵּרוּ עֵינַיִם לָהֶם וְלֹא יִרְאוּ: [6]אָזְנַיִם לָהֶם וְלֹא יִשְׁמָעוּ אַף לָהֶם וְלֹא יְרִיחוּן: [7]יְדֵיהֶם וְלֹא יְמִישׁוּן רַגְלֵיהֶם וְלֹא יְהַלֵּכוּ לֹא־יֶהְגּוּ בִּגְרוֹנָם: [8]כְּמוֹהֶם יִהְיוּ עֹשֵׂיהֶם כֹּל אֲשֶׁר בֹּטֵחַ בָּהֶם: [9]יִשְׂרָאֵל בְּטַח בַּיְיָ עֶזְרָם וּמָגִנָּם הוּא. [10]בֵּית אַהֲרֹן בִּטְחוּ בַיְיָ עֶזְרָם וּמָגִנָּם הוּא: [11]יִרְאֵי יְיָ בִּטְחוּ בַיְיָ עֶזְרָם וּמָגִנָּם הוּא:

[12]יְיָ זְכָרָנוּ יְבָרֵךְ. יְבָרֵךְ אֶת־בֵּית יִשְׂרָאֵל יְבָרֵךְ אֶת־בֵּית אַהֲרֹן: [13]יְבָרֵךְ יִרְאֵי יְיָ הַקְּטַנִּים עִם הַגְּדֹלִים: [14]יֹסֵף יְיָ עֲלֵיכֶם עֲלֵיכֶם וְעַל בְּנֵיכֶם: [15]בְּרוּכִים אַתֶּם לַיְיָ עֹשֵׂה שָׁמַיִם וָאָרֶץ: [16]הַשָּׁמַיִם שָׁמַיִם לַיְיָ וְהָאָרֶץ נָתַן לִבְנֵי אָדָם: [17]לֹא הַמֵּתִים יְהַלְלוּ־יָהּ וְלֹא כָּל־יֹרְדֵי דוּמָה: [18]וַאֲנַחְנוּ נְבָרֵךְ יָהּ מֵעַתָּה וְעַד עוֹלָם הַלְלוּ־יָהּ:

154

Psalm 116

¹⁹I love that God hears my voice, my plea, ²⁰that He turns His ear to me, so I will cry out during my days. I am encompassed by the sorrows of death; ²¹the straits of Sheol have found me as I find trouble and misery. ²²And I call out Adonai's name: O Adonai, remove me from this! ²³Adonai is merciful and righteous, and our God is compassionate. Adonai guards the simple. ²⁴I am lowly, but I have salvation. ²⁵O my soul, return to your rest, for Adonai has rewarded you. ²⁶For You, Adonai, have saved me from death, my eye from tears, my foot from stumbling. ²⁷I will walk before Adonai in the lands of the living. ²⁸I believe what I speak, I who have been afflicted. ²⁹I said all men are liars only in haste.

³⁰What shall I give back to Adonai for all that He has rewarded me? ³¹I lift up a cup of deliverance and call upon Adonai's name. ³²Before all His people, I will fulfill my vows to Adonai. ³³The death of His righteous is grievous in Adonai's eyes. ³⁴Adonai, I am Your servant; I am Your servant, the son of Your maidservant, and You have loosened my bonds. ³⁵I will offer a *todah* offering to You and call upon Adonai's name. Before all His people, ³⁶I will fulfill my vows to Adonai, ³⁷in the courtyards of Adonai's house, inside of Jerusalem. Halleluyah!

Psalm 117

³⁸Praise Adonai, all nations, laud Him, all peoples, ³⁹for His love toward us is great, and Adonai's truth is everlasting. Halleluyah!

אָ ¹⁹ הָבְתִּי כִּי יִשְׁמַע יְיָ אֶת־קוֹלִי
תַּחֲנוּנָי: ²⁰ כִּי הִטָּה אָזְנוֹ לִי וּבְיָמַי
אֶקְרָא: ²¹ אֲפָפוּנִי חֶבְלֵי־מָוֶת וּמְצָרֵי
שְׁאוֹל מְצָאוּנִי צָרָה וְיָגוֹן אֶמְצָא:
²² וּבְשֵׁם יְיָ אֶקְרָא אָנָּה יְיָ מַלְּטָה נַפְשִׁי:
²³ חַנּוּן יְיָ וְצַדִּיק וֵאלֹהֵינוּ מְרַחֵם:
²⁴ שֹׁמֵר פְּתָאִים יְיָ דַּלּוֹתִי וְלִי יְהוֹשִׁיעַ:
²⁵ שׁוּבִי נַפְשִׁי לִמְנוּחָיְכִי כִּי יְיָ גָּמַל
עָלָיְכִי: ²⁶ כִּי חִלַּצְתָּ נַפְשִׁי מִמָּוֶת
אֶת־עֵינִי מִן דִּמְעָה אֶת־רַגְלִי מִדֶּחִי:
²⁷ אֶתְהַלֵּךְ לִפְנֵי יְיָ בְּאַרְצוֹת הַחַיִּים:
²⁸ הֶאֱמַנְתִּי כִּי אֲדַבֵּר אֲנִי עָנִיתִי מְאֹד:
²⁹ אֲנִי אָמַרְתִּי בְחָפְזִי כָּל־הָאָדָם כֹּזֵב:
³⁰ מָה אָשִׁיב לַיְיָ כָּל־תַּגְמוּלוֹהִי עָלָי:
³¹ כּוֹס יְשׁוּעוֹת אֶשָּׂא וּבְשֵׁם יְיָ אֶקְרָא:
³² נְדָרַי לַיְיָ אֲשַׁלֵּם נֶגְדָה־נָּא לְכָל־
עַמּוֹ: ³³ יָקָר בְּעֵינֵי יְיָ הַמָּוְתָה לַחֲסִידָיו:
³⁴ אָנָּה יְיָ כִּי אֲנִי עַבְדֶּךָ אֲנִי עַבְדְּךָ
בֶּן־אֲמָתֶךָ פִּתַּחְתָּ לְמוֹסֵרָי: ³⁵ לְךָ אֶזְבַּח
זֶבַח תּוֹדָה וּבְשֵׁם יְיָ אֶקְרָא: ³⁶ נְדָרַי לַיְיָ
אֲשַׁלֵּם נֶגְדָה־נָּא לְכָל־עַמּוֹ: ³⁷ בְּחַצְרוֹת
בֵּית יְיָ בְּתוֹכֵכִי יְרוּשָׁלַיִם הַלְלוּ־יָהּ:

הַ ³⁸ לְלוּ אֶת־יְיָ כָּל־גּוֹיִם שַׁבְּחוּהוּ
כָּל־הָאֻמִּים: ³⁹ כִּי גָבַר עָלֵינוּ
חַסְדּוֹ וֶאֱמֶת יְיָ לְעוֹלָם הַלְלוּ־יָהּ:

Verses 60–63 are each recited twice.

Psalm 118

[40]Give thanks to Adonai, for He is good, for His love is everlasting. [41]Let Israel say, "For His love is everlasting." [42]Let the house of Aaron say, "For His love is everlasting." [43]Let those who revere Adonai say, "For His love is everlasting." [44]From the straits I called on God, and in the expanse was answered by God. [45]Adonai is mine. I shall not fear. What can a human do to me? [46]Adonai is mine with those who help me, and I will see those who hate me. [47]It is better to seek refuge in Adonai than to trust in man. [48]It is better to seek refuge in Adonai than to trust in nobility. [49]All the nations surrounded me, and with Adonai's name I will cut them down. [50]They completely surrounded me, and with Adonai's name I will cut them down. [51]They surrounded me like bees—they shall be extinguished like the fire of thorns, and with Adonai's name I will cut them down. [52]You cast me down to fall, but Adonai helps me. [53]My strength and my might are God, who is my salvation. [54]The voice of joy and celebration resounds in the tents of the righteous. [55]Adonai's right hand triumphs. Adonai's right hand has exalted me. Adonai's right hand triumphs. [56]I will not die but live, and I will tell of God's deeds. [57]Adonai has punished me but not let me die. [58]Open the gates of righteousness for me that I might enter them. I will thank God. [59]This is the gate to God—the righteous will enter it. [60]I will thank You, for You have answered me and given me salvation. [61]The stone that the builders rejected is now the cornerstone. [62]This is from Adonai—it is wonderful to behold. [63]This is the day that Adonai made. Let us rejoice on it and be happy!

הֹ[40]וֹדוּ לַייָ כִּי טוֹב כִּי לְעוֹלָם חַסְדּוֹ:
[41]יֹאמַר נָא יִשְׂרָאֵל כִּי לְעוֹלָם חַסְדּוֹ: [42]יֹאמְרוּ נָא בֵית אַהֲרֹן כִּי לְעוֹלָם חַסְדּוֹ: [43]יֹאמְרוּ נָא יִרְאֵי יְיָ כִּי לְעוֹלָם חַסְדּוֹ: [44]מִן הַמֵּצַר קָרָאתִי יָּהּ עָנָנִי בַמֶּרְחָב יָהּ: [45]יְיָ לִי לֹא אִירָא מַה־יַּעֲשֶׂה לִי אָדָם: [46]יְיָ לִי בְּעֹזְרָי וַאֲנִי אֶרְאֶה בְשֹׂנְאָי: [47]טוֹב לַחֲסוֹת בַּיְיָ מִבְּטֹחַ בָּאָדָם:[48]טוֹב לַחֲסוֹת בַּיְיָ מִבְּטֹחַ בִּנְדִיבִים: [49]כָּל־גּוֹיִם סְבָבוּנִי בְּשֵׁם יְיָ כִּי אֲמִילַם: [50]סַבּוּנִי גַם־סְבָבוּנִי בְּשֵׁם יְיָ כִּי אֲמִילַם: [51]סַבּוּנִי כִדְבֹרִים דֹּעֲכוּ כְּאֵשׁ קוֹצִים בְּשֵׁם יְיָ כִּי אֲמִילַם: [52]דַּחֹה דְחִיתַנִי לִנְפֹּל וַיְיָ עֲזָרָנִי: [53]עָזִּי וְזִמְרָת יָהּ וַיְהִי־לִי לִישׁוּעָה: [54]קוֹל רִנָּה וִישׁוּעָה בְּאָהֳלֵי צַדִּיקִים יְמִין יְיָ עֹשָׂה חָיִל: [55]יְמִין יְיָ רוֹמֵמָה יְמִין יְיָ עֹשָׂה חָיִל: [56]לֹא אָמוּת כִּי אֶחְיֶה וַאֲסַפֵּר מַעֲשֵׂי יָהּ: [57]יַסֹּר יִסְּרַנִּי יָּהּ וְלַמָּוֶת לֹא נְתָנָנִי: [58]פִּתְחוּ־לִי שַׁעֲרֵי־צֶדֶק אָבֹא בָם אוֹדֶה יָהּ: [59]זֶה הַשַּׁעַר לַייָ צַדִּיקִים יָבֹאוּ בוֹ: [60]אוֹדְךָ כִּי עֲנִיתָנִי וַתְּהִי־לִי לִישׁוּעָה: [61]אֶבֶן מָאֲסוּ הַבּוֹנִים הָיְתָה לְרֹאשׁ פִּנָּה: [62]מֵאֵת יְיָ הָיְתָה זֹּאת הִיא נִפְלָאת בְּעֵינֵינוּ: [63]זֶה הַיּוֹם עָשָׂה יְיָ נָגִילָה וְנִשְׂמְחָה בוֹ:

[64]Please, Adonai, redeem us!

Please, Adonai, redeem us!

Please, Adonai, save us!

Please, Adonai, save us!

אָנָּא יְיָ הוֹשִׁיעָה נָּא: [64]

אָנָּא יְיָ הוֹשִׁיעָה נָּא:

אָנָּא יְיָ הַצְלִיחָה נָּא:

אָנָּא יְיָ הַצְלִיחָה נָּא:

Each verse (65–68) is recited twice:

[65]Blessed is the one who comes with Adonai's name. We bless you from Adonai's house.

[66]God is Adonai, and He has shined light upon us. Bind the festival offering with cords up to the altar's horns.

[67]You are my God and I will thank You, truly my God—I will exalt You.

[68]Give thanks to Adonai, for He is good. For His kindness is everlasting.

בָּרוּךְ הַבָּא בְּשֵׁם יְיָ [65]

בֵּרַכְנוּכֶם מִבֵּית יְיָ:

אֵל יְיָ וַיָּאֶר לָנוּ [66]

אִסְרוּ־חַג בַּעֲבֹתִים

עַד קַרְנוֹת הַמִּזְבֵּחַ:

אֵלִי אַתָּה וְאוֹדֶךָּ [67]

אֱלֹהַי אֲרוֹמְמֶךָּ:

הוֹדוּ לַיְיָ כִּי טוֹב [68]

כִּי לְעוֹלָם חַסְדּוֹ:

Concluding the Hallel

[69]All of Your creatures will praise You, Adonai. [70]And Your pious righteous ones who do Your will, and in joy the entire house of Israel will thank, bless, praise, glorify, exalt, adore, sanctify, and laud You, our king, [71]for it is good to thank You, and fitting to sing to You, for You have always and will always be God.

יְהַלְלוּךְ יְיָ אֱלֹהֵינוּ כָּל־מַעֲשֶׂיךָ. [69]

וַחֲסִידֶיךָ צַדִּיקִים עוֹשֵׂי רְצוֹנֶךָ וְכָל־ [70]

עַמְּךָ בֵּית יִשְׂרָאֵל בְּרִנָּה יוֹדוּ וִיבָרְכוּ

וִישַׁבְּחוּ וִיפָאֲרוּ וִירוֹמְמוּ וְיַעֲרִיצוּ

וְיַקְדִּישׁוּ וְיַמְלִיכוּ אֶת־שִׁמְךָ מַלְכֵּנוּ

כִּי לְךָ טוֹב לְהוֹדוֹת וּלְשִׁמְךָ נָאֶה [71]

לְזַמֵּר כִּי מֵעוֹלָם וְעַד עוֹלָם אַתָּה אֵל:

B. Psalm 136 (The Great *Hallel*) and Conclusion

Psalm 136

[72]Give thanks to Adonai, for He is good. For His love is everlasting.

[73]Give thanks to the God of gods. For His love is everlasting.

[74]Give thanks to the Lord of lords. For His love is everlasting.

[75]To the One who alone does great wonders. For His love is everlasting.

הוֹדוּ לַיְיָ כִּי טוֹב. כִּי לְעוֹלָם חַסְדּוֹ: [72]

הוֹדוּ לֵאלֹהֵי הָאֱלֹהִים. [73]

כִּי לְעוֹלָם חַסְדּוֹ:

הוֹדוּ לַאֲדֹנֵי הָאֲדֹנִים. [74]

כִּי לְעוֹלָם חַסְדּוֹ:

לְעֹשֵׂה נִפְלָאוֹת גְּדֹלוֹת לְבַדּוֹ. [75]

כִּי לְעוֹלָם חַסְדּוֹ:

76To the One who wisely created the sky. For His love is everlasting.

77To the One who spread out the earth on the water. For His love is everlasting.

78To the One who created the great lights. For His love is everlasting.

79The sun to be ruler by day. For His love is everlasting.

80The moon and stars to be rulers by night. For His love is everlasting.

81To the One who struck Egypt through their first-born. For His love is everlasting.

82And who brought Israel out from their midst. For His love is everlasting.

83With a strong hand and an outstretched arm. For His love is everlasting.

84To the One who split the Red Sea. For His love is everlasting.

85And brought Israel through it. For His love is everlasting.

86And shook Pharaoh and his army in the Red Sea. For His love is everlasting.

87To the One who led His people through the desert. For His love is everlasting.
88To the One who struck great kings. For His love is everlasting.

89And killed mighty kings. For His love is everlasting.

76לְעֹשֵׂה הַשָּׁמַיִם בִּתְבוּנָה.
כִּי לְעוֹלָם חַסְדּוֹ:

77לְרוֹקַע הָאָרֶץ עַל הַמָּיִם.
כִּי לְעוֹלָם חַסְדּוֹ:

78לְעֹשֵׂה אוֹרִים גְּדֹלִים.
כִּי לְעוֹלָם חַסְדּוֹ:

79אֶת־הַשֶּׁמֶשׁ לְמֶמְשֶׁלֶת בַּיּוֹם.
כִּי לְעוֹלָם חַסְדּוֹ:

80אֶת־הַיָּרֵחַ וְכוֹכָבִים לְמֶמְשְׁלוֹת
בַּלָּיְלָה. כִּי לְעוֹלָם חַסְדּוֹ:

81לְמַכֵּה מִצְרַיִם בִּבְכוֹרֵיהֶם.
כִּי לְעוֹלָם חַסְדּוֹ:

82וַיּוֹצֵא יִשְׂרָאֵל מִתּוֹכָם.
כִּי לְעוֹלָם חַסְדּוֹ:

83בְּיָד חֲזָקָה וּבִזְרוֹעַ נְטוּיָה.
כִּי לְעוֹלָם חַסְדּוֹ:

84לְגֹזֵר יַם־סוּף לִגְזָרִים.
כִּי לְעוֹלָם חַסְדּוֹ:

85וְהֶעֱבִיר יִשְׂרָאֵל בְּתוֹכוֹ.
כִּי לְעוֹלָם חַסְדּוֹ:

86וְנִעֵר פַּרְעֹה וְחֵילוֹ בְיַם־סוּף.
כִּי לְעוֹלָם חַסְדּוֹ:

87לְמוֹלִיךְ עַמּוֹ בַּמִּדְבָּר.
כִּי לְעוֹלָם חַסְדּוֹ:

88לְמַכֵּה מְלָכִים גְּדֹלִים.
כִּי לְעוֹלָם חַסְדּוֹ:

89וַיַּהֲרֹג מְלָכִים אַדִּירִים.
כִּי לְעוֹלָם חַסְדּוֹ:

90Sichon, king of the Amorites. For His love is everlasting.

91Og, king of Bashan. For His love is everlasting.

92And gave their land as a heritage. For His love is everlasting.

93A heritage to Israel His servant. For His love is everlasting.

94Who remembered us when we were low. For His love is everlasting.

95And set us free from our enemies. For His love is everlasting.

96Who gives food to all creatures. For His love is everlasting.

97Give thanks to the God of heaven. For His love is everlasting.

Concluding the Great Hallel

98The breath of every living being will praise You, and the spirit of every mortal being will always glorify and extol You, our king. 99You have always been and will always be God, and other than You we have no king to save us and redeem us, ransom us and rescue us and sustain us, and love us at every time of sorrow and hardship. 100We have no king other than You! God of the first and the last, God of all creatures, master of all generations, glorified through great praise, He treats His world with love and His creatures with compassion. 101Adonai neither rests nor sleeps. He awakens those who sleep, and rouses those who slumber, and grants speech to the mute, and frees the captives, and supports the falling, and raises those who are bent over. 102It is You alone whom we gratefully acknowledge.

90לְסִיחוֹן מֶלֶךְ הָאֱמֹרִי.
כִּי לְעוֹלָם חַסְדּוֹ:

91וּלְעוֹג מֶלֶךְ הַבָּשָׁן. כִּי לְעוֹלָם חַסְדּוֹ:

92וְנָתַן אַרְצָם לְנַחֲלָה.
כִּי לְעוֹלָם חַסְדּוֹ:

93נַחֲלָה לְיִשְׂרָאֵל עַבְדּוֹ.
כִּי לְעוֹלָם חַסְדּוֹ:

94שֶׁבְּשִׁפְלֵנוּ זָכַר לָנוּ. כִּי לְעוֹלָם חַסְדּוֹ:

95וַיִּפְרְקֵנוּ מִצָּרֵינוּ. כִּי לְעוֹלָם חַסְדּוֹ:

96נֹתֵן לֶחֶם לְכָל־בָּשָׂר.
כִּי לְעוֹלָם חַסְדּוֹ:

97הוֹדוּ לְאֵל הַשָּׁמָיִם. כִּי לְעוֹלָם חַסְדּוֹ:

98נִשְׁמַת כָּל־חַי תְּבָרֵךְ אֶת־שִׁמְךָ יְיָ אֱלֹהֵינוּ. וְרוּחַ כָּל־בָּשָׂר תְּפָאֵר וּתְרוֹמֵם זִכְרְךָ מַלְכֵּנוּ תָּמִיד. 99מִן הָעוֹלָם וְעַד הָעוֹלָם אַתָּה אֵל. וּמִבַּלְעָדֶיךָ אֵין לָנוּ מֶלֶךְ גּוֹאֵל וּמוֹשִׁיעַ פּוֹדֶה וּמַצִּיל וּמְפַרְנֵס וּמְרַחֵם בְּכָל־עֵת צָרָה וְצוּקָה. 100אֵין לָנוּ מֶלֶךְ אֶלָּא־אַתָּה: אֱלֹהֵי הָרִאשׁוֹנִים וְהָאַחֲרוֹנִים. אֱלוֹהַּ כָּל־בְּרִיּוֹת אֲדוֹן כָּל־תּוֹלָדוֹת הַמְהֻלָּל בְּרֹב הַתִּשְׁבָּחוֹת הַמְנַהֵג עוֹלָמוֹ בְּחֶסֶד וּבְרִיּוֹתָיו בְּרַחֲמִים. 101וַיְיָ לֹא יָנוּם וְלֹא יִישָׁן. הַמְּעוֹרֵר יְשֵׁנִים וְהַמֵּקִיץ נִרְדָּמִים. וְהַמֵּשִׂיחַ אִלְּמִים. וְהַמַּתִּיר אֲסוּרִים וְהַסּוֹמֵךְ נוֹפְלִים וְהַזּוֹקֵף כְּפוּפִים. 102לְךָ לְבַדְּךָ אֲנַחְנוּ מוֹדִים.

[103]Even if our mouths were filled with song like the sea, and our tongues with joy like the sea's many roaring waves, and our lips with praise like the wide expanse of the sky, and even if our eyes shone like the sun and the moon, and even if our hands were spread wide like the eagles in the sky, and even if our feet were light like gazelles, we would be unable to properly acknowledge You with thanks, Adonai our God and our ancestors' God, or to praise Your name for even one-thousandth of the thousands of thousands upon thousands and millions upon millions of great things You did for our ancestors and for us: [104]You freed us from Egypt, Adonai our God. You redeemed us from the house of bondage. You nourished us in famines and provided for us in abundance. You delivered us from the sword and saved us from the plague. You freed us from severe stubborn diseases. [105]Until now Your kindness has helped us and Your love has not abandoned us. Never forsake us, Adonai our God. [106]Therefore, the limbs You apportioned us and the breath and spirit that You breathed into our nostrils, and the tongue that You put into our mouths, it is all of these that will thank, bless, praise, glorify, exalt, adore, sanctify, and extol You, our king. [107]For to You every mouth will offer thanks, and to You every tongue will swear allegiance, and to You every knee will bend, and before You everyone of height will bow, and every heart will revere You, and every lung sing to Your name, in accordance with what is written: All my bones will say: Adonai, who is like You! You save the weak from those who are stronger than them, and the poor and needy from those who rob them.

אִלּוּ פִינוּ מָלֵא שִׁירָה כַּיָּם וּלְשׁוֹנֵנוּ [103] רִנָּה כַּהֲמוֹן גַּלָּיו וְשִׂפְתוֹתֵינוּ שֶׁבַח כְּמֶרְחֲבֵי רָקִיעַ וְעֵינֵינוּ מְאִירוֹת כַּשֶּׁמֶשׁ וְכַיָּרֵחַ. וְיָדֵינוּ פְרוּשׂוֹת כְּנִשְׁרֵי שָׁמַיִם. וְרַגְלֵינוּ קַלּוֹת כָּאַיָּלוֹת. אֵין אֲנַחְנוּ מַסְפִּיקִים לְהוֹדוֹת לְךָ יְיָ אֱלֹהֵינוּ וֵאלֹהֵי אֲבוֹתֵינוּ וּלְבָרֵךְ אֶת־שְׁמֶךָ עַל אַחַת מֵאֶלֶף אֶלֶף אַלְפֵי אֲלָפִים וְרִבֵּי רְבָבוֹת פְּעָמִים הַטּוֹבוֹת שֶׁעָשִׂיתָ עִם אֲבוֹתֵינוּ וְעִמָּנוּ: [104] מִמִּצְרַיִם גְּאַלְתָּנוּ יְיָ אֱלֹהֵינוּ. וּמִבֵּית עֲבָדִים פְּדִיתָנוּ. בְּרָעָב זַנְתָּנוּ. וּבְשָׂבָע כִּלְכַּלְתָּנוּ. מֵחֶרֶב הִצַּלְתָּנוּ וּמִדֶּבֶר מִלַּטְתָּנוּ. וּמֵחֳלָיִם רָעִים וְנֶאֱמָנִים דִּלִּיתָנוּ: [105] עַד הֵנָּה עֲזָרוּנוּ רַחֲמֶיךָ. וְלֹא עֲזָבוּנוּ חֲסָדֶיךָ. וְאַל תִּטְּשֵׁנוּ יְיָ אֱלֹהֵינוּ לָנֶצַח. [106] עַל כֵּן אֵבָרִים שֶׁפִּלַּגְתָּ בָּנוּ. וְרוּחַ וּנְשָׁמָה שֶׁנָּפַחְתָּ בְּאַפֵּינוּ וְלָשׁוֹן אֲשֶׁר שַׂמְתָּ בְּפִינוּ. הֵן הֵם יוֹדוּ וִיבָרְכוּ וִישַׁבְּחוּ וִיפָאֲרוּ וִירוֹמְמוּ וְיַעֲרִיצוּ וְיַקְדִּישׁוּ וְיַמְלִיכוּ אֶת־שִׁמְךָ מַלְכֵּנוּ: [107] כִּי כָל־פֶּה לְךָ יוֹדֶה. וְכָל־לָשׁוֹן לְךָ תִשָּׁבַע וְכָל־בֶּרֶךְ לְךָ תִכְרַע. וְכָל־קוֹמָה לְפָנֶיךָ תִשְׁתַּחֲוֶה. וְכָל־לְבָבוֹת יִירָאוּךָ וְכָל־קֶרֶב וּכְלָיוֹת יְזַמְּרוּ לִשְׁמֶךָ. כַּדָּבָר שֶׁכָּתוּב: כָּל־עַצְמֹתַי תֹּאמַרְנָה יְיָ מִי כָמוֹךָ. מַצִּיל עָנִי מֵחָזָק מִמֶּנּוּ וְעָנִי וְאֶבְיוֹן מִגֹּזְלוֹ:

108Who can compare to You! Who can equal You! And who can match You, great, mighty, and awesome God, God on high, creator of heaven and earth. 109We will exalt You and laud You and glorify You and praise Your holy name. For it is said, "For David, O my soul, praise Adonai, and my very being, His holy name."

110God in Your tremendous power, great in Your glorious name, mighty forever and awe inspiring in Your awe, You are king, seated on a high and exalted throne.

111Abiding forever, His name is exalted and holy. And it is written: Acclaim Adonai all you righteous, for it is fitting for the upright to offer praise.

112You will be lauded by the mouths of the upright.

You will be praised by the words of the righteous.

You will be exalted by the tongues of the faithful.

You will be sanctified by the lungs of holy creatures.

113With songs of joy, our king, your name shall be glorified by the vast multitudes of your people, the house of Israel, in every generation, 114for it is the obligation of every creature before You, Adonai our God and our ancestors' God, to thank, magnify, laud, glorify, acclaim, exalt, and praise You, even beyond all the words of the songs and hymns of David son of Jesse Your anointed servant.

115Let Your name be forever praised, our king, great and holy king and God, in the heavens and on earth.

108 מִי יִדְמֶה־לָּךְ וּמִי יִשְׁוֶה־לָּךְ וּמִי יַעֲרָךְ־לָךְ. הָאֵל הַגָּדוֹל הַגִּבּוֹר וְהַנּוֹרָא אֵל עֶלְיוֹן קֹנֵה שָׁמַיִם וָאָרֶץ. 109 נְהַלֶּלְךָ וּנְשַׁבֵּחֲךָ וּנְפָאֶרְךָ וּנְבָרֵךְ אֶת־שֵׁם קָדְשֶׁךָ. כָּאָמוּר: לְדָוִד בָּרְכִי נַפְשִׁי אֶת־יְיָ וְכָל־קְרָבַי אֶת־שֵׁם קָדְשׁוֹ:

110 הָאֵל בְּתַעֲצֻמוֹת עֻזֶּךָ הַגָּדוֹל בִּכְבוֹד שְׁמֶךָ הַגִּבּוֹר לָנֶצַח וְהַנּוֹרָא בְּנוֹרְאוֹתֶיךָ: הַמֶּלֶךְ הַיּוֹשֵׁב עַל כִּסֵּא רָם וְנִשָּׂא:

111 שׁוֹכֵן עַד מָרוֹם וְקָדוֹשׁ שְׁמוֹ. וְכָתוּב: רַנְּנוּ צַדִּיקִים בַּיְיָ לַיְשָׁרִים נָאוָה תְהִלָּה:

112 בְּפִי יְשָׁרִים תִּתְהַלָּל.

וּבְדִבְרֵי צַדִּיקִים תִּתְבָּרַךְ.

וּבִלְשׁוֹן חֲסִידִים תִּתְרוֹמָם.

וּבְקֶרֶב קְדוֹשִׁים תִּתְקַדָּשׁ:

113 וּבְמַקְהֲלוֹת רִבְבוֹת עַמְּךָ בֵּית יִשְׂרָאֵל בְּרִנָּה יִתְפָּאַר שִׁמְךָ מַלְכֵּנוּ בְּכָל־דּוֹר וָדוֹר. 114 שֶׁכֵּן חוֹבַת כָּל־הַיְצוּרִים לְפָנֶיךָ יְיָ אֱלֹהֵינוּ וֵאלֹהֵי אֲבוֹתֵינוּ לְהוֹדוֹת לְהַלֵּל לְשַׁבֵּחַ לְפָאֵר לְרוֹמֵם לְהַדֵּר לְבָרֵךְ לְעַלֵּה וּלְקַלֵּס עַל כָּל־דִּבְרֵי שִׁירוֹת וְתִשְׁבְּחוֹת דָּוִד בֶּן־יִשַׁי עַבְדְּךָ מְשִׁיחֶךָ:

115 יִשְׁתַּבַּח שִׁמְךָ לָעַד מַלְכֵּנוּ הָאֵל הַמֶּלֶךְ הַגָּדוֹל וְהַקָּדוֹשׁ בַּשָּׁמַיִם וּבָאָרֶץ.

116For song and praise, veneration and melody, strength and power, eternity, greatness and might, exaltation and glory, holiness and dominion, blessings and thanks befit You, Adonai our God and our ancestors' God, from now and ever more! 117Blessed are You, Adonai, God, greatly lauded king and God, God of grateful acknowledgment, Lord of wonders, who chooses melodious songs, our king, our God, eternal life.

116כִּי לְךָ נָאֶה יְיָ אֱלֹהֵינוּ וֵאלֹהֵי אֲבוֹתֵינוּ. שִׁיר וּשְׁבָחָה הַלֵּל וְזִמְרָה עֹז וּמֶמְשָׁלָה נֶצַח גְּדֻלָּה וּגְבוּרָה תְּהִלָּה וְתִפְאֶרֶת קְדֻשָּׁה וּמַלְכוּת. בְּרָכוֹת וְהוֹדָאוֹת מֵעַתָּה וְעַד עוֹלָם: 117בָּרוּךְ אַתָּה יְיָ אֵל מֶלֶךְ גָּדוֹל בַּתִּשְׁבָּחוֹת אֵל הַהוֹדָאוֹת אֲדוֹן הַנִּפְלָאוֹת הַבּוֹחֵר בְּשִׁירֵי זִמְרָה מֶלֶךְ אֵל חֵי הָעוֹלָמִים:

Bendigamos	Let Us Bless

Bendigamos · **Let Us Bless**

Bendigamos al Altísimo,
    Al Señor que nos crió,
Démosle agradecimiento
    Por los bienes que nos dió.

Alabado sea su Santo Nombre,
    Porque siempre nos apiadó.
Load al Señor que es bueno,
    Que para siempre su merced.

Bendigamos al Altísimo,
    Por su Ley primeramente,
Que liga a nuestra raza
    Con el cielo continuamente,

Alabado sea su Santo Nombre,
    Porque siempre nos apiadó.
Load al Señor que es bueno,
    Que para siempre su merced.

Bendigamos al Altísimo,
    Por el pan segundamente,
Y también por los manjares
    Que comimos juntamente.

Pues comimos y bebimos alegremente
    Su merced nunca nos faltó,
Load al Señor que es bueno,
    Que para siempre su merced.

Bendita sea la casa esta,
    El hogar de su presencia,
Donde guardamos su fiesta,
    Con alegría y permanencia.

Alabado sea su Santo Nombre,
    Porque siempre nos apiadó.
Load al Señor que es bueno,
    Que para siempre su merced.

הוֹדוּ לַיְיָ כִּי טוֹב
כִּי לְעוֹלָם חַסְדּוֹ:

Let us bless the Most High
    The Lord who raised us,
Let us give Him thanks
    For the good things which He has given us.

Praised be His Holy Name,
    Because He always took pity on us.
Praise the Lord, for He is good,
    For His mercy is everlasting.

Let us bless the Most High
    First for His Law,
Which binds our race
    With heaven continually,

Praised be His Holy Name,
    Because He always took pity on us.
Praise the Lord, for He is good,
    For His mercy is everlasting.

Let us bless the Most High,
    Secondly for the bread
And also for the foods
    Which we have eaten together.

For we have eaten and drunk happily
    His mercy has never failed us.
Praise the Lord, for He is good,
    For His mercy is everlasting.

Blessed be this house,
    The home of His presence,
Where we keep His feast,
    With happiness and permanence.

Praised be His Holy Name,
    Because He always took pity on us.
Praise the Lord, for He is good,
    For His mercy is everlasting.

Give thanks to Adonai, for He is good,
    for His love is everlasting.

Bendigamos ("Let Us Bless"), a Spanish table-hymn sung by some Sefardi Jews following Grace After Meals. The song's origin remains uncertain, but has been attributed to the seventeenth-century Marrano communities in the southwest of France. Translated by Alan D. Corré.

ARNOW (THE WORLD OF MIDRASH)

"Hallel" Some sages maintained that David composed the *Hallel*, but others found it inconceivable that Israel had not already sung these psalms of praise in Egypt while slaughtering the first paschal sacrifice (Pes. 117a). This view alludes to an earlier midrashic tradition that the Israelites first uttered *Hallel* on their last night in Egypt.[1] Likely the most ancient liturgical rite associated with Passover, *Hallel* was sung at the Temple as the paschal sacrifice was slaughtered (M. Pes. 5:7), and again later, following the festival meal when the last of the paschal offering had been   *(p. 175)*

BRETTLER (OUR BIBLICAL HERITAGE)

"Psalm 115" Psalm 115 is divided into two parts when recited: verses 1–11, which may be seen as an introduction or call to worship, and verses 12–18, the prayer itself. The former concludes with Israel, Aaron, and those   *(p. 176)*

GRAY (MEDIEVAL COMMENTATORS)

"Hallel" R. Yochanan interpreted *lo karav zeh el zeh kol halailah*, "the one could not come near the other all through the night" (Exod. 14:20) in light of Isaiah 6:3: *v'kara zeh el zeh v'amar*, "And one would call to the other." His implicit interpretation is that the "one" who did not "come near the other" at night was a ministering angel, who nightly sings God's praises in concert with others.   *(p. 177)*

GREEN (PERSONAL SPIRITUALITY)

[56] *"I will not die but live"* The Seder is the only evening occasion when we recite the psalms of *Hallel*. They are filled with exultation and joy, but woven through them also is the theme of confrontation with death. The psalmist has looked death in the face, cried out to God, and been redeemed. This personal struggle with mortality is woven together with the tale of the people's redemption, "when Israel went forth from Egypt," which is what makes the text appropriate to the Pesach table.

But the Seder, as the   *(p. 177)*

[For prayer instructions, see pages 156–157.]

15. "PRAISE"—*HALLEL*, PART TWO, PSALMS 115–118, 136

A. Psalms 115–118 and Conclusion

Psalm 115

[1]Not for us, Adonai, not for us, but for Your name glorify Your love and truth. [2]Why should the nations say, Where is their God?—[3]while our God is in heaven, doing whatever He pleases. [4]Their idols are silver and gold, the work of human hands. [5]They have a mouth and cannot speak. They have eyes and cannot see. [6]They have ears and cannot hear. They have a nose and cannot smell. [7]Their hands, and they cannot touch. Their legs, and they cannot walk.

J. HOFFMAN (TRANSLATION)

[1]*"Not for us"* The Hebrew *lanu* ("for us") is more general, including also "to us," etc. The juxtaposition of "not *lanu*" after "pour Your anger over them" lends a second meaning to the beginning of the psalm. While "not *lanu*" begins the psalm with the notion "not for us," it also completes the petition "pour Your anger over" with "not on us."

[1]*"Glorify"* More literally, "show glory."   *(p. 178)*

L. HOFFMAN (TRANSLATION)

[1] *"Not for us, Adonai, not for us"* We saw above (see *"Hallel," My People's Passover Haggadah*, Volume 2, pp. 97, 106) that originally only Psalms 113–114 were recited; when the meal was moved to the end of the night, other psalms were added to complete the night with praise. But why Psalms 115–118 specifically?

To begin with, when new biblical readings are added liturgically, it is commonplace to pick up where the old reading leaves off. The best example is Rosh Hashanah, which was originally celebrated in Eretz Yisrael for *(p. 182)*

(p. 182)

SIGNPOST: "PRAISE"—*HALLEL*, PART TWO; PSALMS 115–118, 136

WE BEGAN OUR PRAISE OF GOD WITH THE FIRST HALF OF THE HALLEL (PSS. 113–114) BEFORE DINNER (MY PEOPLE'S PASSOVER HAGGADAH, VOLUME 2, PP. 93–94). WE CONTINUE IT NOW WITH PSALMS 115–118. TOGETHER THESE SIX PSALMS ARE CALLED THE EGYPTIAN HALLEL, ALTHOUGH THE RABBIS ALSO IDENTIFIED THIS SECOND GROUP OF PSALMS WITH THE ERA OF MESSIANIC REDEMPTION, THE ULTIMATE EXPRESSION OF HOPE. WE CONCLUDE WITH PSALM 136, CALLED THE GREAT HALLEL AND ITS CONCLUDING BLESSING. FOR COMPLETE COMMENTARY, SEE MY PEOPLE'S PRAYER BOOK, VOLUME 10, SHABBAT MORNING: SHACHARIT AND MUSAF (MORNING AND ADDITIONAL SERVICES), PP. 22–68.

———◆———

‏לֹא לָנוּ יְיָ לֹא לָנוּ כִּי לְשִׁמְךָ תֵּן כָּבוֹד עַל חַסְדְּךָ‎[1] ‏עַל אֲמִתֶּךָ: לָמָּה יֹאמְרוּ הַגּוֹיִם אַיֵּה־נָא אֱלֹהֵיהֶם:‎[2] ‏וֵאלֹהֵינוּ בַשָּׁמָיִם כֹּל אֲשֶׁר חָפֵץ עָשָׂה: עֲצַבֵּיהֶם‎[3][4] ‏כֶּסֶף וְזָהָב מַעֲשֵׂה יְדֵי אָדָם: פֶּה לָהֶם וְלֹא יְדַבֵּרוּ‎[5] ‏עֵינַיִם לָהֶם וְלֹא יִרְאוּ: אָזְנַיִם לָהֶם וְלֹא יִשְׁמָעוּ‎[6] ‏אַף לָהֶם וְלֹא יְרִיחוּן: יְדֵיהֶם וְלֹא יְמִישׁוּן רַגְלֵיהֶם‎[7] ‏וְלֹא יְהַלֵּכוּ‎

KUSHNER AND POLEN (CHASIDIC VOICES)

[66] *"Bind the festival offering with cords up to the altar's horns"* Yehuda Aryeh Lieb of Ger (*S'fat Emet, Pesach*, 5636), cites *Sefer Y'tsirah* (1:1), which notes that all creation is subsumed under the three categories of space, time, and spirit. For each one of these there is a paradigm: space, naturally, is Eretz Yisrael and the Temple; time is the festivals; and spirit is the Jewish People. And, continues, the Gerer, it is the human *(p. 185)*

(p. 185)

LANDES (HALAKHAH)

"Hallel, Part Two" Passover is suffused with the singing of *Hallel*. As we have seen, the ancient *pesach* was offered in the Temple and eaten in the *chavurah* with the constant singing of *Hallel*. Some sing two of its psalms at the *(p. 185)*

(p. 185)

ZIERLER (FEMINIST VOICES)

[103] *"Even if our mouths were filled with song like the sea"* The stunning array of metaphors presented in this prayer indicates the importance and power of metaphorical language as a tool for prayer. The only way that we can begin to apprehend God is through the signs and symbols of language, through the "as if" of metaphor. The feminist desire to add feminine God language to our prayers stems from our *(p. 185)*

(p. 185)

They cannot vocalize in their throat. [8]Those who make them, all who trust in them, shall be like them. [9]Israel, trust in Adonai, who is their help and shield. [10]House of Aaron, trust in Adonai, who is their help and shield. [11]You who revere Adonai, trust in Adonai, who is their help and shield.

[12]Adonai who remembers us will bless us, bless us and bless the house of Israel. [13]He will bless the house of Aaron. He will bless those who revere Adonai, the small with the great. [14]Adonai will increase you, you and your children. [15]You are the blessed of Adonai, maker of heaven and earth. [16]Heaven is Adonai's heaven, and the earth He gave to people. [17]The dead cannot praise God, nor can anyone who descends into silence. [18]We will praise God from now and ever more: Halleluyah!

Psalm 116

[19]I love that God hears my voice, my plea, [20]that He turns His ear to me, so I will cry out during my days. I am encompassed by the sorrows of death; [21]the straits of Sheol have found me as I find trouble and misery. [22]And I call out Adonai's name: O Adonai, remove me from this! [23]Adonai is merciful and righteous, and our God is compassionate. Adonai guards the simple. [24]I am lowly, but I have salvation. [25]O my soul, return to your rest, for Adonai has rewarded you. [26]For You, Adonai, have saved me from death, my eye from tears, my foot from stumbling.

לֹא־יֶהְגּוּ בִּגְרוֹנָם: [8]כְּמוֹהֶם יִהְיוּ עֹשֵׂיהֶם כֹּל אֲשֶׁר בֹּטֵחַ בָּהֶם: [9]יִשְׂרָאֵל בְּטַח בַּיָי עֶזְרָם וּמָגִנָּם הוּא. [10]בֵּית אַהֲרֹן בִּטְחוּ בַיָי עֶזְרָם וּמָגִנָּם הוּא: [11]יִרְאֵי יָי בִּטְחוּ בַיָי עֶזְרָם וּמָגִנָּם הוּא:

[12]יָי זְכָרָנוּ יְבָרֵךְ. יְבָרֵךְ אֶת־בֵּית יִשְׂרָאֵל יְבָרֵךְ אֶת־בֵּית אַהֲרֹן: [13]יְבָרֵךְ יִרְאֵי יָי הַקְּטַנִּים עִם הַגְּדֹלִים: [14]יֹסֵף יָי עֲלֵיכֶם עֲלֵיכֶם וְעַל בְּנֵיכֶם: [15]בְּרוּכִים אַתֶּם לַיָי עֹשֵׂה שָׁמַיִם וָאָרֶץ: [16]הַשָּׁמַיִם שָׁמַיִם לַיָי וְהָאָרֶץ נָתַן לִבְנֵי אָדָם: [17]לֹא הַמֵּתִים יְהַלְלוּ־יָה וְלֹא כָּל־יֹרְדֵי דוּמָה: [18]וַאֲנַחְנוּ נְבָרֵךְ יָה מֵעַתָּה וְעַד עוֹלָם הַלְלוּ־יָה:

[19]אָהַבְתִּי כִּי יִשְׁמַע יָי אֶת־קוֹלִי תַּחֲנוּנָי: [20]כִּי הִטָּה אָזְנוֹ לִי וּבְיָמַי אֶקְרָא: [21]אֲפָפוּנִי חֶבְלֵי־מָוֶת וּמְצָרֵי שְׁאוֹל מְצָאוּנִי צָרָה וְיָגוֹן אֶמְצָא: [22]וּבְשֵׁם יָי אֶקְרָא אָנָּה יָי מַלְּטָה נַפְשִׁי: [23]חַנּוּן יָי וְצַדִּיק וֵאלֹהֵינוּ מְרַחֵם: [24]שֹׁמֵר פְּתָאִים יָי דַּלֹּתִי וְלִי יְהוֹשִׁיעַ: [25]שׁוּבִי נַפְשִׁי לִמְנוּחָיְכִי כִּי יָי גָּמַל עָלָיְכִי: [26]כִּי חִלַּצְתָּ נַפְשִׁי מִמָּוֶת אֶת־עֵינִי מִן דִּמְעָה אֶת־רַגְלִי מִדֶּחִי:

27I will walk before Adonai in the lands of the living. 28I believe what I speak, I who have been afflicted. 29I said all men are liars only in haste.

30What shall I give back to Adonai for all that He has rewarded me? 31I lift up a cup of deliverance and call upon Adonai's name. 32Before all His people, I will fulfill my vows to Adonai. 33The death of His righteous is grievous in Adonai's eyes. 34Adonai, I am Your servant; I am Your servant, the son of Your maidservant, and You have loosened my bonds. 35I will offer a *todah* offering to You and call upon Adonai's name. Before all His people, 36I will fulfill my vows to Adonai, 37in the courtyards of Adonai's house, inside of Jerusalem. Halleluyah!

Psalm 117

38Praise Adonai, all nations, laud Him, all peoples, 39for His love toward us is great, and Adonai's truth is everlasting. Halleluyah!

Psalm 118

40Give thanks to Adonai, for He is good, for His love is everlasting. 41Let Israel say, "For His love is everlasting." 42Let the house of Aaron say, "For His love is everlasting." 43Let those who revere Adonai say, "For His love is everlasting." 44From the straits I called on God, and in the expanse was answered by God. 45Adonai is mine. I shall not fear. What can a human do to me?

²⁷אֶתְהַלֵּךְ לִפְנֵי יְיָ בְּאַרְצוֹת הַחַיִּים: ²⁸הֶאֱמַנְתִּי כִּי אֲדַבֵּר אֲנִי עָנִיתִי מְאֹד: ²⁹אֲנִי אָמַרְתִּי בְחָפְזִי כָּל־הָאָדָם כֹּזֵב:

³⁰מָה אָשִׁיב לַייָ כָּל־תַּגְמוּלוֹהִי עָלָי: ³¹כּוֹס יְשׁוּעוֹת אֶשָּׂא וּבְשֵׁם יְיָ אֶקְרָא: ³²נְדָרַי לַייָ אֲשַׁלֵּם נֶגְדָה־נָּא לְכָל־עַמּוֹ: ³³יָקָר בְּעֵינֵי יְיָ הַמָּוְתָה לַחֲסִידָיו: ³⁴אָנָּה יְיָ כִּי אֲנִי עַבְדֶּךָ אֲנִי עַבְדְּךָ בֶּן־אֲמָתֶךָ פִּתַּחְתָּ לְמוֹסֵרָי: ³⁵לְךָ אֶזְבַּח זֶבַח תּוֹדָה וּבְשֵׁם יְיָ אֶקְרָא: ³⁶נְדָרַי לַייָ אֲשַׁלֵּם נֶגְדָה־נָּא לְכָל־עַמּוֹ: ³⁷בְּחַצְרוֹת בֵּית יְיָ בְּתוֹכֵכִי יְרוּשָׁלַיִם הַלְלוּ־יָהּ:

³⁸הַלְלוּ אֶת־יְיָ כָּל־גּוֹיִם שַׁבְּחוּהוּ כָּל־הָאֻמִּים: ³⁹כִּי גָבַר עָלֵינוּ חַסְדּוֹ וֶאֱמֶת יְיָ לְעוֹלָם הַלְלוּ־יָהּ:

⁴⁰הוֹדוּ לַייָ כִּי טוֹב כִּי לְעוֹלָם חַסְדּוֹ: ⁴¹יֹאמַר נָא יִשְׂרָאֵל כִּי לְעוֹלָם חַסְדּוֹ: ⁴²יֹאמְרוּ נָא בֵית אַהֲרֹן כִּי לְעוֹלָם חַסְדּוֹ: ⁴³יֹאמְרוּ נָא יִרְאֵי יְיָ כִּי לְעוֹלָם חַסְדּוֹ: ⁴⁴מִן הַמֵּצַר קָרָאתִי יָּהּ עָנָנִי בַמֶּרְחָב יָהּ: ⁴⁵יְיָ לִי לֹא אִירָא מַה־יַּעֲשֶׂה לִי אָדָם:

[46]Adonai is mine with those who help me, and I will see those who hate me. [47]It is better to seek refuge in Adonai than to trust in man. [48]It is better to seek refuge in Adonai than to trust in nobility. [49]All the nations surrounded me, and with Adonai's name I will cut them down. [50]They completely surrounded me, and with Adonai's name I will cut them down. [51]They surrounded me like bees—they shall be extinguished like the fire of thorns, and with Adonai's name I will cut them down. [52]You cast me down to fall, but Adonai helps me. [53]My strength and my might are God, who is my salvation. [54]The voice of joy and celebration resounds in the tents of the righteous. [55]Adonai's right hand triumphs. Adonai's right hand has exalted me. Adonai's right hand triumphs. [56]I will not die but live, and I will tell of God's deeds. [57]Adonai has punished me but not let me die. [58]Open the gates of righteousness for me that I might enter them. I will thank God. [59]This is the gate to God—the righteous will enter it. [60]I will thank You, for You have answered me and given me salvation. [61]The stone that the builders rejected is now the cornerstone. [62]This is from Adonai—it is wonderful to behold. [63]This is the day that Adonai made. Let us rejoice on it and be happy!

[64]Please, Adonai, redeem us!

Please, Adonai, redeem us!

Please, Adonai, save us!

Please, Adonai, save us!

יְיָ לִי בְּעֹזְרָי וַאֲנִי אֶרְאֶה בְשֹׂנְאָי: [46]
טוֹב לַחֲסוֹת בַּיְיָ מִבְּטֹחַ בָּאָדָם: [48]טוֹב [47]
לַחֲסוֹת בַּיְיָ מִבְּטֹחַ בִּנְדִיבִים: [49]כָּל־
גּוֹיִם סְבָבוּנִי בְּשֵׁם יְיָ כִּי אֲמִילַם:
סַבּוּנִי גַם־סְבָבוּנִי בְּשֵׁם יְיָ כִּי [50]
אֲמִילַם: [51]סַבּוּנִי כִדְבֹרִים דֹּעֲכוּ כְּאֵשׁ
קוֹצִים בְּשֵׁם יְיָ כִּי אֲמִילַם: [52]דַּחֹה
דְחִיתַנִי לִנְפֹּל וַיְיָ עֲזָרָנִי: [53]עָזִּי וְזִמְרָת
יָהּ וַיְהִי־לִי לִישׁוּעָה: [54]קוֹל רִנָּה
וִישׁוּעָה בְּאָהֳלֵי צַדִּיקִים יְמִין יְיָ עֹשָׂה
חָיִל: [55]יְמִין יְיָ רוֹמֵמָה יְמִין יְיָ עֹשָׂה
חָיִל: [56]לֹא אָמוּת כִּי אֶחְיֶה וַאֲסַפֵּר
מַעֲשֵׂי יָהּ: [57]יַסֹּר יִסְּרַנִּי יָּהּ וְלַמָּוֶת לֹא
נְתָנָנִי: [58]פִּתְחוּ־לִי שַׁעֲרֵי־צֶדֶק אָבֹא
בָם אוֹדֶה יָהּ: [59]זֶה הַשַּׁעַר לַיְיָ צַדִּיקִים
יָבֹאוּ בוֹ: [60]אוֹדְךָ כִּי עֲנִיתָנִי וַתְּהִי־לִי
לִישׁוּעָה: [61]אֶבֶן מָאֲסוּ הַבּוֹנִים הָיְתָה
לְרֹאשׁ פִּנָּה: [62]מֵאֵת יְיָ הָיְתָה זֹּאת
הִיא נִפְלָאת בְּעֵינֵינוּ: [63]זֶה הַיּוֹם עָשָׂה
יְיָ נָגִילָה וְנִשְׂמְחָה בוֹ:

אָנָּא יְיָ הוֹשִׁיעָה נָּא: [64]
אָנָּא יְיָ הוֹשִׁיעָה נָּא:
אָנָּא יְיָ הַצְלִיחָה נָּא:
אָנָּא יְיָ הַצְלִיחָה נָּא:

⁶⁵Blessed is the one who comes with Adonai's name.

We bless you from Adonai's house.

⁶⁶God is Adonai, and He has shined light upon us.

Bind the festival offering with cords up to the altar's horns.

⁶⁷You are my God and I will thank You, truly my God—I will exalt You.

⁶⁸Give thanks to Adonai, for He is good. For His kindness is everlasting.

Concluding the Hallel

⁶⁹All of Your creatures will praise You, Adonai. ⁷⁰And Your pious righteous ones who do Your will, and in joy the entire house of Israel will thank, bless, praise, glorify, exalt, adore, sanctify, and laud You, our king, ⁷¹for it is good to thank You, and fitting to sing to You, for You have always and will always be God.

B. **Psalm 136 (The Great *Hallel*) and Conclusion**

Psalm 136

⁷²Give thanks to Adonai, for He is good. For His love is everlasting.

⁷³Give thanks to the God of gods. For His love is everlasting.

⁷⁴Give thanks to the Lord of lords. For His love is everlasting.

⁷⁵To the One who alone does great wonders. For His love is everlasting.

בָּרוּךְ הַבָּא בְּשֵׁם יְיָ ⁶⁵
בֵּרַכְנוּכֶם מִבֵּית יְיָ:
אֵל יְיָ וַיָּאֶר לָנוּ ⁶⁶
אִסְרוּ־חַג בַּעֲבֹתִים
עַד קַרְנוֹת הַמִּזְבֵּחַ:
אֵלִי אַתָּה וְאוֹדֶךָּ ⁶⁷
אֱלֹהַי אֲרוֹמְמֶךָּ:
הוֹדוּ לַיְיָ כִּי טוֹב ⁶⁸
כִּי לְעוֹלָם חַסְדּוֹ:

יְהַלְלוּךָ יְיָ אֱלֹהֵינוּ כָּל־מַעֲשֶׂיךָ. ⁶⁹
וַחֲסִידֶיךָ צַדִּיקִים עוֹשֵׂי רְצוֹנֶךָ וְכָל־ ⁷⁰
עַמְּךָ בֵּית יִשְׂרָאֵל בְּרִנָּה יוֹדוּ וִיבָרְכוּ
וִישַׁבְּחוּ וִיפָאֲרוּ וִירוֹמְמוּ וְיַעֲרִיצוּ
וְיַקְדִּישׁוּ וְיַמְלִיכוּ אֶת־שִׁמְךָ מַלְכֵּנוּ
כִּי לְךָ טוֹב לְהוֹדוֹת וּלְשִׁמְךָ נָאֶה ⁷¹
לְזַמֵּר כִּי מֵעוֹלָם וְעַד עוֹלָם אַתָּה אֵל:

הוֹדוּ לַיְיָ כִּי טוֹב. כִּי לְעוֹלָם חַסְדּוֹ: ⁷²
הוֹדוּ לֵאלֹהֵי הָאֱלֹהִים. ⁷³
כִּי לְעוֹלָם חַסְדּוֹ:
הוֹדוּ לַאֲדֹנֵי הָאֲדֹנִים. ⁷⁴
כִּי לְעוֹלָם חַסְדּוֹ:
לְעֹשֵׂה נִפְלָאוֹת גְּדֹלוֹת לְבַדּוֹ. ⁷⁵
כִּי לְעוֹלָם חַסְדּוֹ:

169

76To the One who wisely created the sky. For His love is everlasting.

77To the One who spread out the earth on the water. For His love is everlasting.

78To the One who created the great lights. For His love is everlasting.

79The sun to be ruler by day. For His love is everlasting.

80The moon and stars to be rulers by night. For His love is everlasting.

81To the One who struck Egypt through their first-born. For His love is everlasting.

82And who brought Israel out from their midst. For His love is everlasting.

83With a strong hand and an outstretched arm. For His love is everlasting.

84To the One who split the Red Sea. For His love is everlasting.

85And brought Israel through it. For His love is everlasting.

86And shook Pharaoh and his army in the Red Sea. For His love is everlasting.

87To the One who led His people through the desert. For His love is everlasting.

88To the One who struck great kings. For His love is everlasting.

לְעֹשֵׂה הַשָּׁמַיִם בִּתְבוּנָה. 76
כִּי לְעוֹלָם חַסְדּוֹ:

לְרוֹקַע הָאָרֶץ עַל הַמָּיִם. 77
כִּי לְעוֹלָם חַסְדּוֹ:

לְעֹשֵׂה אוֹרִים גְּדֹלִים. 78
כִּי לְעוֹלָם חַסְדּוֹ:

אֶת־הַשֶּׁמֶשׁ לְמֶמְשֶׁלֶת בַּיּוֹם. 79
כִּי לְעוֹלָם חַסְדּוֹ:

אֶת־הַיָּרֵחַ וְכוֹכָבִים לְמֶמְשָׁלוֹת 80
בַּלָּיְלָה. כִּי לְעוֹלָם חַסְדּוֹ:

לְמַכֵּה מִצְרַיִם בִּבְכוֹרֵיהֶם. 81
כִּי לְעוֹלָם חַסְדּוֹ:

וַיּוֹצֵא יִשְׂרָאֵל מִתּוֹכָם. 82
כִּי לְעוֹלָם חַסְדּוֹ:

בְּיָד חֲזָקָה וּבִזְרוֹעַ נְטוּיָה. 83
כִּי לְעוֹלָם חַסְדּוֹ:

לְגֹזֵר יַם־סוּף לִגְזָרִים. 84
כִּי לְעוֹלָם חַסְדּוֹ:

וְהֶעֱבִיר יִשְׂרָאֵל בְּתוֹכוֹ. 85
כִּי לְעוֹלָם חַסְדּוֹ:

וְנִעֵר פַּרְעֹה וְחֵילוֹ בְיַם־סוּף. 86
כִּי לְעוֹלָם חַסְדּוֹ:

לְמוֹלִיךְ עַמּוֹ בַּמִּדְבָּר. 87
כִּי לְעוֹלָם חַסְדּוֹ:

לְמַכֵּה מְלָכִים גְּדֹלִים. 88
כִּי לְעוֹלָם חַסְדּוֹ:

⁸⁹And killed mighty kings. For His love is everlasting.

⁹⁰Sichon, king of the Amorites. For His love is everlasting.

⁹¹Og, king of Bashan. For His love is everlasting.

⁹²And gave their land as a heritage. For His love is everlasting.

⁹³A heritage to Israel His servant. For His love is everlasting.

⁹⁴Who remembered us when we were low. For His love is everlasting.

⁹⁵And set us free from our enemies. For His love is everlasting.

⁹⁶Who gives food to all creatures. For His love is everlasting.

⁹⁷Give thanks to the God of heaven. For His love is everlasting.

Concluding the Great Hallel

⁹⁸The breath of every living being will praise You, and the spirit of every mortal being will always glorify and extol You, our king. ⁹⁹You have always been and will always be God, and other than You we have no king to save us and redeem us, ransom us and rescue us and sustain us, and love us at every time of sorrow and hardship. ¹⁰⁰We have no king other than You! God of the first and the last, God of all creatures, master of all generations, glorified through great praise, He treats His world with love and His creatures with compassion.

⁸⁹וַיַּהֲרֹג מְלָכִים אַדִּירִים.

כִּי לְעוֹלָם חַסְדּוֹ:

⁹⁰לְסִיחוֹן מֶלֶךְ הָאֱמֹרִי.

כִּי לְעוֹלָם חַסְדּוֹ:

⁹¹וּלְעוֹג מֶלֶךְ הַבָּשָׁן.

כִּי לְעוֹלָם חַסְדּוֹ:

⁹²וְנָתַן אַרְצָם לְנַחֲלָה.

כִּי לְעוֹלָם חַסְדּוֹ:

⁹³נַחֲלָה לְיִשְׂרָאֵל עַבְדּוֹ.

כִּי לְעוֹלָם חַסְדּוֹ:

⁹⁴שֶׁבְּשִׁפְלֵנוּ זָכַר לָנוּ.

כִּי לְעוֹלָם חַסְדּוֹ:

⁹⁵וַיִּפְרְקֵנוּ מִצָּרֵינוּ.

כִּי לְעוֹלָם חַסְדּוֹ:

⁹⁶נֹתֵן לֶחֶם לְכָל־בָּשָׂר.

כִּי לְעוֹלָם חַסְדּוֹ:

⁹⁷הוֹדוּ לְאֵל הַשָּׁמָיִם.

כִּי לְעוֹלָם חַסְדּוֹ:

⁹⁸נִשְׁמַת כָּל־חַי תְּבָרֵךְ אֶת־שִׁמְךָ יְיָ אֱלֹהֵינוּ. וְרוּחַ כָּל־בָּשָׂר תְּפָאֵר וּתְרוֹמֵם זִכְרְךָ מַלְכֵּנוּ תָּמִיד. ⁹⁹מִן הָעוֹלָם וְעַד הָעוֹלָם אַתָּה אֵל. וּמִבַּלְעָדֶיךָ אֵין לָנוּ מֶלֶךְ גּוֹאֵל וּמוֹשִׁיעַ פּוֹדֶה וּמַצִּיל וּמְפַרְנֵס וּמְרַחֵם בְּכָל־עֵת צָרָה וְצוּקָה. ¹⁰⁰אֵין לָנוּ מֶלֶךְ אֶלָּא־אַתָּה: אֱלֹהֵי הָרִאשׁוֹנִים וְהָאַחֲרוֹנִים. אֱלוֹהַּ כָּל־בְּרִיּוֹת אֲדוֹן כָּל־תּוֹלָדוֹת הַמְהֻלָּל בְּרֹב הַתִּשְׁבָּחוֹת הַמְנַהֵג עוֹלָמוֹ בְּחֶסֶד וּבְרִיּוֹתָיו בְּרַחֲמִים.

[101]Adonai neither rests nor sleeps. He awakens those who sleep, and rouses those who slumber, and grants speech to the mute, and frees the captives, and supports the falling, and raises those who are bent over. [102]It is You alone whom we gratefully acknowledge.

[103]Even if our mouths were filled with song like the sea, and our tongues with joy like the sea's many roaring waves, and our lips with praise like the wide expanse of the sky, and even if our eyes shone like the sun and the moon, and even if our hands were spread wide like the eagles in the sky, and even if our feet were light like gazelles, we would be unable to properly acknowledge You with thanks, Adonai our God and our ancestors' God, or to praise Your name for even one-thousandth of the thousands of thousands upon thousands and millions upon millions of great things You did for our ancestors and for us: [104]You freed us from Egypt, Adonai our God. You redeemed us from the house of bondage. You nourished us in famines and provided for us in abundance. You delivered us from the sword and saved us from the plague. You freed us from severe stubborn diseases. [105]Until now Your kindness has helped us and Your love has not abandoned us. Never forsake us, Adonai our God. [106]Therefore, the limbs You apportioned us and the breath and spirit that You breathed into our nostrils, and the tongue that You put into our mouths, it is all of these that will thank, bless, praise, glorify, exalt, adore, sanctify, and extol You, our king.

172

[101] וַיְיָ לֹא יָנוּם וְלֹא יִישָׁן. הַמְעוֹרֵר יְשֵׁנִים וְהַמֵּקִיץ נִרְדָּמִים. וְהַמֵּשִׂיחַ אִלְּמִים. וְהַמַּתִּיר אֲסוּרִים וְהַסּוֹמֵךְ נוֹפְלִים וְהַזּוֹקֵף כְּפוּפִים. [102] לְךָ לְבַדְּךָ אֲנַחְנוּ מוֹדִים.

[103] אִלּוּ פִינוּ מָלֵא שִׁירָה כַּיָּם וּלְשׁוֹנֵנוּ רִנָּה כַּהֲמוֹן גַּלָּיו וְשִׂפְתוֹתֵינוּ שֶׁבַח כְּמֶרְחֲבֵי רָקִיעַ. וְעֵינֵינוּ מְאִירוֹת כַּשֶּׁמֶשׁ וְכַיָּרֵחַ. וְיָדֵינוּ פְרוּשׂוֹת כְּנִשְׁרֵי שָׁמָיִם. וְרַגְלֵינוּ קַלּוֹת כָּאַיָּלוֹת. אֵין אֲנַחְנוּ מַסְפִּיקִים לְהוֹדוֹת לְךָ יְיָ אֱלֹהֵינוּ וֵאלֹהֵי אֲבוֹתֵינוּ וּלְבָרֵךְ אֶת־שְׁמֶךָ עַל אַחַת מֵאֶלֶף אֶלֶף אַלְפֵי אֲלָפִים וְרִבֵּי רְבָבוֹת פְּעָמִים הַטּוֹבוֹת שֶׁעָשִׂיתָ עִם אֲבוֹתֵינוּ וְעִמָּנוּ: [104] מִמִּצְרַיִם גְּאַלְתָּנוּ יְיָ אֱלֹהֵינוּ. וּמִבֵּית עֲבָדִים פְּדִיתָנוּ. בְּרָעָב זַנְתָּנוּ. וּבְשָׂבָע כִּלְכַּלְתָּנוּ. מֵחֶרֶב הִצַּלְתָּנוּ וּמִדֶּבֶר מִלַּטְתָּנוּ וּמֵחֳלָיִם רָעִים וְנֶאֱמָנִים דִּלִּיתָנוּ: [105] עַד הֵנָּה עֲזָרוּנוּ רַחֲמֶיךָ. וְלֹא עֲזָבוּנוּ חֲסָדֶיךָ. וְאַל תִּטְּשֵׁנוּ יְיָ אֱלֹהֵינוּ לָנֶצַח. [106] עַל כֵּן אֵבָרִים שֶׁפִּלַּגְתָּ בָּנוּ. וְרוּחַ וּנְשָׁמָה שֶׁנָּפַחְתָּ בְּאַפֵּינוּ וְלָשׁוֹן אֲשֶׁר שַׂמְתָּ בְּפִינוּ. הֵן הֵם יוֹדוּ וִיבָרְכוּ וִישַׁבְּחוּ וִיפָאֲרוּ וִירוֹמְמוּ וְיַעֲרִיצוּ וְיַקְדִּישׁוּ וְיַמְלִיכוּ אֶת־שִׁמְךָ מַלְכֵּנוּ:

107For to You every mouth will offer thanks, and to You every tongue will swear allegiance, and to You every knee will bend, and before You everyone of height will bow, and every heart will revere You, and every lung sing to Your name, in accordance with what is written: All my bones will say: Adonai, who is like You! You save the weak from those who are stronger than them, and the poor and needy from those who rob them. 108Who can compare to You! Who can equal You! And who can match You, great, mighty, and awesome God, God on high, creator of heaven and earth. 109We will exalt You and laud You and glorify You and praise Your holy name. For it is said, "For David, O my soul, praise Adonai, and my very being, His holy name."

110God in Your tremendous power, great in Your glorious name, mighty forever and awe inspiring in Your awe, You are king, seated on a high and exalted throne.

111Abiding forever, His name is exalted and holy. And it is written: Acclaim Adonai all you righteous, for it is fitting for the upright to offer praise.

112You will be lauded by the mouths of the upright.

You will be praised by the words of the righteous.

You will be exalted by the tongues of the faithful.

You will be sanctified by the lungs of holy creatures.

107 כִּי כָל־פֶּה לְךָ יוֹדֶה. וְכָל־לָשׁוֹן לְךָ תִשָּׁבַע וְכָל־בֶּרֶךְ לְךָ תִכְרַע. וְכָל־קוֹמָה לְפָנֶיךָ תִשְׁתַּחֲוֶה. וְכָל־לְבָבוֹת יִירָאוּךָ וְכָל־קֶרֶב וּכְלָיוֹת יְזַמְּרוּ לִשְׁמֶךָ. כַּדָּבָר שֶׁכָּתוּב: כָּל־עַצְמוֹתַי תֹּאמַרְנָה יְיָ מִי כָמוֹךָ. מַצִּיל עָנִי מֵחָזָק מִמֶּנּוּ וְעָנִי וְאֶבְיוֹן מִגֹּזְלוֹ: 108 מִי יִדְמֶה־לָּךְ וּמִי יִשְׁוֶה־לָּךְ וּמִי יַעֲרָךְ־לָךְ. הָאֵל הַגָּדוֹל הַגִּבּוֹר וְהַנּוֹרָא אֵל עֶלְיוֹן קֹנֵה שָׁמַיִם וָאָרֶץ. 109 נְהַלֶּלְךָ וּנְשַׁבֵּחֲךָ וּנְפָאֶרְךָ וּנְבָרֵךְ אֶת־שֵׁם קָדְשֶׁךָ. כָּאָמוּר: לְדָוִד בָּרְכִי נַפְשִׁי אֶת־יְיָ וְכָל־קְרָבַי אֶת־שֵׁם קָדְשׁוֹ:

110 הָאֵל בְּתַעֲצֻמוֹת עֻזֶּךָ הַגָּדוֹל בִּכְבוֹד שְׁמֶךָ הַגִּבּוֹר לָנֶצַח וְהַנּוֹרָא בְּנוֹרְאוֹתֶיךָ: הַמֶּלֶךְ הַיּוֹשֵׁב עַל כִּסֵּא רָם וְנִשָּׂא:

111 שׁוֹכֵן עַד מָרוֹם וְקָדוֹשׁ שְׁמוֹ. וְכָתוּב: רַנְּנוּ צַדִּיקִים בַּיְיָ לַיְשָׁרִים נָאוָה תְהִלָּה:

112 בְּפִי יְשָׁרִים תִּתְהַלָּל. וּבְדִבְרֵי צַדִּיקִים תִּתְבָּרַךְ. וּבִלְשׁוֹן חֲסִידִים תִּתְרוֹמָם. וּבְקֶרֶב קְדוֹשִׁים תִּתְקַדָּשׁ:

113With songs of joy, our king, Your name shall be glorified by the vast multitudes of Your people, the house of Israel, in every generation, 114for it is the obligation of every creature before You, Adonai our God and our ancestors' God, to thank, magnify, laud, glorify, acclaim, exalt, and praise You, even beyond all the words of the songs and hymns of David son of Jesse Your anointed servant.

115Let Your name be forever praised, our king, great and holy king and God, in the heavens and on earth. 116For song and praise, veneration and melody, strength and power, eternity, greatness and might, exaltation and glory, holiness and dominion, blessings and thanks befit You, Adonai our God and our ancestors' God, from now and ever more! 117Blessed are You, Adonai, God, greatly lauded king and God, God of grateful acknowledgment, Lord of wonders, who chooses melodious songs, our king, our God, eternal life.

113וּבְמַקְהֲלוֹת רִבְבוֹת עַמְּךָ בֵּית יִשְׂרָאֵל בְּרִנָּה יִתְפָּאַר שִׁמְךָ מַלְכֵּנוּ בְּכָל־דּוֹר וָדוֹר. 114שֶׁכֵּן חוֹבַת כָּל־הַיְצוּרִים לְפָנֶיךָ יְיָ אֱלֹהֵינוּ וֵאלֹהֵי אֲבוֹתֵינוּ לְהוֹדוֹת לְהַלֵּל לְשַׁבֵּחַ לְפָאֵר לְרוֹמֵם לְהַדֵּר לְבָרֵךְ לְעַלֵּה וּלְקַלֵּס עַל כָּל־דִּבְרֵי שִׁירוֹת וְתִשְׁבְּחוֹת דָּוִד בֶּן־יִשַׁי עַבְדְּךָ מְשִׁיחֶךָ:

115יִשְׁתַּבַּח שִׁמְךָ לָעַד מַלְכֵּנוּ הָאֵל הַמֶּלֶךְ הַגָּדוֹל וְהַקָּדוֹשׁ בַּשָּׁמַיִם וּבָאָרֶץ. 116כִּי לְךָ נָאֶה יְיָ אֱלֹהֵינוּ וֵאלֹהֵי אֲבוֹתֵינוּ. שִׁיר וּשְׁבָחָה הַלֵּל וְזִמְרָה עֹז וּמֶמְשָׁלָה נֶצַח גְּדֻלָּה וּגְבוּרָה תְּהִלָּה וְתִפְאֶרֶת קְדֻשָּׁה וּמַלְכוּת. בְּרָכוֹת וְהוֹדָאוֹת מֵעַתָּה וְעַד עוֹלָם: 117בָּרוּךְ אַתָּה יְיָ אֵל מֶלֶךְ גָּדוֹל בַּתִּשְׁבָּחוֹת אֵל הַהוֹדָאוֹת אֲדוֹן הַנִּפְלָאוֹת הַבּוֹחֵר בְּשִׁירֵי זִמְרָה מֶלֶךְ אֵל חֵי הָעוֹלָמִים:

eaten. *Song of Songs Rabbah* (2:40), a midrashic collection compiled in the sixth century, refers to the gusto with which *Hallel* had been intoned throughout Jerusalem when the Temple stood: "'Let me hear your voice' (Song of Songs 2:14). This refers to the melodious recitation of *Hallel*. When the people of Israel recite *Hallel*, their voice ascends on high. And so the saying, 'The Pesach [offering] in the house and the *Hallel* breaks the roof!'"[2] Why do we recite a "half *Hallel*" (omitting the first eleven verses of Pss. 115 and 116) for the last six days of Passover and the full *Hallel* for the entire festival of Sukkot? *Pesikta D'rav Kahana* (Supplement 2:8) explains that in contrast to Sukkot, Scripture gives no command to rejoice on Passover—"because the Egyptians died during Passover." We read only a partial *Hallel* for the last six days of Passover "because … 'If your enemy falls, do not exult' (Prov. 24:17)."[3]

[1] *"Not for us"* The Talmud interprets this verse (and possibly other elements of the first half of this psalm that depict abandonment by God) as referring to a period known as the "birth pangs of the messiah" (Pes. 118a). This period preceding the ultimate messianic redemption would be preceded by such overwhelming suffering that one great sage said, "Let [the messiah] come, and let me not [live to] see him" (San. 98b). The *Midrash on Psalms* (44:1) uses the verse as the basis of a bitter protest to God. "What a work You performed in bringing *them* out of Egypt and dividing the sea for *them*! But you have not done such things for *us*. As Scripture says, 'Not for us, Adonai.' … How does helping our ancestors profit us? When shall we benefit? When will you show us a good sign?"

[16] *"Heaven is Adonai's heaven, and the earth He gave to people"* Drawing such a clear boundary between the divine and human realms troubled the Sages. Besides, elsewhere the Bible states, "The earth is Adonai's and all that it holds" (Ps. 24:1). The Talmud resolves the contradiction by noting that before eating, we recite a blessing attributing the source of all bounty to God. Only after this acknowledgment do the fruits of this world revert to us, as it were, to enjoy (Ber. 35a). Further blurring the divine/human boundary was the fact that Moses "went up to God" (Exod. 19:3) but "Adonai came down upon Mount Sinai" (Exod. 19:20). "Moses changed the earthly into heavenly and the heavenly into earthly" (*Deut. Rab.* 10:2).[4] In this midrash the boundary between the earthly and heavenly realms seems to disappear, and the power to bring godliness into the world lies in human hands.

[33] *"The death of His righteous is grievous in Adonai's eyes"* The *Midrash on Psalms* (116:8) describes a king who set forth with his soldiers into the wilderness. When the supplies started to run out, the king got hungry, and a steward gave him bread. Arriving in a town, the inhabitants fed the king, who then returned home and forgot the steward. One day the steward appeared before the king and reminded him of the bread he had given him. The king offered him a succession of promotions, to which the steward objected, "'Do you think that is why I gave you bread?' Finally the king said, 'Look, you are my equal. Can you ask more of me than that?' That is how God speaks

to the righteous. 'Look, you are My equals ... "If you produce what is noble out of the worthless, you shall be My spokesman [i.e., My representative on earth, doing what I do]" (Jer. 15:19). Even as I create worlds and resurrect the dead, so shall you.'" Serving God empowers us to help redeem the world. With the "death of His righteous" ones, God loses not just a collaborator, but an equal partner!

[38] *"Praise Adonai, all nations ... for His love toward us is great"* Why should other nations praise God because of God's mercy to us? Rabbi Yosei ben Chalafta (second century CE) taught it was because of "the mighty and wondrous deeds that God wrought for *them*." Against the usual reading of the text and contrary to the more common rabbinic tendency of highlighting the exclusive favor God shows Israel, Yosei ben Chalafta argues that God bestows wonders on *all* nations. Perhaps as an illustration, he also taught that "Egypt is destined to bring a gift to the messiah. The messiah will think he should not accept it from them, but God will instruct him, 'Accept it from them: they furnished hospitality to My children in Egypt'" (Pes. 118b).

[62] *"This is from Adonai"* "This verse alludes to the congregation of Israel who were enslaved to clay and bricks but were then lifted up in clouds of glory. The Egyptians were amazed at them, saying, 'Until now you were enslaved in all kinds of drudgery, and now you are lifted up in all kinds of glory.' The congregation of Israel replied, saying, 'You are amazed at us! We are amazed at ourselves....' But the Holy Spirit replied, 'This is from Adonai ...'" (*Midrash on Psalms* 118:21).[5] Sometimes our good fortune simply defies rational explanation!

———◆———

BRETTLER (OUR BIBLICAL HERITAGE)

who fear God (vv. 9–11), while the latter begins with these three groups (vv. 12–13), advocating that they be blessed by God. Both Psalm 115:9–11 and 118:2–4 contain references to "Israel," "house of Aaron," and "those who revere Adonai," in this order. These refer to three specific groups of people, from larger to smaller. The house of Aaron refers to the priests, the *kohanim*. It is uncertain who "those who revere Adonai" are—does this refer to anyone who worships the God of Israel, or is it a technical term, referring to a specific subgroup?

"Psalm 116" Psalm 116 is also divided into two parts when recited: verses 1–11 (here, vv. 19–29), in which the psalmist thanks God for saving him, and verses 12–19 (here, vv. 30–37), in which he discusses the vow offering that he will bring to the Temple as a thanksgiving offering. Though they can be separated, these two parts form a logical whole.

"Psalm 117" Psalm 117 is a post-exilic psalm and the shortest chapter of the Bible, only two verses long. Like some other psalms, it *imagines* that the entire world is assembled at the Temple to praise God. Many of the psalms that celebrate God's

kingship share this imagined setting; see, for example, Psalm 97:1, "Adonai is king! Let the earth exult, the many islands rejoice!"

"Psalm 118" Psalm 118, like Psalm 115, which opened this section, contains references to Israel, Aaron, and those who revere God (118:2–4; here, vv. 41–44). Like many psalms, the verbal tenses present significant difficulties: Is the psalmist calling to Adonai while in straits, asking to be saved (v. 5; here, v. 44), or has he already been saved (v. 21; here, v. 60)? If he has been saved, should the verses cast in the past be read as quotations from before? Or is he still in trouble, but so certain that Adonai will save him that he speaks as if he is already saved? Verse 27 (here, v. 66) of this psalm, "God is Adonai, and He has shined light upon us. Bind the festival offering with cords up to the altar's horns," is also very important—the second half of the verse contains ritual instructions, suggesting when it was recited.

70 *"And Your pious righteous ones [vachasidekha]"* In a variety of biblical texts, it is unclear if *chasidim* refers to a general category of people who follow Adonai or if this is a technical term for a particular group called *chasidim*.

——◆——

GRAY (MEDIEVAL COMMENTATORS)

R. Yochanan went on to say that the ministering angels wanted to come together to recite a song of praise at the time of the parting of the sea, but God protested, "The work of My hands is drowning in the sea, and you wish to recite a song!" (Meg. 10b). The *Kol Bo* (R. Aharon b. R. Jacob Hakohen of Lunel, France and Spain, thirteenth to fourteenth century, *siman* 52) quoted this midrash to explain why we recite an abbreviated *Hallel* during Pesach week (after the first two days) rather than the full *Hallel* that we recite during Sukkot week. The diminished *Hallel*, he explains, reflects God's rebuke of the angels and the consequent diminution of our loud praise of God.

——◆——

GREEN (PERSONAL SPIRITUALITY)

great family celebration of all Jews, is also a time when mortality is on our minds. As the tale is passed down from one generation to the next, we inevitably think about those empty places at our table, belonging to those who told *us* the tale and now are no longer with us. We think of the future Seder tables of our children and grandchildren, when we too will be present only as a past memory.

Paradoxically, this is the closest we Jews can come to a taste of immortality. More than others, we see our lives as a link between generations. The meaning Judaism gives to our lives lies mostly in transmitting Torah to children and grandchildren. We have a tale to tell, a message to pass down. As we look at our descendants—both physical and spiritual—sitting around the table, we dare to think that the message will survive. In that message, and in the unique ways it will be told by generations to come, we will remain present, long after our physical selves are missing from this family's Seder table.

———◆———

J. HOFFMAN (TRANSLATION)

[2] *"Where is their God?"* Literally, "where *na* is their God." Frequently, *na* introduces a sense of formality; for this reason, we sometimes translate it as "sir" (see "sir," *My People's Passover Haggadah*, Volume 2, p. 21). Here we suspect it is used to augment the poetry. Having no equivalent word in English, we leave *na* untranslated.

[3] *"Doing whatever He pleases"* Surprisingly, "doing whatever He pleases" sounds pejorative in many English dialects and therefore fails to capture the positive aspect of the Hebrew. We simply want to indicate that while other gods can do nothing, our God can do anything. But all of the reasonable ways to express that in English sound like a negative judgment to some. Compare "doing whatever He wants," which some feel represents not absolute power (such as a beneficent king might wield) but rather disregard for others.

[5] *"Cannot"* Literally, "do not." Hebrew frequently uses the simple indicative ("do not") where English requires a modal ("cannot").

[6] *"A nose"* The introduction of the article "a" here partially breaks the poetry of the Hebrew. Unfortunately, "they have nose" is not grammatical in English (though it is in many other languages, including Hebrew).

[7] *"Their hands"* Our change in English grammar matches the Hebrew, which also switches to sentence fragments here, probably for poetic reasons.

[9] *"Their"* This transition from second person ("Israel, trust …") to third ("their") is as odd in Hebrew as it is in English. A single vowel change in the Hebrew would give us the more expected, "Israel trusts in Adonai, their …."

[11] *"Revere"* Or "fear." We no longer have an English word to capture the combination of reverence and fear expressed by the Hebrew.

[12] *"Bless us, bless us"* Literally, "bless, bless." But we need "us" in English. We repeat "bless us" in English because the repetition of "bless" *(y'varekh)* in Hebrew creates a poetic impact that we want to capture in English. Below (v. 14), "you" will be repeated, augmenting the impact.

[17] *"Silence"* The Septuagint gives us "Hades."

[19] *"I love that God"* Or "I would love it if God ..." Hebrew frequently does not distinguish between statements and hopes.

[20] *"During my days"* Others, "while I live." That is probably the point, but we want to retain the indirect reference to life, coming as it does before a direct reference to death.

[22] *"Remove me from this"* Others paraphrase, "save my life" or "deliver my life." The Hebrew literally reads "remove my life." We add "from this."

[25] *"Soul"* This is the same word we just translated as "me" (and that others translate as "life"). All three translations are inaccurate, but we have no good option here.

[26] *"You, Adonai"* Hebrew, just "you," but the Hebrew shifts from feminine (used for "soul") to masculine (used for "Adonai"), so the point is clear in Hebrew. We have no other way to make the transition clear, so we have to spell out "Adonai."

[28] *"What"* Or, "how ..."

[28] *"Afflicted"* Literally, "greatly afflicted." The Hebrew includes an adverb *(m'od)* to modify "afflicted," but while "greatly afflicted" is more literal, the shorter version seems to reflect the poetry better.

[31] *"Deliverance"* Literally, "deliverances." Maybe "deliverance-cup" would be better.

[31] *"Adonai's name"* We translate here on the assumption that Adonai's name itself was assumed to have power.

[32] *"Before all His people"* We move "before all His people" to the beginning of the line. In Hebrew, it comes second. But we want to make it clear that it is not the vows that are before the people, but the fulfilling of them.

[32] *"Fulfill"* Others, the literal "pay." But in English, vows are fulfilled, not paid.

[33] *"Grievous"* Following *JPS*. The Hebrew is literally "precious." But we reject the literal translation—"The death of His righteous is precious in Adonai's eyes"—because it seems so obviously wrong. Another possibility is that we have misunderstood the first part. Perhaps it does not mean "the death of His righteous." Indeed, the grammar and even the vocabulary are odd. One possibility is, "What is precious in Adonai's eyes can (seem to) be death to His righteous," that is, that His righteous might misconstrue something valuable and wrongly consider it dangerous.

[34] *"Loosened my bonds"* Brenton's nineteenth-century English translation of the Septuagint offers the nicely poetic "burst my bonds asunder." We use "loosened" here, but the Hebrew may be stronger, and "opened" may in fact be more accurate. It is difficult to know.

[35] *"Todah"* That is, "thanks" offering.

[35] *"Offering"* Hebrew, *zevach,* which above we left transliterated. (See *"Zevach," My People's Passover Haggadah,* Volume 2, p. 123.)

[37] *"Inside of Jerusalem"* Or "inside of you, Jerusalem." That is, the psalmist may be addressing Jerusalem directly. It is hard to tell from the poetic Hebrew.

[40] *"For He is good"* Another reading supported by the Hebrew is "for it is good to do so."

[41] *"Love"* Frequently, "mercy." *JPS* gives us "steadfast love," though "steadfast love" lasting "forever" seems redundant. At issue are the nuances of the Hebrew word *chesed*. We know it refers to something good, but beyond that, specific details are difficult to confirm.

[44] *"From the straits"* Literally, "from the strait," perhaps meant to be understood metaphorically, as in *JPS*, "in distress." The Midrash connects the word for "Egypt" *(mitsrayim)* to the word straits *(meitsarim)*.

[44] *"Was answered by God"* Literally, "God answered me." We use the passive here to make it possible to put "God" at the end of both "From the straits ..." and "in the expanse ...," mirroring the poetic Hebrew word order. In rearranging the English, however, we split up *merchav* ("expanse") and *yah* ("God"). This is unfortunate because some texts have one word where we have two. The one-word version means "He answered me in God's expanse" or "He answered me in the expanse." The Septuagint gives us the latter. (In a debate in the Talmud [Pes. 117a], Rabbah similarly argues for the one-word *merchavyah*.)

[45] *"Mine"* Literally, "to me." The line continues "[what can a human do] to me," creating a poetic impact we cannot capture in English. ("Adonai is with me.... What can a human do with me?" is tempting, because it captures the word play, but it seems to stray too far from the meaning of the Hebrew.) This half-line and the next ("I shall not fear") are used to end the famous synagogue poem *Adon Olam*.

[45] *"A human"* Others, "man," but in the generic sense of "human." Another possibility here is "mortal."

[46] *"Adonai is mine with those who help me"* So reads the Hebrew. The point may simply be, as in the Septuagint, "Adonai is my helper." King James gives us, "The LORD taketh my part with them that help me."

[46] *"See those who hate me"* Frequently emended, as in *JPS*, "I will see the downfall of ..."

[49] *"Adonai's name"* Or, perhaps, "... with the name 'Adonai.'"

[49] *"Cut them down"* Following *JPS*. The verb here comes from the same root as the verb "to circumcise." The King James "I will destroy them" is probably the point. But the use of a verb describing circumcision, that is, cutting around, in response to nations that gather around ("surround") is unlikely to be an accident.

[50] *"They completely surrounded me"* Roughly following Brenton. The Hebrew verb "surround," which comes from the root *s.b.b*, is one of the rare verbs that can be declined in two different ways with no difference in meaning. Here we see both of them, *sabuni* and *s'vavuni*, literally, "they surrounded me [*sabuni*, one possible verb

form] and surrounded me [*s'vavuni*, the other one]." A similar example in English would be "they dived and they dove."

[51] *"Bees"* The Septuagint elaborates: "... surrounded me like bees around a honeycomb."

[51] *"Extinguished like the fire of thorns"* So reads the Hebrew. Though the point is clear, it's difficult to understand the metaphor of "the fire of thorns." This may have been an ancient idiom, along the lines of our modern "as dead as a doornail," doornails being no deader than any other hardware, but nonetheless appearing in the idiom.

[53] *"My strength and my might are God, who is my salvation"* See *My People's Prayer Book*, Volume 3, *P'sukei D'zimrah (Morning Psalms)*, p. 174, for a discussion of this interesting and difficult phrase.

[54] *"Resounds"* Following *JPS*. In English, the literal translation "is" wouldn't do justice to the poetic nature of the Hebrew.

[55] *"Right hand"* We translate almost literally (simply "right" would be more literal), though in so doing, we miss some of the impact of the Hebrew, which was written at a time when the metaphor of the "right hand" was more widespread. We find remnants of the asymmetry of right and left in English: "right" (correct, proper), "adroit" (skillful; literally [from French], "to the right"), "gauche" (boorish; literally [from French], "left"), "sinister" (evil; literally, [from Latin] "left"), "left-handed compliment" (a "compliment" with a veiled slight), etc.

[55] *"Triumphs"* Or, perhaps, "is valiant." The Hebrew literally reads, "does *chayil*." *Chayil* is the same interesting word used to describe one's wife in Proverbs, frequently recited on Shabbat (see *My People's Prayer Book*, Volume 7, *Shabbat at Home*, p. 74).

[55] *"Has exalted me"* Or "lifted me up." We prefer "exalted" here so that this line will match the ending of the psalm. (See below, "I will exalt You.") Another possibility is simply "[Adonai's hand] is raised." It is common in Hebrew to omit direct objects (here, "me") even where they are required in English. This is one of the rare instances in which it is difficult to know if a direct object was indeed intended. We base our translation on the Septuagint, which similarly reads, "lifted me up."

[58] *"Open"* The command is plural, though the addressees are not specified.

[58] *"Thank"* Or "thankfully acknowledge." We prefer the shorter translation in keeping with the opening of the psalm.

[61] *"Cornerstone"* Literally, "head of the corner." *JPS*'s "chief cornerstone" seems redundant, though our "stone ... is now the cornerstone" is repetitive in a way that the poetic Hebrew is not.

[64] *"Please"* This is the best we can do, but we still miss the impact of the Hebrew, which, poetically, starts with *ana* and ends with *na*. Both of these words generally add a

tone of formality. See *My People's Passover Haggadah*, Volume 2, "Where is their God," p. 178, and "Sir," p. 21. (We do not use "sir" here because, although it may be a reasonable way to address a magistrate, we do not use it for God.)

[65] *"With Adonai's name"* Commonly, "in Adonai's name" (or "in the name of Adonai"). But to "come in the name of" in English means to come as a representative of, and that is not what the Hebrew means. This line represents roughly the same use of "Adonai's name" as we saw above (e.g., "with Adonai's name I will cut them down").

[66] *"Festival offering"* Literally, just "festival."

[66] *"Altar's horns"* We read in Leviticus that the great sacrificial altar was adorned with horns.

[67] *"Truly my God"* We add the word "truly" to distinguish this clause from the preceding one. In Hebrew, the first one uses *el* for "God," while the current clause uses *elohim* for "God." We need two different ways of expressing "God" to make the poetry work, so we resort to adding "truly."

[67] *"I will exalt you"* This line hearkens back to "Adonai's right hand has exalted me" (v. 55).

[70] *"Pious righteous ones"* We would prefer just "pious righteouses" or "pious" and then another noun, but we seem not to have anything appropriate in English.

[70] *"Laud"* Better, "declare You king," but we need a single word here to maintain the impact of the Hebrew.

——◆——

L. HOFFMAN (HISTORY)

just one day, featuring the reading of Genesis 21, "God visited Sarah [to announce her pregnancy with Isaac]." When the Babylonians added a second day, they automatically chose the very next chapter, Genesis 22, which, by chance only, contains the story of the *Akedah*. So too with the extra psalms for *Hallel*. Since the pre-meal praise had stopped at the end of Psalm 114, the post-meal addition began with Psalm 115.

So much for the beginning; but what prompted the Rabbis to conclude with Psalm 118? It was probably the messianic connotations of that psalm. Blessed is the one who comes with Adonai's name *(Barukh haba b'shem Adonai)*." The original template for the Seder, after all, was not only to go from "degradation to praise," but to end with "redemption." The pre-meal *Hallel* had ended with a blessing of redemption (see "Redeemer of Israel," *My People's Passover Haggadah*, Volume 2, p. 113). So the post-meal psalms were planned to end with the same theme.

[64–65] *"Please … save …. Blessed is the one who comes with Adonai's name [Barukh haba b'shem Adonai]"* The Gospels cite this verse as the way Jesus was welcomed into

Jerusalem. "The multitude going ahead of him and behind him cried out, 'Please save!' to the son of David. 'Blessed is he who comes in the name of Adonai'" (Matt. 21:9). In the late Middle Ages, some Jews at the Seder welcomed Elijah with the same messianic call. Thirteenth-century Italian Jews greeted a child at his circumcision that way and then placed him in Elijah's chair, as a visual symbol of their hope that he might turn out to be Elijah returning or even the messiah himself.

[69]*"[They] will praise You [Y'hall'lukha]"* Every *Hallel* ends with a *Birkat Hashir* ("Blessing of Song"). With the last psalm of the Egyptian *Hallel* (Ps. 118) completed, we say one of them, "[They] will praise You." Another occurs after the Great *Hallel* (see below, "The breath of every living being"). Some versions of the Haggadah postpone this version of the blessing until the end of the Great *Hallel* and then say both versions together.

[72]*"Give thanks to Adonai [Psalm 136]"* The word *Hallel* ("praise") is the name given to sets of psalms used liturgically as praise of God (see "*Hallel*," *My People's Passover Haggadah*, Volume 2, p. 97). Earlier we said the Egyptian *Hallel*: Psalms 113–114 before dinner, and Psalms 115–118 after it. Here we encounter a second *Hallel*, *Hallel Hagadol*, "The Great *Hallel*." It comes as some surprise to see Psalm 136 alone called a *Hallel*, since, unlike the others, it is a single psalm, not an entire set. It may have been part of such a set originally, however, since talmudic opinion (Pes. 118a) links it to the psalm before, saying that the Great *Hallel* begins with Psalm 135:1 or (another opinion) Psalm 135:3. Others in the Talmud, however, do stipulate Psalm 136 alone, and that is our practice today.

Almost as an aside, the same talmudic discussion advocates Psalm 23 either as an alternative Great *Hallel* or a psalm to be said alongside it. The standard Haggadah omits it, but at least one rabbinic luminary of the Middle Ages, the *Maharil* (Jacob Moellin of Germany, 1365–1427), played it safe and said it anyway.

More interesting than the Great *Hallel* itself are the instructions in which it is embedded. Its roots lie in the Talmud's recollection of Rabbi Tarfon saying, "Over a fourth cup, finish the [Egyptian] *Hallel* and say *Hallel Hagadol*." But Rabbi Tarfon's statement has been doctored. He actually advised reciting these *Hallels* over a *fifth* cup, not just a fourth one! Knowing that the Seder has four cups, not five, our most famous medieval commentator, *Rashi* (France, d. 1105), "corrected" the text to read "fourth," and our printed version of the Talmud follows *Rashi*'s mistaken emendation. But manuscripts make plain that the original said "fifth." What then is the fifth cup?

It was possibly related to Rabbi Tarfon's perspective on redemption. Palestinian tradition identified each of the normal four cups of wine with a separate act of redemption in Israel's past. Rabbi Tarfon poured a fifth cup—to be tasted only if the messiah arrived that night. It was therefore a fifth cup that went unconsumed.

His custom continued, although not with everyone. That is why *Rashi* assumed the Talmud's citation of it to be a mistake. Eventually, medieval Jews began awaiting the coming of Elijah, at which time the tradition of the fifth cup seems to have been revived and given a new name: Elijah's cup. Later still, some rabbis of note (the same *Maharil* who included Psalm 23, for example) kept six cups: the usual four, Rabbi Tarfon's fifth, and the cup for Elijah as a sixth. In our time, the *Maharil*'s practice recurs in the

American Reform Haggadah of 1974.

[98] *"The breath of every living being"* Rabbinic liturgy employs the rhetorical technique of bracketing: citing large chunks of biblical material, like psalms, but attaching prologues and epilogues in blessing form to contextualize them within rabbinic theology. People called to the Torah for an *aliyah,* for example, recite blessings before and after asserting the role of Torah in rabbinic tradition. Before reading, we say God chose us and gave us Torah *(bachar banu ... v'natan lanu et torato)*; after, we claim the Torah is true *(emet),* and the vehicle for eternal life *(chayei olam).*

So too, any *Hallel* (there are three of them—see *"Hallel," My People's Passover Haggadah,* Volume 2, p. 97) usually begins and ends with a blessing.

The Seder's two *Hallel*s (the Egyptian *Hallel,* Psalms 113–114 before dinner [Volume 2, pp. 93–94] and Psalms 115–118 after dinner, [Volume 2, pp. 154–157]; and the Great *Hallel,* Psalm 136 following [Volume 2, pp. 157–159]) now conclude with a blessing reiterating the overall liturgical centrality of praising God. The Mishnah refers to this blessing as the "Blessing of Song" *(Birkat Hashir).*

Like so much of Jewish liturgy in the period before universal literacy and the widespread availability of prayer books, more than a single version of this blessing circulated. The Talmud (Pes. 118a) cites two of them, *Y'hall'lukha* ("They shall praise You") and *Nishmat kol cha'i* ("The breath of every being"). Many more must have existed as well, one of which, *Yishtabach* ("[All life] shall praise [Your name]"), we use as the conclusion for the daily *Hallel* in synagogue (see *My People's Prayer Book,* Volume 3, *P'sukei D'zimrah* [*Morning Psalms*], pp. 177–182). *Nishmat kol cha'i* and *Yishtabach* together conclude the same prayer on Shabbat and holidays (see *My People's Prayer Book,* Volume 10, *Shabbat Morning: Shacharit and Musaf,* pp. 41–43).

The Haggadah utilizes all three, but splits them up between the two *Hallel*s, so that the Egyptian *Hallel* concludes with *Y'hall'lukhah* (see above, "[They] will praise You [*Y'hall'lukha*]"), and the Great *Hallel* ends with *Nishmat kol cha'i* and *Yishtabach.*

The Egyptian *Hallel* is said in synagogue too, and there it receives an opening blessing: either "Blessed is God ... who commanded us to *read* the *Hallel*" *(likro et hahallel)* or "... to *complete* the *Hallel*" *(ligmor et hahallel).*

Here the opening blessing is lacking. Concerned, after the fact, about the missing blessing, the Geonim (c. 750–1038) observed that the *Hallel* of the Seder is not so much a reading *(k'ri'ah)* as it is a song *(shir).* But this is an ex post facto halakhic justification. Medieval practice actually varied. Some Haggadot included the blessing that commands us "to read the *Hallel*" for psalms said before dinner and "to complete the *Hallel*" for the psalms said after it.

More likely, then, the missing blessing in our practice is a consequence of the fact that early on, it became customary for people to interrupt their Seder to hear the *Hallel* read communally in synagogue (see *"Hallel," My People's Passover Haggadah,* Volume 2, pp. 97, 106–107). There they did indeed say a blessing before it. Eventually, it moved to the home, but the blessing remained only in the synagogue version, for those who still went there.

KUSHNER AND POLEN (CHASIDIC VOICES)

spirit that binds space and time together. And just this is the hidden teaching in the psalm verse: "Bind the festival offering [time] with cords [yearning for connectedness with God] to the altar [place]." The cord symbolizes connectedness, which is epitomized by the love of God. Thus, it is this yearning for God that ties everything together.

Furthermore, these bonds of love link past and present in Jewish history. Every era of our history has its own unique contribution. When, for example, the Temple stood, loving God was a public and tangible act, and we did not need to worry about inwardness as much as we do today. Thus, when we bind the generations, we bind our inwardness today with our ancestors' loving actions in the past, effectively fusing both dimensions of time together.

—◆—

LANDES (HALAKHAH)

synagogue before the Seder. Now we conclude the *Hallel* of the Haggadah, with the addition of *Hallel Hagadol*, "The Great *Hallel*." The Talmud knows more than one practice. Our custom follows Rabbi Judah, who said Psalm 136.

The rules of *Hallel* are as follows:

1. It is said sitting but not reclining.
2. It is proper to hold the cup and, if possible, to raise it during the recital.
3. If there are at least three present, one should lead and the others respond, as a form of joy and song. This especially should be done with Psalm 136, which contains the refrain *ki l'olam chasdo* ("for His mercy endures forever").
4. The fourth cup is drunk at the end while reclining.

—◆—

ZIERLER (FEMINIST VOICES)

recognition that none of what we say is literal and is at best an approximation. God is no person, no more "He" than "She." But if we take seriously the metaphorical logic of *ilu finu*, that "even if our mouths were filled with song like the sea … we would be unable to properly acknowledge [God] with thanks," how can we limit our praise and thanksgiving to a uni-gendered God? How dare we approach God with anything less than a full range of human language and experience?

———◆ ◆ ◆———

16. FORMAL CONCLUSION

A. The Fourth Cup and Final Blessing

Fourth cup of wine

כּוֹס רְבִיעִי

Lift the fourth cup of wine and recite:

[1] Blessed are You, Adonai our God, ruler of the world, who creates the fruit of the vine.

בָּרוּךְ אַתָּה יְיָ אֱלֹהֵינוּ מֶלֶךְ הָעוֹלָם בּוֹרֵא פְּרִי הַגָּפֶן:

Drink the wine while reclining ceremoniously to the left.

Final Blessing

On Friday night include the words in parentheses.

[2] Blessed are You, Adonai our God, ruler of the world, for the vine and for the fruit of the vine; for the produce of the field; and for a precious, bountiful, and spacious land that You loved and gave our ancestors as their inheritance, to eat of its fruit and to enjoy its bounty. [3] Adonai our God, have mercy on Israel Your people, and on Jerusalem Your city, and on Zion where Your glory dwells, and on Your altar and on Your Temple. [4] And rebuild Jerusalem Your holy city quickly in our day. And bring us back up into it, and let us be happy with it that we might eat of its fruit, and enjoy its bounty, and praise You for it in holiness and purity. [5] (And love us and strengthen us on this Shabbat day) and let us be happy on this Festival of Matzot, for You are and do good to everyone. [6] And we gratefully acknowledge You for the land and the fruit of the vine. [7] Blessed are You, Adonai our God, for the land and for the fruit of the vine.

[2] בָּרוּךְ אַתָּה יְיָ אֱלֹהֵינוּ מֶלֶךְ הָעוֹלָם עַל הַגֶּפֶן וְעַל פְּרִי הַגֶּפֶן וְעַל תְּנוּבַת הַשָּׂדֶה וְעַל אֶרֶץ חֶמְדָּה טוֹבָה וּרְחָבָה שֶׁרָצִיתָ וְהִנְחַלְתָּ לַאֲבוֹתֵינוּ לֶאֱכוֹל מִפִּרְיָהּ וְלִשְׂבּוֹעַ מִטּוּבָהּ. [3] רַחֶם יְיָ אֱלֹהֵינוּ עַל יִשְׂרָאֵל עַמֶּךָ וְעַל יְרוּשָׁלַיִם עִירֶךָ וְעַל צִיּוֹן מִשְׁכַּן כְּבוֹדֶךָ וְעַל מִזְבְּחֶךָ וְעַל הֵיכָלֶךָ. [4] וּבְנֵה יְרוּשָׁלַיִם עִיר הַקֹּדֶשׁ בִּמְהֵרָה בְיָמֵינוּ וְהַעֲלֵנוּ לְתוֹכָהּ. וְשַׂמְּחֵנוּ בָהּ וְנֹאכַל מִפִּרְיָהּ וְנִשְׂבַּע מִטּוּבָהּ. וּנְבָרֶכְךָ עָלֶיהָ בִּקְדֻשָּׁה וּבְטָהֳרָה [5] (וּרְצֵה וְהַחֲלִיצֵנוּ בְּיוֹם הַשַּׁבָּת הַזֶּה) וְשַׂמְּחֵנוּ בְּיוֹם חַג הַמַּצּוֹת הַזֶּה. כִּי אַתָּה יְיָ טוֹב וּמֵטִיב לַכֹּל. [6] וְנוֹדֶה לְּךָ עַל הָאָרֶץ וְעַל פְּרִי הַגֶּפֶן: [7] בָּרוּךְ אַתָּה יְיָ עַל הָאָרֶץ וְעַל פְּרִי הַגֶּפֶן:

186

B. Prayer for "Acceptance" of the Seder *(NIRTSAH)*

[8]The Passover celebration has concluded appropriately,

[9]With all its laws and rules.

[10]As we have had the honor to celebrate it, so we may have the honor to do it.

[11]Pure One, dwelling in Your home,

Lift up this uncountable assembly.

Draw near and lead the vineyard plants,

Redeemed to Zion in joy.

C. A Messianic Hope

[12]NEXT YEAR IN JERUSALEM!

נִרְצָה

[8]חֲסַל סִדּוּר פֶּסַח כְּהִלְכָתוֹ.

[9]כְּכָל־מִשְׁפָּטוֹ וְחֻקָּתוֹ:

[10]כַּאֲשֶׁר זָכִינוּ לְסַדֵּר אוֹתוֹ.

כֵּן נִזְכֶּה לַעֲשׂוֹתוֹ:

[11]זָךְ שׁוֹכֵן מְעוֹנָה.

קוֹמֵם קְהַל מִי מָנָה:

קָרֵב נַהֵל נִטְעֵי כַנָּה.

פְּדוּיִם לְצִיּוֹן בְּרִנָּה:

[12]לְשָׁנָה הַבָּאָה בִּירוּשָׁלָיִם:

ARNOW (THE WORLD OF MIDRASH)

"Nirtsah" The Seder's final "official" element is known as *nirtsah* ("accepted"), a word that appears in this form only twice in the Bible. In Leviticus 1:4, the context involves specific actions that render a sacrifice acceptable—a relevant concern for the Seder, which developed as a substitute for the paschal sacrifice. It appears again in Isaiah 40:2, a verse that figures in a poignant midrash exploring the parallels between the suffering of Job and Israel (*Pesikta D'rav Kahana* 16:6). As the hand of God struck Job (19:21), so it struck Israel with the destruction of the Temple: "Speak tenderly to Jerusalem, and declare to her that the term of her service is over, that   *(p. 191)*

BALIN (MODERN HAGGADOT)

[12] *"Next year in Jerusalem"* In 1965, a newly published Passover Haggadah edited by Lewis M. Moroze and with illustrations by William Vigoda was dedicated to the memory of James Chaney, Andrew Goodman, and Michael Schwirmer, the civil rights activists who had been murdered in Mississippi by the Ku Klux Klan the year prior. This Haggadah asks Seder participants to remember that they were once slaves and thus enjoined to "hold high the torch of liberty and rededicate themselves to the never-ending battle for freedom...."[1] The Seder ends with a "Fourth and Final Toast" to freedom, after which all recite in unison: *(p. 191)*

BRETTLER (OUR BIBLICAL HERITAGE)

"Nirtsah" This poem consists of eight lines—like many biblical poems, each line is of approximately the same length, but there is no true meter. Unlike biblical poems, end-rhyme characterizes this composition: the first four lines end in *-to*, the last four in *-na*. The use of *nizkeh* at the end of the first four lines and *zakh* at the beginning of the fifth line ties the two sections together.

[9]*"Laws and rules"* Although this phrase is frequent in the Bible, this verse probably alludes to   *(p. 192)*

[For prayer instructions, see page 186.]

16. FORMAL CONCLUSION

A. The Fourth Cup and Final Blessing

[1]Blessed are You, Adonai our God, ruler of the world, who creates the fruit of the vine.

[2]Blessed are You, Adonai our God, ruler of the world, for the vine and for the fruit of the vine; for the produce of the field; and for a precious, bountiful, and spacious land that You loved and gave our ancestors as their inheritance, to eat of its fruit and to enjoy its bounty. [3]Adonai our God, have mercy on Israel Your people, and on Jerusalem Your city, and on Zion

GILLMAN (THEOLOGICALLY SPEAKING)

"Next year in Jerusalem" The theme of redemption is everywhere in the concluding portions of the Seder. It is introduced in the redemption blessing that concludes the telling of the story before the festive meal; it was symbolized by the introduction of Elijah, the herald of redemption; and it will appear at the very end of the Haggadah when God kills the Angel of Death. Here it appears in the exclamation, "Next year in Jerusalem!"

From the time of the   *(p. 193)*

J. HOFFMAN (TRANSLATION)

[2] *"For"* Hebrew, *al*, the same word we translated "about" above (see "About," *My People's Passover Haggadah*, Volume 2, p. 62).

[2] *"The vine"* Better might be "vines," which is the point. (Using "the" to refer generically to something is common. See "Frogs," Volume 2, p. 62.) But the blessing progresses from *hagefen* ("the vine") to *p'ri hagefen* ("fruit of the vine"), and we want to *(p. 194)*

(p. 194)

SIGNPOST: FORMAL CONCLUSION

THE SEDER ENDS WITH A FINAL CUP AND A BLESSING. WE PRAY THEN THAT OUR SEDER SERVICE HAS BEEN ACCEPTABLE TO GOD AND SUM UP THIS NIGHT'S HOPES AND ASPIRATIONS IN THE FINAL SYMBOLIC LINE: "NEXT YEAR IN JERUSALEM!"

———◆———

כּוֹס רְבִיעִי

[1] בָּרוּךְ אַתָּה יְיָ אֱלֹהֵינוּ מֶלֶךְ הָעוֹלָם בּוֹרֵא פְּרִי הַגָּפֶן:

[2] בָּרוּךְ אַתָּה יְיָ אֱלֹהֵינוּ מֶלֶךְ הָעוֹלָם עַל הַגֶּפֶן וְעַל פְּרִי הַגֶּפֶן וְעַל תְּנוּבַת הַשָּׂדֶה וְעַל אֶרֶץ חֶמְדָּה טוֹבָה וּרְחָבָה שֶׁרָצִיתָ וְהִנְחַלְתָּ לַאֲבוֹתֵינוּ לֶאֱכֹל מִפְּרְיָהּ וְלִשְׂבּוֹעַ מִטּוּבָהּ. [3] רַחֵם יְיָ אֱלֹהֵינוּ עַל יִשְׂרָאֵל עַמֶּךָ וְעַל יְרוּשָׁלַיִם עִירֶךָ וְעַל צִיּוֹן

L. HOFFMAN (HISTORY)

[2] *"For the vine and for the fruit of the vine"* Meals conclude with *Birkat Hamazon*, usually translated as "Grace after Meals." A literal translation would be *"Blessing* of the Food." It consists of four blessings today, but the singular noun, "blessing," alerts us to the fact that at first only one blessing was said. In all probability, several such single-blessings versions once existed. "For the vine and for the fruit of the vine" is such a blessing, now reserved for the occasions of eating food *(p. 196)*

(p. 196)

LANDES (HALAKHAH)

[8] *"The Passover celebration has concluded appropriately"* We conclude by announcing that "the Passover celebration has concluded appropriately." This ending arouses great emotion. Its wording, "as we have had the honor to celebrate it (tonight), so we may have the honor to do it (in the future)"(v. 10), reflects the halakhic principle of *s'khar mitzvah mitzvah* ("the reward for [doing] a *mitzvah* is [the opportunity to do] a [another] *mitzvah*"). It reflects the confidence of Halakhah that the law can be fulfilled, that it is not an impossible burden, a trap leading toward sin, as claimed by Paul and other detractors. And in the last words, the image of divinity and a resurrected people are proclaimed—telling us that the observance of these laws has a transcendent and transformative value. Inculcation of such yearning, confidence, and joyful vision of the transcendent requires the ritual *mitzvot* of Passover and the act of *(p. 197)*

(p. 197)

where Your glory dwells, and on Your altar and on Your Temple. [4]And rebuild Jerusalem Your holy city quickly in our day. And bring us back up into it, and let us be happy with it that we might eat of its fruit, and enjoy its bounty, and praise You for it in holiness and purity. [5](And love us and strengthen us on this Shabbat day) and let us be happy on this Festival of Matzot, for You are and do good to everyone. [6]And we gratefully acknowledge You for the land and the fruit of the vine. [7]Blessed are You, Adonai our God, for the land and for the fruit of the vine.

B. Prayer for "Acceptance" of the Seder (NIRTSAH)

[8]The Passover celebration has concluded appropriately,

[9]With all its laws and rules.

[10]As we have had the honor to celebrate it, so we may have the honor to do it.

[11]Pure One, dwelling in Your home,

Lift up this uncountable assembly.

Draw near and lead the vineyard plants,

Redeemed to Zion in joy.

C. A Messianic Hope
[12]NEXT YEAR IN JERUSALEM!

מִשְׁכַּן כְּבוֹדֶךָ וְעַל מִזְבַּחֶךָ וְעַל הֵיכָלֶךָ. [4]וּבְנֵה יְרוּשָׁלַיִם עִיר הַקֹּדֶשׁ בִּמְהֵרָה בְיָמֵינוּ וְהַעֲלֵנוּ לְתוֹכָהּ. וְשַׂמְּחֵנוּ בָהּ וְנֹאכַל מִפִּרְיָהּ וְנִשְׂבַּע מִטּוּבָהּ. וּנְבָרֶכְךָ עָלֶיהָ בִּקְדֻשָּׁה וּבְטָהֳרָה [5](וּרְצֵה וְהַחֲלִיצֵנוּ בְּיוֹם הַשַּׁבָּת הַזֶּה) וְשַׂמְּחֵנוּ בְּיוֹם חַג הַמַּצּוֹת הַזֶּה. כִּי אַתָּה יְיָ טוֹב וּמֵטִיב לַכֹּל. [6]וְנוֹדֶה לְךָ עַל הָאָרֶץ וְעַל פְּרִי הַגָּפֶן. [7]בָּרוּךְ אַתָּה יְיָ עַל הָאָרֶץ וְעַל פְּרִי הַגָּפֶן:

נִרְצָה

[8]חֲסַל סִדּוּר פֶּסַח כְּהִלְכָתוֹ. [9]כְּכָל־מִשְׁפָּטוֹ וְחֻקָּתוֹ: [10]כַּאֲשֶׁר זָכִינוּ לְסַדֵּר אוֹתוֹ. כֵּן נִזְכֶּה לַעֲשׂוֹתוֹ: [11]זָךְ שׁוֹכֵן מְעוֹנָה. קוֹמֵם קְהַל מִי מָנָה: קָרֵב נַהֵל נִטְעֵי כַנָּה. פְּדוּיִם לְצִיּוֹן בְּרִנָּה:

[12]לְשָׁנָה הַבָּאָה בִּירוּשָׁלָיִם:

ARNOW (THE WORLD OF MIDRASH)

her iniquity is expiated [*nirtsah*, i.e., atonement has been accepted]; for she has received at the hand of Adonai double for all her sins" (Isa. 40:2). And as Job received double reward for his suffering, so too, the midrash concludes, will Israel.

[11] *"Redeemed to Zion in joy"* This expression paraphrases Isaiah: "The redeemed ... shall return to Zion in joy" (35:10). The same image appears midrashically in a juxtaposition of Psalm 136 (see *My People's Passover Haggadah*, Volume 2, p. 157) with the famous passage in Ecclesiastes, "To everything there is a season ..." (3:1–8). [1] "A time to dance" (Eccl. 3:4) corresponds to "a strong hand and an outstretched arm" (Ps. 136:12). This teaches that [with the Exodus] Israel rejoiced and danced, as it says, "He led His people out in gladness ... with joyous song" (Ps. 105:43). So it will be in their future redemption ... as it says, "And the redeemed ... shall return to Zion with joy ..." (Isa. 35:10). [2] For millennia our ancestors prayed for restoration of the Jewish homeland. That we live in an age when millions of Jews celebrate Passover in the State of Israel certainly merits joyous dance and song!

[12] *"Next year in Jerusalem"* "There are ten portions of beauty in the world, nine in Jerusalem and one in the rest of the world. There are ten portions of wisdom in the world, nine in the Land of Israel and one in the rest of the world" (*Esther Rabbah* 1:17). Discounting a measure of rabbinic hyperbole, the fact remains that until the nineteenth century, for most Jews, the yearning for return to Jerusalem found fulfillment in prayer rather than tangible action. The warning of Rabbi Chelbo, a third-century sage from the Land of Israel, helps explain why. To a passage from Song of Songs (8:4), "Do not wake or rouse love until it please," he offered the following comment: Israel "should not attempt to go up from the diaspora by means of their own force. For if they do, why should the king messiah come to gather the exiles of Israel?" (*Song of Songs Rabbah* 2:20). This view illustrates a traditional resistance that Zionists have had to overcome.

———◆———

BALIN (MODERN HAGGADOT)

L'shono h'abo b'nai Chorin,

Next year may we all be the children of freedom. [2]

For Elie Wiesel, Nobel laureate and premier advocate for preserving the memories of the Holocaust, the final line of the Seder serves as a call to remember and review the tragedies of the Jewish people:

This article of faith, this song of hope which reverberates from century to century ... from massacre to massacre, is restated here tonight. Jews are being murdered again? Next year the killing will stop. Jews are again being starved and persecuted? Next year the story of their persecution will be told. Always next year. Next year in Jerusalem. [3]

Am Yisrael Hai ("The people Israel lives") is the provocative title of a Haggadah published in South Africa in 1981. It is a paean to the State of Israel, represented in its pages as the embodiment of the undying spirit of the Jewish people. The seven-branched menorah, the state symbol, appears on every page with the caption "*am yisrael hai.*" On the title page is the prescient statement of Theodor Herzl:

> In Basel [at the first Zionist Congress, 1897], I established the Jewish state. If I were to say that aloud today, universal laughter would be the response. Maybe in five years, certainly in fifty, everybody will recognize it. If you will it, it will not turn out to be fiction.[4]

While the traditional text of the Haggadah is intact, sketches of coins of ancient Israel, of Zionist and Israeli leaders, and of scenes of Israeli life are sprinkled throughout. Under a photograph of the *Kotel* (the Western Wall), a caption reads: "In our days—the beginning of redemption."[5]

Though triumphant in tone, the Haggadah recalls as well Jewish degradation. Two snapshots appearing among the final pages of *Am Yisrael Hai* speak eloquently of the cycle of servitude and redemption: the first shows throngs of South Africans gathered at the annual Mourning Assembly in Memory of Six Million Martyrs at the West-Park Cemetery Monument in Johannesburg. The second displays a pilot of one of the Israeli Air Force C135 planes on its return from Entebbe with released hostages. Make no mistake about it, according to the aptly titled *Am Yisrael Hai*, Jews throughout time have triumphed over adversity, as first told in the Haggadah of old.

◆

BRETTLER (OUR BIBLICAL HERITAGE)

Numbers 9:14; however, the order of the terms in question is reversed: "And when a stranger who resides with you would offer a Passover sacrifice to Adonai, he must offer it in accordance with the rules and laws of the Passover sacrifice."

[11] *"Pure One"* Although the term *zach* is used in the Bible in reference to people and oil, it is never used of God.

[11] *"Home"* In biblical Hebrew, the feminine *m'onah* refers to a wild animal's lair; in medieval Hebrew, it is used as a synonym for the masculine *ma'on*, which in the Bible also means "a home," or "the heaven" as God's home.

[11] *"Uncountable assembly"* The Hebrew, *mi manah*, is a reference to Balaam's oracle in Numbers 23:10, "Who can count [*mi manah*] the dust of Jacob, / Number the dust-cloud of Israel?" It thus functions here as a name for Israel.

[11] *"Vineyard plants"* Also referring to Israel, based on Psalm 80:16, "the stock planted by Your right hand."

[11] *"Redeemed to Zion in joy"* A paraphrase of Isaiah 35:10 and 51:11: "And the ransomed of Adonai shall return, / And come with shouting to Zion, / Crowned with joy everlasting."

[12] *"Next year in Jerusalem"* Although the previous poem is mostly a paraphrase of biblical verses, this wish has no biblical precedent, in part because much of the Bible was written when Israel was in its land. This sentiment here is not a generic wish for restoration, but is likely connected specifically to the Passover celebration, since a fully proper commemoration can only occur in Jerusalem, with a restored Temple, where the paschal lamb may be eaten. It is thus different in tone and meaning than the request at the beginning of the seder, in the *Ha lachma anya*, to enjoy next Passover as free people in Israel—there the freedom is emphasized, while here, as in "From the *zevachs* and the *pesachs*" (see *My People's Passover Haggadah*, Volume 2, p. 120) the wish is for cultic restoration.

———◆———

GILLMAN (THEOLOGICALLY SPEAKING)

prophets, the dream of a return to Zion was an intrinsic part of the vision of the end of days. Jewish eschatology (from the Greek, *eschaton*, "the last events," and *logos*, "the study of") at its richest includes three dimensions: a universal dimension, what will happen to the world as a whole (the end of warfare, social justice, and the worship of God by all peoples); a national dimension, what will happen to the Jewish people (the end of the exile and the rebuilding of the Temple); and a personal dimension, what will happen to the individual person (the resurrection of the dead and the final judgment). We saw how that national dimension appeared earlier in Rabbi Akiva's version of the redemption benediction before the festive meal. It appears once again in this exclamation.

The return to Zion was the centerpiece of the national dimension from the time of the first exile after the destruction of the First Temple. It became central once again after the destruction of the Second Temple at the hands of Rome. That second, more extended exile ended with the creation of the modern State of Israel, though many Jews had in fact returned to settle there in the pre-state years.

But why do we continue to conclude our Seder with this exclamation? For centuries, our ancestors could claim that they were not free to return, and the words constituted a prayer. Now however, most of us who are not in Jerusalem choose not to be. Why then do we continue to use this formula, and further, why do those Jews who have settled in Jerusalem continue to recite it?

One possible answer to both questions is that the phrase has been altered by the addition of one word so that the exclamation becomes, "Next year in Jerusalem rebuilt!" (in Hebrew, *Y'rushalayim hab'nuiah*). That reworded statement expresses the hope that one day in the future, Jerusalem may be a flourishing city where its diverse populations could live in peace with one another. That's the Jerusalem we yearn to return to.

But others continue to use the ancient formula and understand it in its original sense as an eschatological vision. It's not the current, living city of Jerusalem that we dream of but rather the heavenly Jerusalem, the Jerusalem of the mystics who posited an idealized Jerusalem poised above and parallel to the earthly Jerusalem. Only in the age to come, after the coming of the messiah, will the heavenly Jerusalem merge with and become identical to the earthly Jerusalem. When we exclaim, "Next year in Jerusalem!" it is this event that we anticipate.

Note that we also conclude the liturgy of the *N'illah* ("Concluding") service at the end of Yom Kippur with the very same exclamation. In both instances, the reference is to the ultimate redemption to come. At the end of Yom Kippur, we are cleansed of our sins, and at the end of the Seder, we are once again free from Egyptian bondage, whatever the political realities in which the community labors. Both are redemptive moments—one for the individual, the second, the Seder, for the community.

——◆——

J. HOFFMAN (TRANSLATION)

preserve that literary device in our translation.

[2] *"Produce"* Hebrew, *t'nuvah*, a biblical word. In 1926, young pioneers in Israel chose the name *t'nuvah* for the name of their food-distribution cooperative. It has since become Israel's largest food manufacturer.

[2] *"Precious"* Or "desirable."

[2] *"Bountiful"* Others, "good." But while *tov* can mean "good," immediately below we find that our ancestors (or maybe us) "eat of its *tov*." "Bounty" fits.

[2] *"To eat of its fruit"* It's not entirely clear who is doing the eating. It may be "our ancestors," or it may be "us." We would prefer to translate "that we might ..." (or "that they might ..."), but we don't want to wrongly limit the meaning of the Hebrew.

[2] *"Enjoy"* Literally, "sate." Once again, we would prefer something along the lines of "that we might eat our fill...," but without knowing who is doing the eating, we are forced to translate loosely to avoid the nearly ungrammatical "to sate oneself...."

[3] *"Have mercy"* Or "love."

[3] *"On"* Hebrew, *al*, the same word we translated as "for," above (Volume 2, p. 189).

[4] *"Bring us back up"* Literally, "raise us." We add "back," as we frequently do.

[4] *"Let us be happy"* Others, "gladden us," which seem too stilted to us. The other possibility is "make us happy."

[5] *"Are and do good"* Translated more or less literally. The first word, *tov*, is the one translated in verse 2 as "bounty." Here the word clearly means just "good." As for "do

good," we might prefer "do well," but the verb in Hebrew comes from the root "good," and we want to preserve the similarity.

"Acceptance" While our translation captures the point of the Hebrew, it is awkward in a way that the simple Hebrew *nirtsah* is not.

[8] *"Celebration"* Or "Seder." *Seder*, in Hebrew, means "order." (See also *My People's Passover Haggadah*, Volume 1, "The Checking of Leaven," p. 94.) The related verb *sider* means "(to) order," and the noun from that verb is *sidur*, "ordering." (The prayer book is called a Siddur because it puts the prayers in order.) We choose "celebration" here, though, because we will need "celebrate" in the next line.

[8] *"Appropriately"* Or "according to its halakhah."

[10] *"Celebrate"* Hebrew, *l'sader*. See above, "celebration."

[11] *"Your home"* Literally, "at home." The Hebrew here, *ma'on*, probably alludes to *m'on betekha*, which in turn is a somewhat cryptic reference to the Temple.

[11] *"Lift up"* Hebrew, *komem*. The related adjective, *kom'miyut*, "upright," appears only in Leviticus 26:13: "I am Adonai your God who brought you out of the Land of Egypt … and I helped you walk *kom'miyut*." The *komem* here, then, obliquely refers to the Exodus from Egypt. This is the first of three oblique references that reveal a hidden message in the poem.

[11] *"Uncountable"* Hebrew, "who can count?" The syntax is odd here. The phrase itself appears in Balaam's first blessing of Israel, in Numbers 23:10. It thereby obliquely references a curse turning into a blessing. This is actually the third oblique reference, although it appears second in our translation, because English, unlike Hebrew, puts adjectives before the nouns they modify.

[11] *"Assembly"* Hebrew, *adat*, but many versions read, *k'hal adat*, that is, "assembly of the congregation [of]." The phrase appears twice in the Bible; the first appearance, in Exodus 12:6, is in the context of the laws instituting the Passover celebration. This is the second oblique reference, though (see above) it appears third in English. Taken together, the three oblique references—"lift up," "assembly," and finally "uncountable"—reflect the Exodus from Egypt, then Passover, and finally turning curse into a blessing. This beautiful progression creates a most wonderfully poetic conclusion to the Passover Seder.

[11] *"Vineyard plants"* We see this imagery in Psalm 80, where the "vineyard planted by [God's] right hand" is the people of Israel. The common Shabbat song *D'ror Yikra* (see *My People's Prayer Book*, Volume 7, *Shabbat at Home*, p. 127), though using different vocabulary, similarly envisions redemption through the metaphor of planting a vine in a vineyard.

[11] *"Redeemed to Zion"* Or "Redeemed for Zion."

L. HOFFMAN (HISTORY)

other than bread. (The usual *Birkat Hamazon* occurs after our meal, which ends with a final piece of bread, the *afikoman*, *My People's Passover Haggadah*, Volume 2, p. 115.)

This final blessing once constituted the end of the Seder. In the Middle Ages, other things were tacked on: a "second" conclusion ("The Passover celebration has concluded appropriately" and "Next year in Jerusalem," which follow; see below); and some optional afterdinner songs.

⁸ *"The Passover celebration has concluded appropriately"* This is a stanza from a liturgical poem composed for *Shabbat Hagadol*, the Shabbat preceding Passover, when it was customary to review all the necessary Halakhah pertinent to the holiday. The author was Joseph Tov Elem, an eleventh-century French halakhist and poet, known also by his French name, Joseph Bonfils (Tov Elem and Bonfils mean the same thing—"good youth"). Depending on local practice, it is now said either where we have it here, or after the concluding songs that follow.

It entered the Seder in the fourteenth century, as an expression of hope that having celebrated our Seder in perfect order, we will merit being allowed to sacrifice the Passover offering in perfect form in a Temple rebuilt. Technically, the prayer is called *Nirtsah*, meaning "accepted," a reference to Passover's beginnings as a sacrifice; like the *pesach* itself, our Seder too, we hope, is "accepted" by God.

The poem implies that the reason our Seder is accepted is that we have done it in the right order. Ritual depends on order, of course, and certainly the sacrificial system of antiquity was heavily prescribed as to order. But why, precisely in the eleventh century, did someone write a poem for the Shabbat before the Seder designed to guarantee that the Seder be conducted in proper order? This is the same period when our familiar mnemonic *Kadesh urchats ...* was composed (see "*Kadesh urchats* ['Sanctify and wash']," *My People's Passover Haggadah*, Volume 1, p. 107). And that was not the only mnemonic to be written then; there were others, including one by Joseph Tov Elem himself.

This virtual obsession with order again betrays the close-knit cultural reliance of Jews and Christians on each other. Christian ritual was rooted in its Jewish origins. In the Middle Ages, influence went in the opposite direction. For example, the wafer-like substance used as the eucharistic host became identified as Jesus' actual body; people consumed it with great care that no crumbs fell to the floor. So Jews ate their *afikoman* that way, as eating it became equivalent to a sacramental rite. As the wafer stood for Jesus, so the *afikoman* began to stand for the messiah—its being "hidden away" *(tsafun)* was taken as the messiah remaining in hiding until the right moment.

Part of the turn to what is almost a magical identification of symbols with what they stand for was a certain compulsion to make sure every little detail of using them was done properly, lest the "magic" fail. The obsession with proper order fit the larger religious environment that emphasized proper detail lest the deeper purposes of the ritual fail.

12 *"Next year in Jerusalem"* It is hard to say when this hope to be returned to Jerusalem was composed, but the first evidence of it in the Haggadah comes from the fourteenth century. By the fifteenth century, Rabbi Sholom of Austria calls it "customary." It was a fitting conclusion to the last line of the *Nirtsah* prayer, "Draw near and lead the vineyard plants, redeemed to Zion in joy."

———◆———

LANDES (HALAKHAH)

lifting the poor and the powerless out of their bondage to poverty, fear, and depression. Such I have learned from my parents, grandparents, and teachers, and so I transmit to my children, and God willing to theirs, and to my students. And that is my blessing for all of us.

————◆ ◆ ◆————

17. FOUR SEDER SONGS

A. *Ki Lo Na'eh, Ki Lo Ya'eh* ("For It Fits and Befits Him")

כִּי לוֹ נָאֶה. כִּי לוֹ יָאֶה:

[1] Mighty in majesty, chosen in truth, His troops will tell Him,

(Refrain:) [2] "You and You; You, yes, You; You, indeed, You; You Adonai, are royal. For it fits and befits Him."

[3] Preeminent in majesty, glorious in truth, His dedicated will tell Him …

[4] Pure in majesty, potent in truth, His servants will tell Him …

[5] Unique in majesty, great in truth, His students will tell Him …

[6] Ruling in majesty, revered in truth, His attendants will tell Him …

[7] Humble in majesty, redeemer in truth, His righteous will tell Him …

[8] Holy in majesty, merciful in truth, His throngs will tell Him …

[9] Powerful in majesty, sustainer in truth, His upright will tell Him …

[1] אַדִּיר בִּמְלוּכָה. בָּחוּר כַּהֲלָכָה.
גְּדוּדָיו יֹאמְרוּ לוֹ …

[2] לְךָ וּלְךָ. לְךָ כִּי לְךָ. לְךָ אַף לְךָ. לְךָ יְיָ
הַמַּמְלָכָה: כִּי לוֹ נָאֶה. כִּי לוֹ יָאֶה …

[3] דָּגוּל בִּמְלוּכָה. הָדוּר כַּהֲלָכָה.
וָתִיקָיו יֹאמְרוּ לוֹ …

[4] זַכַּאי בִּמְלוּכָה. חָסִין כַּהֲלָכָה.
טַפְסְרָיו יֹאמְרוּ לוֹ …

[5] יָחִיד בִּמְלוּכָה. כַּבִּיר כַּהֲלָכָה.
לִמּוּדָיו יֹאמְרוּ לוֹ …

[6] מָרוֹם בִּמְלוּכָה. נוֹרָא כַּהֲלָכָה.
סְבִיבָיו יֹאמְרוּ לוֹ …

[7] עָנָו בִּמְלוּכָה. פּוֹדֶה כַּהֲלָכָה.
צַדִּיקָיו יֹאמְרוּ לוֹ …

[8] קָדוֹשׁ בִּמְלוּכָה. רַחוּם כַּהֲלָכָה.
שִׁנְאַנָּיו יֹאמְרוּ לוֹ …

[9] תַּקִּיף בִּמְלוּכָה. תּוֹמֵךְ כַּהֲלָכָה.
תְּמִימָיו יֹאמְרוּ לוֹ …

B. *Adir Hu* ("He Is Mighty")

אַדִּיר הוּא

[10] He is mighty.
(Refrain:) May He soon rebuild His house. Quickly, quickly, soon, in our days. God, rebuild, God, rebuild, soon rebuild Your house.

[10] אַדִּיר הוּא …
יִבְנֶה בֵיתוֹ בְּקָרוֹב. בִּמְהֵרָה. בִּמְהֵרָה.
בְּיָמֵינוּ בְּקָרוֹב. אֵל בְּנֵה. אֵל בְּנֵה. בְּנֵה
בֵיתְךָ בְּקָרוֹב …

[11]He is chosen. He is wonderful. He is preeminent …

11בָּחוּר הוּא. גָּדוֹל הוּא. דָּגוּל הוּא . . .

[12]He is glorious. He is dedicated. He is virtuous …

12הָדוּר הוּא. וָתִיק הוּא. זַכַּאי הוּא . . .

[13]He is loving. He is pure. He is unique …

13חָסִיד הוּא. טָהוֹר הוּא. יָחִיד הוּא . . .

[14]He is great. He is wise. He is king …

14כַּבִּיר הוּא. לָמוּד הוּא. מֶלֶךְ הוּא . . .

[15]He is revered. He is exalted. He is strong …

15נָאוֹר הוּא. סַגִּיב הוּא. עִזּוּז הוּא . . .

[16]He is redeeming. He is righteous. He is holy …

16פּוֹדֶה הוּא. צַדִּיק הוּא. קָדוֹשׁ הוּא . . .

[17]He is merciful. He is almighty. He is powerful …

17רַחוּם הוּא. שַׁדַּי הוּא. תַּקִּיף הוּא . . .

c. *Echad Mi Yode'a?* ("Who Knows One?")

אֶחָד מִי יוֹדֵעַ?

[18]Who knows one? I know one. One is our God in heaven and on earth.

18אֶחָד מִי יוֹדֵעַ? אֶחָד אֲנִי יוֹדֵעַ. אֶחָד אֱלֹהֵינוּ שֶׁבַּשָּׁמַיִם וּבָאָרֶץ:

[19]Who knows two? I know two. Two is the tablets of the covenant. One is our God in heaven and on earth.

19שְׁנַיִם מִי יוֹדֵעַ? שְׁנַיִם אֲנִי יוֹדֵעַ. שְׁנֵי לֻחוֹת הַבְּרִית. אֶחָד אֱלֹהֵינוּ שֶׁבַּשָּׁמַיִם וּבָאָרֶץ:

[20]Who knows three? I know three. Three is the patriarchs. Two is the tablets of the covenant. One is our God in heaven and on earth.

20שְׁלֹשָׁה מִי יוֹדֵעַ? שְׁלֹשָׁה אֲנִי יוֹדֵעַ. שְׁלֹשָׁה אָבוֹת. שְׁנֵי לֻחוֹת הַבְּרִית. אֶחָד אֱלֹהֵינוּ שֶׁבַּשָּׁמַיִם וּבָאָרֶץ:

21Who knows four? I know four. Four is the matriarchs. Three is the patriarchs. Two is the tablets of the covenant. One is our God in heaven and on earth.

21אַרְבַּע מִי יוֹדֵעַ? אַרְבַּע אֲנִי יוֹדֵעַ. אַרְבַּע אִמָּהוֹת. שְׁלֹשָׁה אָבוֹת. שְׁנֵי לֻחוֹת הַבְּרִית. אֶחָד אֱלֹהֵינוּ שֶׁבַּשָּׁמַיִם וּבָאָרֶץ:

22Who knows five? I know five. Five is the books of the Torah. Four is the matriarchs. Three is the patriarchs. Two is the tablets of the covenant. One is our God in heaven and on earth.

22חֲמִשָּׁה מִי יוֹדֵעַ? חֲמִשָּׁה אֲנִי יוֹדֵעַ. חֲמִשָּׁה חֻמְשֵׁי תוֹרָה. אַרְבַּע אִמָּהוֹת. שְׁלֹשָׁה אָבוֹת. שְׁנֵי לֻחוֹת הַבְּרִית. אֶחָד אֱלֹהֵינוּ שֶׁבַּשָּׁמַיִם וּבָאָרֶץ:

23Who knows six? I know six. Six is the orders of the Mishnah. Five is the books of the Torah. Four is the matriarchs. Three is the patriarchs. Two is the tablets of the covenant. One is our God in heaven and on earth.

23שִׁשָּׁה מִי יוֹדֵעַ? שִׁשָּׁה אֲנִי יוֹדֵעַ. שִׁשָּׁה סִדְרֵי מִשְׁנָה. חֲמִשָּׁה חֻמְשֵׁי תוֹרָה. אַרְבַּע אִמָּהוֹת. שְׁלֹשָׁה אָבוֹת. שְׁנֵי לֻחוֹת הַבְּרִית. אֶחָד אֱלֹהֵינוּ שֶׁבַּשָּׁמַיִם וּבָאָרֶץ:

24Who knows seven? I know seven. Seven is the days of the week. Six is the orders of the Mishnah. Five is the books of the Torah. Four is the matriarchs. Three is the patriarchs. Two is the tablets of the covenant. One is our God in heaven and on earth.

24שִׁבְעָה מִי יוֹדֵעַ? שִׁבְעָה אֲנִי יוֹדֵעַ. שִׁבְעָה יְמֵי שַׁבַּתָּא. שִׁשָּׁה סִדְרֵי מִשְׁנָה. חֲמִשָּׁה חֻמְשֵׁי תוֹרָה. אַרְבַּע אִמָּהוֹת. שְׁלֹשָׁה אָבוֹת. שְׁנֵי לֻחוֹת הַבְּרִית. אֶחָד אֱלֹהֵינוּ שֶׁבַּשָּׁמַיִם וּבָאָרֶץ:

25Who knows eight? I know eight. Eight is days of circumcision. Seven is the days of the week. Six is the orders of the Mishnah. Five is the books of the Torah. Four is the matriarchs. Three is the patriarchs. Two is the tablets of the covenant. One is our God in heaven and on earth.

25שְׁמוֹנָה מִי יוֹדֵעַ? שְׁמוֹנָה אֲנִי יוֹדֵעַ. שְׁמוֹנָה יְמֵי מִילָה. שִׁבְעָה יְמֵי שַׁבַּתָּא. שִׁשָּׁה סִדְרֵי מִשְׁנָה. חֲמִשָּׁה חֻמְשֵׁי תוֹרָה. אַרְבַּע אִמָּהוֹת. שְׁלֹשָׁה אָבוֹת. שְׁנֵי לֻחוֹת הַבְּרִית. אֶחָד אֱלֹהֵינוּ שֶׁבַּשָּׁמַיִם וּבָאָרֶץ:

26Who knows nine? I know nine. Nine is the months of birth. Eight is days of circumcision. Seven is the days of the week. Six is the orders of the Mishnah. Five is the books of the Torah. Four is the matriarchs. Three is the patriarchs. Two is the tablets of the covenant. One is our God in heaven and on earth.

²⁶תִּשְׁעָה מִי יוֹדֵעַ? תִּשְׁעָה אֲנִי יוֹדֵעַ. תִּשְׁעָה יַרְחֵי לֵדָה. שְׁמוֹנָה יְמֵי מִילָה. שִׁבְעָה יְמֵי שַׁבַּתָּא. שִׁשָּׁה סִדְרֵי מִשְׁנָה. חֲמִשָּׁה חֻמְשֵׁי תוֹרָה. אַרְבַּע אִמָּהוֹת. שְׁלֹשָׁה אָבוֹת. שְׁנֵי לֻחוֹת הַבְּרִית. אֶחָד אֱלֹהֵינוּ שֶׁבַּשָּׁמַיִם וּבָאָרֶץ:

27Who knows ten? I know ten. Ten is the commandments. Nine is the months of birth. Eight is days of circumcision. Seven is the days of the week. Six is the orders of the Mishnah. Five is the books of the Torah. Four is the matriarchs. Three is the patriarchs. Two is the tablets of the covenant. One is our God in heaven and on earth.

²⁷עֲשָׂרָה מִי יוֹדֵעַ? עֲשָׂרָה אֲנִי יוֹדֵעַ. עֲשָׂרָה דִבְּרַיָּא. תִּשְׁעָה יַרְחֵי לֵדָה. שְׁמוֹנָה יְמֵי מִילָה. שִׁבְעָה יְמֵי שַׁבַּתָּא. שִׁשָּׁה סִדְרֵי מִשְׁנָה. חֲמִשָּׁה חֻמְשֵׁי תוֹרָה. אַרְבַּע אִמָּהוֹת. שְׁלֹשָׁה אָבוֹת. שְׁנֵי לֻחוֹת הַבְּרִית. אֶחָד אֱלֹהֵינוּ שֶׁבַּשָּׁמַיִם וּבָאָרֶץ:

28Who knows eleven? I know eleven. Eleven is the stars. Ten is the commandments. Nine is the months of birth. Eight is days of circumcision. Seven is the days of the week. Six is the orders of the Mishnah. Five is the books of the Torah. Four is the matriarchs. Three is the patriarchs. Two is the tablets of the covenant. One is our God in heaven and on earth.

²⁸אַחַד עָשָׂר מִי יוֹדֵעַ? אַחַד עָשָׂר אֲנִי יוֹדֵעַ. אַחַד עָשָׂר כּוֹכְבַיָּא. עֲשָׂרָה דִבְּרַיָּא. תִּשְׁעָה יַרְחֵי לֵדָה. שְׁמוֹנָה יְמֵי מִילָה. שִׁבְעָה יְמֵי שַׁבַּתָּא. שִׁשָּׁה סִדְרֵי מִשְׁנָה. חֲמִשָּׁה חֻמְשֵׁי תוֹרָה. אַרְבַּע אִמָּהוֹת. שְׁלֹשָׁה אָבוֹת. שְׁנֵי לֻחוֹת הַבְּרִית. אֶחָד אֱלֹהֵינוּ שֶׁבַּשָּׁמַיִם וּבָאָרֶץ:

29Who knows twelve? I know twelve. Twelve is the tribes. Eleven is the stars. Ten is the commandments. Nine is the months of birth. Eight is days of circumcision. Seven is the days of the week. Six is the orders of the Mishnah.

²⁹שְׁנֵים עָשָׂר מִי יוֹדֵעַ? שְׁנֵים עָשָׂר אֲנִי יוֹדֵעַ. שְׁנֵים עָשָׂר שִׁבְטַיָּא. אַחַד עָשָׂר כּוֹכְבַיָּא. עֲשָׂרָה דִבְּרַיָּא. תִּשְׁעָה יַרְחֵי לֵדָה. שְׁמוֹנָה יְמֵי מִילָה. שִׁבְעָה יְמֵי שַׁבַּתָּא. שִׁשָּׁה סִדְרֵי מִשְׁנָה.

Five is the books of the Torah. Four is the matriarchs. Three is the patriarchs. Two is the tablets of the covenant. One is our God in heaven and on earth.

חֲמִשָּׁה חֻמְשֵׁי תוֹרָה. אַרְבַּע אִמָּהוֹת. שְׁלֹשָׁה אָבוֹת. שְׁנֵי לֻחוֹת הַבְּרִית. אֶחָד אֱלֹהֵינוּ שֶׁבַּשָּׁמַיִם וּבָאָרֶץ:

[30]שְׁלֹשָׁה עָשָׂר מִי יוֹדֵעַ? שְׁלֹשָׁה עָשָׂר אֲנִי יוֹדֵעַ. שְׁלֹשָׁה עָשָׂר מִדַּיָּא. שְׁנֵים עָשָׂר שִׁבְטַיָּא. אַחַד עָשָׂר כּוֹכְבַיָּא. עֲשָׂרָה דִבְּרַיָּא. תִּשְׁעָה יַרְחֵי לֵדָה. שְׁמוֹנָה יְמֵי מִילָה. שִׁבְעָה יְמֵי שַׁבַּתָּא. שִׁשָּׁה סִדְרֵי מִשְׁנָה. חֲמִשָּׁה חֻמְשֵׁי תוֹרָה. אַרְבַּע אִמָּהוֹת. שְׁלֹשָׁה אָבוֹת. שְׁנֵי לֻחוֹת הַבְּרִית. אֶחָד אֱלֹהֵינוּ שֶׁבַּשָּׁמַיִם וּבָאָרֶץ:

[30]Who knows thirteen? I know thirteen. Thirteen is the attributes. Twelve is the tribes. Eleven is the stars. Ten is the commandments. Nine is the months of birth. Eight is days of circumcision. Seven is the days of the week. Six is the orders of the Mishnah. Five is the books of the Torah. Four is the matriarchs. Three is the patriarchs. Two is the tablets of the covenant. One is our God in heaven and on earth.

חַד גַּדְיָא

D. *Chad Gadya* ("One Kid")

[31]One kid, one kid that father bought for two *zuzim*; *one kid, one kid*.

[31]חַד גַּדְיָא חַד גַּדְיָא. דְּזַבִּן אַבָּא בִּתְרֵי זוּזֵי. חַד גַּדְיָא חַד גַּדְיָא:

[32]The cat came and ate the kid that father bought for two *zuzim*; *one kid, one kid*.

[32]וְאָתָא שֻׁנְרָא וְאָכַל לְגַדְיָא. דְּזַבִּן אַבָּא בִּתְרֵי זוּזֵי. חַד גַּדְיָא חַד גַּדְיָא:

[33]The dog came and bit the cat that ate the kid that father bought for two *zuzim*; *one kid, one kid*.

[33]וְאָתָא כַלְבָּא. וְנָשַׁךְ לְשֻׁנְרָא. דְּאָכַל לְגַדְיָא. דְּזַבִּן אַבָּא בִּתְרֵי זוּזֵי. חַד גַּדְיָא חַד גַּדְיָא:

[34]The stick came and beat the dog that bit the cat that ate the kid that father bought for two *zuzim*; *one kid, one kid*.

[34]וְאָתָא חוּטְרָא. וְהִכָּה לְכַלְבָּא. דְּנָשַׁךְ לְשֻׁנְרָא. דְּאָכַל לְגַדְיָא. דְּזַבִּן אַבָּא בִּתְרֵי זוּזֵי. חַד גַּדְיָא חַד גַּדְיָא:

35The fire came and burned the stick that beat the dog that bit the cat that ate the kid that father bought for two *zuzim*; *one kid, one kid.*

³⁵וְאָתָא נוּרָא. וְשָׂרַף לְחוּטְרָא. דְּהִכָּה לְכַלְבָּא. דְּנָשַׁךְ לְשֻׁנְרָא. דְּאָכַל לְגַדְיָא. דְּזַבַּן אַבָּא בִּתְרֵי זוּזֵי. חַד גַּדְיָא חַד גַּדְיָא:

36The water came and quenched the fire that burned the stick that beat the dog that bit the cat that ate the kid that father bought for two *zuzim*; *one kid, one kid.*

³⁶וְאָתָא מַיָּא. וְכָבָה לְנוּרָא. דְּשָׂרַף לְחוּטְרָא. דְּהִכָּה לְכַלְבָּא. דְּנָשַׁךְ לְשֻׁנְרָא. דְּאָכַל לְגַדְיָא. דְּזַבַּן אַבָּא בִּתְרֵי זוּזֵי. חַד גַּדְיָא חַד גַּדְיָא:

37The ox came and drank the water that quenched the fire that burned the stick that beat the dog that bit the cat that ate the kid that father bought for two *zuzim*; *one kid, one kid.*

³⁷וְאָתָא תוֹרָא. וְשָׁתָה לְמַיָּא. דְּכָבָה לְנוּרָא. דְּשָׂרַף לְחוּטְרָא. דְּהִכָּה לְכַלְבָּא. דְּנָשַׁךְ לְשֻׁנְרָא. דְּאָכַל לְגַדְיָא. דְּזַבַּן אַבָּא בִּתְרֵי זוּזֵי. חַד גַּדְיָא חַד גַּדְיָא:

38The slaughterer came and slaughtered the ox that drank the water that quenched the fire that burned the stick that beat the dog that bit the cat that ate the kid that father bought for two *zuzim*; *one kid, one kid.*

³⁸וְאָתָא הַשּׁוֹחֵט. וְשָׁחַט לְתוֹרָא. דְּשָׁתָה לְמַיָּא. דְּכָבָה לְנוּרָא. דְּשָׂרַף לְחוּטְרָא. דְּהִכָּה לְכַלְבָּא. דְּנָשַׁךְ לְשֻׁנְרָא. דְּאָכַל לְגַדְיָא. דְּזַבַּן אַבָּא בִּתְרֵי זוּזֵי. חַד גַּדְיָא חַד גַּדְיָא:

39The Angel of Death came and slaughtered the slaughterer that slaughtered the ox that drank the water that quenched the fire that burned the stick that beat the dog that bit the cat that ate the kid that father bought for two *zuzim*; *one kid, one kid.*

³⁹וְאָתָא מַלְאַךְ הַמָּוֶת. וְשָׁחַט לַשּׁוֹחֵט. דְּשָׁחַט לְתוֹרָא. דְּשָׁתָה לְמַיָּא. דְּכָבָה לְנוּרָא. דְּשָׂרַף לְחוּטְרָא. דְּהִכָּה לְכַלְבָּא. דְּנָשַׁךְ לְשֻׁנְרָא. דְּאָכַל לְגַדְיָא. דְּזַבַּן אַבָּא בִּתְרֵי זוּזֵי. חַד גַּדְיָא חַד גַּדְיָא:

40The Holy One of blessing came and slaughtered the Angel of Death who came and slaughtered the slaughterer that slaughtered the ox that drank the water that quenched the fire that burned the stick that beat the dog that bit the cat that ate the kid that father bought for two *zuzim*; one kid, one kid.

40וְאָתָא הַקָּדוֹשׁ בָּרוּךְ הוּא. וְשָׁחַט לְמַלְאָךְ הַמָּוֶת. דְּשָׁחַט לְשׁוֹחֵט. דְּשָׁחַט לְתוֹרָא. דְּשָׁתָה לְמַיָּא. דְּכָבָה לְנוּרָא. דְּשָׂרַף לְחוּטְרָא. דְּהִכָּה לְכַלְבָּא. דְּנָשַׁךְ לְשׁוּנְרָא. דְּאָכַל לְגַדְיָא. דְּזַבַּן אַבָּא בִּתְרֵי זוּזֵי. חַד גַּדְיָא חַד גַּדְיָא:

בַּח וְהוֹדָיָה
הַלֵּל וְזִמְרָה
נֵצַח וּגְדֻלָּה
פְּרוֹמוֹשֶׁן וּסְטְרַײְפִּים
לְחַכְמֵי הַבִּשּׁוּל בַּ-524
הַהוֹפְכִים
אֶג-פָּאוֹדֶר לְצַפִּיחַת בִּדְבַשׁ,
סַרְדִינִים לְלִוְיָתָן
בּוּלִי-בִּיף' לְשׁוֹר-הַבָּר
וְקַפּ-אוֹפּ-טִי' לְיַיִן הַמְשׁוּמָר

The "Messianic" Meal
Haggadah, Surveyors Battalion 524 of the Land of Israel, Italy, 1946
"Praise, veneration and melody, eternity and greatness [paraphrasing Yishtabach—see My People's Passover Haggadah, Volume 2, p. 174], promotion and stripes to the Ingenious Ones of Cuisine of the 524th [Surveyors Battalion] who transformed egg powder into 'wafers made with honey' [Exod. 16:31, i.e., manna], sardines into the Leviathan [a mythic fish that legend reserves for the messianic meal that God will prepare for the righteous], Bully Beef [canned beef rations] into the Wild Ox [another mythic beast for the messianic meal], and a cup of tea into preserved wine [yayin ham'shumar, wine said to be preserved in its grapes since the six days of creation for the righteous in the world to come]."
Collection of Stephen P. Durchslag

תפריט

מנה ראשונה

דגים

מרק

בשר ותוספות

לפתן

קנוח סעודה

Menu
Haggadah, Surveyors Battalion 524 of the Land of Israel, Italy, 1946
Yiddish and Hebrew:
"First Course—A hardboiled egg with original Portuguese
sardines and various vegetables.
Fish—Gefilte fish just like in your mother's home.
Soup—Hot broth with pesachdikeh k'neidlech.
Meat and Accompaniments—Roasted wild ox (only for the righteous and newly religious)
with fried potatoes and many assorted greens.
Compote—Compote with ice cream.
Dessert—A holiday home-style tart, kosher for Passover, even to the highest standards, with
fragrant black coffee."
Collection of Stephen P. Durchslag

ARNOW (THE WORLD OF MIDRASH)

[2] *"You Adonai, are royal"* A midrashic reading alludes to God's struggle against evil. The Talmud applies 1 Chronicles 29:11, "You Adonai, are royal," *l'kha Adonai hamamlakhah,*[1] to God's ultimate victory over Amalek. We learn that "Adonai will be at war with Amalek throughout the ages" (Exod. 17:16).[2] So long as evil, the seed of Amalek, remains in the world, God's rule will not be complete.[3]

[10] *"Rebuild, soon rebuild Your house"* According to *Tanna D'vei Eliyahu,* as a reward for Israel's great faith, God makes the angels wait to praise God until after Israel has done so. God explains that despite their human frailties *(p. 214)*

BALIN (MODERN HAGGADOT)

"Echad Mi Yode'a? [Who Knows One?]" Since the founding of the American Jewish Historical Society in 1892, Jews have attempted to demonstrate their patriotism by accentuating the achievements of those co-religionists who exerted themselves on behalf of liberty and justice for all. No better example exists than *The Bicentennial Passover Haggadah* issued in commemoration of the two hundredth anniversary of the founding of the United States, which (among other gems) contains an updated version of *Echad Mi Yode'a?* called a "Bicentennial Ballad" with the following lyrics: *(p. 215)*

BRETTLER (OUR BIBLICAL HERITAGE)

"Ki Lo Na'eh Ki Lo Ya'eh [For It Fits and Befits Him]" This poem is a triple acrostic, that is, an alphabet poem. (See *My People's Prayer Book,* Volume 3, P'sukei D'zimrah,* p. 116.) Since there are 22 letters in the Hebrew alphabet, the final letter *tav* is used three times, since 24 (= 22 + 2 additional uses of *tav*) is divisible by 3. The third phrase of each stanza notes various heavenly or earthly groups that praise God; on heavenly groups, see the description in Isaiah 6, where seraphs recite "Holy, holy, holy is the Lord of hosts. The whole *(p. 217)*

17. FOUR SEDER SONGS

A. *Ki Lo Na'eh, Ki Lo Ya'eh* ("For It Fits and Befits Him")

[1]Mighty in majesty, chosen in truth,
His troops will tell Him,
(Refrain:) [2]*"You and You; You, yes, You; You, indeed, You; You Adonai, are royal. For it fits and befits Him."*
[3]Preeminent in majesty, glorious in truth,
His dedicated will tell Him …
[4]Pure in majesty, potent in truth,
His servants will tell Him …

GILLMAN (THEOLOGICALLY SPEAKING)

[40]*"Slaughtered the Angel of Death"* It is thoroughly appropriate that we conclude the celebration of our festival of redemption with the ultimate redemption, the redemption from death. Not for a moment should we believe that this song is introduced into the Haggadah only to keep the children awake to the end. Its message is properly theological: God's power is ultimate. God is even more powerful than death. *(p. 217)*

J. HOFFMAN (TRANSLATION)

"For It Fits and Befits Him" Literally, *"Ki it is na'eh* to Him and it is *ya'eh* to Him." On *ki*, see below, "Yes." *Na'eh* and *ya'eh* are near synonyms, both meaning roughly "befitting, appropriate, proper," etc. They rhyme and sound similar in Hebrew, so we try to find words in English that likewise rhyme and sound similar. We are lucky that "fit" and "befit" come pretty close. (We would prefer it if there were a word, say, "git," that meant the same thing as "fit," but we are not so lucky as that.) *(p. 218)*

SIGNPOST: FOUR SEDER SONGS

IN THEORY THE SEDER IS OVER. BUT JEWS HAVE PREFERRED TO LINGER AWHILE, SAVORING FREEDOM. OVER THE CENTURIES, EXTRA SONGS HAVE BEEN ATTACHED TO THE HAGGADAH. WE INCLUDE THE BEST KNOWN OF THEM. CHAD GADYA, THE LAST OF THESE, ENDS WITH ANOTHER VISION OF ULTIMATE HOPE: GOD VANQUISHING THE ANGEL OF DEATH.

כִּי לוֹ נָאֶה. כִּי לוֹ יָאֶה:

אַ֫דִּיר בִּמְלוּכָה. בָּחוּר כַּהֲלָכָה. [1]

גְּדוּדָיו יֹאמְרוּ לוֹ . . . לְךָ וּלְךָ. לְךָ כִּי לְךָ. לְךָ אַף [2] לְךָ. לְךָ יְיָ הַמַּמְלָכָה: כִּי לוֹ נָאֶה. כִּי לוֹ יָאֶה . . .

דָּגוּל בִּמְלוּכָה. הָדוּר כַּהֲלָכָה. [3] וָתִיקָיו יֹאמְרוּ לוֹ . . .

זַכַּאי בִּמְלוּכָה. חָסִין כַּהֲלָכָה. [4] טַפְסְרָיו יֹאמְרוּ לוֹ . . .

L. HOFFMAN (HISTORY)

"Ki Lo Na'eh, Ki Lo Ya'eh [For It Fits and Befits Him]" Our Haggadah follows Ashkenazi tradition in its choice of songs, the first being *Ki Lo Na'eh* ("For It Fits and Befits Him"). Two other songs from antiquity often precede it, however: *Az Rov Nissim* ("Then Many Miracles")—sometimes referred to by its refrain, *Vay'hi ba'chatsi halailah* ("It happened at midnight")— *(p. 221)*

KUSHNER AND POLEN (CHASIDIC VOICES)

"Who Knows One?" Rabbi Ya'akov Yosef of Polnoye *(Toldot Ya'akov Yosef, Vayakhel)* teaches that one who is wise understands that there is nothing in the world that is truly separate from God. Everything is a single unity. The universe and God are (as in the classical image) like a snail "whose garment comes from itself." It wears what it is. The universe in all its fullness is a manifestation of God. And thus, to really speak and comprehend the words "I know one" is not just a child's counting game; it becomes the ultimate theological expression of faith.

First we must understand the unity, then we examine the apparent multiplicity of variegated forms, and finally, we return to a deeper understanding of the great unity. We read in Isaiah 41:4, "I am the first and I am the last." Indeed, atop the kabbalistic *s'firot* tree, the place of *Keter* or *Ein Sof*, and symbolizing still the *(p. 224)*

⁵Unique in majesty, great in truth, His students will tell Him …

יָחִיד בִּמְלוּכָה. **כַּ**בִּיר כַּהֲלָכָה.
לִמּוּדָיו יֹאמְרוּ לוֹ ...

⁶Ruling in majesty, revered in truth, His attendants will tell Him …

מָרוֹם בִּמְלוּכָה. **נוֹ**רָא כַּהֲלָכָה.
סְבִיבָיו יֹאמְרוּ לוֹ ...

⁷Humble in majesty, redeemer in truth, His righteous will tell Him …

עָנָו בִּמְלוּכָה. **פּוֹ**דֶה כַּהֲלָכָה.
צַדִּיקָיו יֹאמְרוּ לוֹ ...

⁸Holy in majesty, merciful in truth, His throngs will tell Him …

קָדוֹשׁ בִּמְלוּכָה. **רַ**חוּם כַּהֲלָכָה.
שִׁנְאַנָּיו יֹאמְרוּ לוֹ ...

⁹Powerful in majesty, sustainer in truth, His upright will tell Him …

תַּקִּיף בִּמְלוּכָה. **תּוֹ**מֵךְ כַּהֲלָכָה.
תְּמִימָיו יֹאמְרוּ לוֹ ...

B. *Adir Hu* ("He Is Mighty")

אַדִּיר הוּא

¹⁰He is mighty.
(Refrain:) May He soon rebuild His house. Quickly, quickly, soon, in our days. God, rebuild, God, rebuild, soon rebuild Your house.

אַדִּיר הוּא ...
יִבְנֶה בֵיתוֹ בְּקָרוֹב. בִּמְהֵרָה. בִּמְהֵרָה.
בְּיָמֵינוּ בְּקָרוֹב. אֵל בְּנֵה. אֵל בְּנֵה. בְּנֵה
בֵיתְךָ בְּקָרוֹב ...

¹¹He is chosen. He is wonderful. He is preeminent …

בָּחוּר הוּא. **גָּ**דוֹל הוּא. **דָּ**גוּל הוּא ...

¹²He is glorious. He is dedicated. He is virtuous …

הָדוּר הוּא. **וָ**תִיק הוּא. **זַ**כַּאי הוּא ...

¹³He is loving. He is pure. He is unique …

חָסִיד הוּא. **טָ**הוֹר הוּא. **יָ**חִיד הוּא ...

¹⁴He is great. He is wise. He is king …

כַּבִּיר הוּא. **לָ**מוּד הוּא. **מֶ**לֶךְ הוּא ...

15He is revered. He is exalted. He is strong …

15נָאוֹר הוּא. סַגִּיב הוּא. עִזּוּז הוּא …

16He is redeeming. He is righteous. He is holy …

16פּוֹדֶה הוּא. צַדִּיק הוּא. קָדוֹשׁ הוּא …

17He is merciful. He is almighty. He is powerful …

17רַחוּם הוּא. שַׁדַּי הוּא. תַּקִּיף הוּא …

c. *Echad Mi Yode'a?*
   ("Who Knows One?")

אֶחָד מִי יוֹדֵעַ?

18Who knows one? I know one. One is our God in heaven and on earth.

18אֶחָד מִי יוֹדֵעַ? אֶחָד אֲנִי יוֹדֵעַ.
אֶחָד אֱלֹהֵינוּ שֶׁבַּשָּׁמַיִם וּבָאָרֶץ:

19Who knows two? I know two. Two is the tablets of the covenant. One is our God in heaven and on earth.

19שְׁנַיִם מִי יוֹדֵעַ? שְׁנַיִם אֲנִי יוֹדֵעַ. שְׁנֵי
לְחוֹת הַבְּרִית. אֶחָד אֱלֹהֵינוּ שֶׁבַּשָּׁמַיִם
וּבָאָרֶץ:

20Who knows three? I know three. Three is the patriarchs. Two is the tablets of the covenant. One is our God in heaven and on earth.

20שְׁלֹשָׁה מִי יוֹדֵעַ? שְׁלֹשָׁה אֲנִי יוֹדֵעַ.
שְׁלֹשָׁה אָבוֹת. שְׁנֵי לְחוֹת הַבְּרִית. אֶחָד
אֱלֹהֵינוּ שֶׁבַּשָּׁמַיִם וּבָאָרֶץ:

21Who knows four? I know four. Four is the matriarchs. Three is the patriarchs. Two is the tablets of the covenant. One is our God in heaven and on earth.

21אַרְבַּע מִי יוֹדֵעַ? אַרְבַּע אֲנִי יוֹדֵעַ.
אַרְבַּע אִמָּהוֹת. שְׁלֹשָׁה אָבוֹת. שְׁנֵי
לְחוֹת הַבְּרִית. אֶחָד אֱלֹהֵינוּ שֶׁבַּשָּׁמַיִם
וּבָאָרֶץ:

22Who knows five? I know five. Five is the books of the Torah. Four is the matriarchs. Three is the patriarchs. Two is the tablets of the covenant. One is our God in heaven and on earth.

22חֲמִשָּׁה מִי יוֹדֵעַ? חֲמִשָּׁה אֲנִי יוֹדֵעַ.
חֲמִשָּׁה חֻמְשֵׁי תוֹרָה. אַרְבַּע אִמָּהוֹת.
שְׁלֹשָׁה אָבוֹת. שְׁנֵי לְחוֹת הַבְּרִית. אֶחָד
אֱלֹהֵינוּ שֶׁבַּשָּׁמַיִם וּבָאָרֶץ:

²³Who knows six? I know six. Six is the orders of the Mishnah. Five is the books of the Torah. Four is the matriarchs. Three is the patriarchs. Two is the tablets of the covenant. One is our God in heaven and on earth.

²⁴Who knows seven? I know seven. Seven is the days of the week. Six is the orders of the Mishnah. Five is the books of the Torah. Four is the matriarchs. Three is the patriarchs. Two is the tablets of the covenant. One is our God in heaven and on earth.

²⁵Who knows eight? I know eight. Eight is days of circumcision. Seven is the days of the week. Six is the orders of the Mishnah. Five is the books of the Torah. Four is the matriarchs. Three is the patriarchs. Two is the tablets of the covenant. One is our God in heaven and on earth.

²⁶Who knows nine? I know nine. Nine is the months of birth. Eight is days of circumcision. Seven is the days of the week. Six is the orders of the Mishnah. Five is the books of the Torah. Four is the matriarchs. Three is the patriarchs. Two is the tablets of the covenant. One is our God in heaven and on earth.

²³שִׁשָּׁה מִי יוֹדֵעַ? שִׁשָּׁה אֲנִי יוֹדֵעַ. שִׁשָּׁה סִדְרֵי מִשְׁנָה. חֲמִשָּׁה חֻמְשֵׁי תוֹרָה. אַרְבַּע אִמָּהוֹת. שְׁלֹשָׁה אָבוֹת. שְׁנֵי לֻחוֹת הַבְּרִית. אֶחָד אֱלֹהֵינוּ שֶׁבַּשָּׁמַיִם וּבָאָרֶץ:

²⁴שִׁבְעָה מִי יוֹדֵעַ? שִׁבְעָה אֲנִי יוֹדֵעַ. שִׁבְעָה יְמֵי שַׁבַּתָּא. שִׁשָּׁה סִדְרֵי מִשְׁנָה. חֲמִשָּׁה חֻמְשֵׁי תוֹרָה. אַרְבַּע אִמָּהוֹת. שְׁלֹשָׁה אָבוֹת. שְׁנֵי לֻחוֹת הַבְּרִית. אֶחָד אֱלֹהֵינוּ שֶׁבַּשָּׁמַיִם וּבָאָרֶץ:

²⁵שְׁמוֹנָה מִי יוֹדֵעַ? שְׁמוֹנָה אֲנִי יוֹדֵעַ. שְׁמוֹנָה יְמֵי מִילָה. שִׁבְעָה יְמֵי שַׁבַּתָּא. שִׁשָּׁה סִדְרֵי מִשְׁנָה. חֲמִשָּׁה חֻמְשֵׁי תוֹרָה. אַרְבַּע אִמָּהוֹת. שְׁלֹשָׁה אָבוֹת. שְׁנֵי לֻחוֹת הַבְּרִית. אֶחָד אֱלֹהֵינוּ שֶׁבַּשָּׁמַיִם וּבָאָרֶץ:

²⁶תִּשְׁעָה מִי יוֹדֵעַ? תִּשְׁעָה אֲנִי יוֹדֵעַ. תִּשְׁעָה יַרְחֵי לֵדָה. שְׁמוֹנָה יְמֵי מִילָה. שִׁבְעָה יְמֵי שַׁבַּתָּא. שִׁשָּׁה סִדְרֵי מִשְׁנָה. חֲמִשָּׁה חֻמְשֵׁי תוֹרָה. אַרְבַּע אִמָּהוֹת. שְׁלֹשָׁה אָבוֹת. שְׁנֵי לֻחוֹת הַבְּרִית. אֶחָד אֱלֹהֵינוּ שֶׁבַּשָּׁמַיִם וּבָאָרֶץ:

27Who knows ten? I know ten. Ten is the commandments. Nine is the months of birth. Eight is days of circumcision. Seven is the days of the week. Six is the orders of the Mishnah. Five is the books of the Torah. Four is the matriarchs. Three is the patriarchs. Two is the tablets of the covenant. One is our God in heaven and on earth.

28Who knows eleven? I know eleven. Eleven is the stars. Ten is the commandments. Nine is the months of birth. Eight is days of circumcision. Seven is the days of the week. Six is the orders of the Mishnah. Five is the books of the Torah. Four is the matriarchs. Three is the patriarchs. Two is the tablets of the covenant. One is our God in heaven and on earth.

29Who knows twelve? I know twelve. Twelve is the tribes. Eleven is the stars. Ten is the commandments. Nine is the months of birth. Eight is days of circumcision. Seven is the days of the week. Six is the orders of the Mishnah. Five is the books of the Torah. Four is the matriarchs. Three is the patriarchs. Two is the tablets of the covenant. One is our God in heaven and on earth.

30Who knows thirteen? I know thirteen. Thirteen is the attributes. Twelve is the tribes. Eleven is the stars.

עֲשָׂרָה מִי יוֹדֵעַ? עֲשָׂרָה אֲנִי יוֹדֵעַ. 27
עֲשָׂרָה דִבְּרַיָּא. תִּשְׁעָה יַרְחֵי לֵדָה.
שְׁמוֹנָה יְמֵי מִילָה. שִׁבְעָה יְמֵי שַׁבַּתָּא.
שִׁשָּׁה סִדְרֵי מִשְׁנָה. חֲמִשָּׁה חֻמְשֵׁי
תוֹרָה. אַרְבַּע אִמָּהוֹת. שְׁלֹשָׁה אָבוֹת.
שְׁנֵי לֻחוֹת הַבְּרִית. אֶחָד אֱלֹהֵינוּ
שֶׁבַּשָּׁמַיִם וּבָאָרֶץ:

אַחַד עָשָׂר מִי יוֹדֵעַ? אַחַד עָשָׂר אֲנִי 28
יוֹדֵעַ. אַחַד עָשָׂר כּוֹכְבַיָּא. עֲשָׂרָה
דִבְּרַיָּא. תִּשְׁעָה יַרְחֵי לֵדָה. שְׁמוֹנָה יְמֵי
מִילָה. שִׁבְעָה יְמֵי שַׁבַּתָּא. שִׁשָּׁה סִדְרֵי
מִשְׁנָה. חֲמִשָּׁה חֻמְשֵׁי תוֹרָה. אַרְבַּע
אִמָּהוֹת. שְׁלֹשָׁה אָבוֹת. שְׁנֵי לֻחוֹת
הַבְּרִית. אֶחָד אֱלֹהֵינוּ שֶׁבַּשָּׁמַיִם
וּבָאָרֶץ:

שְׁנֵים עָשָׂר מִי יוֹדֵעַ? שְׁנֵים עָשָׂר אֲנִי 29
יוֹדֵעַ. שְׁנֵים עָשָׂר שִׁבְטַיָּא. אַחַד עָשָׂר
כּוֹכְבַיָּא. עֲשָׂרָה דִבְּרַיָּא. תִּשְׁעָה יַרְחֵי
לֵדָה. שְׁמוֹנָה יְמֵי מִילָה. שִׁבְעָה יְמֵי
שַׁבַּתָּא. שִׁשָּׁה סִדְרֵי מִשְׁנָה. חֲמִשָּׁה
חֻמְשֵׁי תוֹרָה. אַרְבַּע אִמָּהוֹת. שְׁלֹשָׁה
אָבוֹת. שְׁנֵי לֻחוֹת הַבְּרִית. אֶחָד
אֱלֹהֵינוּ שֶׁבַּשָּׁמַיִם וּבָאָרֶץ:

שְׁלֹשָׁה עָשָׂר מִי יוֹדֵעַ? שְׁלֹשָׁה עָשָׂר 30
אֲנִי יוֹדֵעַ. שְׁלֹשָׁה עָשָׂר מִדַּיָּא. שְׁנֵים
עָשָׂר שִׁבְטַיָּא. אַחַד עָשָׂר כּוֹכְבַיָּא.

Ten is the commandments. Nine is the months of birth. Eight is days of circumcision. Seven is the days of the week. Six is the orders of the Mishnah. Five is the books of the Torah. Four is the matriarchs. Three is the patriarchs. Two is the tablets of the covenant. One is our God in heaven and on earth.

עֲשָׂרָה דִבְּרַיָּא. תִּשְׁעָה יַרְחֵי לֵדָה. שְׁמוֹנָה יְמֵי מִילָה. שִׁבְעָה יְמֵי שַׁבַּתָּא. שִׁשָּׁה סִדְרֵי מִשְׁנָה. חֲמִשָּׁה חֻמְשֵׁי תוֹרָה. אַרְבַּע אִמָּהוֹת. שְׁלֹשָׁה אָבוֹת. שְׁנֵי לֻחוֹת הַבְּרִית. אֶחָד אֱלֹהֵינוּ שֶׁבַּשָּׁמַיִם וּבָאָרֶץ:

D. *Chad Gadya* ("One Kid")

חַד גַּדְיָא

31One kid, one kid that father bought for two *zuzim*; *one kid, one kid.*

‏31‏ חַד גַּדְיָא חַד גַּדְיָא. דְּזַבַּן אַבָּא בִּתְרֵי זוּזֵי. חַד גַּדְיָא חַד גַּדְיָא:

32The cat came and ate the kid that father bought for two *zuzim*; *one kid, one kid.*

‏32‏ וַאֲתָא שׁוּנְרָא וְאָכַל לְגַדְיָא. דְּזַבַּן אַבָּא בִּתְרֵי זוּזֵי. חַד גַּדְיָא חַד גַּדְיָא:

33The dog came and bit the cat that ate the kid that father bought for two *zuzim*; *one kid, one kid.*

‏33‏ וַאֲתָא כַלְבָּא. וְנָשַׁךְ לְשׁוּנְרָא. דְּאָכַל לְגַדְיָא. דְּזַבַּן אַבָּא בִּתְרֵי זוּזֵי. חַד גַּדְיָא חַד גַּדְיָא:

34The stick came and beat the dog that bit the cat that ate the kid that father bought for two *zuzim*; *one kid, one kid.*

‏34‏ וַאֲתָא חוּטְרָא. וְהִכָּה לְכַלְבָּא. דְּנָשַׁךְ לְשׁוּנְרָא. דְּאָכַל לְגַדְיָא. דְּזַבַּן אַבָּא בִּתְרֵי זוּזֵי. חַד גַּדְיָא חַד גַּדְיָא:

[35]The fire came and burned the stick that beat the dog that bit the cat that ate the kid that father bought for two *zuzim; one kid, one kid.*

[36]The water came and quenched the fire that burned the stick that beat the dog that bit the cat that ate the kid that father bought for two *zuzim; one kid, one kid.*

[37]The ox came and drank the water that quenched the fire that burned the stick that beat the dog that bit the cat that ate the kid that father bought for two *zuzim; one kid, one kid.*

[38]The slaughterer came and slaughtered the ox that drank the water that quenched the fire that burned the stick that beat the dog that bit the cat that ate the kid that father bought for two *zuzim; one kid, one kid.*

[39]The Angel of Death came and slaughtered the slaughterer that slaughtered the ox that drank the water that quenched the fire that burned the stick that beat the dog that bit the cat that ate the kid that father bought for two *zuzim; one kid, one kid.*

³⁵וַאֲתָא נוּרָא. וְשָׂרַף לְחוּטְרָא. דְּהִכָּה לְכַלְבָּא. דְּנָשַׁךְ לְשֻׁנְרָא. דְּאָכַל לְגַדְיָא. דְּזַבֵּן אַבָּא בִּתְרֵי זוּזֵי. חַד גַּדְיָא חַד גַּדְיָא:

³⁶וַאֲתָא מַיָּא. וְכָבָה לְנוּרָא. דְּשָׂרַף לְחוּטְרָא. דְּהִכָּה לְכַלְבָּא. דְּנָשַׁךְ לְשֻׁנְרָא. דְּאָכַל לְגַדְיָא. דְּזַבֵּן אַבָּא בִּתְרֵי זוּזֵי. חַד גַּדְיָא חַד גַּדְיָא:

³⁷וַאֲתָא תוֹרָא. וְשָׁתָה לְמַיָּא. דְּכָבָה לְנוּרָא. דְּשָׂרַף לְחוּטְרָא. דְּהִכָּה לְכַלְבָּא. דְּנָשַׁךְ לְשֻׁנְרָא. דְּאָכַל לְגַדְיָא. דְּזַבֵּן אַבָּא בִּתְרֵי זוּזֵי. חַד גַּדְיָא חַד גַּדְיָא:

³⁸וַאֲתָא הַשּׁוֹחֵט. וְשָׁחַט לְתוֹרָא. דְּשָׁתָה לְמַיָּא. דְּכָבָה לְנוּרָא. דְּשָׂרַף לְחוּטְרָא. דְּהִכָּה לְכַלְבָּא. דְּנָשַׁךְ לְשֻׁנְרָא. דְּאָכַל לְגַדְיָא. דְּזַבֵּן אַבָּא בִּתְרֵי זוּזֵי. חַד גַּדְיָא חַד גַּדְיָא:

³⁹וַאֲתָא מַלְאַךְ הַמָּוֶת. וְשָׁחַט לַשּׁוֹחֵט. דְּשָׁחַט לְתוֹרָא. דְּשָׁתָה לְמַיָּא. דְּכָבָה לְנוּרָא. דְּשָׂרַף לְחוּטְרָא. דְּהִכָּה לְכַלְבָּא. דְּנָשַׁךְ לְשֻׁנְרָא. דְּאָכַל לְגַדְיָא. דְּזַבֵּן אַבָּא בִּתְרֵי זוּזֵי. חַד גַּדְיָא חַד גַּדְיָא:

⁴⁰The Holy One of blessing came and slaughtered the Angel of Death who came and slaughtered the slaughterer that slaughtered the ox that drank the water that quenched the fire that burned the stick that beat the dog that bit the cat that ate the kid that father bought for two *zuzim; one kid, one kid.*

⁴⁰וְאָתָא הַקָּדוֹשׁ בָּרוּךְ הוּא. וְשָׁחַט לְמַלְאַךְ הַמָּוֶת. דְּשָׁחַט לְשׁוֹחֵט. דְּשָׁחַט לְתוֹרָא. דְּשָׁתָה לְמַיָּא. דְּכָבָה לְנוּרָא. דְּשָׂרַף לְחוּטְרָא. דְּהִכָּה לְכַלְבָּא. דְּנָשַׁךְ לְשׁוּנְרָא. דְּאָכַל לְגַדְיָא. דְּזַבֵּן אַבָּא בִּתְרֵי זוּזֵי. חַד גַּדְיָא חַד גַּדְיָא:

ARNOW (THE WORLD OF MIDRASH)

"... every day Israel anticipates my sovereignty and the rebuilding of My house. And each and every day they call Me 'builder of Jerusalem'⁴ [i.e., in the *Amidah*, recited thrice daily, and also in Grace after Meals]." The midrash concludes: "Amen, *bimheira b'yameinu*, rebuild soon."⁵ The Temple rebuilt not only symbolized the restoration of intimacy with God—there the *Shekhinah* will dwell—but was a harbinger of messianic times.⁶ According to one midrashic timeline, first God rebuilds the Temple, and then, in the month of Nisan, the messiah arrives.⁷ Of what use will the Temple be in the messianic world without sin and therefore with no need for atonement through sacrifice? Only the thanksgiving offering will continue (*Lev. Rab.* 9:7).

18–30 *"Echad Mi Yode'a?"* This song is based on midrashic sources from the sixth or seventh century. These texts elaborate on the retribution God metes out when, as recounted in the Book of Chronicles, King David conducts a census without divine authorization. Given his choice of punishment, David elects "three *days* of the sword of Adonai, pestilence in the land, the angel of Adonai wreaking destruction ..." (1 Chron. 21:12). (Here a day refers to a twelve-hour period, three days equaling thirty-six hours.) The midrash now elaborates: "Masters at pleading argued on Israel's behalf, each one asking God to set aside a single hour. The seven days of the week, the eight days from birth to circumcision ... the five books of Torah, and the three patriarchs—thus twenty three. And ... the Ten Commandments and the two tables [tablets] of the covenant—a total of thirty five." In any event, there remained only one hour of pestilence.⁸ Still, seventy thousand perished. The song's inclusion in the Haggadah makes sense for two reasons. As the midrash implies, despite losses, Israel was spared from more than 97 percent of its allotted suffering, an outcome that Jews over the millennia would surely have envied. Second, the midrashic source concerns a story to which the Haggadah alludes when it mentions, "His sword drawn in his outstretched hand against Jerusalem" (1 Chron. 21:16; see *My People's Passover Haggadah*, Volume 2, p. 29). It is this sword that the midrash's pleaders stay. David sinned by counting his troops, a practice the Bible forbids (Exod. 30:12–15). Against the grain of Jewish custom, which is often superstitious about counting, this song encourages us to count—to count what matters, not the size of our armies, but the objects of our faith.

[40] *"And slaughtered the Angel of Death"* "But as for the tree of the knowledge of good and evil, you must not eat of it; for as soon as you do, you shall die" (Gen. 2:17). Talmudic traditions connect the Angel of Death with the evil inclination (the *yetser hara*) and envision God slaying both in the messianic era.[9] *Deuteronomy Rabbah* (2:30) elaborates: "God said: 'In this world, because the evil inclination is present, people kill one another and die, but in the time to come I will uproot the evil inclination from your midst and there will be no death in the world,' [as Scripture says], 'He will swallow up death forever' (Isa. 25:8)." The world of *Chad Gadya* finally ends. A midrash known as the *Letters of Rabbi Akiva* puts it this way: "'Then My people will dwell ... in untroubled places of rest' (Isa. 32:18)—without the Angel of Death...."[10] The Seder's last words bring us back to the beginning, to Eden and the world of peace and eternal life.

——◆——

BALIN (MODERN HAGGADOT)

One is the good ship Peartree which in 1654 brought the first Jewish settlers to these shores. Two are the early settlers Jacob Barsimon and Asser Levy who demanded the right to serve in the defense of their country.... Five are the synagogues of Philadelphia, Newport, Charleston, Richmond and Savannah praised by George Washington on his ascendancy to the presidency [saying]: May the same Deity who long since delivering the Hebrews from their Egyptian Oppressors ... whose providential agency has lately been conspicuous in establishing these United States continue to water them with the dews of heaven and to make the inhabitants of every denomination to participate in the blessings of that people whose God is Jehovah.... Eight are the words "And thou shalt proclaim liberty throughout the land!" taken from our Bible [Lev. 25:17] by the founders of our Republic and fashioned by them into a ring for the Liberty Bell.... Twelve and more are the American Nobel laureates [of Jewish descent] who have from this land broadened the horizons of health, science and peace.[1]

[31–40] *"Chad Gadya [One Kid]"* *Haggadah for the Liberated Lamb* (1988) is for "vegetarians and ... everyone concerned with unbridled cruelty." Complete with recipes for vegetarian liver and a "Seder roast," it suggests replacing the *z'ro'a* with olives, grapes, and grains, which "symbolize the commandments of compassion for the oppressed found in the Bible."[2] It maintains that God chose Moses to lead the Israelites because of his heroic behavior toward animals, as in the midrash where Moses returns a strayed lamb to its flock. Despite its zealous campaign against cruelty toward animals *(tsa'ar ba'alei chayim)*, the *Haggadah for the Liberated Lamb* ends with the traditional rendering of *Chad Gadya*, the song about the kid, which was gobbled by the cat, which was bitten by the dog, which was beaten by a stick.

Chava Alberstein, the popular, political, and prolific Israeli singer who has recorded nearly fifty albums over forty years, is an icon of folk music whose defiant songs include a version of *Chad Gadya*, written in 1989 in response to the first intifada (Palestinian uprising).[3] Her provocative adaptation opens with the original Aramaic, accompanied by a simple Hebrew translation and followed by verses implicitly criticizing Israeli policies toward the Palestinians. Alberstein prods the listener:

> And why are you singing *Chad Gadya*?
> Spring isn't here yet and Passover hasn't arrived.
> And what has changed for you,
> what has changed?" [*mah hashtanah*]
> I have changed
> this year.
> For on all the nights, all the nights [*she bekhol halelot*]
> I asked only four questions [*arbah koshiot*].
> This night I have another question:
>
> How long will the cycle of horror last
> the pursuer and the pursued
> the striker and the stricken
> When will this madness end?
> And what has changed for you, what has changed?[4]

In reaction to the powerful lyrics, Alberstein received death threats, and government-controlled radio stations barred the recording until public pressure ultimately caused the ban to be lifted.[5]

To this day, the song reverberates in Israeli culture. Most recently, Amos Gitai, the award-winning film director, used Alberstein's *Chad Gadya* as the book end for his movie *Free Zone*. The film, which was originally shown at the Cannes Film Festival in 2005, depicts the complex relationship of three women (an American, an Israeli, and a Palestinian) who encounter each other in the tax-free zone between Jordan and Saudi Arabia. The movie opens with a ten-minute single shot of the Israeli-born star Natalie Portman as she cries while listening to Chava Alberstein sing her version of *Chad Gadya*. The song provides a fitting accompaniment to Gitai's raw depiction of the uneasy co-existence and tangled reality of the Middle East.[6]

◆

BRETTLER (OUR BIBLICAL HERITAGE)

earth is full of His glory" (6:3). This is the motif of the K'dushah section of the Amidah (see *My People's Prayer Book*, Volume 2, *The Amidah*, pp. 84ff.). The phrase "You and You; You, yes, You; You, indeed, You; You Adonai, are royal" is from the late prayer ascribed to David in 1 Chronicles 29:11.

10–17 "*Adir Hu* [*He Is Mighty*]*"* Another acrostic poem praising God (see above, *"Ki Lo Na'eh"*). Most of the epithets are biblical and are used of God in the Bible; some are biblical but not used of God (e.g., *dagul*), while others are post-biblical (e.g., *vatik*). Following common biblical usage, the Temple is here called "His [= God's] house"; many biblical writers believed that the God or the divine presence actually resided in the Temple, with the ark and cherubim forming a throne for the deity.

18–30 "*Echad Mi Yode'a?* [*Who Knows One?*]*"* The Book of Proverbs contains several numerical sayings (e.g., 30:21–23, "The earth shudders at three things, / At four which it cannot bear: / A slave who becomes king; / A scoundrel sated with food; / A loathsome woman who gets married; / A slave-girl who supplants her mistress"). These are isolated sayings and do not count up from the numeral one, as this song, which has no close biblical model, does. In offering examples, the poem mostly uses numbers from the biblical world (e.g., the three patriarchs and four matriarchs and the eleven stars of Joseph's dream), though there is reference to the rabbinic world (the six orders of Mishnah) and the natural world (the nine months of birth) as well.

31–40 "*Chad Gadya* [*One Kid*]*"* This poem, in structure and content, is totally foreign to the biblical world, mentioning, for example, "the Angel of Death," who is absent from the Bible. (The Bible also does not mention any cats!) However, the main point of the poem, that God is powerful and stands above all and controls all, is very biblical and is emphasized in particular in sections of the Book of Job. For example, Job begins his response to Adonai's second speech from the whirlwind by noting, "I know that You can do everything, / That nothing You propose is impossible for You" (Job 42:2).

———◆———

GILLMAN (THEOLOGICALLY SPEAKING)

That God, at the end of days, will resurrect the dead is a central teaching of Judaism at least since the second century BCE. Most Bible scholars claim that Daniel 12:2— "Many of those that sleep in the dust of the earth will awake, some to eternal life, others to reproaches, to everlasting abhorrence"—is the sole explicit biblical reference to life after death. That verse, part of a more extended passage (Dan. 10–12), conventionally dated to 165 BCE, is part of an eschatological vision that anticipated the approaching conflict between the Syrian-Greeks and the Maccabees, whose victory we now celebrate on Hanukkah.[1]

But this concluding stanza goes a significant step beyond the doctrine of resurrection: not only does God have the power to resurrect the dead, God even has the power to destroy death forever.

The assumption that underlies this claim is that death itself is a residue of the chaos that God, in time, will banish from creation. That is not a popular assumption today. Many of our contemporaries would argue that death is a blessing, a way to keep nature fresh and young. Every creature dies and is replaced with a new creation. This is clearly not the view of our tradition. There is no clear indication, in the Bible itself, on why or how death entered the world—though the conventional view is that it is the result of Adam's sin as recorded in Genesis 3—but in time, the Bible proclaimed that death does not mark the end of God's ability to affect our destiny. If it did, then death would be more powerful than God, and we should properly worship death—which would be intolerable. In proclaiming that God has the power to resurrect the dead and now, in this last stanza of our song, that God slaughters the Angel of Death, the Bible and the later Jewish tradition celebrated God's power as ultimate.

These very last words of the Haggadah sound the last note of the theme of redemption and, at the same time, represent the climax of the trajectory that took us from the disgrace to the glory, from the bad things to the praise.

———◆———

J. HOFFMAN (TRANSLATION)

[1] *"Mighty in majesty"* Alas, by juxtaposing "mighty" and "majesty" we create alliteration in English where there is none in the original Hebrew. Additionally, the first word, *adir*, was chosen not only for its meaning but also to take its place in the alphabetic acrostic around which the song is built. Here we have *alef*. "Chosen" (see immediately below) gives us *bet*, and so forth. Although the choice between one English word and another (e.g., "mighty" versus "strong") is somewhat arbitrary, we try to use the same English words for the same Hebrew ones in this song and the next, *Adir Hu*.

[1] *"Chosen"* This is probably what the word means. Another, less likely possibility, is "first."

[1] *"In truth"* Hebrew, *kahalakhah*, that is, *k-* ("like") *halakhah*. The word form is similar to *bimlukhah* ("in majesty"), that is, *b-* ("in") *m'lukhah*. Although the words "in" and "like" are completely different in English, *b-* and *k-* (their Hebrew counterparts) are more similar than they sound to those who don't know Hebrew. (And they are made to sound even less similar to English speakers than they otherwise might, because, for complicated grammatical reasons, *b-* here becomes *bi*, and *k-* becomes *ka*.) We therefore choose "in majesty" and "in truth" to convey this similarity, even though our translations are slightly closer to each other than the original Hebrew words are.

[1] *"Troops"* This somewhat rare Hebrew word (which happens to mean "regiment or battalion" in Modern Israeli Hebrew) refers at times to secular military groups and at

times to God's forces. Here, as with the other words that precede "tell Him," it probably refers to "angels."

[2] *"You and You"* Literally, "to You and to You," because the end of the line ("You … are royal") is expressed in Hebrew as "royalty is Yours," and "Yours" is expressed in Hebrew as "to You." This sort of dative subject (in which the subject "has" rather than "is") is common across the world's languages. For example, in Modern French, rather than "I am hungry" we find "I have hunger." It is a mistake to translate these datives ("to him," "to me," "I have," etc.) literally. However, our translation, which changes the literal "to You" into the correct "You," misses the (very obscure) allusions of the other instances of "to You." For example, "You, indeed, You," may be a reference to Psalms 74 and 89, where we find, "Yours is the day, indeed, Yours is the night" (Ps. 74:16) and "Yours is the sky, indeed, the earth is Yours" (Ps. 89:12). Finally, the fact that seven *l'lkha*'s appear in each chorus is probably significant.

[2] *"Yes"* Hebrew, *ki*, the word we translated as "for" in the title and chorus, as well as, for example, in the Great *Hallel*. The word *ki* sometimes has the force of "because," sometimes of emphasis, and sometimes of "but." In English, "You, for You," conveys the wrong meaning, so we translate "yes." The full line, "You, yes, You," may be an allusion to Isaiah 62:4 ("You will no longer be called Forsaken … but [*ki*] you will be called I Desired Her"), where Isaiah uses the imagery of a woman—first rejected, then taken back—to express salvation. Or the line may reflect Jeremiah 10:7, "*Ki* it fits You [to revere You]." Jeremiah is the only place in Scripture we find the verb *ya'eh*, which appears in this song's title and chorus.

[2] *"You, Adonai, are royal"* Others, the awkward, "Yours is the royalty," or even "to You is the royalty."

[3] *"Preeminent"* Following *JPS*'s translation of Song of Songs (5:10), where we find that "my lover is … preeminent." "Preeminent" refers to special status without indicating what the source of that status might be. Another possibility is that *dagul* refers to some particular quality that we have not been able to discern.

[3] *"Dedicated"* Or, perhaps, "learned."

[4] *"Potent"* Or simply "strong." But we will need "strong" for *aziz*, below, in *Adir Hu*. Furthermore, the Hebrew *chasin* is a rare word—appearing in the Bible only in Psalm 89:9—and we prefer to translate rare words in Hebrew with rare words in English. (As it happens, *chasin* in Modern Hebrew means "immune." The cognate Arabic root can also have a sense of "beautiful.")

[4] *"Servants"* Or "attendants," but will want that word below. *JPS* translates "marshals."

[5] *"Great"* That is, "mighty," as in a "great force," not a "great movie." We would prefer "mighty," but we have already used that English word for a different Hebrew one.

[5] *"Students"* Others, "disciples."

[6] *"Attendants"* From the Hebrew root *s.v.v*, "to surround." These attendants are probably closer to the one they serve than the "servants" mentioned above.

[10] *"Rebuild"* Literally, "build." As we have noted before, Hebrew has no "re-" prefix, so we must add it where context dictates.

[10] *"House"* Others, almost universally, "temple." Of course the word *bayit* here refers to the Temple, but it does so obliquely, so we want a similar word in English that refers to but is not the name of the Temple. "House" is close.

[10] *"God, rebuild"* We usually avoid this sort of fragment, because while it is grammatical in Hebrew to omit a direct object (as in, "rebuild," meaning "rebuild it"), English does not allow this possibility. But in the context of a song, we feel it's okay.

[11] *"Wonderful"* We would prefer "great," but we will need "great" for *kabir* (below, v. 14), in keeping with our translation for *kabir* above (Volume 2, p. 208).

[15] *"Exalted"* To fit the word *sagiv* into the acrostic, the poet uses a *sin* where the word would normally be spelled with a *samech*. This change reflects a time when spelling was a matter of opinion. (We also see confirmation that, when the poem was written, *sin* and *samech* already had the same sound.)

[17] *"Almighty"* Hebrew, *shaddai*. *Shaddai* may be a proper name (as in *JPS*), or, as King James suggests, it may be an adjective. The word itself is interesting. It seems to be the singular first-person possessive of the plural word *shaddim*, that is, "my *shad*s." (Similarly, *adonai* is the singular first-person possessive of the plural *adonim*, that is, "my *adon*s"; *adon* means "lord.") *Shad* probably means "strength," though an identical-sounding word means "(female) breast." The translation "almighty" reflects the first word and its core meaning of "strength." Some people think that *shaddai* comes from the second meaning and therefore think that *shaddai* incorporates concepts such as "sustainer."

[18] *"Who knows one?"* In Hebrew, the words for the numbers (*echad*, "one," here) are moved to the beginning of the questions and of the answers, effectively highlighting the numbers. For example, the Hebrew here literally reads, "One, who knows?" "One, I know." While Hebrew grammar allows this possibility, standard English grammar does not. The effect is similar to: "One: Who knows one?"

[18] *"In heaven and on earth"* In Hebrew, the same preposition, *b'*, means both "in" and "on" here, creating a slightly more poetic line in Hebrew than the English conveys.

[19] *"Is"* Or "are." The Hebrew could mean either. Here we assume that we are not counting (in this case) the tablets, but rather clarifying what "two" represents.

[19] *"Tablets"* Hebrew, *luchot*, a term used in the Bible predominantly to represent the Ten Commandments.

[22] *"Books"* Hebrew, *chumshei*, roughly "fifths," as the books of the Torah are called in Hebrew. That is, in Hebrew, even the word for "book" here reflects the fact that there are five of them.

[23] *"Orders"* Or "books." We use "orders" here because we already used "book" for the books of the Torah, and we try to use different words in English when there are different words in Hebrew.

[24] *"Week"* The "Hebrew" here is actually Aramaic, *shabata*, literally, "Sabbath." The Aramaic was used instead of the Hebrew to preserve the rhyme scheme. "Sabbath" is frequently used metonymically to refer to a "week."

[25] *"Days of circumcision"* Commonly, "days until circumcision," but we prefer to mirror the Hebrew more closely here, preserving the parallel with other "days of ..." numbers.

[27] *"Commandments"* Again, we have Aramaic.

[28] *"Stars"* Aramaic again. The "stars" are the stars of Joseph's dream.

[29] *"Tribes"* Aramaic.

[30] *"Attributes"* Aramaic, referring to the thirteen attributes of God.

———◆———

L. HOFFMAN (HISTORY)

and *Omets G'vuratekha* ("The Strength of Your Might"). They were composed by two exceptional representatives of the classic age of synagogue poetry in ancient Palestine (c. fifth century), Yannai and Eliezer Kalir. Though composed as parts of much longer poems intended for synagogue recitation (Ashkenazim say them on *Shabbat Hagadol* and on the morning service of the first day of Passover), they entered the Ashkenazi Haggadah somewhere in the twelfth or thirteenth century. At least in recent years, their poetic complexity has mitigated against their being included in many Seders, even if they are included in the Haggadah.

Because of their complexity, which would have required pages of explanation, we refer to them only, but do not include them here. We do, however, include the folk songs common to Ashkenazi Haggadot, beginning with "For It Fits and Befits Him" (*Ki Lo Na'eh*).

Ki Lo Na'eh is mentioned by Rabbi Jacob ben Judah of London (d. 1285) and appears also in thirteenth-century Haggadot from Germany and Italy. Its author is unknown. In form, it is a *piyyut* (a synagogue poem that follows complex technical rules and is often opaque in meaning), but it is not nearly as difficult to understand as the Yannai and Kalir poems. It crosses the line into the folk-song genre because its verses are simple and its refrain can easily be sung. After-dinner songs had to be easily memorizable or at least contain refrains that were.

10–17 *"Adir Hu [He Is Mighty]"* In many Haggadot, the prior song, *Ki Lo Na'eh*, appears before the concluding *Nirtsah* (see "The Passover celebration has concluded appropriately," *My People's Passover Haggadah*, Volume 2, p. 190), so that *Adir Hu* ("He Is Mighty") follows immediately afterward. The *Nirtsah* anticipates the messianic era when Jerusalem and its Temple will be rebuilt. "He Is Mighty" explicitly explains how the one and mighty God will indeed be able to rebuild it. The song appears in the fourteenth century, not originally as a Seder song at all, but as a simple folk tune apt to be sung after any dinner. Jews in medieval Avignon sang it on every holiday.

There are different traditions for singing the twenty-two verses. They all begin with the first verse, *Adir hu*, followed by the refrain. After this some create seven equal stanzas of three items each, while others make stanzas with three, four, ten and then four of the terms. These are the most common customs, but others exist as well. In any case, we begin with *aleph*, the first letter of the alphabet and end with *tav*, the last one.

18–30 *"Echad Mi Yode'a? [Who Knows One?]"* The next song in Ashkenazi Haggadot is "Who Knows One?" (*Echad Mi Yodea?*), a simple number game going from one to thirteen. The relevance of one (referring to God) is evident; but the number thirteen is also critical. The shorthand reference to thirteen "attributes" (*midaya*) returns us back to the one God, by referencing God's thirteen attributes mentioned in Exodus 34:6–7.

Like most of the final songs, this one too is a relatively late addition to the Haggadah, and of unknown origin. It is said to have been discovered in the walls of an old synagogue in Germany, and if so, it may go back to the time of Eliezer of Worms, a fourteenth-century halakhist from the movement known as German pietism (*chasidei ashkenaz*). Some old versions of the song present it as a commentary on the *Sh'ma*, Judaism's primary statement of God's oneness.

More likely, however, it is a Jewish version of an ordinary German folk song entitled "Good Friend, I Ask You" (*Guter Freund Ich Frage Dich*). Its first verse reads, "One is our God who lives in and hovers over heaven" (*Eins ist unser Gott, der da lebt, der da schwebt im Himmel*). The first verse of the Yiddish version of "Who Knows One?" reads exactly like the German original.

31–40 *"Chad Gadya [One Kid]"* Of all the concluding songs, this one has received the most attention. It has been seen as an allegory on Israel's fate, each of the victors in the song representing another (and later) kingdom or ruler to which Jews were subservient. In reality, it was probably meant as nothing more than an amusing song akin to "The House That Jack Built." Like other Jewish folk songs, this one too is based on a popular German table song that may itself be related to an earlier French one.

Nonetheless, it is not surprising to find the specific *content* of the song coming from Jewish tradition; even in folk songs, people use images and ideas that they know best. In this case, the model may be a midrash (*Gen. Rab.* 38:13) with a similar chain of inference: Nimrod tells Abraham to worship fire; Abraham objects, "Better to worship water that puts out fire." Nimrod agrees, so Abraham suggests worshiping clouds that carry water. The midrash continues in that vein until Nimrod loses his temper and refuses to "play the game" anymore. An equally likely influence is Mishnah Avot 2:7, which pictures Hillel watching a skull float downstream, and saying, "Because you have drowned others, others have drowned you; and in the end, those who drowned you will themselves be drowned." Our song is about the almost endless chain of retribution.

What makes the song so very Jewish is the same sort of conclusion that we saw in "Who Knows One?" The end in both instances is God, the single God who is "one" for "Who Knows One?" and who is the final judge and arbiter, even over death, for "An Only Kid."

Chad Gadya was probably composed in the Yiddish vernacular and only then translated into our familiar Aramaic version. Medieval Jews did not know Aramaic, so would be unlikely to have composed a folk song in it. It has been suggested also that the Aramaic has some grammatical problems that a true Aramaic poet would have avoided. The most obvious is the refrain, *diz'van abba* ("that father bought"), which circulated until relatively recently as *d'zaven abba* ("that father sold"). The latter seems unlikely, in context. Another is the phrase *atal shunrah v'achlah l'gadya*, "There came a cat that ate the kid." In Aramaic, "cat" *(shunra)* is masculine, while the modifying verb *achlah* ("ate") is feminine. In German, however (whence we get our Yiddish), "cat" is feminine. Alternatively, the mistakes might be explained as errors that crept in over time to further the rhythm of the song. In any event, most current editions of the Haggadah have been emended to say *diz'van*, "bought," and *achal*, the masculine for "ate."

[38] *"The slaughterer [lashochet]"* Standard texts vocalize this word as *l'shochet*, but we believe it should be *lashochet*. The change involves comparative Hebrew and Babylonian Aramaic grammar.

The definite article in Hebrew is a prefix—a *heh* with a *patach*, pronounced *ha*. *Kelev*, for instance, is "dog," while *hakelev* is "the dog." Babylonian Aramaic uses a suffix, *kametz alef*, providing the ending sound "a," and does not distinguish the definite from the indefinite. The Hebrew *kelev*, for example, is *kalba* in Aramaic, but *kalba* means either "a dog" or "the dog."

In addition, Hebrew and Aramaic form the objective case differently. In Aramaic it is formed by an introductory *lamed* ("l"), whether or not the following noun is definite ("the dog") or indefinite ("a dog"). Hebrew, however, distinguishes the two: "A dog" requires no preceding notification that it is the object of the sentence. "The dog," however, demands the introductory word *et*, giving us *et hakelev*.

The nouns in the poem are generally Aramaic, so when they are objects in the sentences, they receive an introductory *l*. There are, however, some exceptions, notably (for our purposes here), *shochet*, "slaughterer," which is Hebrew. Clearly, the poet wanted to say that "The angel of death killed *the* slaughterer" (not "*a* slaughterer"). Had he used the normal Hebrew formulation, he would have said *et hashochet*. But that would have ruined the poem's overall pattern, so he provided the introductory Aramaic *lamed* instead. When the prefix *l* is attached to an indefinite noun (that does not already have the definite article *ha*), it is pronounced *l'*. When it is added to the already existent prefix *ha*, the two sounds combine to give us *la*.

We should therefore have *lashochet*, not *l'shochet*.

———◆———

KUSHNER AND POLEN (CHASIDIC VOICES)

primal unity out of which the universe has yet to flow, all is one; likewise, the bottom *s'firah*, *Malkhut* or *K'nesset Yisra'el*, is also called "one," because it is mystically referred to as "I," meaning the personhood of God.

This unity ascends from the first chorus, "I know one," all the way to the thirteenth. But even there the repeated chorus returns back to "one." Ya'akov Yosef then cites a teaching ascribed to the Baal Shem Tov maintaining that this is a theological statement: Each one of the increasing numbers is a metaphor for our experience of the world in its increasing complexity. And, when we *arrive* at thirteen, we realize that, according to *gematria*, the numerical value of the word for one, *echad*—spelled, *alef* (1), *chet* (8), and *dalet* (4)—also totals 13. And in this way thirteen becomes one.

"*Chad Gadya [One Kid]*" Rabbi Ya'akov Yosef of Polnoye *(Toldot Ya'akov Yosef, Vayakhel)* offers the following interpretation of *Chad Gadya*, "One Kid." The song was probably intended as a parable of Jewish history, wherein the Jews are the kid, and everyone and everything else are the nations that sought to destroy us. Ya'akov Yosef reads Isaiah 41:4, "I am the first ..." to imply that Jewish history all begins with a "father" (God) who purchased a "kid" (Israel).

But Isaiah adds also, "I am the last." These two dimensions of time, embracing ultimacy (from first to last), encompass all that is: the reality of this world and of the world-to-come. And they, likewise, correspond to the ten *s'firot*. Alas, when the *s'firot* are garbed in earthly garments, we count them separately as ten, but they are, in truth, only different manifestations of the same underlying unity, as we read in Isaiah 30:20, "Your Master will no longer hide in his garments, and your eyes will behold your Master" (Jewish Publication Society translation, 1917). Of the "two" eras (this world and the world-to-come) that are really not two, but one, this verse is an allusion to the world-to-come: in messianic times the power of the Angel of Death will be no more. And this is the implication of Zechariah 14:9, "On that day Adonai will be one, and God's name will be one."

This is a radical teaching—In the eschaton it will be revealed that even the "Angel of Death"—another way of saying the evil inclination, even the demonic—was a hidden aspect of the Divine. The unity of which Zechariah speaks is a mystical unity of all that leaves nothing outside—even that which seems to us now as incapable of assimilation into the sacred. This is the unity of *abba* and *Hakadosh Barukh Hu*, of first and last, the unity of the personal God of Israel with the transcendent One.[1]

———◆ ◆ ◆———

Appendix I

Two Early Seders: Mishnah and Tosefta

The Mishnah and the Tosefta, law codes or teaching manuals dating from around 200 CE, contain our earliest descriptions of how the Rabbis believed the night of Passover should be celebrated in the post-Temple era. The Tosefta has commonly been held to be a commentary on the Mishnah, although recently some scholars have argued that it contains a pre-Mishnaic layer that the compiler of the Mishnah subsequently reworked. As will become apparent, the rituals described by both sources share common elements, but differ in important ways (see Arnow, Passover for the Early Rabbis, *My People's Passover Haggadah*, Volume 1, pp. 16–17). The diagram below highlights the unique and common elements (italicized) of each as well as their contrasting order.[1]

Mishnah	Tosefta
Required: 4 cups of wine and reclining	*Required: 4 cups of wine and reclining*
Kiddush	*Kiddush*
Matzah, lettuce, charoset	Hors d'oeuvres of innards
Questions, answers, midrash, symbols defined	_____
Hallel, part 1	*Hallel, part 1*
_____	*Matzah, lettuce, charoset*
Meal	*Meal*
Grace	_____
Hallel, part 2	*Hallel, part 2*
Blessing of Song	All-night study session

      The translation below of the Mishnah is based on the early thirteenth-century Kaufmann manuscript, generally credited as the best of such manuscripts because it lacks a number of additions that gradually crept into the Mishnah from the Talmud and from the Haggadah itself. Some of the more significant differences between this and the widely available, "standard" Vilna text of the Mishnah are highlighted in notes.[2] The numbering of *mishnayot* in the Kaufmann manuscript has been slightly altered for easier comparison with other editions of the Mishnah. The translation of the

Tosefta is based on Hebrew rendering of this source prepared by Saul Liberman.[3] Except for italicized transliterated Hebrew words, the presence of italics denotes material that appears in *both* the Tosefta and Mishnah. Note that certain material appears in both sources but not necessarily in the exact same location.

Mishnah

10:1 *On the eve of Passover, close to [the time of] minchah [the daily afternoon offering, about 3:30], a person should not eat until it gets dark. Even a poor person in Israel should not eat until [he] reclines. [Those who serve] should not give him fewer than four cups of wine* even if [the funds come] from the charity plate.

10:2 *[They] mixed for him the first cup [of wine]. The House of Shammai say, "[He] says the blessing over the day [the festival] and afterward [he] says the blessing over the wine." And the House of Hillel say, "[He] says the blessing over the wine and afterward [he] says the blessing over the day."*

10:3 *[They] served him—[he] dips the lettuce [chazeret, the vegetable used for the bitter herbs] before he reaches the bread condiment.* [They] served him unleavened bread and lettuce and charoset,[4] even though the charoset is not a [biblical] commandment. Rabbi Leazer ben Rabbi Tzadok says, "[It is a] commandment. In the Temple [they] serve him the carcass of the Passover offering.

10:4 *[They] poured for him the second cup—and here the child asks, and if the child lacks intelligence, he[5] instructs him. Why is this night different from all other nights?[6] In that on all other nights we dip things one time, this*

Tosefta

10:1 *On the eve of Passover, close to [the time of] minchah [the daily afternoon offering, about 3:30], a person should not eat until it gets dark. Even a poor person in Israel should not eat until [he] reclines.* And *[those who serve] should not give him fewer than four cups of wine,* which contain the amount of a fourth [of log = 1.5 eggs, in liquid measure], whether it is raw or diluted, whether it is fresh or old [from the previous year]. Rabbi Yehudah says, "And as long as it has the taste and appearance of wine" [= taste, even though possibly diluted; appearance, even though old].

10:2, 3 *[They] mixed for him the first cup [of wine]. The House of Shammai say, "[He] says the blessing over the day [the festival] and afterward [he] says the blessing over the wine,"* for the day causes the wine to come, and the day has already become sanctified and the wine has not yet come [= the day, which automatically comes at the appropriate time irrespective of the presence of wine, has already started]. *And the House of Hillel say, "[He] says the blessing over the wine and afterward [he] says the blessing over the day,"* for the wine causes [provides the occasion for] the Sanctification of the day to be recited. Another matter [= another reason]: The blessing over the wine is constant and the blessing over the day is not constant [and that which is constant, not

Mishnah (cont.)

night, two times. In that on all other nights we eat leaven and matzah, this night, only matzah. In that on all other nights we eat meat roasted, steamed, or cooked [in a liquid, boiled], this night, only roasted. According to the child's intelligence, his father instructs him. [He] starts with the disgrace and ends with the glory; and [he] expounds from, "My father was a wandering Aramean" [Deut. 26:5], until he finishes the entire portion.

10:5 Rabban Gamaliel used to say, "Anyone who doesn't explain these three things on Passover has not fulfilled his obligation: *Pesach* [the Passover offering], matzah [unleavened bread], and *merorim* [bitter herbs]." *Pesach*—It is for the Holy One of Blessing's passing over the houses of our ancestors in Egypt. *Merorim*—They are for the Egyptians embittering the lives of our ancestors in Egypt. *Matzah*—It is because they were redeemed.[7] We must therefore thank, praise, honor, glorify, exalt, and elevate[8] the One who did all these miracles for us and who brought us from slavery to freedom.[9] So let us exclaim: "Halleluyah!" [Psalm 113].

10:6 *Up to what point does he recite [the Hallel]? The House of Shammai say, "Until 'as a mother rejoicing with her children'" [the end of Psalm 113]. And the House of Hillel say, "Until 'stones into springs of water'" [the end of Psalm 114]. And he seals with [the term or prayer for] "redemption." [He ends with a blessing formula with the motif of redemption.]* Rabbi Tarfon says, "Who redeemed us

Tosefta (cont.)

intermittent, takes precedence]. And the halakhah follows the words of the House of Hillel.

10:4 A man is commanded to make his children and his wife happy on the holiday. With what does he make them happy? With wine, as it is written, "and wine gladdens the heart" (Ps. 104:15). Rabbi Yehudah says, "Women with what is appropriate for them, and children with what is appropriate for them."

10:5 The waiter dips innards [in salt water] and serves them to the guests [even before darkness, since this hors d'oeuvre whets the appetite and does not satiate the guests]. Even though there is no proof on this matter, there is a mention [= a hint] of it: "Plow a line and do not sow among the thorns" (Jer. 4:3). [= One starts with something to direct that which is to follow; the line will direct the seeding, and the hors d'oeuvre will direct the food.]

10:6, 7, 8, and part of 9 [As to] one who leads in reciting the *Hallel*—they go to him and read [with him] and he does not go to them. [As to] one who leads in reciting to his minor sons and daughters—he must respond with them in the places that they respond [i.e., he must read with them the portions with which they respond, for as minors, they cannot perform the act on his behalf]. In what place does he respond? [When] he reaches, "Blessed is the One who comes"—he responds with them, "with Adonai's name." Townspeople who lack someone to lead then in reciting the

Mishnah (cont.)

and redeemed our ancestors from Egypt, and brought us to this night"— and [he] does not seal [with a concluding formula]. Rabbi Akiva says, "[One adds to the blessing:] 'So too, Adonai our God and our ancestors' God, bring us to festivals that are approaching in peace, that we might be happy as we rebuild Your city, and joyful as we serve You; to eat from the *pesach*s and the *zevach*s and the blood from which will reach the wall of Your altar and please You. And we will thankfully acknowledge You with a new song for our redemption.'"

10:7 [They] mixed for him the third cup [of wine]—[he] says the blessing over his food. [At] the fourth [cup]— [he] finishes the *Hallel* [through Psalm 118] and says over it the blessing over the song. Between the former cups, if [he] wants to drink [further] he may drink. Between the third and the fourth, [he] should not drink.

10:8 *After [eating from] the Passover offering, they do not end [with] afikoman* [revelry]. [If they] fell asleep: [if it was] some of them—[they] may eat [again because the remaining individuals of the group, who stayed awake, maintained the group]; and [if it was] all of them— [they] may not eat [again]. Rabbi Yosei says, "If [they] dozed—[they] may eat [again]. And if [they] slumbered— [they] may not eat [again]."

10:9 After midnight the Passover offering imparts uncleanness to the hands; *piggul* [i.e., an offering prepared

Tosefta (cont.)

Hallel—[they] go to the house of the assembly and read the first portion [Psalms 113–114], and [they] go home and eat and drink, and [they] return and finish the *Hallel*. And if they are unable [to return to the house of assembly] they finish all of it [i.e., they finish all the *Hallel* before going home the first time]. The *Hallel* is not abbreviated or expanded. Rabbi Elazar ben Parata used to keep the praises plain [literally, "flat," that is, he did not double them]. Rabbi [Yehudah Hanasi] used to repeat the praises.

10:9 continued … Rabbi Elazar said, "[They] grab unleavened bread [from each other] for [the sake of] the child [to astonish him] so that he will not fall asleep." Rabbi Yehudah says, "Even if [the adult] has eaten only one hors d'oeuvre, even if [he] has dipped only one [piece of] lettuce [and is still hungry], [he and the others] grab unleavened bread for [the sake of] the child, so that he will not fall asleep."

10:9 continued … *Up to what point does he recite [the Hallel]? The House of Shammai say, "Until 'as a mother rejoicing with her children'" [the end of Psalm 113]. And the House of Hillel say, "Until 'stones into springs of water'" [the end of Psalm 114]. And he seals with [the term or prayer for] "redemption." [He ends with a blessing formula with the motif of redemption.]* Said the House of Shammai to the House of Hillel, "And have [the Israelites] already gone forth that [they] mention the Exodus from Egypt?" [The communal meal over the paschal lamb,

Mishnah (cont.)

with the intention of eating it after its proper time] and *notar* [i.e., food left over beyond its proper time] impart uncleanness to the hands. [If one] said the blessing over the Passover offering [*Birkat Hapesach*], [he] is exempt from that over the festive offering [*shel'zevach*]; that [blessing] over the festive offering, [he] is not exempt for that over the Passover offering—the words of Rabbi Ishmael. Rabbi Akiva says, "[Saying] the former does not exempt [one from saying] the latter, and [saying] the latter does not exempt [one from saying] the former."

Tosefta (cont.)

as depicted in Exod. 12, precedes the actual Exodus from Egypt. Hence in re-creating the events, it is inappropriate at the evening meal to give thanks for the Exodus.] Said the House of Hillel to them, "Even if he waits until the cock crows [early in the morning, to mention the redemption, it is still inappropriate]. Lo, these [Israelites] did not go forth until the sixth hour of the day [= later, after the hour at which the cock crows]. [Therefore, following your logic,] how can [one] mention "redemption" [later or in the special selection of the Psalms in the morning service] while [the Israelites] have not yet been redeemed [and yet people do mention 'redemption' at that time]!"

10:9 concluded and 10 The *unleavened bread and* the *lettuce and* the *charoset, even though the charoset is not a [biblical] commandment. Rabbi Elazar ben Rabbi Tsadok says, "[It is a] commandment. In the Temple [they] serve him the carcass of the Passover offering.* A case: Rabbi Elazar ben Rabbi Tsadok said to the merchants of Lod, "Come, take the prescribed [*mitzvah*] spices."

10:11, 12 *After [eating from] the Passover offering, they do not end [with] afikoman,* such as nuts, dates, and parched grain. A person is obliged to engage himself in the [study of the] *halakhot* [= laws] of Passover all night, even with [only] his son, even with [only] himself, even with [only] his student. A case concerning: Rabban Gamaliel and the elders were eating ceremoniously [reclining] in the house of Baitos the son of Zonin in Lod,

Tosefta (cont.)

and [they] were engaged in the halakhot of the Passover offering all night, until the cock's call. [They] raised up [the table] from in front of them, and [they] stirred and went along to the house of study.

10:13 What is the blessing over the Passover offering [*Birkat Hapesach*]? "Blessed [are You, Adonai our God, ruler of the world,] who sanctified us with His commandments and commanded us to eat the Passover offering." What is the blessing over the festive offering [*Birkat Hazevach*]? "Blessed [are You, Adonai our God, ruler of the world,] who sanctified us with His commandments and commanded us to us to eat the festive offering."

The Kaufmann Mishnah, Thirteenth Century
Pesachim, Chapter 10
Ms. Kaufmann A.50, page 122
Library, Hungarian Academy of Sciences

מלמדן מה נשתנה הלילה הזה
מכל הלילות שבכל הלילות אנו
מטבלים אפילו פעם אחת הלילה
הזה שתי פעמים שבכל הלילות
אנו אוכלים חמץ ומצה הלילה
הזה כולו מצה שבכל הלילות אנו
אוכלים בשר צלי שלוק ומבושל
הלילה הזה כולו צלי לפי דעתו של בן
אביו מלמדו מתחיל בגנות ומסיים
בשבח ודורש מארמי אבד אבי
עד שהוא גומר כל הפרשה. רבן
גמליאל אומ כל שלא אמ שלושה
דברים אלו בפסח לא יצא ידי חובתו
פסח מצה ומרורים פסח על שם
שפסח המקום על בתי אבותינו במצרים
מרורים על שם שמררו המצריים את
חיי אבותינו במצרים מצה על שם
שנגאלו לפיכך אנו חייבים להודות
להלל לשבח לפאר לרומם לגדל לל
שעשה לנו ולאבותינו את כל הניסים
האלו והוציאנו מעבדות לחירות
ונאמר לפניו הללויה. ו עד איכן
הוא אומר שמי אומרים עד אם
הבנים שמחה ובית הלל עד חלמיש
למעינו מים וחותם בגאולה. ז ר
טרפון או אשר גאלנו וגאל את
אבותינו ממצ והגיענו הלילה הזה
ואינו חותם ר עקיבה אומ כן אחינו
ר אבותינו יגיענו לרגלים הבאים

לקראתכו לשלום שמחים בבנין עירך
ואוכלמן הפסחים ומן הזבחים אשר
יגיע דמם על קיר מזבחך לרצון ונודה
לך על גאולתינו בו אתה יי גאל ישראל
ח מזגו לו כוס שלישי מברך על
מזונו רביעי גומר את ההלל ואומ
עליו ברכת השיר בין הכוסות האילו
אם רצה לשתות ישתה בין שלישי
לרביעי לא ישתה. ט אין מפטירין אחר
הפסח אפיקימן ישנו מקצתן יאכלו
וכולם יאכלו ר יוסה או אם נתנמנמו
יאכלו ואם נרדמו לא יאכלו. י
הפסח אחר חצות מטמא את הידיים
הפיגל והנותר מטמאים את הידיים
בירך ברכת הפסח פטר את הזבח
את שלובח לא פטר את שלפסח דעירי
ר ישמעא ר עקיבה או לא ופוטרת
וו ולא וופוטרתו.

חסל פסח פר י

כיפורים א

שבעת ימים קודם ליום הכיפורים
מפרישין כהן גדל מביתו ללשכת
הפרהזדרין ומתקינין לו כהן אחר
תחתיו טמא יאריעבו פסל ר יהודה
או את אשה אחרת מתקינים לו שמא
תמות אשתו שנבערו ובעד במתי הוא
אשתו אמרו לו וחכמ אין לדבר סוף
ב כל שבעת הימים הוא ורק
אות הדה ומקטיר אותה קטורת ומטיב

The Kaufmann Mishnah, continued
Ms. Kaufmann A.50, page 123
Library, Hungarian Academy of Sciences

תוספתא מסכת פסחים פרק י

(1) ערב פסחים סמוך למנחה לא יאכל אדם עד שתחשך. אפי' עני שבישראל לא יאכל עד שיסב ולא יפחתו לו מארבע כוסות של יין שיש בהן כדי רביעית. בין חי בין מזוג בין חדש בין ישן. ר' יהודה או' ובלבד שיהא בו טעם יין ומראה.

(2) מזגו לו כוס ראשון בית שמיי או' מברך על היום ואחר כך מברך על היין שהיום גורם ליין שיבא וכבר קדש היום ועדיין יין לא בא. ובית הלל או' מברך על היין ואחר כך מברך על היום שהיין גורם לקדושת היום שתאמר.

(3) דבר אחר ברכת היין תדירא וברכת היום אינה תדירה. והלכה כדברי בית הלל.

(4) מצוה על אדם לשמח בניו ובני ביתו ברגל. במה משמחן ביין דכת' ויין ישמח לבב אנוש. ר' יהודה או' נשים בראוי להם וקטנים בראוי להם.

(5) השמש מכביש בבני מעים ונותן לפני האורחין אע"פ שאין ראיה

לדבר זכר לדבר נירו לכם ניר ואל תזרעו אל קוצים.

(6) המקרא את ההלל הם הולכין אצלו וקורין והוא אין הולך אצלם.

(7) המקרא את בניו ובנותיו קטנים צריך להיות עונה עמהן במקום שעונין. באי זה מקום הוא עונה הגיע לברוך הבא אום' עמהן בשם ה' הגיע לברכנוכם אום' עמהן מבית ה'.

(8) בני העיר שאין להן מי שיקרא את ההלל הולכין לבית הכנסת וקורין פרק ראשון והולכין ואוכלין ושותין וחוזרין ובאין וגומרין את כולו ואם אי אפשר להן גומרין את כולו. ההלל אין פוחתין ממנו ואין מוסיפין עליו.

(9) ר' לעזר בן פרטא היה פושט בו דברים ר' היה כופל בו דברים. ר' לעזר אמ' חוטפין מצה לתינוקות בשביל שלא ישנו. ר' יהודה או' אפי' לא אכל אלא פרפרת אחת אפי' לא טבל אלא חזרת אחת חוטפין מצה לתינוקות בשביל שלא ישנו. עד היכן הוא אום' בית שמיי או' עד אם הבנים שמחה. ובית הלל או' עד חלמיש למעינו מים וחותם בגאולה.

אמרו בית שמיי לבית הלל וכי כבר
יצאו שמזכירין יציאת מצרים אמרו
להם בית הלל אפילו הוא ממתין עד
קרות הגבר הרי אילו לא יצאו עד
שש שעות ביום היאך אומר את
הגאולה ועדין לא נגאלו. המצה
והחזרת והחרוסת אף על פי שאין
חרוסת מצוה ר' לעזר בי ר' צדוק
אומ' מצוה. במקדש מביאין לפניו
גופו של פסח.

(10) מעשה ואמ' להם ר' לעזר בר'
[צדוק] לתגרי לוד בואו וטלו לכם
תבלי מצוה.

(11) אין מפטירין אחר הפסח
אפיקומן כגון אגוזין תמרים וקליות.
חייב אדם לעסוק בהלכות הפסח כל
הלילה אפלו בינו לבין בנו אפלו
בינו לבין עצמו אפלו בינו לבין
תלמידו.

(12) מעשה ברבן גמליאל וזקנים
שהיו מסובין בבית ביתוס בן זונין
בלוד והיו עסוקין בהלכות הפסח כל
הלילה עד קרות הגבר הגביהו
מלפניהן ונועדו והלכו להן לבית
המדרש.

(13) אי זו היא ברכת הפסח ברוך
אשר קדשנו במצותיו וצונו לוכל
הפסח. אי זו היא ברכת הזבח ברוך
אשר קדשנו במצותיו וצונו לוכל
הזבח.

Appendix II

A Haggadah from the Cairo Genizah

INTRODUCTION

This manuscript of the Haggadah was looted from the Cairo Genizah in the late nineteenth century. It was then purchased by David Werner Amram, a law professor at the University of Pennsylvania and a collector of rare Hebrew books, who donated it to Dropsie College (now the Center for Advanced Jewish Studies at the University of Pennsylvania). The Dropsie Haggadah is especially important because all Haggadot in use today reflect the practice of Jews in early medieval Babylonia, whereas this one reflects the liturgical custom of the Land of Israel. It can be dated no later than the tenth or eleventh century, some time before the first Crusade, from which many Jews fled, virtually putting an end, at least temporarily, to Jewish settlement in Palestine. By the time Jews returned to reestablish themselves, they had already adopted Babylonian custom.

The manuscript contains a number of unusual blessings over food, such as "creator of various delicacies." The fact that these appear elsewhere in rabbinic literature alongside the foods they are to introduce allows us to identify the foods that were served for the Seder at which this Haggadah would have been used. Besides the usual green vegetable that we have (parsley dipped in salt water), hors d'oeuvres may have included: rice, mixed with eggs and honey; dates, figs or grapes; sweetbreads and skewers of grilled meats and sausages, possibly with more eggs.

Also noteworthy, the Haggadah's *Mah Nishtanah* contains three rather than four "questions," and the "Wandering Aramean" midrash is relatively unelaborated.

The accompanying Hebrew reflects the content of each line of each page as it appears in the manuscript along with occasional vowels and diacritical markings also present in the original.[1] The pagination follows standard terms of manuscript reference, *recto* being the right hand page, and *verso* the reverse side of it. These are noted in both the Hebrew and the English translation. To facilitate reference, we have added "verse numbers" and subheadings (in brackets); to save space, we have omitted Psalms 113 and 114 (in Hebrew and in English) since they do not differ from our standard biblical wording.

The translation and accompanying commentary are by Joel M. Hoffman. The manuscript (Halper 211) can be viewed on line in its entirety: http://sceti.library.upenn.edu/pages/index.cfm?so_id=2242. (See illustration in *My People's Passover Haggadah*, Volume 1, p. 146.)

Sanctification of Passover

קדוש פסח

[1]Blessed are You, Adonai our God, ruler of the world, creator of the fruit of the vine.

[2]Blessed are You, Adonai our God, ruler of the world, who sanctified Israel His people above all nations and loved them above all peoples. Adonai our God gave us Sabbaths for rest, festivals and times of the year for rejoicing. [3]He gave us this day of Shabbat, the Festival of Matzot for happiness, and for the holidays and for holy occasions, [2r] for on it Adonai our God brought miracles and mighty acts to those who love Him, and wonders to those who like Him. [4]Blessed are You, Adonai, who sanctifies Israel, Shabbat, and the Festival of Matzot, and holidays of happiness and the times of the year and holy occasions.

1v [1] ברוך אתה יי אלהנו מלך
העלם בורא פרי הגפן
[2] ברוך אתה יי אלהינו מלך
העלם אשר קדש ישראל
עמו מכל העמים ורצה
בהם מכל הלשונות [3] ויתן
לנו יי אלהנו שבתת לִמְנוּחה
חגים וזמנים לששון את
יום השבת הזה את יום
חג המצות לשמחה
וליום טוב ולמקראי קדש
2r כי בו עשה יי אלהינו נסים
וגבורות לא[ו]הביו
ונפלאות לבני ידידיו
[4] ברוך אתה יי מקדש
ישראל השבת וחג המצות
ומועדי שמחה והזמנים
ומקראי קדש

"Sanctification of Passover" Or, "Kiddush for Passover." The word *kiddush*, "sanctification," is also a technical term for the "sanctification" prayer, which, in English we call "Kiddush." This is basically the same prayer we use for Shabbat and other holidays.

[2] *"All nations"* Literally, "all the nations." The Hebrew here differs slightly from our main text, which reads, literally, "every nation." But the Hebrew for "all" and for "every" is identical, so the Hebrew is closer than the English would indicate. On the addition in English of "other," see "the nations," *My People's Passover Haggadah*, Volume 1, p. 130.

[2] *"All peoples"* For more, see "people," Volume 1, p. 130.

[3] *"He gave us"* We add this for the same reason we added "You gave us" in Volume 1, on p. 130 ("You gave us").

3 *"Festival"* Literally, "day of the Festival. We omit the second word "day" because "day of the Festival of Matzot" is awkward in a way that the Hebrew is not.

3 *"The holidays"* Literally, "good day." See "holidays," *My People's Passover Haggadah,* Volume 1, p. 130.

3 *"Brought"* Literally, "did."

3 *"Miracles"* Or "wonders." Miracles are extra-scientific and are therefore possible only in a scientific culture. (There are, thus, wonders but no miracles in the Bible.) It is difficult to know the degree to which the Genizah manuscript reflects a community that had incorporated science. But because we will need "wonders" immediately below, we choose "miracles" here.

3 *"Mighty acts"* We would prefer a single word in English here, but nothing appropriate suggests itself.

3 *"Those who love Him"* Literally, "his lovers," but "lovers" in English does not mean what we want it to. (And "adorers" is not a word.)

3 *"Those who like Him"* Literally, "his friends." We use the same phrasing here that we did for "those who love Him" to reproduce the Hebrew parallel structure in English.

4 *"Holidays"* Hebrew, *mo'ed,* a different word in Hebrew than we just translated as "holidays."

[Other Blessings]

1 Blessed are You, Adonai our God, ruler of the world, who has kept us alive, sustained us, and brought us to this time of year.

[2v] 2 Blessed are You, Adonai our God, ruler of the world, who sanctified us with His commandments and commanded us about washing our hands.

3 Blessed are You, Adonai our God, ruler of the world, creator of the fruit of the earth.

4 Blessed are You, Adonai our God, ruler of the world, creator of the fruit of the tree.

5 Blessed are You, Adonai our God, ruler of the world, who [3r] created mountains and valleys

2r...¹ ברוך אתה יי אלהנו מלך
העלם שהחינו וקימנו
והגיענו לזמן הזה
2v ²ברוך אתה יי אלהינו
מלך העלם אשר קדשנו
במצותיו וצונו על נטילת
ידים ³ ברוך אתה
יי אלהנו מלך העלם בורא
פרי האדמה
⁴ ברוך אתה יי אלהנו מלך
העלם בורא פרי העץ
⁵ ברוך אתה יי
אלהנו מלך העלם אשר
3r ברא הרים ובקעות

237

and planted every fruit tree in them.

[6]Blessed are You, Adonai, for the land and for the fruit of the tree.

[7]Blessed are You, Adonai our God, ruler of the world, creator of various delicacies.

[8]Blessed are You, Adonai our God, ruler of the world, who created various delicacies to delight [3v] many people.

[9]Blessed are You, Adonai, for the land and for delicacies.

[10]Blessed are You, Adonai our God, ruler of the world, creator of various souls.

[11]Blessed are You, Adonai our God, ruler of the world, who created pure souls in which to bring the soul of all that lives to life.

[4r] [12]Blessed are You, Adonai, eternal life.

ונטע בהם עץ כל
פרי ⁶ברוך אתה יי על
הארץ ועל פרי העץ.
⁷ברוך אתה יי אלהנו
מלך העלם בורא
מיני מעדנים
⁸ברוך אתה יי אלהנו
מלך העלם אשר ברא
מיני מעדנים לעדן בהם
 נפשות רבות ⁹ברוך אתה 3v
יי על הארץ ועל מעדנים
¹⁰ברוך אתה יי
אלהנו מלך העלם
בורא מיני נפשות
¹¹ברוך אתה
יי אלהנו מלך העלם
אשר ברא נפשות
טהרות להחיות
בהם נפש כל חי
⁴ʳ ¹²ברוך אתה יי חי
העולמים

³ *"Fruit of the earth"* Of course, fruits come from trees and vines, not from the earth. The Hebrew *p'ri* is, in fact, more general than our "fruit," but because the translation "fruit" works so well elsewhere, we are stuck with it here.

⁷ *"Delicacies"* Hebrew, *ma'adanim*, the plural of *ma'adan*. (In Modern Hebrew, a *ma'adan* is a treat, such as chocolate pudding.) We find a similar blessing in the Jerusalem Talmud and, for example, the Rule of the Congregation ("1QSᵇ") from the Dead Sea Scrolls. The word may refer to a specifically tasty sort of food, as we assume here, or it may simply be a dialectal variant meaning "food."

⁸ *"To delight"* In Hebrew, the word for "to delight" here, *l'aden*, shares a root with *ma'adan* (see immediately above). The Hebrew words are more similar than our English translations.

[8] *"People"* Hebrew, *nefesh*, on which see "people," *My People's Passover Haggadah*, Volume 1, p. 130.

[10] *"Souls"* Or "people." The Hebrew word (*nefesh*) captures elements of both. For more, see *My People's Prayer Book*, Volume 1, *The Sh'ma and Its Blessings*, pp. 100 and 102. The Hebrew word here recurs in the following two blessings.

[11] *"The soul of all that lives"* From Job 12:10.

◆

[Questions of the Night and Telling the Passover Story]

[1] Why is this night different from all other nights?

[2] —In that on all other nights we don't dip things one time, this night, two times;

[3] —In that on all other nights we eat leaven and matzah, this night, only matzah;

[4v] [4] —In that on all other nights we eat our meat roasted, grilled, and boiled, this night, only roasted.

[5] A father teaches his son according to his son's intelligence, beginning with disgrace and ending with glory and says, [6] "In the past, your ancestors—Terach, Abraham's father and Nachor's father—lived across the river and served [5r] other gods. And I took your father, Abraham, from across the river and I led him throughout the entire Land of

4r... [1] מה נשתנה

הלילה הזה מכל

הלילות [2]שבכל

הלילות אין אנו מטבלין פעם אחת

והלילה הזה שתי

פעמים [3]שבכל

הלילות אנו אוכלים

4v חמץ ומצה הלילה הזה כלו מצה

[4]שבכל הלילות אנו אכלים

בשר צלי שלוק ומבשל

הלילה הזה כלי צלי

[5]לפי דעתו שלבן אביו

מלמדו מתחיל בגנות

ומסיים בשבח

ואומר [6]בעבר

הנהר ישבו אבותיכם

מעלם תרח אבי אברהם

ואבי נחור ויעבדו

5r אלהים אחרים ואקח

את אביכם את

אברהם מעבר הנהר

ואולך אתו בכל ארץ

239

Canaan and I multiplied his descendants by giving him Isaac, and by giving Isaac Jacob and Esau, and by giving Esau the hill country of Seir as his inheritance while Jacob and his children went down to Egypt."

[5v] [7]Blessed is the One who keeps His promise to Israel. Blessed is He.

[8]After all, the Holy One foresees the end … to do to our father Jacob, for wicked Pharaoh's decree only concerned the males, while Laban wanted to uproot everyone, as it says:

[9]As what He said to Abraham our father between the pieces. As it says,

[10]"He told Abram, [6r] 'Know that your descendants will be strangers in a land that is not theirs; they shall be enslaved and oppressed for four hundred years.'"

[11]This kept our ancestors and us going. Not just one group has risen up against us to destroy us, and the Holy One of Blessing saves us from their hand.

[12]But rather in every generation they rise up against us to destroy us.

[13]Note well what Laban the Aramean wanted to do to our father Jacob, for wicked Pharaoh's decree only concerned the males, while Laban wanted to uproot everyone, as it says:

[14]"My father was a wandering Aramean. He descended to Egypt" compelled

*In the manuscript this line appears in the margin.

כנען וארבה את זרעו
ואתן לו את יצחק ואתן
ליצחק את יעקב ואת
עשו ואתן לעשו את
הר שעיר לרשת אתו
ויעקב ובניו ירדו מצרימה
5v [7] ברוך שומר הבטחתו
של ישראל ברוך הוא
[8] שהקודש מחשב את
הקץ לעשות ליעקב אבינו
שפרעה הרשע לא גזר
אלא על הזכרים לבן בקש
לעקר את הכל שנאמר
[9] כמשאמר לאברהם
אבינו בין הבתרים שנ'
[10] ויאמר לאברם ידוע
6r תדע כי גר יהיה זרעך בארץ
לא להם ועבדום וענו אותם
ארבע מאות שנה: [11] היא שע'
שעמדה לאבותינו ולנו שלא
אחד בלבד עמד עלינו
לכלותינו והקב֫ה֫ מצילינו מידם
[12] אלא בכל דור ודור עומדים עלינו לכלותינו *
[13] צא ולמד מה בקש לבן
הארמי לעשות ליעקב אבינו
שפרעה הרשע לא גזר אלא
על הזכרים ולבן בקש לעקור
את הכל שנאמר [14] ארמי אובד
אבי וירד מצרימה אנוסה

240

[6v] by the word "and lived there in small numbers and there he became a large, mighty and populous nation. [15]The Egyptians were evil toward us and afflicted us and imposed harsh labor upon us."

[16]"We cried out to Adonai our ancestors' God, and Adonai heard our voice and saw our misery and our work and our distress. [17]Adonai brought us out of Egypt" not by an angel and not by a seraph and not by a messenger, but rather the Holy One of Blessing Himself.

[18]"With a strong hand"—[7r] this is two; "with an outstretched arm"—this is two; "with great awe"—this is two; "with signs"—this is two; "with wonders"—this is two. [19]These are the ten plagues that God of Blessing brought upon the Egyptians in Egypt. And these are the plagues:

6v עַל פִּי הַדָּבָר וַיָּגָר שָׁם בִּמְתֵי

מְעָט וַיְהִי שָׁם לְגוֹי גָּדוֹל עָצוּם

15 וָרָב וַיָּרֵעוּ אוֹתָנוּ הַמִּצְרִים

וַיְעַנּוּנוּ וַיִּתְּנוּ עָלֵינוּ עֲבוֹדָה

16 קָשָׁה· וַנִּצְעַק אֶל יְיָ אֱלֹהֵי

אֲבוֹתֵינוּ וַיִּשְׁמַע יְיָ אֶת קוֹלֵינוּ

וַיַּרְא אֶת עָנְיֵנוּ וְאֶת עֲמָלֵינוּ

17 וְאֶת לַחֲצֵינוּ וַיּוֹצִיאֵינוּ יְיָ

מִמִּצְרִים לֹא עַל יְדֵי מַלְאָךְ לֹא

עַל יְדֵי שָׂרָף לֹא עַל יְדֵי שָׁלִיחַ

18 אֶלָּא הַקָּבָּ״ה בְּעַצְמוֹ בְּיָד

חֲזָקָה שְׁתַּיִם וּבִזְרוֹעַ נְטוּיָה

7r שְׁתַּיִם בְּמוֹרָא גָּדוֹל שְׁתַּיִם

בְּאוֹתוֹת שְׁתַּיִם וּבְמוֹפְתִים

19 שְׁנַיִם אֵלּוּ עֶשֶׂר מַכּוֹת שֶׁהֵבִיא

הַמָּקוֹם בָּרוּךְ הוּא עַל הַמִּצְרִים

בְּמִצְרִים וְאֵלּוּ הֵן

[4]*"Our meat"* Literally, just "meat." We add the word "our" to make it possible in English to put the adjectives after the noun.

[4]*"Grilled"* This represents one possible understanding of the Hebrew cookery term. But along with "boiled," next, these are guesses. (We are more sure of "roasted" because the tradition for roasting a shankbone has been preserved.) Blake Leyerle raises the interesting possibility that our three Hebrew terms may correspond with three Greek terms: *optanos* ("roasted") for *ts'li*, *hepsanos* ("boiled") for *m'vushal*, and *opson* ("cooked" or "prepared") for *shaluk*.

[5]*"Father"* Or perhaps, "parent," though the cultural context makes this more inclusive option unlikely.

[5]*"Son"* Or perhaps "child."

[5] *"His son's"* Literally, "his." The Hebrew words are arranged to make it clear who "his" refers to.

[7] *"His promise to Israel"* The Hebrew here differs slightly from our main text. Here we have, literally, "keeps Israel's promise," but the manuscript text here nonetheless refers to a promise made by God, not by Israel. It is common for languages and dialects to differ in this sort of way. For example, in English, "my promise" is only a promise I make, not one made to me; by contrast, "my photograph" could be a photo I took or one taken of me.

[8] *"Holy One"* Hebrew, simply, *hakadosh*. Perhaps this was supposed to be, as in the main text, "Holy One of Blessing."

[9] *"Between the pieces"* Translated literally. In the main text, we paraphrase "covenant between the pieces" as "splitting covenant." The shorter version we have here is the more intriguing, potentially referring to what God may have told Abraham between the pieces.

[14] *"Compelled"* For reasons that are not clear, the word seems to be feminine *(anusa)*. This may be a scribal error or represent a grammatical form we do not understand. Or it may reflect a Hebrew pronunciation at odds with the Masoretic pronunciation, which forms the basis of "standard" Hebrew; see "slaying," *My People's Passover Haggadah*, Volume 2, p. 243.

[17] *"The Holy One of Blessing"* The Hebrew here is abbreviated. We find only the first letter of each word of the phrase, and dots over the resulting word. (Dots were frequently used to indicate abbreviations.) We note the fact only because there seems to be no reason for the abbreviation.

[19] *"God"* Hebrew, *hamakom*. See "God of Blessing," Volume 2, p. 244.

———◆———

[The Ten Plagues in Egypt]

[1]Blood. [2]Frogs.	7r... [1]דם [2]צפרדיע *
[3]Lice. [4]Swarms. [5]Blight. [6]Boils. [7]Hail.	[3]כנים [4]ערוב [5]דבר [6]שחין [7]ברד
[8]Locusts. [9]Darkness. [10]Slaying of the first-born.	[8]ארבה [9]חושך [10]מכות בכורות

*In the manuscript these two words are part of the previous line.

[10] *"Slaying"* The Hebrew here looks like it reads "slayings," that is, *makot (mem-kaf-vav-tav)*, instead of *makat (mem-kaf-tav*, as we have in the main text). More likely, however, the *vav* here is evidence of different traditions for pronouncing Hebrew. Our current pronunciation is based upon work done in Tiberias toward the end of the first millennium. Jews elsewhere almost certainly pronounced their words differently. Here we see potential evidence that the word was pronounced not *makat* but rather *makot*. (For more on the various pronunciations of Hebrew, and where our current understanding comes from, see Joel M. Hoffman, *In the Beginning: A Short History of the Hebrew Language* [New York: NYU Press, 2004].)

—◆—

[Symbols of the Night and "In Each and Every Generation"]

[1] He brought us out of there, as it says, "It was us that He brought out of there."

[2] Rabban Gamaliel says, "Anyone who doesn't explain these three things on Passover has not fulfilled his obligation: Passover, [7v] matzah, and bitter herbs."

[3] The Passover is for the God of Blessing's passing over the houses of our ancestors in Egypt, as it says, "You shall say the Passover sacrifice is for Adonai, who passed over the houses of the children of Israel in Egypt when He struck Egypt but saved our houses. The people then bowed down low."

[4] The bitter herbs are for the Egyptians embittering the lives of our ancestors in Egypt, as it says, "They embittered their lives with hard work with mortar and brick, and with all manner of

7r...[1] והוציאנו משם שנאמר

ואותנו הוציא משם. [2] רבן

גמליאל אומר כל שלא אמר

שלושה דברים אילו בפסח

לא יצא ידי חובתו · פסח

7v מצה ומרורים · [3] פסח על שום

שפסח המקום ברוך הוא על

בתי אבותינו במצרים שנא'

ואמרתם זבח פסח הוא לייי

אשר פסח על בתי בני ישראל

במצרים בנגפו אתמצרים

ואת בתינו הציל ויקוד העם

וישתחוו · [4] מרורים על

שום שמררו המצרים את

חיי אבותינו במצרים שנא'

וימררו את חייהם בעבודה

קשה בחומר ובלבנים ובכל

[8r] work in the field; they did all of their work under duress."

⁵The matzah is for having been redeemed, as it says, "They baked the dough that they brought out of Egypt into cakes of matzah, because it had not leavened, because they were evicted from Egypt and they could not delay, and they hadn't prepared any provisions."

⁶In each and every generation people must regard themselves as though they personally left Egypt, as it says, "Tell your child [8v] on that day: it is because of what Adonai did for me when I left Egypt."

⁷We must therefore thank, praise, honor, glorify, exalt, extol, and exult the One who did all of these miracles for us and for our ancestors, and brought us from slavery to freedom. ⁸So let us exclaim: "Halleluyah!"

עבודה בשדה את כל עבו' 8r
עבודתם אשר עבדו בהם
בפרך · ⁵מצה על שום
שנגאלו · שנאמר ויאפו
את הבצק אשר הוציאו
ממצרים עוגות מצות כי לא
חמץ כי גרשו ממצרים
ולא יכלו להתמהמה וגם
צדה לא עשו להם · ⁶בכל
דור ודור חייב אדם לראות
את עצמו כאילו הוא יצא
ממצרים. שנא' והגדת לבנך
ביום ההוא לאמר בעבור זה 8v
עשה יי לי בצאתי ממצרים
⁷לפיכך אנו חייבים להודות
להלל לשבח לפאר לרומם
לגדל לנצֵחַ למי שעשה לנו
ולאבותינו את כל הנסים
האלו והוציאנו מעבדות
לחרות ⁸ונאמר לפניו הללויה

¹ *"It was us that He brought out of there"* Or just, "He brought us out of there." The Hebrew word order (taken directly from Deuteronomy 6:23) is different than in the phrase that precedes it ("He brought us out of there"). To mark the difference, we use different translations in English, too. If it were grammatical in English, here we would prefer, "us He brought out of there."

² *"Passover"* That is, the Passover sacrifice, *pesach* in Hebrew.

² *"Bitter herbs"* Here we find a plural word, *m'rorim*. By contrast, the main text has just the collective noun *maror*. Because we translated *maror* as "bitter herbs," we have no way of capturing the small dialectal difference we see here.

³ *"God of Blessing's"* Hebrew, *hamakom baruch hu*. We have used "Holy One of Blessing" for the (more common) *hakadosh baruch hu*. Here we see *kadosh* ("Holy One") replaced with *makom*.

[5] *"Having been redeemed"* Literally, "they were redeemed." We rephrase so we can continue the "is for …" pattern, matching the Hebrew *al shum*….

[7] *"Extol"* We would prefer a more common word here for the Hebrew *l'gadel* (from the common Hebrew root *g.d.l*, "great"), but we have used up all of the common words. "Magnify" would be great, but we used it for a different word in the main text. "Aggrandize" would be fine except for its very negative connotations.

[7] *"Exult"* Or, "eternalize," but that word in English seems to apply primarily to the dead. The Hebrew comes from a root that denotes both "victory" and "eternity."

———◆———

The first two Psalms of Hallel, Psalms 113 and 114, have been omitted.

[Blessings of Redemption]

[…9v] [1]Blessed is the One who redeemed us and redeemed our ancestors from Egypt, and brought us to this night to eat matzah and bitter herbs.

[10r] [2]So too, Adonai our God and our ancestors' God, bring us to festivals that are approaching in peace, that we might be happy as we rebuild Your city, joyful as we serve You.

[3]There we will eat from the *zevachs* and the *pesachs* the blood from which will reach the wall of Your altar and please You. [4]And we will gratefully acknowledge You with a new song for our redemption. [5]Blessed are You, Adonai, redeemer of Israel.

[6]Blessed are You, Adonai our God, ruler of the world, who sanctified us with His commandments and commanded us about eating matzah and bitter herbs on this night in honor of the mighty acts of the King

ב [1] ...9v

אשר גאלנו וגאל את אבותינו
ממצרים והגיענו ללילה הזה
לאכל בו מצות ומרורים
10r [2]כן אלהנו ואלהי אבותינו יגיענו
לרגלים הבאים לקראתינו
לשלום שמחים בבנין עירך
[3]שם ששים בעבודתך ונאכל
מן הזבחים ומן הפסחים
שיגיע דמם על קיר מזבחך
לרצון [4]ונודה לך שיר חדש
על גאולתינו [5]ברוך אתה יי
גאל ישראל : [6]ברוך אתה יי אלהנו
מלך העלם אשר קדשנו
במצותיו וצונו על אכילת
מצה ומרור בלילה הזה
להזכיר גבורתו שלמלך

[10v] over the kings of kings, blessed be He, who brought miracles to our ancestors at this time of year for Abraham, Isaac, and Jacob.

⁷Blessed are You, Adonai, who remembers the covenant.

⁸Blessed are You, Adonai our God, ruler of the world, who brings bread out of the earth. Amen.

¹⁰v מלכי המלכים ברוך הוא
שעשה נסים לאבתינו בזמן
הזה בעבור אברהם יצחק
ויעקב ⁷ברוך אתה יי זוכר
הברית: ⁸ברוך אתה יי אל׳
מלך העלם המוצא לחם מן
הארץ אמן

¹ *"Blessed is the One"* The manuscript has a lone *bet*, the first letter of *baruch* ("Blessed"). This was probably meant as an abbreviation for "Blessed is the One," as we have here, though it could have been the longer, "Blessed are You, Adonai our God, ruler of the world."

¹ *"Bitter herbs"* Once again, the word is plural in the manuscript. See *"Maror," My People's Passover Haggadah*, Volume 2, p. 244.

³ *"From which"* The Hebrew subordinative word that gives us "from which" is *she-* here, while it is *asher* in the main text. The words are identical in meaning, and we point out the difference only so readers of the English can see every place that the manuscript differs from the main text.

⁶ *"Bitter herbs"* The Hebrew here is singular. See above, "Bitter herbs."

⁶ *"In honor of"* Others, "to remember." See *"memorial," My People's Passover Haggadah*, Volume 1, p. 130.

⁶ *"The mighty acts of"* We would prefer to use the simple possessive here, but "the King over the kings of kings' mighty acts" is too hard to parse.

———◆———

Blessing

¹Let us bless the One from whom we have eaten and from whose bounty we live.

²Blessed are You, Adonai our God, ruler of the world: on Passover You once redeemed those who sought Your majestic glory, and You saved and redeemed the males.

³"Make it into loaves." [11r] As it says, "And Abraham hurried to his tent toward Sarah and said, 'Hurry! Three measures of flour! Knead it and make it into loaves.'"

⁴And it says, "You open your hand

ברכה
¹...¹⁰v נברך שאכלנו משלו ומטבו
חיינו ²ברוך אתה יי אלהנו מלך
העלם אז בפסח גאלתה
דורשי הוד כבודו הצלת
והושעת זכור ³עשי עוגות
¹¹r כן׳ וימהר אברהם האהלה
אל שרה ויאמר מהרי שלש
סאים קמח סלת לושי ועשי
עוגות ⁴ונ׳ פותח את ידיך

and satisfy the desire of everything that lives."

⁵Blessed are You, Adonai, who provides for everyone.

⁶This is the Passover rite: the purification of friends, who all left happy to keep the month of Aviv, as it says, ⁷"Keep the month of Aviv and offer a *pesach* to Adonai your God, for in the month of Aviv Adonai your God brought you out of Egypt at night."

⁸And it says, [11v] "Eat your fill and bless Adonai your God for the good land that He gave you, and remember…."

⁵בָּרוּךְ וּמַשְׂבִּיעַ לְכָל חַי רָצוֹן
אַתָּה יי' 'הַזָּן' אֶת הַכֹּל
⁶זֹאת חֻקַּת הַפֶּסַח טַהֲרַת
יְדִידִים כֻּלָּם יָצְאוּ שְׂמֵחִים
לִשְׁמוֹר אֶת חֹדֶשׁ הָאָבִיב
כנ' ⁷שָׁמוֹר אֶת חֹדֶשׁ הָאָבִיב
וְעָשִׂיתָ פֶּסַח לַיי' אֱלֹהֶיךָ כִּי
בְּחֹדֶשׁ הָאָבִיב הוֹצִיאֲךָ יי'
אֱלֹהֶיךָ מִמִּצְרַיִם לַיְלָה ⁸וּן'
11v וְאָכַלְתָּ וְשָׂבַעְתָּ וּבֵרַכְתָּ אֶת יי'
אֱלֹהֶיךָ עַל הָאָרֶץ הַטֹּבָה אֲשֶׁר
נָתַן לָךְ וְזָכַרְתָּ . . .

"Blessing" Or, perhaps, *B'rakhah.* Above ("Sanctification of Passover") we noted that *Kiddush* can mean "sanctification," generically, or "*Kiddush,*" specifically. Presumably, *B'rakhah* works the same way, even though *Kiddush* is a commonly used modern word while the same is not true for *B'rakhah.* If the word was a technical term, then perhaps a modern equivalent such as *Birkat Hamazon* or "grace" captures the spirit of the original text.

² *"Once"* That is, "long ago," not "one time."

² *"Your majestic glory"* We translate more or less literally, though this may have been an expression, akin to the modern English "your honor" (to a judge).

² *"The males"* Literally, "a male."

³ *"Loaves"* Others, "cakes." But these were essentially bread, not cakes as we know them.

³ *"Flour"* The Hebrew, from Genesis 18:6, indicates a particular type of flour.

⁴ *"You open"* The Hebrew is actually just a second-person singular verb (as in, "[You] open"), not an imperative ("open!"), because the text cites Psalm 145:16: "[You] open Your hand…." So we add the subject "You."

⁵ *"Provides"* Or perhaps the more specific "provides food."

⁵ *"Everyone"* The Hebrew, *kol,* potentially includes animals as well as people.

⁶ *"Rite"* Or, "law."

⁷ *"Offer"* Literally, "do."

⁷ *"Pesach"* Passover sacrifice.

⁸ *"Eat your fill"* Literally, "eat and be satisfied."

Notes

9. A LONG ANSWER: A MIDRASH ON "MY FATHER WAS A WANDERING ARAMEAN ..."

David Arnow

1. Friedlander, *Pirke De Rabbi Eliezer*, p. 273.
2. BT Shab. 89b and *Gen. Rabbah* 86:2.
3. Esther 1:11, 2:17, 6:8.
4. *MRI, Pischa* 5:14, vol. 1, p. 34, and p. 35 n. 2.
5. *MRI, Pischa* 5:6, vol.1, pp. 33–34.
6. Author's translation of Ps.?27:14.?
7. *Tanchuma*, sec. 4:12 on Exod. 15:1.
8. For "affliction" as separation of husbands and wives, see BT Yoma 74b.
9. Friedlander, *Pirke de Rabbi Eliezer*, p. 379. According to *Pesikta de-Rav Kahana* (7:6/9), Bithya, a first-born, was spared the tenth plague. For a recent discussion of the passage from Mishnah Sanhedrin, see Gilbert S. Rosenthal, "The Strange Tale of a Familiar Text" (*The Journal of the Academy for Jewish Religion*, vol. 3, no. 1, 2007). The oldest manuscripts of this midrash quote the Mishnah as it appears here without "preserving a life *in Israel*..." See Friedlander, *Pirke De Rabbi Eliezer*, p. 379, note 3, and *Pirke De Rabbi Eliezer* by C. M. Horowitz (Jerusalem: Makor Publishing, 1972), p. 175.

Carole B. Balin

1. My thanks to David Arnow for his suggestions on this incipit.
2. I[saac]. S. Moses, ed. *Seder Hagadah: Domestic Service for the Eve of Passover*, 2nd ed. (Chicago: no publisher noted, 1898), pp. 10–11.

Alyssa Gray

1. Jacob Z. Lauterbach, *Mekilta de-Rabbi Ishmael* (Philadelphia: Jewish Publication Society, 1933), Pischa 5:6, vol. 1, pp. 33–34.

10. THE ROLE OF GOD

David Arnow

1. Abraham Joshua Heschel, *Moral Grandeur and Spiritual Audacity*, ed. Susannah Heschel (New York: Straus and Giroux, 1996), p. 163.
2. The Bible itself contains the roots of these beliefs. The Book of Numbers states: "We cried to Adonai and He heard our plea, and He sent a *malakh* [an angel or messenger] who took us out

from Egypt" (20:16). With regard to the last plague we read: "For when Adonai goes through to smite the Egyptians, He will see the blood on the lintel and two doorposts, and Adonai will pass over the door and not let the destroyer [*mashchit*] enter and smite your home" (Exod. 12:23). These ideas were vividly elaborated in extra-cannonical Jewish texts of the late Second Temple period such as the Book of Jubilees (49:2) and the Wisdom of Solomon (18:14–15).

3. *MRI*, *Pischa* 7:28, vol. 1, p. 53.

4. *MRI*, *Bachodesh* 5:20, vol. 2, pp. 231–32.

5. The midrash uses the term "blight" *(dever)* not with regard to the fifth plague, but more broadly as a form of divine punishment.

6. The figure in 1 Chronicles 21:16 holding the sword in his hand is none other than "the angel of Adonai," a key figure in the Two Powers Heresy. As quoted in the Haggadah, one would certainly have the impression that it was God whose hand was outstretched over Jerusalem, as it had been over Egypt (Exod. 14:31).

7. *MRI*, *Shirata* 3:24, vol. 2, p. 24.

8. *MRI*, *Pischa* 14:35 ff. vol. 1, pp. 113–114.

9. *MRI*, *Beshalach* 7:89, vol. 1, p. 249. The midrash reads *mikerev* to mean "from the innards" (in Lev. 1:13 *kerev* means "entrails") rather than simply "from within." See *Midrash on Psalms* 114:6 for this explanation.

10. *MRI*, *Pischa* 16:171, vol. 1, p. 141.

11. Friedlander, *Pirke De Rabbi Eliezer*, p. 312.

12. This view is widely, but erroneously, attributed to Abarbanel's commentary on the Haggadah, *Zevach Pesach*. As pointed out by Goldschmidt (*Seder Haggadah Shel Pesach* [Tel Aviv: Schocken, 1947], pp. 21–22) and Akiva ben Ezra (*Minhage Hagim* [Jerusalem: M. Nyuman, 1962], pp. 241–43), the origins of this interpretation are relatively recent. As Ben Ezra notes, numerous customs support the notion that the wine removed from our cups represents a dangerous substance. In various places the spilt wine was secretly poured on the doorstep of a *soneh yisra'el*, "one who hates Israel," as it was believed that contact with the wine would result in death of a member of one's household.

13. See Jacob Moellin Segal, *Sefer Maharil* (Jerusalem: Jerusalem Institute, 1989), Seder HaHaggadah, p. 27.

14. For more on this subject, see *My People's Passover Haggadah*, Volume 2, p. 175 *(Hallel)*.

15. Although the Pharaoh of the Exodus is not the one to which Ezekiel is referring, rabbinic literature freely interprets biblical verses pertaining to one in terms of the other.

16. The description in Exodus (8:13) notes that the lice are "in" rather than "on" man and beast, as if they have penetrated like arrows.

17. In Exodus (8:17) the word is spelled without a *vav*. William Braude offers a somewhat different explanation of the wordplay. See his translation of *Pesikta Rabbati* (New Haven: Yale University Press, 1968), vol. 2, p. 447, n. 108.

18. Enelow, *Mishnah of Rabbi Eliezer*, chap. 19, p. 355.

19. *MRI*, *Pischa* 13:31, vol. 1, p. 98.

20. *Pesikta D'rav Kahana* (7:6/9) asserts that first-born daughters were also slain.

21. The midrash makes a play on words involving "immeasurable," עַד בְּלִי דַי, and "until your lips shall wear away," עַד שֶׁיִּבְלוּ.

22. *MRI*, *Beshalach* 2:108, vol. 1, p. 195.

23. *MRI*, *Shirata* 7:20, vol. 2, p. 55.

24. *Jerusalem Bible* translation.

25. *MRI*, *Beshalach* 1:5, vol. 1, p. 169.

26. Friedlander, *Pirke De Rabbi Eliezer*, p. 342.

Carole B. Balin

1. *Seder of the Children of Abraham* appears in *Shalom Seders. Three Haggadot,* compiled by New Jewish Agenda, introduction by Arthur Waskow (New York: Adama Books, 1984).
2. Ibid., p. 61–62.
3. Ibid., p. 63.
4. Noam Zion and David Dishon, *A Different Night: The Family Participation Haggadah* (Jerusalem: Shalom Hartman Institute, 1997), p. 107.

Alyssa Gray

1. See Ephraim Kanarfogel, *"Peering Through the Lattices": Mystical, Magical, and Pietistic Dimensions in the Tosafist Period* (Detroit, MI: Wayne State University Press, 2000), p. 137.
2. *Sefer Maharil: Minhagim: Seder Ha-Haggadah,* par. 27.
3. *Darkhei Moshe* to *Tur Orach Chayim* 473.
4. Kanarfogel, *Peering,* p. 137.
5. Ibid., p. 138.
6. *Magen Avraham* to *Shulchan Arukh,* O. Ch. 473:7, n. 29.
7. *Be'er Heiteiv* to *Shulchan Arukh,* O. Ch. 473:7, n. 26.
8. Shab. 146a and A. Z. 22b.
9. *Orchot Chayim* in *Haggadah Shel Pesach* (Torat Chayim) (Jerusalem: Mossad Harav Kook, 1998).

Wendy I. Zierler

1. Alan Unterman, Rivka Horwitz, Joseph Dan, and Sharon Koren, *"Shekhinah,"* in *Encyclopaedia Judaica,* 2nd ed., eds. Michael Berenbaum and Fred Skolnik (Detroit: Macmillan Reference, 2007), vol. 18, pp. 440–44.
2. Isaiah Tishby, *The Wisdom of the Zohar,* trans. David Goldstein (Oxford: Littman Library, 1989), p. 382.
3. Lynn Gottlieb, *She Who Dwells Within* (New York: HarperSanFrancisco, 1995), p. 22.
4. Margaret Moers Wenig, "Their Lives a Page Plucked from a Holy Book," in *The Woman's Passover Companion,* p. 123.
5. *San Diego Women's Haggadah,* 2nd ed. (San Diego: Women's Institute for Continuing Jewish Education, 1986), p. 41.
6. Arnold M. Rothstein, "Anthropocentrism and New Forms of Idolatry," *Journal of Reform Judaism* (Spring 1981): 26–32.
7. E. M. Broner and Naomi Nimrod, *The Women's Haggadah* (San Francisco: Harper SanFrancisco, 1994), pp. 56–65.

11. SUMMING IT ALL UP ...

David Arnow

1. *Melchilta dej-Rabbi Shimon bar Yohai,* trans. W. David Nelson (Philadelphia: Jewish Publication Society, 2006), *Pischa* 14:1, p. 46 (hereafter cited in notes as *MRSBY*).
2. *MRSBY, Pischa* 16:3, p. 56.
3. *MRI, Pischa* 14:49, vol. 1, p. 110.
4. *MRI, Shirata* 8:94, vol. 2, p. 66.

Alyssa Gray

1. *Ran* on Alfasi to Pes. 25b. in *Rif,* s.v. *"kol."*
2. *M'yuchas L'Rashbam,* in *Haggadah Shel Pesach* (Torat Chayim).
3. *Rashbam* to Pes. 116b, s.v. *"tsarikh l'hagbiha."*

4. Martin I. Lockshin, ed. and trans., *Rashbam's Commentary on Exodus: An Annotated Translation* (Atlanta: Scholars Press, 1997), p. 110, n. 42.

5. *Pischa* 14:49, Lauterbach, *Mekhilta de-Rabbi Ishmael*, vol. 1, p. 110.

6. *Sefer Maharil, Seder Ha-Haggadah*, par. 26.

Wendy I. Zierler

1. Pauline Wengeroff, *Rememberings*, trans. Henny Wenkart (College Park: University Press of Maryland, 2000), p. 37.

12. "Praise": *Hallel*, Part One

David Arnow

1. The expression appears in BT Pes. 116b in connection with the Seder.

2. J. D. Eisenstein, *Ozar Midrashim* (New York: published by the author, 1915), p. 127.

3. The midrash renders the last phrase of Ps. 114:1, "from a people that was glad." Its reading is based on a rearrangement of the letters עלז, which means "glad" as in Zeph. 3:14, "be glad (וְעָלְזִי) with your heart...." This serves as the basis for connecting Ps. 114:1 and 105:38.

4. *MRI, Beshalach* 6:65, vol. 1, p. 237.

5. *MRI, Beshalach* 6:1–35, vol. 1, pp. 232–34.

6. *MRI, Bachodesh* 5:95, vol. 2, p. 236.

Alyssa Gray

1. See *Ramban's* glosses on *Rambam's Sefer Hamitzvot, shoresh* 1, par. 9.

2. See Joseph Tabory, *The Passover Ritual Throughout the Generations* (Tel-Aviv: Hakibbutz Hameuchad, 1996), pp. 307–8 (Hebrew).

3. The notion that there are seven heavens originated outside of rabbinic Judaism. Evidence for the notion is found in the enigmatic apocryphal work II (Slavonic Apocalypse of) Enoch, of uncertain date, as well as in Islamic legend. The idea most likely entered Islam from earlier sources. The early kabbalistic work *Sefer Y'tsirah* ("Book of Formation") also mentions the seven heavens, and the notion persists in kabbalistic literature.

4. Tosafot to Pes. 116a, s.v. "*l'fikhakh*."

13. Redemption: Blessing and Meal

David Arnow

1. Eisenstein, *Ozar Midrashim*, p. 451, *Aseret ha-Dibrot*.

2. The link between table and altar derives from Ezek. 41:22, which refers to an altar as "the table that stands before Adonai."

3. The four cups in the Joseph story: Gen. 40:11, 40:13. The four cups of retribution: Jer. 25:15, 51:6–7; Pss. 11:6, 75:9. The four cups of conolation: Pss. 16:5, 23:5, and 116:3 (the latter is the plural and counts for two cups of consolation).

4. *Orchot Chayim Eliezer*, p. 29. Sec. 12, in Eisenstein, *Ozar Midrashim*.

5. *Jerusalem Bible* translation.

6. Philo, *The Special Laws*, vol. 7, ed. F. H. Coulson (Cambridge: Harvard University Press, 1937), pp. 399–405.

7. The Palestinian Talmud (Pes. 70a, 10:37:d) only says that *charoset* should be murky or soft as a "remembrance of the blood."

8. See, for example, Pes. 119b.

Carole B. Balin

1. *Haggadah Ketzarah* (Vilna, 1907) and *Passover Haggadah, According to the Custom of the Karaite Jews of Egypt* (printed by the Karaite Jews of America, 2000).

2. David Geffen, ed., *American Heritage Haggadah: The Passover Experience* (Jerusalem: Gefen Publishing House, 1992), p. 21.

3. David Einhorn, ed. "Domestic Service on the Eve of Passover," in *Olat Tamid: Book of Prayers for Israelitish Congregations*, 5th ed. (New York: E. Thalmessinger Press, 1872), p. 383.

4. As told in Noam Zion and David Dishon, *A Different Night: The Family Participation Haggadah* (Jerusalem: Shalom Hartman Institute, 1997), p. 113.

5. Translation by Yosef Hayim Yerushalmi, *Haggadah and History* (Philadelphia: Jewish Publication Society, 1975), plate 144.

Alyssa Gray

1. *Rif* to Pes. 25b–26a, in *Rif*; *Rosh* to Pes. ch. 10, *siman* 30.

2. For Tabory's analysis, see http://www.biu.ac.il/JH/Parasha/eng/pesach/tabori.html.

3. It is found in *Machzor Vitry* (*Hilkhot Pesach, siman* 74, p. 286), in *Rashi*'s collected responsa (*siman* 304), and in the *Sefer Hapardes, siman* 132.

14. MEDIEVAL ADDITIONS

David Arnow

1. *MRI, Pischa* 14:113, vol. 1, p. 115.

2. Author's translation.

3. *MRI, Shirata* 6:69, vol. 2, p. 48.

4. Jer. 10:25 and Ps. 79:6–7 are very similar, and Haggadot from the Middle Ages included either of them.

Carole B. Balin

1. Leopold Stein, *Gebetbuch für Israelitische Gemeinden* (*Seder Ha'avodah*), vol. 1 (Mannheim: Verlag von J. Schneider's Buchhandlung, 1882), p. 184. This is my English translation. See also David Golinkin, "Pesah Potpourri: On the Origin and Development of Some Lesser-Known Pesah Customs," *Conservative Judaism*, vol. 55, no. 3 (Spring 2003), pp. 58–71.

2. *The Union Haggadah* (New York: CCAR, 1907), pp. 82–83.

3. Debra Reed Blank, "*Sh'fokh Hamatkha* and Eliyahu in the Haggadah: Ideology in Liturgy," *Conservative Judaism*, vol. 40, no. 2 (Winter 1987–88), p. 77.

4. "Ceremonial for Opening the Door of Elijah" [An experimental leaflet issued by the CCAR, 1943].

5. Herbert Bronstein, ed., *A Passover Haggadah: The New Union Haggadah* (New York: Central Conference of American Rabbis, 1974), p. 68.

6. Sue Levi Elwell, ed., *The Open Door: A Passover Haggadah* (New York: Central Conference of American Rabbis, 2002), p. 86.

7. Mordecai M. Kaplan, Eugene Kohn, and Ira Eisenstein, eds. *The New Haggadah for the Pesah Seder* (New York: Behrman House, 1941), pp. 105ff.

8. Joy Levitt and Michael Strassfeld, *A Night of Questions: A Passover Haggadah* (Elkins Park, PA: Reconstructionist Press, 2000), pp. 118–22.

9. Philip Birnbaum, ed. *The Passover Haggadah* (New York: Hebrew Publishing Co., 1953), pp. 62–63.

10. Rachel Anne Rabinowicz, ed. *Passover Haggadah: The Feast of Freedom* (New York: Rabbinical Assembly, 1982), p. 101.

11. For further information, see Blank, pp. 73–86.

12. Jakob Petuchowski, Book Review, *Conservative Judaism* 35 (Spring 1982): pp. 81–83.

13. Morris Silverman, ed. *The Passover Haggadah* (Bridgeport, CT: Prayer Book Press, 1972).

14. Rachel Anne Rabinowicz, ed., *Passover Haggadah: The Feast of Freedom* (New York: Rabbinical Assembly, 1982), pp. 94ff.

15. Saul Goodman, ed., *Passover Haggadah* (New York: Sholem Aleichem Folk Institute, 1962), p. 32.

Alyssa Gray

1. Tosafot to Pes. 117b, s.v. "*revi'i.*"

2. For other scholarly attempts to link the fifth cup with Elijah's cup, see the sources cited by Tabory in *The Passover Ritual*, 329n. 83.

3. *Seder Rav Amram (Seder Pesach)* includes only the two verses beginning "Pour out Your wrath" and "For they have consumed Jacob." However, it is quite possible that these verses were added to *Seder Rav Amram* by later copyists who sought to "update" his opus.

Wendy I. Zierler

1. You can find Leila Gal Berner's version in *The Journey Continues: The Ma'ayan Passover Haggadah* (New York: Ma'ayan, 2002), p. 102; *A Night of Questions*, ed. Joy Levitt and Michael Strassfeld (Elkins Park, PA: Reconstructionist Press, 2000), p. 119; and *The Open Door: A Passover Haggadah*, ed. Sue Levi Elwell (New York: CCAR, 2002), pp. 135–36. For another version of *Miriam Han'via'h* see *Shaarei Simcha: Gates of Joy*, ed. Adena Berkowitz and Rivka Haut (Jersey City: Ktav, 2007), p. 84. Other Haggadot include Debbie Friedman's "Miriam's Song," or "Miriam" by Laura Berkson. See, for example, "Congregation Beth Simchat Torah Feminist Minyan Haggadah" (unpublished). Numerous songs and prose pieces about Miriam can be found in *All the Women Followed Her: A Collection of Writings on Miriam the Prophet and the Women of Exodus*, ed. Rebecca Schwartz (Mountainview, CA: Rikudei Miriam Press, 2001), as well as the *Women's Seder Sourcebook: Rituals and Readings for Use at the Passover Seder*, eds., Sharon Cohen Anisfeld, et al. (Woodstock, VT: Jewish Lights, 2003).

15. "PRAISE": *HALLEL*, PART TWO

David Arnow

1. *MRI, Shirata* 2:15, vol. 2, p. 2. This midrash uses a verse from Isaiah (30:29): "For you, there shall be singing as on a night when a festival is hallowed." BT Pes. 95b uses the same verse as a proof text for the requirement to say *Hallel* on the night of Passover.

2. BT Pes. 85b contains a similar saying.

3. BT Arach. 10a–b explains the partial *Hallel* in light of the fact that the additional sacrifices offered on the last six days of Passover were the same each day, while for Sukkot, they differed on each day. Different sacrifices merited a complete *Hallel*.

4. Such boundary blurring had not always been accepted. BT Suk. 5a insists that God remained ten handbreadths above Sinai and that Moses (and Elijah) remained the same distance below heaven!

5. Translation of these scriptural passages follows William G. Braude, *The Midrash on Psalms* (New Haven: Yale University Press, 1959), p. 245.

16. FORMAL CONCLUSION

David Arnow

1. *Jerusalem Bible* translation.

2. *Midrash T'murah* 12, in Eisenstein, *Ozar Midrashim*, p. 582.

Carole B. Balin

1. Lewis M. Moroze, ed. and illus. by William Vigoda, *Passover Haggadah* (Newark, NJ: Danfred Publications, 1965), p. 1.

2. Ibid., p. 20.

3. Elie Wiesel, *A Passover Haggadah*, Mark Podwal, illustrator (New York: Simon and Schuster, 1993), p. 119.

4. *Haggadah shel Pesach "Am Yisrael Hai,"* Solomon Fedler, ed. and David-Noah Fedler, illus., 3rd ed. (Johannesburg: 1981), p. iii.

5. Ibid.

17. FOUR SEDER SONGS

David Arnow

1. The phrase appears in the liturgy and is recited as the Torah is carried through the congregation prior to reading it.

2. BT Ber. 58a.

3. *Tanchuma* on Deut., *Ki Tetse* sec. 18. The midrash interprets the fact that in the phrase *keis yah*, "throne of God" (Exod. 17:16), both words are abbreviated, i.e., not complete, thus symbolizing the incompleteness of God's rule.

4. Ps. 147:2.

5. See Bar Ilan Responsa Project (CDROM15+) Tanna Debe Eliyyahu (Ish Shalom), Pirkei Ha'Yeridot, sec. 3. The midrash is based on Job 38:7: "...the morning stars sang together amd all the divine beings shouted for joy." The midrash understands the "morning stars" to be Israel. Israel thus sings before the angels.

6. *Song of Songs Rabbah* 4:12.

7. *Exodus Rabbah* 14:1.

8. *Pesikta Rabbati* 11:3.

9. BT B. B. 16a, BT Suk. 52a.

10. Solomon Wertheimer, *Otiot d'Rabbi Akiva* (version 2) in *Batei Midrashot* (Jerusalem: Mosad ha-Rav Kook, 1950–1953), vol. 2, p. 417.

Carole B. Balin

1. Abraham Klausner, *The Bicentennial Passover Haggadah* (New York; Emanuel Press Publication, 1976), pp. 27–53.

2. Roberta Kalechofsky, ed., "Introduction," in *Haggadah for the Liberated Lamb* (Marblehead, MA: Micah Publications, 1985), and see 2nd ed. (1988) for recipes.

3. My thanks to Professor Mark Kligman for pointing me to this version of "*Chad Gadya*."

4. "*Chad Gadya*" is a track on "Crazy Flower: A Collection," which was released on 21 April 1998.

5. For more on Chava Alberstein, go to www.npr.org for interview by Madeleine Brand (24 April 2002).

6. For more on Amos Gitai, go to www.amosgitai.com.

Neil Gillman

1. For a more detailed discussion of both the historical and theological import of this verse, see Neil Gillman, *The Death of Death: Resurrection and Immortality in Jewish Thought* (Woodstock, VT: Jewish Lights Publishing, 2000). For a discussion that dates the emergence of this doctrine far earlier in Israelite history, see Jon D. Levenson, *Resurrection and the Restoration of Israel: The Ultimate Victory of the God of Life* (New Haven: Yale University Press, 2006).

Lawrence Kushner and Nehemia Polen

1. Regarding the use of Zech. 14:9 in this context, see *Rashi* on Deut. 6:4 (the *Sh'ma*), where the idea is already articulated in less extreme form.

APPENDIX I

1. See Judith Hauptman, "How Old Is the Haggadah?" *Judaism* 51, no. 1 (Winter 2002): 8.

2. The translation of the Mishnah follows that of Joel M. Hoffman for material that appears in the Passover Haggadah and otherwise has been guided by that of Baruch Bokser. The translation of the Tosefta follows Bokser more closely. See Baruch M. Bokser, *The Origins of the Seder* (New York: Jewish Theological Seminary of America, 2002, originally published in 1984). The Kaufmann manuscript is available online at the Jewish National and University Library, http://jnul.huji.ac.il/dl/talmud.

3. Saul Lieberman, *Tosefta-ki-feshuta* (New York: Jewish Theological Seminary, 1955–1988).

4. Vilna adds: "and two cooked dishes."

5. Vilna reads: "his father."

6. Vilna includes four "questions" addressing why we eat matzah, bitter herbs, and roasted meat; and why we dip twice as opposed to not even once on all other nights.

7. Vilna explains the terms Gamaliel mentions in the order he states them. Here the order differs, with matzah following rather than preceding bitter herbs. Vilna adds: "In each and every generation people must regard themselves as though they personally left Egypt, as it says, 'Tell your child on that very day: "This is what Adonai did for me when I left Egypt"' [Exod. 13:8].

8. Vilna lacks "to elevate," but includes four additional expressions of praise, for a total of nine.

9. Vilna adds: "from sorrow to happiness, from mourning to celebration, and from darkness to great light, and from enslavement to redemption."

APPENDIX II

1. We have followed E. Daniel Goldschmidt's transcription of the manuscript (*Haggadah shel Pesach V'toldoteha*. Jerusalem: Bialik Press, 1960).

List of Abbreviations

A. Z.	Avodah Zarah	Isa.	Isaiah
Arakh.	Arakhin	Jer.	Jeremiah
B. B.	Bava Batra	Josh.	Joshua
B. K.	Bava Kama	Ket.	Ketubot
B. M.	Bava Metsia	Kid.	Kiddushin
Ber.	Berakhot	Lev.	Leviticus
BT	Babylonian Talmud, Bavli	M.	Mishnah
Chron.	Chronicles	M. K.	Moed Katan
Chul.	Chullin	Mal.	Malachi
Dan.	Daniel	Meg.	Megillah
Deut.	Deuteronomy	Men.	Menachot
Eccl.	Ecclesiastes	Mid.	Middot
Eduy.	Eduyot	MRI	Mekhilta de-Rabbi Ishmael
Eruv.	Eruvin	MRSBY	Mekhilta de-Rabbi Shimon bar Yohai
Exod.	Exodus		
Ezek.	Ezekiel	Ned.	Nedarim
Gen.	Genesis	Neh.	Nehemiah
Hab.	Habbakuk	Num.	Numbers
		O. Ch.	Orach Chayim

Pes.	Pesachim		Shab.	Shabbat
Prov.	Proverbs		Shek.	Shekalim
Ps.	Psalms		Sot.	Sotah
PT	Palestinian Talmud, Yerushalmi		Suk.	Sukkah
			Ta'an.	Ta'anit
R. H.	Rosh Hashanah		Ter.	Terumot
Rab.	Rabbah (Midrash Rabbah)		Zech.	Zechariah
Sam.	Samuel		Zeph.	Zephaniah
Sanh.	Sanhedrin			

Glossary

The following glossary presents names and Hebrew words used regularly throughout this volume and provides the way they are pronounced. Sometimes two pronunciations are common, in which case the first is the way the word is sounded in Hebrew, and the second is the way it is sometimes heard in common speech, under the influence of Yiddish, the folk language of Jews in northern and eastern Europe (a combination, mostly, of Hebrew and German). Our goal is to provide the way that many Jews actually use these words, not just the technically correct version.

- The pronunciations are divided into syllables by dashes.

- The accented syllable is written in capital letters.

- "Kh" represents a guttural sound, similar to the German (as in "sprach").

- The most common vowel is "a" as in "father," which appears here as "ah."

- The short "e" (as in "get") is written as either "e" (when it is in the middle of a syllable) or "eh" (when it ends a syllable).

- Similarly, the short "i" (as in "tin") is written as either "i" (when it is in the middle of a syllable) or "ih" (when it ends a syllable).

- A long "o" (as in Moses") is written as "oe" (as in the word "toe") or "oh" (as in the word "Oh!").

Abudarham: David ben Joseph Abudarham, fourteenth-century Spanish commentator on the liturgy. His *Sefer Abudarham* (completed in 1340) is our primary account of Spanish (Sefardi) practice of the time.

Acharonim (pronounced ah-khah-roh-NEEM or, commonly, akh-ROH-nim): The name given to Jewish legal authorities from the middle of the sixteenth century on. The word means, literally, "later ones," as opposed to the "earlier ones," authorities prior to that time who are held in higher regard and are called *Rishonim* (pronounced ree-shoh-NEEM or, commonly, ree-SHOH-nim). Singular: *Acharon* (pronounced ah-khah-ROHN) and *Rishon* (pronounced ree-SHOHN).

Aggadah (pronounced ah-gah-DAH): Literally, "narrative," or "telling," from the same root as *haggadah* ("telling"), but unrelated to the Passover Haggadah; refers to literary "tellings," or tales, like parables, biographical narratives, and short vignettes that are embedded in rabbinic literature less as legal argumentation than as grounds for lessons in extralegal matters such as ethics, history, and theology.

Amidah (pronounced either ah-mee-DAH or, commonly, ah-MEE-dah): One of three commonly used titles for the second of two central units in the worship service, the first being the *Sh'ma* and Its Blessings. It is composed of a series of blessings, many of which are petitionary, except on Sabbaths and holidays, when the petitions are removed out of deference to the holiness of the day. Also called *T'fillah* and *Sh'moneh Esreh. Amidah* means "standing" and refers to the fact that the prayer is said standing up.

Amora(im): See ***Tannaitic***.

Arba'ah Turim: See ***Tur***.

Ari, Ha'ari (pronounced ah-REE, hah-ah-REE): Acronym for Isaac ben Solomon Luria (1534–1572); the initials refer to *Ha'Elohi Rabbi Yitzchak*, "the divine Rabbi Isaac" or *Ha'Ashkenazi Rabbi Isaac*. Renowned kabbalist who lived mostly in Jerusalem, Egypt, and Safed.

Ashkenazi (pronounced ahsh-k'-nah-ZEE, or, commonly, ahsh-k'-NAH-zee): From the Hebrew word *Ashkenaz,* meaning the geographic area of northern and eastern Europe; "Ashkenazi" is the adjective, describing the liturgical rituals and customs practiced there. "Ashkenazim " (plural) refers to Jews from this geographic region. These terms contrast with "Sefardi," meaning the liturgical rituals and customs that are derived from Sefarad, current day Spain and Portugal (see ***Sefardi***), and "Sefardim," who trace their roots there—or, now, also to North Africa or the Middle East, where many exiles went in 1492 (from Spain) and 1497 (from Portugal).

Ashkenazim: See ***Ashkenazi***.

Avot D'rabbi Natan (pronounced ah-VOHT d'-rah-BEE nah-TAHN): A collection of wisdom akin to Mishnah Avot, providing lessons attributed to the chain of Rabbis who predated the Mishnah (the Tannaim, pre-200). Variously dated from the third to the seventh/eighth centuries.

Bavli: See ***Talmud***.

B'dikat chamets (pronounced b'-dee-KAHT khah-MAYTS): The process of searching for leaven on the night before Passover.

Bertinoro, Ovadiah: Italian rabbi (1450?–1516?) whose commentary on the Mishnah has become the standard commentary on that work.

Bet Yosef (pronounced BAIT yoh-SAYF): Commentary to the *Tur* by Joseph Caro, sixteenth century, Land of Israel; and a precursor to his more popular code, the *Shulchan Arukh*. See *Tur* and **Shulchan Arukh**.

Birkat Hamazon (pronounced beer-KAHT hah-mah-ZOHN): Grace after Meals, consisting of four blessings, which thank God for (1) feeding all creatures; (2) giving the Jewish people the Land of Israel; (3) rebuilding Jerusalem; and (4) showing goodness. Embedded within these four blessings are petitions to the "Merciful One" (*harachaman* [pronounced hah-rah-khah-MAHN]). Bracketing the whole is an introduction called *zimmun* (pronounced zee-MOON) and a conclusion on the theme of peace.

Bitul chamets (pronounced bee-TOOL khah-MAYTS): Literally, "nullification of leaven," a phrase related to the ritual of seeking out and burning the leaven in one's possession, so that any leaven still in one's possession is considered "null and void."

Bi'ur chamets (pronounced bee-OOR khah-MAYTS): Literally, "burning the leaven." The act of symbolically burning leavened food *(chamets)* on the night before Passover.

Caro, Joseph: See **Shulchan Arukh**.

Chamets (pronounced khah-MAYTS): Products forbidden on Passover because they are made with wheat, barley, spelt, oats, or rye that may have fermented or leavened through having come in contact with water for more than eighteen minutes.

Charedi (pronounced khah-ray-DEE or, commonly, khah-RAY-dee): Literally "reverently fearful," a diverse group of ultra-Orthodox Jews who reject accommodation with modernity.

Chazon Ish (pronounced khah-ZOHN EESH): A commentary on part of the *Shulchan Arukh* by Avraham Yeshayahu Karelitz (1878–1953, Lithuania and Israel). Karelitz was a student of astronomy, mathematics, anatomy, and botany as well as one of the leading talmudic scholars of his era. Known for his practical approach to matters of Jewish law.

Deuteronomy Rabbah: A midrashic collection containing some twenty-seven homilies corresponding roughly to the triennial cycle of Torah reading that marked Palestinian Jewry prior to the Crusades. With early origins, the text was compiled between 450 and 800.

Dov Baer, The Great Maggid [Preacher] of Mezerich (1710–1772): Leader of Chasidism following the death of the movement's spiritual father, the Baal Shem Tov (1700–1760). Introduced the systematic study of Kabbalah in Chasidism.

Eruv tavshilin (pronounced ay-ROOV tahv-shee-LEEN or, commonly, AY-roov, tahv-SHEE-leen): Literally, "the joining of cooked foods." Ordinarily, food prepared on a festival must be consumed only on the festival itself. Thus when a festival falls directly before the Sabbath, it would be impossible to cook the Sabbath meal. The *eruv tavshilin* solves this problem through a legal fiction: two dishes, one cooked and the other bread (here, matzah), are set aside before Passover, as if Sabbath-meal cooking actually preceded the festival.

Esther Rabbah: A midrashic collection centered on the Book of Esther, containing material dating from the sixth through eleventh centuries.

Exodus Rabbah: A midrashic collection in two parts. Exodus 1–10 (tenth century) is exegetical—it follows the order of the biblical verses on which it comments; Exodus 12–40 (eleventh or twelfth century) is homiletical—it is arranged like a set of sermons.

Gaon (pronounced gah-OHN; plural: *Geonim*, pronounced g'-oh-NEEM): Title for the leading rabbis in Babylon (present-day Iraq) from about 750 to 1038. From a biblical word meaning "glory," equivalent, in a title, to saying "Your Excellence."

Gemara (pronounced g'-mah-RAH, but, popularly, g'-MAH-rah): The commentary on the Mishnah that appears together with the Mishnah on which it comments as the Talmud (Talmud = Mishnah + Gemara). Sometimes, however, used loosely to mean the entire Talmud, the Mishnah included.

Genesis Rabbah: Extraordinarily detailed midrashic collection (fifth or sixth century), sometimes expounding on Genesis word by word.

Genizah (pronounced g'-nee-ZAH or, commonly g'-NEE-zah): Literally, "storing." A place where worn-out ritual objects and books containing the name of God were stored, usually a room connected to a synagogue. The Cairo Genizah, the most famous such storeroom (discovered at the end of the nineteenth century), contained a Haggadah dating back to the tenth or eleventh century CE (see *My People's Passover Haggadah*, Volume 2, Appendix II).

Geonim: See ***Gaon***.

Gra (pronounced GRAH): Acronym for *G*aon *R*abbi *E*lijah of Vilna (1720–1797), known also as the Vilna Gaon, outstanding halakhic authority of Lithuania and virulent opponent of Chasidism.

Gryz (pronounced griz): Acronym for *G*aon *R*abbi *Y*itzchak *Z*e'ev Soloveitchik (1886–1959), also known as Velvel Soloveitchik or the Brisker Rov. Renowned talmudist from the Brisk dynasty, born in Brisk, Lithuania, he emigrated to Palestine during the war and established the Brisk Yeshiva in Jerusalem.

Hagahot Maimuniyot (pronounced hah-gah-HOHT ma'i-moo-nee-YOHT): Literally, "glosses to Maimonides," a set of glosses and brief commentary on Maimonides' compendium of Jewish law, the *Mishneh Torah*, by Rabbi Meir Hakohen of Rothenburg (late thirteenth century).

Halakhot G'dolot (hah-lah-KHOHT g'doh-LOHT): Ninth-century summary of Jewish law, widely but not universally ascribed to Shimon Kayyara, Babylonia (present-day Iraq).

Hallel (pronounced hah-LAYL, or, commonly, HAH-layl): A Hebrew word meaning "praise" and, by extension, the name given to sets of psalms that are recited liturgically in praise of God: Psalms 145–150, the Daily *Hallel*, is recited each morning; Psalm 136, the Great *Hallel*, is recited on Shabbat and holidays and is part of the Passover Seder. Psalms 113–118, the best-known *Hallel*, known more fully as the Egyptian *Hallel*, is recited on holidays and gets its name from Psalm 114:1, which celebrates the moment "when Israel left Egypt."

Hallel Hagadol (pronounced hah-LAYL [or, commonly, HAH-layl] hah-gah-DOHL): Literally, "the Great *Hallel*," which refers to Psalm 136. See ***Hallel***.

Ibn Ezra, Abraham (Rabbi Abraham ibn Ezra, Spain, then various countries, 1089–1164): Grammarian, poet, Bible commentator, astronomer, physician, and philosopher (1089–1164) born in Spain but itinerant from 1140, during which time he wrote most of his works.

Jerusalem Talmud: Another term for the Palestinian Talmud, in Hebrew, the *Yerushalmi*. See ***Talmud***.

Kabbalah (pronounced kah-bah-LAH or, commonly, kah-BAH-lah): A general term for Jewish mysticism, but used properly for a specific mystical doctrine that began in western Europe in the eleventh or twelfth century; recorded in the *Zohar* (see ***Zohar***) in the thirteenth century, and then further elaborated, especially in the Land of Israel (in Safed), in the sixteenth century. From a Hebrew word meaning "to receive" or "to welcome," and secondarily, "tradition," implying the receiving of tradition from one's past.

Kaplan, Mordecai M. (1881–1983): Born in Lithuania, emigrated to the United States in 1890. Kaplan was a rabbi, teacher, theologian, and spiritual father of the Reconstructionist Movement. He rejected most supernatural ideas in Judaism and defined God as the power that made possible the pursuit of fundamental values such as freedom or improving the world.

Kiddush (pronounced kee-DOOSH or, commonly, KIH-d'sh): Literally, "sanctification," hence, a form of *K'dushat Hayom*; in this case, the prayer for the eve of Shabbat and holidays, intended to announce the arrival of sacred time, and accompanied by *Birkat Yayin,* the blessing over wine.

Lamentations Rabbah: Midrashic collection, late fifth century largely about the destruction of the Temple and the question of divine justice in light of innocent suffering.

Lekach Tov: See **Midrash Lekach Tov**.

Levi Yitzchak of Berditchev (1740–1810): Disciple of Dov Baer, the *Maggid* of Mezerich. Levi Yitzchak expanded Chasidism in central Poland, the Ukraine, and Lithuania, center of opposition to the movement.

Leviticus Rabbah: Midrashic collection (fifth or sixth century) on the Book of Leviticus.

Machzor Vitry (pronounced mahkh-ZOHR veet-REE or, commonly, MAHKH-zohr VEET-ree): Literally, the *machzor* (prayer book containing the annual cycle of liturgy) from Vitry (in France). The most significant early French commentary to the liturgy, composed in the tenth and/or eleventh century, primarily by Simchah of Vitry, a student of *Rashi*.

Maharal of Prague: Acronym *(MaHaRaL)* for Judah Loew ben Bezalel (1525–1609), Moreinu *HaRav* Loew, "Our Teacher, the Rabbi Loew." Known for his piety and asceticism, a great scholar of Talmud, philosopher, prolific writer, and a mathematician who enjoyed a social relationship with the famed astronomer Tycho Brahe.

Maharil (pronounced mah-hah-RIL; Rabbi Jacob Moellin, Germany, fourteenth to fifteenth century): Acronym *(MaHaRiL)* for *Morenu* ("our teacher") *HaRav Ya'akov haLevi*, (1360?–1427, Germany), leading talmudist and outstanding authority who helped shape Ashkenazi custom and tradition.

Maimonides, Moses (known also as *Rambam*, pronounced RAHM-bahm): Most important Jewish philosopher of all time; also a physician and very significant legal authority. Born in Spain, he moved to Egypt, where he lived most of his life (1135–1204).

Masoretic text: Literally, the "transmitted" text of the Hebrew Bible. Toward the end of the first millennium CE, a group of Jews in Tiberias standardized the Bible as we know it. Working from the consonantal text and from the traditions they had received, they added vowels, cantillation marks, and copious notes about the text. It is the Masoretic text that appears in most Hebrew Bibles.

Meiri, Menachem ben Solomon (1249–1316, Provence): Renowned commentator on the Talmud and author of an important treatise on ethics and repentance.

Mekhilta (pronounced m'-KHIL-tah): Shortened reference to either of two parallel midrashic works. See **Mekhilta D'rabbi Yishmael** and **Mekhilta D'rabbi Shimon bar Yochai**.

Mekhilta D'rabbi Shimon bar Yochai (pronounced m'khil-TAH d'rah-bee shee-MOHN bahr yoh-KHA'i or, commonly, m'-KHIL-tah d'-rah-bee SHEE-mohn bahr yoh-KHA'i): Tannaitic midrash (pre-200) similar in style and content to the ***Mekhilta D'rabbi Yishmael***.

Mekhilta D'rabbi Yishmael (pronounced m'-khil-TAH d'-rah-BEE yish-mah-AYL or, commonly, m'-KHIL-tah d'-RAH-bee YISH-mah-ayl): One of the tannaitic midrashim, this one on the Book of Exodus (chapter 12 on).

Merkavah (pronounced mehr-kah-VAH or, commonly, mehr KAH-vah): Literally, "chariot"; hence, the name of a school of Jewish mysticism that pictured God seated in a throne-like chariot, surrounded by angels reciting, "Holy, holy, holy."

Midrash (pronounced meed-RAHSH or, commonly, MID-rahsh): From a Hebrew word meaning "to ferret out the meaning of a text," and therefore a rabbinic interpretation of a biblical word or verse. By extension, a body of rabbinic literature that offers classical interpretations of the Bible.

Midrash Hagadol (pronounced meed-RASH hah-gah-DOHL or, commonly, MIHD-rahsh hah-gah-DOHL) Yemenite midrash on the Pentateuch generally thought to have been composed by David ben Amram of Aden between 1300 and 1400, but incorporating many sources.

Midrash Hallel (pronounced meed-RAHSH hah-LAYL or, commonly, MIHD-rahsh HAH-layl): Midrash on Psalms 113–118 composed in the tenth century or later.

Midrash Lekach Tov (pronounced meed-RAHSH LEH-kach TOHV, or, commonly, MIHD-rahsh leh-kach TOV): Late eleventh-century midrashic commentary on the Pentateuch by Tobiah ben Eliezer. Literally, "good instruction" (Prov. 4:2), the midrash alludes to contemporary events such as the Crusades.

Midrash on Proverbs: Mid-ninth-century midrash reflecting customs in Babylonia and Palestine. Polemicizes against the Karaites, a group of Jews who denied the legitimacy of rabbinic law.

Midrash on Psalms: See ***Midrash T'hillim***.

Midrash Samuel: Midrashic collection compiled around the tenth or eleventh century but contains much old material, some of it only found in this collection.

Midrash Sekhel Tov (pronounced meed-RAHSH SAY-khel TOHV or, commonly, MIHD-rahsh say-khel TOV): Midrashic anthology following the weekly Torah reading. Literally, "good understanding" (Ps. 111:10). Composed by Menachem ben Solomon in the first half of the twelfth century. Also considered by some to be the first treatise on the Hebrew language.

Midrash T'hillim (pronounced meed-RAHSH t'-hee-LEEM or, commonly, mid-rahsh TILL-im): Literally, "Midrash to Psalms," a midrashic collection variously dated, with material as early as the third century, but reaching final redaction only centuries later. Also called *Midrash Shocher Tov* (pronounced meed-RAHSH sho-KHAYR TOHV or, commonly, mid-rahs SHO-kheir TOHV), from the opening words of Proverbs 11:27, the first verse it quotes, "Whoever earnestly seeks what is right [*shocher tov*] pursues what is pleasing."

Midrash Vayosha (pronounced meed-RAHSH vah-yoh-SHAH or, commonly, MIHD-rahs vah-YOH-sha)): Eleventh-century midrash on the Song of the Sea (Exod. 15), named for the expression in Exodus 14:30, "Thus Adonai saved" *(vayosha).*

Minhag (pronounced meen-HAHG or, commonly, MIN-hahg): The Hebrew word for custom and, therefore, used liturgically to describe the customary way that different groups of Jews pray. By extension, *minhag* means a "rite," as in *Minhag Ashkenaz,* meaning "the rite of prayer, or the customary way of prayer for Jews in *Ashkenaz"*—that is, northern and eastern Europe.

Mishnah (pronounced meesh-NAH or, commonly, MISH-nah): The first written summary of Jewish law, compiled in the Land of Israel about the year 200 CE and, therefore, our first overall written evidence for the state of Jewish practice in the early centuries.

Mishnah B'rurah (pronounced meesh-NAH b'-roo-RAH or, commonly, MISH-nah B'ROO-rah): Halakhic commentary and compendium on laws in that portion of the *Shulchan Arukh* called *Orach Chayim* ("The Way of Life"), containing most of the laws on liturgy; by Rabbi Israel Meir Hakohen Kagan *(Chafetz Chayim),* Radin, Poland, 1838–1933.

Mishnah of Rabbi Eliezer: Also known as *Midrash Agur* ("The words of Agur …" [Prov. 30:1]), date unknown.

Mitzvah (pronounced meetz-VAH or, commonly, MITZ-vah; plural: *mitzvot,* pronounced meetz-VOTE): A Hebrew word used commonly to mean "good deed," but in the more technical sense, denoting any commandment from God and, therefore, by extension, what God wants us to do. Reciting the *Sh'ma* morning and evening, for instance, is a *mitzvah.*

Mitnagdim (pronounced mit-nagh-DEEM or, commonly, the Yiddishized mis-NAHG-dim): Literally, "opponents" of Chasidism in the eighteenth and nineteenth centuries. Now sometimes used to designate ultra-Orthodox Jews who are not Chasidic.

Mitzvot: See **Mitzvah**.

Mordecai Yosef Leiner of Izbica (1804–1854): Founder of the Izhbitzer Chasidic dynasty and known for his belief in radical determinism—that God determines everything, including the actions of all human beings.

M'zuzah (pronounced m'-zoo-ZAH or, commonly, m'-ZOO-zah): Literally, "doorpost," and hence, a small tubelike object, generally decorated, containing a tiny parchment scroll, that is affixed to the doorpost of the entrances to Jewish homes and to certain rooms within. On the parchment are written two passages from the Book of Deuteronomy 6:4–9 and 11:13–21). These include the requirement to inscribe the teachings of Torah "on the doorposts of your house and on your gates."

Nachmanides (pronounced nahkh-MAH-nih-deez): Also known as Ramban (pronounced rahm-BAHN), an acronym (RaMBaN) for *Rabbi Moses ben Nachman* (1194–1270, Spain and Israel). Bible commentator, halakhist, and kabbalist of extraordinary influence.

Numbers Rabbah: A midrashic collection with two parts: sections 1–14, from the midtwelfth century, and sections 15–23, of unknown origin. Both parts were likely combined in the early thirteenth century.

Olah (pronounced oh-LAH): From the Hebrew word meaning "to go up" and, hence, the Temple offering consisting of an animal wholly offered up to God, because it was entirely consumed by sacrificial fire.

Olam haba (pronounced oh-LAHM hah-BAH or, commonly, OH-lahm hah-BAH): Literally, "the world-to-come," a term for one of the three most common eschatological promises of rabbinic Judaism. The others are *y'mot hamashi'ach* (pronounced y'MOHT hah-mah-SHEE-ahkh), "messianic days" (that is, the era after the coming of the messiah); and *t'chi'at hametim* (pronounced t'chee-YAHT hah-may-TEEM), "the resurrection of the dead."

Omer: See ***S'firat ha'omer***.

Orach Chayim (pronounced oh-RAKH kah-YEEM or, commonly, OH-rakh KHA-yim): Abbreviated as O. Ch. Literally, "The Way of Life," one of four sections in the *Tur* and the *Shulchan Arukh,* two of Judaism's major law codes.

Orchot Chayim (pronounced ohr-KHOT khah-YEEM): Chief work of Rabbi Aharon ben Rabbi Jacob Hakohen of Lunel (Southern France and Spain, thirteenth to fourteenth century). Literally, "Ways of Life."

Pesikta D'rav Kahana (pronounced p'SIK-tah d'RAV kah-HAH-nah): Literally, "the section [or portion] of Rabbi Kahana"; a midrashic collection from the fifth or sixth century organized around the cycle of Torah and *Haftarah* readings for the festivals and special Sabbaths.

Pesikta Rabbati (pronounced p'-SIK-tah rah-BAH-tee): A midrashic collection organized similarly to *Pesikta D'rav Kahana*, but of unknown origin and date, and containing material on apocalyptic themes.

Pirkei D'rabbi Eliezer (pronounced peer-KAY d'rah-BEE eh-lee-EH-zer or, commonly, PEER-kay d'-RAH-bee eh-lee-EH-z'r): Literally, "Chapters of Rabbi Eliezer," so named because it begins with stories about Eliezer ben Hyrcanus (the same Rabbi Eliezer mentioned in the Haggadah). Composed in the first third of the ninth century, and sometimes called a "rewritten Bible" because it includes an extended narrative rather than exposition on words or phrases of Scripture.

Rabad (pronounced rah-BAHD): Acronym (RABaD) for *R*abbi *A*braham *b*en *D*avid, (c. 1125–1198) of Posquieres, Provence. Talmudist, halakhist, and among the first to write systematic commentaries on midrash.

Raban (pronounced rah-BAHN): Acronym (RaBaN) for *R*abbi Eliezer *b*en *N*athan of Mainz, Germany (1090–1170). Rabbinic scholar who also lived in Slavic countries and perhaps Russia whose major work *Sefer Haraban* (the Book by Raban) synopsizes and discusses Jewish law and is the oldest complete book to have survived from German Jewry.

Rabban (pronounced rah-BAHN): Rabbinic title of respect (literally, "our master") reserved for "chief" rabbi, head of the central academy, in first- to second-century Palestine.

Rabbenu Hananel (pronounced rah-BAY-noo CHAH-nah-nayl): Hananel ben Hushiel Kairouan, Tunisia (d. 1055/56). Influential commentator on the Talmud, among the first to highlight comparisons between the Jerusalem and Babylonian Talmuds.

Radak (pronounced rah-DAHK): Acronym (RaDaK) for *R*abbi *D*avid *K*imchi (1160?–1235?) of Narbonne, Provence. Bible scholar, grammarian, philosopher, and strong proponent of Maimonides' philosophy.

Rambam: See ***Maimonides***.

Ramban: See ***Nachmanides***.

Ran (pronounced RAHN): Acronym (RaN) for *R*abbi *N*issim [ben Reuven], Spain, d. 1380, and for his commentary on Isaac Alfasi (the *Rif*).

Rashbam (pronounced rahsh-BAHM): Acronym *(RaSHBaM)* for *Rabbi Sh*muel *ben Meir* (1080/85–c. 1174) of northern France. Grandson and student of *Rashi*, and commentator on the Bible and Talmud.

Rashbetz (pronounced rahsh-BETZ or, commonly, RASH-betz): Acronym (RaSHBeTZ) for *Rabbi Sh*imon *ben Tz*emach Duran (1361–1444) of Majorca. Physician, astronomer, mathematician, philosopher, and prolific rabbinic authority whose works include a commentary on the Haggadah.

Rashi (pronounced RAH-shee): Acronym (RaSHI) for *Rabbi Sh*lomo [Solomon] ben *I*saac, French halakhist and commentator on the Bible and Talmud, 1040–1105; founder of school of Jewish thought and custom, whence various liturgical works came into being, among them *Machzor Vitry* and *Siddur Rashi*.

Ravyah (pronounced rahv-YAH or, commonly RAHV-yah): Acronym (RaVYaH) for *Rabbi Eliezer ven Yoel Halevi* (1140–1225) of Bonn, Germany. Itinerant rabbinic scholar and pietist, whose major work (named for him, *Ravyah*) provides a major synopsis and discussion of Jewish law.

Rif (pronounced RIHF): Acronym (RiF) for *Rabbi Isaac* of *Fez* [Alfasi] (North Africa, 1013–1103) and his code of Jewish law by the same name.

Rishonim (pronounced ree-shoh-NEEM or, commonly, ree-SHOH-nim): The name given to Jewish legal authorities from the completion of the Talmud to the middle of the sixteenth century. The word means, literally, "earlier ones," as opposed to the "later ones," authorities after that time who are held in lower regard and are called *Acharonim* (pronounced ah-khah-roh-NEEM or, commonly, akh-ROH-nim). Singular: *Rishon* (pronounced ree-SHOHN) and *Acharon* (pronounced ah-khah-ROHN).

Ritba (pronounced riht-BAH or, commonly, RIHT-bah): Acronym (RITBA) for *Rabbi Yom Tov ben Abraham* Ishbili (c. 1250–1330), Seville. Talmudist and philosopher regarded in his later life as the spiritual leader of Spanish Jewry. His many works include a commentary on the Haggadah.

Ritzba (pronounced ritz-BAH or, commonly RITZ-bah): Acronym (RITZBA) for *Rabbi Yitz*hak *ben Abraham* (twelfth century), France. Commentator on the Talmud and author of numerous responsa, that is, legal opinions.

R'ma (pronounced r'-MAH): An acronym for Rabbi Moses Isserles, sixteenth-century Poland, chief Ashkenazi commentator on the *Shulchan Arukh*, the sixteenth-century Sefardi code by Joseph Caro.

Rosh (pronounced ROHSH): The *Rosh* (1250–1328), otherwise known as Rabbeinu Asher, or Asher ben Yechiel, was a significant halakhic authority, first in Germany and later in Spain. His son, Jacob ben Asher, codified many of his father's views alongside his own in his influential law code, the *Tur*.

S'firat ha'omer (pronounced s'-fee-RAHT hah-OH-mehr): Literally, "counting the Omer." *Omer* (literally, "sheaf") refers to the sheaves of barley, the harvest of which coincides roughly with Passover. The Omer period extends from the eve of the second day of Passover to the night before Shavuot. Each day is counted liturgically as part of the evening *(Ma'ariv)* service.

S'firot (pronounced s'-fee-ROTE; singular: *s'firah*, pronounced s'-fee-RAH): According to the Kabbalah (Jewish mysticism, see **Kabbalah**), the universe came into being by a process of divine emanation, whereby the divine light, as it were, expanded into empty space, eventually becoming physical matter. At various intervals, this light was frozen in time, as if captured by containers, each of which is called a *s'firah*. Literally, *s'firah* means "number," because early theory conceptualized the stages of creation as primordial numbers.

Saadiah Gaon (882-942, Egypt and Sura, Babylonia): A prolific gaon, who wrote grammar, liturgy (the second great prayer book), philosophy, poetry, and responsa. Also noted polemicist against Palestinian authorities and Karaites.

Seder Rav Amram (pronounced SAY-dehr rahv AHM-rahm): First known comprehensive Jewish prayer book, emanating from Rav Amram Gaon (c. 860 CE), a leading Jewish scholar and head of Sura, a famed academy in Babylonia (modern-day Iraq).

Sefardi (pronounced s'-fahr-DEE or, commonly, s'-FAHR-dee): From the Hebrew word *Sefarad* (pronounced s'-fah-RAHD), meaning the geographic area of modern-day Spain and Portugal; "Sefardi" is the adjective, describing the liturgical rituals and customs that are derived from Sefarad, prior to the expulsion of Jews from there at the end of the fifteenth century. These terms contrast with Ashkenazi (see **Ashkenazi**), meaning the liturgical rituals and customs common to northern and eastern Europe. Nowadays, "Sefardi" refers also to the customs of Jews from North Africa and the Arab lands, whose ancestors came from Spain and Portugal. "Sefardim" (plural) refers to Jews who trace their roots to these areas.

Sefardim: See **Sefardi**.

Sefer Ha'agur (pronounced SAY-fehr hah-ah-GOOR): Chief work of Rabbi Jacob Landau (fifteenth century, Germany), a compilation of German Jewish scholarship on daily religious practice; among the first to use kabbalistic ideas as an aid for resolving questions of Jewish law.

Sefer Or Zarua (pronounced SAY-fehr OHR zah-ROO-ah): Legal compendium by Rabbi Isaac ben Moses of Vienna (c. 1180–c. 1250), often referred to as Isaac Or Zarua.

Sefer Rokeach (pronounced SAY-fehr roh-KAY-ahkh): Principal halakhic work of Rabbi Eleazer ben Judah of Worms (c. 1165–1230, Germany), harmonizing the doctrines of German pietists with halakhah, and a valuable source for Jewish custom of the time.

Sekhel Tov: See ***Midrash Sekhel Tov***.

Septuagint (pronounced sehp-TOO-a-jint): Latin for "seventy," reflecting the myth that King Ptolemy of Egypt asked seventy-two Jews to translate the Torah into Greek; refers, therefore, to the first Greek translation of the Bible, begun (probably) in the third century BCE. The original Septuagint included only the Torah, but now we use the term to include also translations of other biblical books that were added to it.

Shehecheyanu (pronounced sheh-heh-khee-YAH-noo): Literally, "who kept us alive" and, hence, the popular name for a blessing praising God for "having kept us alive, sustained us, and brought us to this time of year." Also called *Birkat Hazman* (pronounced beer-KAHT hah-z'-MAHN), "the Blessing of the Time." It is recited at the onset of festivals and a variety of "first-time" events, such as eating the fruit of a new season. Used more generally by liberal Jews to express thanks at happy occasions.

Sheiltot (pronounced sh'-ayl-TOHT): Chief work of Achai Gaon (680–752), literally "*Questions*," a halakhic-midrashic work arranged according to the weekly Torah portion.

Shekhinah (pronounced sh'-khee-NAH or, commonly, sh-KHEE-nah): From the Hebrew root *sh.kh.n*, meaning "to dwell," and, therefore, in talmudic literature, the "indwelling" aspect of God most immediately empathetic to human experience. As the feminine aspect of God, it appears in Kabbalah as the tenth and final *s'firah*, or emanation.

Shibbolei Haleket (pronounced shih-boh-LAY hah-LEH-keht): Literally, "The Gleaned Ears," chief work of Zedekiah ben Abraham Anav (thirteenth century). The first attempt in Italy to codify Jewish law, it includes a complete commentary on the Haggadah.

Sh'ma (pronounced sh'-MAH): The central prayer in the first of the two main units in the worship service, the second being the *Amidah* (see ***Amidah***). The *Sh'ma* comprises three citations from the Bible, and the larger unit in which it is embedded (called the *Sh'ma* and Its Blessings) is composed of a formal Call to Prayer (the *Bar'khu*) and a series of blessings on the theological themes that, together with the *Sh'ma*, constitute a liturgical creed of faith. *Sh'ma*, meaning "hear," is the first word of the first line of the first biblical citation, "Hear O Israel: Adonai is our God; Adonai is One" (Deut. 6:4), which is the paradigmatic statement of Jewish faith, the Jews' absolute commitment to the presence of a single and unique God in time and space.

Shulchan Arukh (pronounced shool-KHAN ah-ROOKH or, commonly, SHOOL-khan AH-rookh): The name given to the best-known code of Jewish law, compiled by Joseph Caro in the Land of Israel and published in 1565. *Shulchan Arukh* means "The Set Table" and refers to the ease with which the various laws are set forth—like a table prepared with food ready for consumption.

Sifra (pronounced seef-RAH): One the tannaitic midrashim, this one on portions of the Book of Leviticus. It begins with Rabbi Ishmael's thirteen rules of interpretation.

Sifre (pronounced seef-RAY): One of the tannaitic midrashim. We have one on Deuteronomy and one on Numbers. The *Sifre on Deuteronomy* includes what may be the oldest written version—a much shorter one—of the Haggadah's midrash on the "wandering Aramean" *(arami oved avi)*.

Soloveitchik, Joseph B. (1903–992, Russia and United States): Also known as "the *Rov*" (the rabbi [par excellence]). Revered centrist Orthodox teacher, philosopher, and talmudist, who ordained more than two thousand rabbis in his nearly fifty years at Yeshiva University. Author of such classics as *Halakhic Man* and *The Lonely Man of Faith*.

Song of Songs Rabbah: Fifth- or sixth-century midrash that interprets the Song of Songs as an allegory of the relationship between God and the people of Israel.

Talmud (pronounced tahl-MOOD or, more commonly, TAHL-m'd): Each of two great compendia of Jewish law and lore compiled over several centuries and, ever since, the literary core of the rabbinic heritage: the Yerushalmi (pronounced y'-roo-SHAHL-mee), the "Palestinian" or "Jerusalem Talmud," compiled in the Land of Israel, c. 400 CE; and the Bavli (pronounced BAHV-lee), or "Babylonian Talmud," from Babylonia (present-day Iraq), c. 550–650 CE. "The" Talmud, cited without specifying one or the other, denotes the Bavli.

Tamid (pronounced tah-MEED): From the Hebrew *tamid*, meaning "always, regular"; hence, the "regular sacrifice" offered daily in the Temple, both morning and afternoon.

Tanchuma (pronounced tahn-KHOO-mah): A midrashic collection of literary sermons covering the weekly Torah readings; probably compiled in Eretz Yisrael in the eighth to ninth century, but attributed to Rabbi Tanchuma bar Abba, an earlier rabbinic figure.

Tanna D'vei Eliyahu (pronounced TAH-nah d'-VAY ay-lee-YAH hoo): Also known as *Seder Eliyahu Rabbah* (SAY-dehr ay-lee-ah-HOO rah-BAH or, commonly, SAY-dehr ay-lee-YAH-hoo RAH-bah), and *Seder Eliyahu Zuta* (SAY-dehr ay-lee-YAH-hoo ZOO-tah), "the greater and lesser teachings of Elijah," a unique midrashic work narrated in the first person. Contains parables, prayers, and admonitions written in colorful style. Dated third or mid-ninth century.

Tanna(im): See **Tannaitic**.

Tannaitic: Referring to the rabbinic period or literature composed between about 20 CE (the death of Hillel) or 70 CE (the destruction of the Second Temple) and 200 CE (the redaction of the Mishnah). A rabbi who lived is this era is called a Tanna (one who hands down orally, learns, or teaches; plural: Tannaim). This is distinguished from the amoraic period, between 200 CE and about 550 CE (the redaction of the Talmud), and *Amora* (from the Hebrew root "to say"; plural: Amoraim), a rabbi who lived during this later era.

T'chi'at hametim (pronounced t'chee-YAHT hah-may-TEEM): Literally, "the resurrection of the dead," a term for one of the three most common eschatological promises of rabbinic Judaism. The others are *olam haba* (pronounced oh-LAHM hah-BAH or, commonly, OH-lahm hah-BAH), "the world-to-come," and *y'mot hamashi'ach* (pronounced y'MOHT hah-mah-SHEE-ahkh), "messianic days" (that is, the era after the coming of the messiah).

Tosafot (pronounced toh-sah-FOHT or, commonly, TOH-sah-foht): Literally, "additional," referring to "additional" twelfth- to fourteenth-century Franco-German halakhists and commentators, the spiritual (and, to some extent, even familial) descendants of the French commentator *Rashi* (1040–1105).

Tosefta (pronounced toh-SEHF-tah): Tannaitic law code or teaching manual structured along the lines of the Mishnah. A supplement (literally, "addition") to the Mishnah, but perhaps containing a core of pre-Mishnaic (i.e., pre-200 CE) material that was reworked in the Mishnah. It contains a description of the night of Passover that differs from the Mishnah; for example, it lacks the question-and-answer approach to telling the story of the Exodus (see Appendix I, *My People's Passover Haggadah*, Volume 2, pp. 225–234).

Tsitsit (pronounced tsee-TSEET): A Hebrew word meaning "tassels" or "fringes" and used to refer to the tassels affixed to the four corners of the *tallit* (the prayer shawl), as Numbers 15:38 instructs.

Tur (pronounced TOOR): The shorthand title applied to a fourteenth-century code of Jewish law, compiled by Jacob ben Asher in Spain, and the source for much of our knowledge about medieval liturgical practice. *Tur* means "row" or "column." The full name of the code is *Arba'ah Turim* (pronounced ahr-bah-AH too-REEM), "The Four Rows," with each row (or *Tur*) being a separate section of law on a given broad topic.

Vayosha: See **Midrash Vayosha**.

Ya'akov Yosef of Polnoye (died c. 1782): First theoretician of Chasidism and author of *Toledot Ya'akov* (pronounced tohl-DOHT yah-ah-KOHV or, commonly, following Ashkenazi pronunciation, TOHL-dohs YAH-k'v), "The Generations of Jacob," the first Chasidic book ever printed.

Yalkut Shimoni (pronounced YAHL-koot shih-MOH-nee): Vast midrashic anthology on the entire Bible compiled from more than fifty sources, many of which are now lost. Compiled by Shimon Hadarshan (pronounced hah-dahr-SHAHN or, commonly, hah-DAHR-shahn), possibly from Frankfurt, twelfth or thirteenth century.

Judah Aryeh Leib of Ger (1847–1905): Founder of Gerer Chasidic dynasty and known also by the name of his book, the *S'fat Emet* (pronounced si-FAHT EH-meht or, commonly, using Ashkenazi pronunciation, s'-FAHS EH-mehs)—literally, "language of truth" (Prov. 12:19), a commentary on the Torah and festivals.

Yerushalmi: See *Talmud*.

YHVH: The ineffable (so, unpronounceable) four-letter name of God, referred to in English as "the tetragrammaton," and traditionally pronounced *Adonai*.

Zevach Pesach (pronounced ZEH-vakh PEH-sakh): Literally, "The offering of the Passover sacrifice"; Haggadah commentary by Isaac ben Judah Abarbanel (1437–1508, Spain and Italy). Written in 1496, it was widely circulated thereafter.

Zohar (pronounced ZOH-hahr): Classic text of Jewish mysticism (literally, the book of "Splendor") by Spanish Kabbalist Moshe ben Tov de Leon (d. 1305). Traditionally ascribed to Rabbi Shimon bar Yochai, mid-second century.

Annotated Select Bibliography

Anisfeld, Sharon Cohen, Tara Mohr, and Catherine Spector, eds. *The Women's Passover Companion: Women's Reflections on the Festival of Freedom.* Woodstock, VT: Jewish Lights Publishing, 2003.

———. *The Women's Seder Sourcebook: Rituals and Readings for Use at the Passover Seder.* Woodstock, VT: Jewish Lights Publishing, 2003.

These two volumes provide an excellent collection of material on the Seder and Passover from a feminist perspective.

Arnow, David. *Creating Lively Passover Seders: A Sourcebook of Engaging Tales, Texts & Activities.* Woodstock, VT: Jewish Lights Publishing, 2004.

A broad-ranging exploration of the history and development of the Haggadah chock-full of material to enliven any Seder.

———. "Elaborating on the Exodus." *Conservative Judaism* 58, no. 4 (2006): 61–79.

Analyzes the meaning of the Haggadah's injunction to "elaborate on the Exodus" during the Seder and brings to light the first Haggadah in which the now standard phrase makes its appearance.

———. "The Passover *Haggadah*: Moses and the Human Role in Redemption." *Judaism*, forthcoming.

Challenges the myth of Moses' complete absence from the Haggadah by analyzing the two places where he does in fact appear and explores other instances in which the Haggadah points to the human role in the process of redemption.

Bahr, Gordon J. "The Seder of Passover and the Eucharistic Words of Jesus" *Novum Testamentum* 12 (1970).

Classic account linking the Seder to the words of Jesus at the Lord's Supper.

Balin, Carole B. "The Modern Transformation of the Ancient Passover *Haggadah*." In *Passover and Easter: The Origin and History to Modern Times,* edited by Paul F. Bradshaw and Lawrence H. Hoffman. Notre Dame, IN: University of Notre Dame Press, 1999.

Summary discussion of modern Haggadot and how they altered the traditional text and ritual.

Blank, Debra Reed. "*Sh'fokh Hamatkha* and *Eliyahu* in the *Haggadah:* Ideology in Liturgy." *Conservative Judaism* 40, no. 2 (1987): 73–86.
Discussion of the way Haggadot have dealt with *Sh'fokh Chamatkha*.

Bokser, Baruch M. "Changing Views of Passover and the Meaning of Redemption According to the Palestinian Talmud." *Journal of the Association for Jewish Studies* 10, no. 1 (Spring 1985): 1–18.
Contrasts descriptions of Passover night as provided in the Mishnah and the Palestinian Talmud (the *Yerushalmi*) and argues that the latter depicts redemption in more personal terms.

———. "*From Sacrifice to Symbol—Beyond*." The Solomon Goldman Lectures V (1990): 1–19.
Traces the development of how Passover was celebrated from the Bible to the rabbinic period.

———. *The Origins of the Passover Seder: The Passover Rite and Early Rabbinic Judaism.* Berkeley: University of California Press, 1984.
A seminal study based on a careful reading of early rabbinic sources arguing that after the Temple was destroyed in 70 CE, the Seder developed as a substitute for the Passover sacrifice.

———. "Ritualizing the Seder." *Journal of the American Academy of Religion* 56, no. 3 (1988): 443–71.
Discusses the manner in which diverse elements of the Seder became endowed with symbolic meaning and developed into rituals.

Bradshaw, Paul F., and Lawrence H. Hoffman, eds. *Passover and Easter: Origin and History to Modern Times.* Notre Dame, IN: University of Notre Dame Press, 1999.
This collection provides a wealth of scholarship on each of these spring festivals and on the relationships between them.

———. *Passover and Easter: The Symbolic Structures of the Sacred Seasons.* Notre Dame, Indiana: University of Notre Dame Press, 1999.

Brumberg-Kraus, Jonathan. "Meals as *Midrash*: A Survey of Ancient Meals in Jewish Studies Scholarship." *Studies in Jewish Civilization* 15 (2005): 297–317.
Analyzes how Jewish meal rituals replaced sacrifices after the Temple's destruction.

———."'Not by Bread Alone …': The Ritualization of Food and Table Talk in the Passover 'Seder' and in the Last Supper." *Semeia* 86 (1999): 165–91.
Considers the influence of the Greco-Roman *symposium* on the Seder and the Last Supper and contrasts the strategies of ritualization in each.

Francis, Fred O. "The *Baraita* of the Four Sons." *Journal of the American Academy of Religion* 42 (1974): 280–197.

A form-critical analysis of the four sons narrative, tracing it to rhetorical models in classical literature.

Fredman, Ruth Gruber. *The Passover Seder*. New York: New American Library, 1983.

An anthropological analysis of the symbols and rituals of the Seder.

Goldin, Judah. "Not By Means of an Angel and Not By Means of a Messenger." In *Studies in Midrash and Related Literature*, edited by Judah Goldin, Barry L. Eichler, and Jeffrey H. Tigay. Philadelphia: Jewish Publication Society, 1988.

A study of this primary source in rabbinic literature to shed light upon its meaning in the Haggadah and on ancient attitudes toward Moses.

Goldshmidt, E. Daniel. *The Passover Haggadah: Sources and History*. Jerusalem: The Bialik Institute, 1960 (Hebrew).

Pioneer study of the Haggadah's historical development by the last century's foremost expert in Jewish liturgical texts, along with the text of the Haggadah used in *My People's Passover Haggadah*; as well as a reproduction of the Genizah Haggadah that appears in our Appendix II.

Golinkin, David. "Pesah Potpourri: On the Origin and Development of Some Lesser-Known Pesah *Customs*." *Conservative Judaism* 55, no. 3 (2003): 58–71.

Probes the origins of thirteen poorly understood Seder customs, from walking around the table as "wandering Arameans" to exposing the truth about a "friendly" alternative to "Pour out Your wrath," falsely attributed to an early sixteenth-century Haggadah!

Goodman, Philip. *The Passover Anthology*. Philadelphia: Jewish Publication Society, 1961.

An extensive collection of writings covering virtually every aspect of the festival, dated, but nonetheless extremely useful.

Greenbaum, David Ephraim. *Haggadah V'agad'ta*. Israel: Author's personal publication, 2004.

Excellent traditional collection of midrashim associated with the Haggadah.

Guggenheimer, Heinrich. *The Scholars Haggadah*. Northvale, NJ: Jason Aronson, 1998.

Provides the Ashkenazic, Sefardic, and Yemenite liturgies of the Haggadah along with detailed commentary focusing on historical development.

Gutmann, Joseph. "The messiah at the Seder." *Raphael Mahler Jubilee Volume* (Israel: 1974): 29–38.

Discussion of the tradition of showing the coming of Elijah and the messiah in medieval illustrated Haggadot.

Halivni, David. "Biurim Bishe'elot Mah Nishtanah." In *Studies in Aggadah, Targum and Jewish Liturgy*, edited by Jakob J. Petuchowski and Ezra Fleischer, 67–74 (Hebrew section). Jerusalem: Magnes, 1981.

Study of the Four Questions, arguing that although some households in antiquity did not say the questions as we do, some, in fact, did.

Hauptman, Judith. "Boundless Gratitude: Mentioning the Exodus at Night." In *Rereading the Mishnah: A New Approach to Ancient Jewish Texts*. Tubingen: Mohr Siebeck, 2005.

Analyzes the sources of the Haggadah's treatment of this subject and sheds new light both on it as well as the relationship between the Mishnah and the Tosefta.

———. "How Old Is the Haggadah?" *Judaism* 51, no. 1 (Winter 2002): 3–18.

Analyzes the relationship between descriptions of the night of Passover in the Mishnah and Tosefta and argues, contrary to the common view, that the latter actually contains an earlier plan for the Seder that the Mishnah later reworked.

Henshke, David. "'The Lord Brought Us Forth from Egypt': On the Absence of Moses in the Passover Haggadah." *AJS Review*, 31 no. 1 (2007): 61–73.

An exploration of the cultural and theological milieu that shaped the Haggadah's minimization of Moses.

———. "The Wandering Aramean Midrash." *Sidra* 4 (1988): 33–52 (Hebrew).

A careful dissection of the Haggadah's central midrash discussing its structure and composition as well as how its beginning relates to the Mishnah's instruction to "begin with degradation."

Hoffman, Lawrence A. *Beyond the Text: A Holistic Approach to Liturgy*. Bloomington: Indiana University Press, 1987.

The classic treatment of the Haggadah as sacred myth, thoroughly explored in ancient and modern contexts.

———. "A Symbol of Salvation in the Passover Seder." In *Passover and Easter: The Origin and History to Modern Times*, edited by Paul F. Bradshaw and Lawrence H. Hoffman. Notre Dame, IN: University of Notre Dame Press, 1999.

An argument for the symbolic significance of matzah as a replacement for the Passover sacrifice, and its impact on understanding the words of Jesus as the Institutional Narrative of Christian liturgical tradition.

Kasher, Menachem. *Hagadah Shelemah*. Jerusalem: Torah Shelemah Institute, 1967 (Hebrew).

An essential resource for research on the Haggadah, by one of the last century's greatest experts in rabbinic literature; particularly useful as a compendium of citations on the Seder and the Haggadah, from representative texts throughout rabbinic tradition.

————. *Israel Passover Haggadah.* New York: Sentry Press, 1950.

A commentary on the Haggadah in both Hebrew and English making use of a wide array of rabbinic sources.

Katsenelenbogen, Mordecai Leyb, ed. *Haggadat Torat Chaim.* Jerusalem: Mossad Harav Kook, 1998 (Hebrew).

The Haggadah with well-annotated commentary of the *Rishonim*, a dozen medieval commentators.

Kulp, Joshua. "The Origins of the Seder and Haggadah." *Currents in Biblical Research* 4, No. 1 (2005): 109–35.

A recent overview of the Haggadah's early development that considers influences of the Temple's destruction, the Bar Kokhba rebellion, competition with emerging Christian groups, as well as the Greek *symposium.*

————. *The Historical Haggadah: Sources and Commentary on the Historical Development of the Seder and the Haggadah.* Schechter Institute of Jewish Studies Press, forthcoming.

Circulating for several years in draft form, an invaluable treatment of the Haggadah's development; a great contribution because of its scholarship and the fact that it is written in English.

Laufer, Nathan. *Leading the Passover Journey: The Seder's Meaning Revealed, the Haggadah's Story Retold.* Woodstock, VT: Jewish Lights Publishing, 2005.

Exegetical discussion of the Seder, step by step, especially rich in reporting the traditions of Rabbi Joseph B. Soloveitchik, the Rov.

Levey, Samson H. "Ben Zoma The Sages and Passover." *Journal of Reform Judaism* 28, no. 2 (Spring, 1981): 33–40.

Classic account explaining the tradition of Ben Zoma as signs of a Jewish-Christian heresy.

Leyerle, Blake. "Meal Customs in the Greco-Roman World." In *Passover and Easter: The Origin and History of Modern Times,* edited by Paul F. Bradshaw and Lawrence H. Hoffman. Notre Dame, IN: University of Notre Dame press, 1999.

Summary of Greco-Roman meal customs relevant to the Seder.

Metzger, Mendel. *La Haggada enluminée.* Leiden: E. J. Brill, 1999.

Contains superb and thorough discussion (and reproductions) of illuminations from medieval Haggadot.

Mihaly, Eugene. "The Passover Haggadah as PaRaDiSe." *CCAR Journal* 13, no. 5 (April 1966): 3–27.

A classic treatment of the different layers of meaning and interpretation contained within the Haggadah.

Mor, Sagit. "The Laws of the Passover Sacrifice or the Narrative of the Exodus: Two Traditions of Designing the Night of Passover after the Destruction of the Temple." *Tzion* 68 (2003): 297–311 (Hebrew).

Contrasts stories in the Tosefta and the Haggadah about what to emphasize on the night of Passover, arguing that the Haggadah's stress on telling the story represents a more adaptive approach than studying the laws of the now-absent sacrifice.

Propp, William H. C. *The Anchor Bible: Exodus 1–18 and Exodus 19–40*. New York: Doubleday, 1999, 2006.

These two volumes, together almost 1,500 pages, include the most up-to-date and comprehensive study of the Book of Exodus, a treasure for anyone interested in the biblical origins of Passover.

Raphael, Chaim. *A Feast of History*. New York. Gallery Books, 1972.

Rich popular introduction to the Haggadah, with excellent illustrations from illuminations through the ages.

Rovner, Jay. "An Early Passover Haggadah According to the Palestinian Rite." *Jewish Quarterly Review* 90, no. 3–4 (2000): 337–96.

In this series of articles the author traces the development of the Haggadah, bringing to light previously unpublished manuscripts nearly a thousand years old. The works provide many insights into the Haggadah's long evolution with special attention devoted to the wandering Aramean midrash (also known as *Mikra Bikkurim Midrash*, "the Midrash on the Declaration of First Fruits"). The last article includes a synoptic table comparing five versions of this midrash.

————. "A New Version of the Eretz Israel *Haggadah* Liturgy and the Evolution of the Eretz Israel '*Miqra*' Bikkurim' Midrash." *Jewish Quarterly Review* 92, no. 3–4 (2002): 421–53.

————. "Two Early Witnesses to the Formation of the *Miqra Bikurim Midrash* and Their Implications for the Evolution of the Haggadah." *Hebrew Union College Annual* 75 (2005): 75–120.

Safrai, Shmuel and Safrai Ze'ev. *The Haggadah of the Sages*. Jerusalem: Carta, 1998 (Hebrew).

An essential resource for research on the development of the Haggadah; features superb scientific discussion of available manuscripts and literary traditions.

Silber, David. *The Passover Haggadah/The Wandering Aramean*. New York: Drisha Institute Tape Project (audiotape), 1994. Available at www.drisha.org.

Two lectures by a brilliant teacher about the meaning of redemption and the Haggadah's treatment of the theme of covenantal promise and fulfillment.

Smith, Dennis E. *From Symposium to Eucharist: The Banquet in the Early Christian World*. Minneapolis: Augsburg Press, 2003.

Wonderful background discussion of the development and influence of Greco-Romnan dining customs on the Seder, with a full chapter devoted just to "The Jewish Banquet."

Stein, Siegfried. "The Influence of the Symposia Literature on the Literary Form of the Haggadah." *Journal of Jewish Studies* 7, nos. 1 and 2 (1957): 13–44.
    The classic work on the relationship between the Greek *symposium* and *symposium* literature and its influence on the Haggadah.

Tabory, Joseph. *The Passover Ritual Throughout the Generations*. Israel: Hakibbutz Hameuchad Publishing House, 1996 (Hebrew).
    Another essential resource by one of the great scholars of the Haggadah, particularly strong in exploring the origins of customs such as the four cups of wine, washing, dipping, etc.

———. "Toward a History of the Paschal Meal." *In Passover and Easter: The Origin and History to Modern Times,* edited by Paul F. Bradshaw and Lawrence H. Hoffman. Notre Dame, IN: University of Notre Dame Press, 1999.
    An analysis of sources, arguing that the Seder began as a sacrificial meal, but then went through two distinct Jewish stages of a Greco-Roman *symposium.*

Yerushalmi, Hayim Yosef. *Haggadah and History: A Panorama in Facsimile of Five Centuries of the Printed Haggadah.* Philadelphia: Jewish Publication Society, 1975.
    An incomparable presentation of images from the collections of Harvard University and the Jewish Theological Seminary of America of printed Haggadot.

Yuval, Israel J. "Easter and Passover as Early Jewish-Christian Dialogue." In *Passover and Easter: The Origin and History of Modern Times*, edited by Paul F. Bradshaw and Lawrence H. Hoffman. Notre Dame, IN: University of Notre Dame Press, 1999.
    Discussion of sources from late antiquity suggesting that much of the Seder is a response to the confrontation of Judaism with early Christianity.

———. "Passover in the Middle Ages." In *Passover and Easter: The Origin and History to Modern Times,* edited by Paul F. Bradshaw and Lawrence H. Hoffman. 1999.
    Excellent survey of medieval customs, particularly as they shed light on Jewish-Christian relations in Europe

Werner, Eric. *A Voice Still Heard: The Sacred Songs of Ashkenazic Jews.* University Park: Pennsylvania State University, 1976.
    Contains classical study of the music of the Haggadah, by the American founder of Jewish musicology.

Wolfson, Ron. *Passover: The Family Guide to Spiritual Celebration.* 2nd ed. Woodstock. VT: Jewish Lights Publishing, 2003.
    A wonderful source of ideas for people planning family Seders.

ANNOTATED SELECT BIBLIOGRAPHY

Zevin, S. Y. *The Festivals in Halachah*. Vol. 1. New York: Mesorah, 1969.
   Excellent discussion in English of traditional Halakhah relevant to the Seder and the Haggadah.

About the Contributors

DAVID ARNOW

David Arnow, PhD, a psychologist by training, has been writing about the Passover Seder for twenty years. He is widely recognized for his innovative work to make the Seder a truly exciting encounter each year with Judaism's central ideas. He is the author of *Creating Lively Passover Seders: A Sourcebook of Engaging Tales, Texts and Activities* (Jewish Lights Publishing) and the creator of its website, www.livelyseders.com. He lectures widely and writes on a broad variety of topics of Jewish interest.

CAROLE B. BALIN

Carole B. Balin is professor of Jewish history at Hebrew Union College–Jewish Institute of Religion in New York. She was educated at Wellesley College, ordained at HUC-JIR, and earned her PhD at Columbia University. She specializes in modern Jewish history, specifically Eastern European Jewish history. She is the author of *To Reveal Our Hearts: Jewish Women Writers in Tsarist Russia* (HUC Press), co-editor with Wendy Zierler of a forthcoming collection of the Hebrew writings of Hava Shapiro (Resling Press), and co-author with Eugene Borowitz of a forthcoming revision of *Liberal Judaism* (URJ Press).

MARC BRETTLER*

Marc Brettler, PhD, is Dora Golding Professor of Biblical Studies in the Department of Near Eastern and Judaic Studies at Brandeis University. His major areas of research are biblical historical texts, religious metaphors, and gender issues in the Bible. Brettler is author of *God Is King: Understanding an Israelite Metaphor* (Sheffield Academic Press), *The Creation of History in Ancient Israel* (Routledge), *The Book of Judges* (Routledge), *How to Read the Bible* (Jewish Publication Society), and *How to Read the Jewish Bible* (Oxford University Press), as well as a variety of articles on the Bible. He is also associate editor of the new edition of the *Oxford Annotated Bible* and coeditor of the *Jewish Study Bible* (Oxford University Press).

* Contributor to the *My People's Prayer Book: Traditional Prayers, Modern Commentaries* Series, winner of the National Jewish Book Award.

NEIL GILLMAN

Neil Gillman, rabbi and PhD, is professor of Jewish philosophy at The Jewish Theological Seminary in New York, where he has served as chair of the department of Jewish philosophy and dean of the Rabbinical School. He is author of *Sacred Fragments: Recovering Theology for the Modern Jew* (Jewish Publication Society), winner of the National Jewish Book Award; *The Death of Death: Resurrection and Immortality in Jewish Thought* (Jewish Lights), a finalist for the National Jewish Book Award and a *Publishers Weekly* "Best Book of the Year"; *The Way Into Encountering God in Judaism* (Jewish Lights); *Traces of God: Seeing God in Torah, History, and Everyday Life* (Jewish Lights), and *The Jewish Approach to God: A Brief Introduction for Christians* (Jewish Lights).

ALYSSA GRAY*

Alyssa Gray, PhD, JD, is associate professor of codes and responsa literature at Hebrew Union College–Jewish Institute of Religion in New York. She has also taught at The Jewish Theological Seminary in New York. She has written on the topics of martyrdom and sexuality in rabbinic literature, Talmudic redaction, Talmudic *aggadah*, liturgy, and women and *tzedakah* in medieval Jewish law. She is the author of *A Talmud in Exile: The Influence of Yerushalmi Avodah Zarah on the Formation of Bavli Avodah Zarah* (Brown Judaic Studies) and the co-editor (with Bernard Jackson) of *Studies in Mediaeval Halakhah in Honor of Stephen M. Passamaneck* (Deborah Charles). Her current research focuses on wealth and poverty in classical rabbinic literature.

ARTHUR GREEN

Arthur Green is rector of the Hebrew College Rabbinical School and Irving Brudnick Professor of Jewish philosophy and religion. He is also professor emeritus of Jewish thought at Brandeis University. He is former president of the Reconstructionist Rabbinical College. He is a rabbi, a historian of Jewish mysticism, and a theologian. His works include *Tormented Master: The Life and Spiritual Quest of Rabbi Nahman of Bratslav* (Jewish Lights); *Keter: The Crown of God in Early Jewish Mysticism; Seek My Face: A Jewish Mystical Theology* (Jewish Lights); *These Are the Words: A Vocabulary of Jewish Spiritual Life* (Jewish Lights); *Ehyeh: A Kabbalah for Tomorrow* (Jewish Lights), and *A Guide to the Zohar*. His translations and interpretations of Hasidic Thought include *Upright Practices and The Light of the Eyes*, by Rabbi Menahem Nahum of Chernobyl; *Your Word Is Fire: The Hasidic Masters on Contemplative Prayer* (with B. W. Holtz; Jewish Lights), and *The Language of Truth: Teachings from the Sefat Emet*.

JOEL M. HOFFMAN*

Joel M. Hoffman, Ph.D., lectures around the globe on popular and scholarly topics spanning history, Hebrew, prayer, and Jewish continuity. He has served on the faculties of Brandeis University, the Academy for Jewish Religion, and, currently, Hebrew Union

College–Jewish Institute of Religion in New York, where he teaches advanced classes on Hebrew and on translation. Hoffman's research in theoretical linguistics brings him to a new approach to ancient Hebrew, viewing it not merely as a dead language, but as a spoken language of antiquity. Hoffman is the author of *In the Beginning: A Short History of the Hebrew Language* (NYU Press). In addition to his graduate-level teaching, Hoffman serves as scholar-in-residence at Temple Shaaray Tefila in Bedford, New York, and finds time to teach youngsters a few afternoons a week.

LAWRENCE A. HOFFMAN*

Lawrence A. Hoffman, Ph.D., was ordained and received his doctorate from Hebrew Union College–Jewish Institute of Religion. He has served in its New York campus for more than three decades, most recently as the Barbara and Stephen Friedman Professor of Liturgy, Worship and Ritual. Widely recognized for his scholarship and classroom teaching, Hoffman has combined research with a passion for the spiritual renewal of contemporary Judaism. He has written and edited over twenty-five books, including *The Art of Public Prayer, 2nd Edition: Not for Clergy Only* (SkyLight Paths), now used nationally by Jews and Christians as a handbook for liturgical planners in church and synagogue, as well as a revision of *What Is a Jew?*, the best-selling classic that remains the most widely read introduction to Judaism ever written in any language. He is editor of the *My People's Prayer Book: Traditional Prayers, Modern Commentaries* Series, winner of the National Jewish Book Award; and author of *Israel—A Spiritual Travel Guide: A Companion for the Modern Jewish Pilgrim* and *The Way Into Jewish Prayer* (both Jewish Lights Publishing). Hoffman is a founder of Synagogue 2000 (now renamed Synagogue 3000), a transdenominational project designed to transform synagogues into the moral and spiritual centers of the twenty-first century. His latest book, *Rethinking Synagogues: A New Vocabulary for Congregational Life* (Jewish Lights), an outgrowth of that project, was a finalist for the National Jewish Book Award.

LAWRENCE KUSHNER*

Lawrence Kushner is the Emanu-El scholar at congregation Emanu-El in San Francisco, an adjunct faculty member at Hebrew Union College–Jewish Institute of Religion, and a visiting professor of Jewish spirituality at the Graduate Theological Union in Berkeley, California. He served as spiritual leader of Congregation Beth El in Sudbury, Massachusetts, for twenty-eight years and is widely regarded as one of the most creative religious writers in America. Ordained a rabbi by Hebrew Union College–Jewish Institute of Religion, Kushner led his congregants in publishing their own prayer book, *V'taher Libenu* (Purify Our Hearts), the first gender-neutral liturgy ever written. Through his lectures and many books, including *The Way Into Jewish Mystical Tradition; Invisible Lines of Connection: Sacred Stories of the Ordinary; The Book of Letters: A Mystical Hebrew Alphabet; Honey from the Rock: An Introduction to Jewish Mysticism; God Was in This Place and I, i Did Not Know: Finding Self, Spirituality, and Ultimate*

Meaning; Eyes Remade for Wonder: A Lawrence Kushner Reader; and *Jewish Spirituality: A Brief Introduction for Christians*, all published by Jewish Lights, he has helped shape the Jewish community's present focus on personal and institutional spiritual renewal.

DANIEL LANDES*

Daniel Landes is director and Rosh HaYeshivah of the Pardes Institute of Jewish Studies in Jerusalem and was an adjunct professor of Jewish law at Loyola University Law School in Los Angeles. Ordained a rabbi by Rabbi Isaac Elchanan Theological Seminary, Landes was a founding faculty member of the Simon Wiesenthal Center and the Yeshiva of Los Angeles, and served as a judge in the Los Angeles Orthodox Beith Din. He has lectured and written various popular and scholarly articles on the subjects of Jewish thought, social ethics, and spirituality.

NEHEMIA POLEN*

Nehemia Polen is professor of Jewish thought and director of the Hasidic Text Institute at Boston's Hebrew College. He is the author of *The Holy Fire: The Teachings of Rabbi Kalonymus Shapira, the Rebbe of the Warsaw Ghetto* (Jason Aronson) as well as many academic and popular articles on Chasidism and Jewish spirituality, and coauthor of *Filling Words with Light: Hasidic and Mystical Reflections on Jewish Prayer* (Jewish Lights). He received his Ph.D. from Boston University, where he studied with and served as teaching fellow for Nobel laureate Elie Wiesel. In 1994 he was Daniel Jeremy Silver Fellow at Harvard University, and he has also been a Visiting Scholar at the Hebrew University in Jerusalem. He was ordained a rabbi at the Ner Israel Rabbinical College in Baltimore, Maryland, and served as a congregational rabbi for twenty-three years. In 1998–1999 he was a National Endowment for the Humanities Fellow, working on the writings of Malkah Shapiro (1894–1971), the daughter of a noted Chasidic master, whose Hebrew memoirs focus on the spiritual lives of women in the context of prewar Chasidism in Poland. This work is documented in his book *The Rebbe's Daughter* (Jewish Publication Society), winner of the National Jewish Book Award.

WENDY I. ZIERLER*

Wendy I. Zierler is Associate Professor of Modern Jewish Literature and Feminist Studies at Hebrew Union College–Jewish Institute of Religion. Prior to joining HUC–JIR she was a research fellow in the English Department of Hong Kong University. She holds PhD and MA degrees in comparative literature from Princeton University, and a BA from Yeshiva University, Stern College. She is the author of *And Rachel Stole the Idols: The Emergence of Hebrew Women's Writing* (Wayne State University Press) and co-editor with Carole B. Balin of a forthcoming collection of the Hebrew writings of Hava Shapiro (Resling Press). At HUC she teaches courses dealing with modern Jewish and Hebrew literature, popular culture and theology, and gender and Judaism.

Index

For major passages in the Haggadah, see also the Table of Contents.

A

Aaron, Vol.2:12, 66
Abarbanel, Don Isaac, Vol.1:187
Abraham, Vol.1:167, 214, 216, 217, 224,
    Vol.2:61, 69, 222–223
Abudarham, David, Vol.1:176
  checking of leaven, Vol.1:97–98
  covenant, Vol.1:228–229
  four children, Vol.1:189
  Hillel sandwich, Vol.1:190
  hospitality, Vol.1:128, Vol.2:176
  recounting Passover story, Vol.1:187
  slavery, Vol.1:166
acculturation, Vol.1:50
activism, Vol.1:192, 197
Adam, Vol.2:44, 67, 77
Adir Hu, Vol.2:198–199, 208, 217–218, 222
Adler, Rachel, Vol.1:76
afikoman, Vol.1:29, 140, 185, Vol.2:111, 115,
    118–119, 122–123, 128–129, 134–136
  eating, Vol.1:199–201
  Levi Yitzchak of Berditchev, Vol.1:203–204
  translation, Vol.1:195
agrarian rituals, Vol.1:10, 11, 134
akedah, Vol.2:182
Akiva, Rabbi, Vol.1:160, 207–208, Vol.2:2,
    55, 112, 117, 121, 125
aliyah laregel, Vol.1:139
American history, Vol.2:206, 215
amidah, Vol.2:217
Amram, Vol.2:11
Amram, David Werner, Vol.2:235
angels
  evil, Vol.2:64

  kinds of, Vol.2:51, 57, 81
  types of, Vol.2:36
animals, plagues, Vol.2:29, 38, 46–47, 61–63
anthropomorphic descriptions of God, Vol.2:36, 55
Aramaic, Vol.1:97, 144–145
Aramean, wandering, Vol.2:1, 4–5, 13, 16–17, 26
ArtScroll Mesorah Series, Vol.1:84
Asher, Vol.2:9
assimilation, Vol.1:50
astrology, Vol.1:134
Av, Ninth of, Vol.1:41
"*Avadim Hayyinu*", Vol.1:161–163
Aviv, Vol.1:13
avodah, Vol.1:214

B

Baker, Cynthia, Vol.1:77
barekh, Vol.2:111, 115
Batya, Vol.2:11–12
B'dikat Chamets, Vol.1:92
Ben Zoma, Vol.1:177, 188, 198, 209
biblical criticism on Haggadah, Vol.1:74
binah, Vol.1:222, 229–230
Birkat Hazman, Vol.1:134
bi'ur, Vol.1:102
blessings
  God, source of, Vol.1:177
  Haggadah, Vol.1:188–189
  havdalah, Vol.1:111–112
  kiddush, Vol.2:111–112
  leaven, Vol.2:92–95
  shehecheyanu, Vol.1:113
blight, plague of, Vol.2:30, 39, 43–44, 46, 53,
    59, 62–63

blood
    plague of, Vol.2:30, 39, 45–46, 52–53, 59, 65–66
    relationship to wonders, Vol.2:29–30, 38–39, 45
    role of in Haggadah, Vol.2:6, 14, 18–19, 23, 27–28
    sacrificial offerings, Vol.2:120
B'nai Brak, seder in, Vol.1:176, 184, 191, 196–197, 207
boils, plague of, Vol.2:30, 39, 46, 63
Borochov, Ber, Vol.1:180–181
Boyarin, Daniel, Vol.1:210
"bread of affliction", Vol.1:119–121, 123–124, 126–127, 135, 141
    language, Vol.1:144–145
    Yachats, Vol.1:140
bread, symbolism of, Vol.1:27, 28
Broide, Simcha Ziskind, Vol.1:149, 155
Broner, E.M., Vol.1:71

C

Cairo Genizah Haggadah, Vol.2:235–247
calendar, Vol.1:23, 131–132, 178
Canaan, Vol.2:1, 6, 119
candles, Vol.1:111, 115, 129
Chad Gadya, Vol.2:202–204, 206, 212–218, 222–224
Chamets. see leaven
Chanukah, Vol.1:190–191
Chanover, Hyman, Vol.1:83
charoset, Vol.1:27, 39, 41, Vol.2:113, 129, 131–132
chavurah, Vol.1:25, 142
chazeret, Vol.1:150
Chazon Ish, Vol.1:137
cherut, Vol.1:136–137, 155
Chesler, Phyllis, Vol.1:71
children, telling Passover story, Vol.1:172, 186, 201
    Maimonides, Moses, Vol.1:190
chosen people, Vol.1:118, 123, 124–125
Christianity
    comparison between Passover and Easter, Vol.2:83
    condemnation of, Vol.1:35
    Crusades, Vol.2:149–151
    in *Hallel*, Vol.2:182–183

    liturgy, Vol.1:33
    nations of, Vol.2:139
    parallelism, Vol.1:31–32
    polemic against, Vol.2:37, 65–66, 75
    relations with Judaism, Vol.1:21, 32–33, 35
    rituals, Vol.2:196
    view on redemption, Vol.2:27
church and state, separation of, Vol.1:66
circumcision, Vol.2:10, 17, 27–28
Civil War, Vol.2:120
colonization, Vol.1:49–50
communism, Vol.1:120
conclusion of seder, Vol.2:186–197
Conservative Judaism, Vol.1:58–60
    Haggadah, Vol.1:82–84
    identity, Vol.1:66
covenant between God and Israel, Vol.1:31, 217, 221, 222, 224, 226, Vol.2:10, 16–17, 88
    Abudarham, David, Vol.1:228–229
    Rashbetz, Vol.1:222, 229
    translation, Vol.1:222
Cowen, Lillie G., Vol.1:87
creation, Vol.2:165
creativity in Seder, Vol.1:19, 69
customs of Seder, Vol.2:51

D

The Dancing with Miriam Haggadah, Vol.1:158
darkness, plague of, Vol.2:30, 39, 47, 53, 59, 66
David, King of Israel, Vol.2:102
Dayyenu, Vol.2:32–34, 37, 41, 49–50, 59–61, 64–68, 70–71
Deborah, Vol.1:222
demographics, Jewish, Vol.1:65
desert, wandering in the, Vol.2:33–34, 41–43, 49, 51
disgrace of slavery, Vol.1:214, 217
Documentary Hypothesis, Vol.1:10
Dreyfus, Alfred, Vol.1:54

E

Easter, Vol.1:23, 33–34
Echad Mi Yode'a?, Vol.2:199–202, 206–207, 209–211, 214–215, 217, 220–222, 224
egg (Seder plate), Vol.1:38, Vol.2:133–134

Egypt, *see also*: Exodus story, slavery
  comparison to Eden, Vol.2:77
  idol worship, Vol.1:215, 218
  Jacob's descent to, Vol.2:1–2, 4, 6, 8
  leaving, Vol.1:187–188
Einhorn, David, Vol.1:81
Elazar ben Azariah, Vol.1:176–177, 188, 198,
    208–209
Eliezer (ben Hycranus), Vol.1:76, 207, 208,
    Vol.2:53, 68
Elijah ben Solomon, Vol.1:43; *see also Gra*
Elijah, welcoming, Vol.2:137–142, 144–151,
    153, 183
Emancipation, Vol.1:79
Enlightenment, Vol.1:79
Eruv Tavshilin, Vol.1:92–93, 96
  feminism, Vol.1:104–105
Esau, Vol.1:216, 217–218
ethnicity, Vol.1:55, 66
Eucharist, Vol.1:25–26
Eve, Vol.2:60, 67, 71, 77
Exodus story, Vol.1:109–110, 122–123
  feminism, Vol.1:71–72
  memorial of, Vol.1:122–123
  miracles, Vol.2:99–104, 107, 139, 152
  nationhood, Vol.1:143
explanation of Haggadah, level of, Vol.2:12,
    24–25
Ezekiel, Vol.2:10, 13, 14, 27, 28, 43

F

faith, Vol.1:32, 228
  God, Vol.2:84–85
  Thirteen Principles of Faith, Vol.1:162, 165
Feinstein, Moshe, Vol.1:137
feminism
  charoset, Vol.2:129
  checking of leaven, Vol.1:95, 104
  comparison to Israel, Vol.2:26–28
  Dayyenu, Vol.2:70–71
  Eruv Tavshilin, Vol.1:104–105
  Exodus story, Vol.1:71–72
  Hallel, Vol.2:97, 108, 165, 185
  karpas, Vol.1:143
  paschal sacrifice, Vol.2:75
  revelation of the *Shekhinah*, Vol.2:37
  role of women in Exodus, Vol.2:92
  Seder plate, Vol.1:105

Ten Plagues, Vol.2:69–70
  traditional text, Vol.1:73
  women of Egypt, Vol.2:12–13
Festival of Matzot, Vol.1:122
fidya, Vol.1:10
Finkelstein, Louis, Vol.1:83, 197
firstborn, killing of
  both people and animals, Vol.2:61, 63
  Dayyenu, Vol.2:32, 34, 41–43
  hardening Pharaoh's heart, Vol.2:47–48,
    56–57
  plague of, Vol.2:29–30, 36, 38–39, 53,
    65–66, 74, 77–78
five, symbolism of, Vol.1:197
flood, Vol.2:10
four children, Vol.1:177, 179–183, 184–185,
    199, 210
  Abudarham, David, Vol.1:189
  gender characteristics, Vol.1:210
  Gra, Vol.1:203
  Levi Yitzchak of Berditchev, Vol.1:203
  Maggid of Mezerich, Vol.1:203
  Mekhilta D'rabbi Yishmael, Vol.1:201–202
  Ritba, Vol.1:189–190
  translation, Vol.1:193–194
Four Questions. *see Mah Nishtanah*
freedom, Vol.1:118, 119, 122, 126, 127–128,
    128
  wine, four cups, Vol.1:136–137
  women's role in, Vol.1:158–159
The Freedom Seder, Vol.1:151
frogs, plague of, Vol.2:30, 39, 46, 53, 59, 62,
    66

G

Gabriel, Vol.2:48
Gamaliel, Rabban, Vol.1:172, 176, 177, 208,
    209, Vol.2:74, 75, 83
gender characteristics, Vol.1:168
gender identity, Vol.1:105
gerim, Vol.1:224–225
German Jews, Vol.1:56
Gershom, Vol.1:109
God, *see also*: *HaMakom*
  anthropomorphic descriptions of, Vol.2:36
  gender characteristics, Vol.1:168
  HaMakom, Vol.1:192
  redemption, Vol.1:165–166, 222, 230

and slavery, Vol.1:226
source of blessing, Vol.1:177
suffering, Vol.1:226–227
Goshen, Vol.2:1, 6
Gospels, Vol.1:23
Gra, Vol.1:203
Greenberg, Irving, Vol.1:228

H

Ha lachma anya. see "bread of affliction"
Hagahot Maimuniyot, Vol.1:98
Haggadah
ArtScroll Mesorah Series, Vol.1:84
biblical criticism, Vol.1:74
blessing over, Vol.1:188–189
Cairo Genizah, Vol.2:235–247, 235–247
Conservative Judaism, Vol.1:58, 61–62,
82–84
definition, Vol.1:3–4
denominational Haggadah, Vol.1:68
four sons, illustrations, Vol.1:179
historical change, Vol.1:51–52
interpretations, Vol.1:4–7
Jewish identity, Vol.1:49–52
midrashim, history of, Vol.2:24–25
Mishnah, Vol.2:225–235
mitzvot, Vol.1:53
Orthodox, Vol.1:67, 84
peoplehood, concept of, Vol.1:69
Reconstructionist Haggadah, Vol.1:62–64, 82
Reform Judaism, Vol.1:57, 59, 80, 81–82
script, Vol.1:18
statehood, Vol.1:181–182
suffering, Vol.1:227
Tosefta, Vol.2:225–234
translations, Vol.1:79–80
women's role in, Vol.1:75–76, 206
zionism, Vol.1:181
Haggadah for Passover (Finkelstein), Vol.1:83
A Haggadah for the School, Vol.1:83
Haggadah Lem'lamdim, Vol.1:151
Haggdah for a Secular Celebration of Pesach,
Vol.1:151–152
hail, plague of, Vol.2:30, 39, 47, 53, 59, 63, 66
Hallel, Vol.1:16, Vol.2:91, 93–94, 96–108,
145–147, 154–162, 164–185
HaMakom, Vol.1:184, 188, 192, 198–199,
209

hands, ritual washing, Vol.1:138–139
Hananel, Rabbenu, Vol.1:166–167
haseivah, Vol.1:158–159; *see also* reclining
Hauptman, Judith, Vol.1:16, 75–76
havdalah, Vol.1:112, 125, 132–133
Hegyon Lev, Vol.1:82–83
herbs, bitter, Vol.1:40–41, 150
Heschel, Susannah, Vol.1:43, 105; *see also maror*
High Holy Days, Vol.2:67
Hillel, Vol.2:118, 120, 122, 126–128,
131–132
Hillel sandwich, Vol.1:41, 190, *see korekh*
history, American, Vol.2:206
holiness, Vol.1:124–125, 131
Holocaust, Vol.1:164, 227, Vol.2:56, 143, 191
homosexuality, Vol.1:105, 144, 210
hospitality, Vol.1:141–142
hunger, Vol.1:145

I

identity, ethnic, Vol.1:55–56
identity, Jewish, Vol.1:47, 62
changes, Vol.1:64–68
Haggadah, Vol.1:49–52
observance level, Vol.1:65
redemption, Vol.1:192–193
Seder observance, Vol.1:67–68
wicked son, Vol.1:187
identity of the Children of Israel (ancient Egypt),
Vol.2:1, 6, 9, 13, 17, 21–22, 25–26
idol worship, Vol.1:213, 214, 216, Vol.2:15,
19, 43, 58, 154, 164
Rachel (matriarch), Vol.1:215
slavery, Vol.1:219
translation, Vol.1:215, 218
Ilan, Tal, Vol.1:205
Imma Shalom, Vol.1:208
interfaith Seder, Vol.1:151
interpretations, multiple, Vol.2:62
Israel, Land of, Vol.2:33–34, 42–43, 54, 68,
191–193; *see also* statehood
Israeli-Palestinian conflict, Vol.2:36, 50
Isserles, Moses, Vol.1:43

J

Jacob, Vol.1:216, 217–218
descent to Egypt, Vol.2:1–2, 4, 6, 8, 13, 17,
25–26

Laban's treatment of, Vol.2:4, 8, 15, 16–17, 28
marriage to Rachel, Vol.2:11
Jacobs, Joseph, Vol.1:86–87, 88
Jastrow, Marcus, Vol.1:82–83
Jesus, Vol.1:22–25, 27
Jewish Federations, Vol.1:62
Jewish Theological Seminary, Vol.1:58
Job, Vol.1:226, Vol.2:56, 187, 191, 217
John, Vol.1:22
Joseph, Vol.2:8–10, 25
Josephus, Vol.1:15, 135
Joshua, Vol.1:214, 217, Vol.2:57
Josiah, Vol.1:11–12
Judah, tribe of, Vol.2:100

K

Kabbalah, Vol.1:45–46, 230, Vol.2:69, 85, 129
Kaddish, Vol.1:29
kadesh, Vol.1:111–112, 114, 124–125
Kant, Emmanuel, Vol.1:54
Kaplan, Mordecai, Vol.1:62–64, 187
karpas, Vol.1:42, 113, 139–140, 143
Katz, Jacob, Vol.1:179
Ki Lo Na'eh, Vol.2:198, 206–208, 218–221
kiddush, Vol.1:111–112, 134, 136, 137, 138
translation, Vol.1:129–130
kiddush l'vanah, Vol.1:178
kingship, Vol.2:8
Klausner, Abraham J., Vol.1:164
Kol Dichfin: The Open Door, A Passover Haggadah, Vol.1:82
korekh, Vol.2:110–111, 115, 120, 122, 124–125, 128, 131–133; *see also* Hillel sandwich
Koslowsky, Nota, Vol.1:180
Ktav Sofer, Vol.1:157
Kushner, Harold, Vol.1:227
k'zayit, measurement of, Vol.1:139–140, Vol.2:132–133

L

Laban the Aramean, Vol.2:1, 4–5, 8, 13, 16–17, 24–26, 28
Last Supper, Vol.1:23–24
law, Jewish
hands, ritual washing, Vol.1:139
leaven, Vol.1:96–97, 101–104
maggid, Vol.1:140–142
reclining during seder, Vol.1:155–157

Seder, Vol.1:53–54
yachats, Vol.1:140
Lazarus, Emma, Vol.1:222
Leah, Vol.2:28
leaven
Abudarham, David, Vol.1:97, 98
Aramaic, Vol.1:97
biblical verses, Vol.1:96–97
blessing over, Vol.1:100–101
burning of, Vol.1:98
checking for, Vol.1:92
definition, Vol.1:100
feminism, Vol.1:95, 104
Maimonides, Moses, Vol.1:94, 97
metaphors, Vol.1:101
nullification, Vol.1:97–100
possession, Vol.1:99–100
search for, Vol.1:95, 101–104
Shulchan Arukh, Vol.1:101–102
leprosy, Vol.2:11
"Let all who are hungry...", Vol.1:124, 127
Levi Yitzchak of Berditchev, Vol.1:203–204
Levine, Yael Katz, Vol.1:105
Levinson, Bernard, Vol.1:12
liberation, personal, Vol.1:191–192
lice, plague of, Vol.2:30, 39, 46, 53, 59, 66
liturgy, see: prayer
Livni, Zvi, Vol.1:181
locusts, plague of, Vol.2:30, 39, 47, 53, 59, 63, 66
Lord's Prayer, Vol.1:29
love, between God and Israel, Vol.1:122
Luria, Isaac, Vol.1:43, 45–46

M

Mah Nishtanah, Vol.1:17, 37–38, 147–149
historical change, Vol.1:154–155
Jewish law, Vol.1:155
Maimonides, Moses, Vol.1:155
translation, Vol.1:148, 153
maggid, Vol.1:123, 140–142, 144
Maggid of Mezerich, Vol.1:203, 205
maidservants, Vol.1:164
Maimonides, Moses
checking of leaven, Vol.1:94, 97
hands, ritual washing, Vol.1:139
kiddush, Vol.1:138
Mah Nishtanah, Vol.1:155

rejoicing, Vol.1:141

telling Passover story, Vol.1:190

Thirteen Principles of Faith, Vol.1:162, 165

wine, four cups, Vol.1:136

Mamet, David, Vol.1:180

manna, Vol.2:33–34, 42–43, 49, 51, 54

Marks, David Woolf, Vol.1:80–81

maror, Vol.1:28, 40–41, 150

blessing over, Vol.2:110, 115

commentary on, Vol.2:78, 83–84, 117, 119–120, 122

link to matzah, Vol.2:80–81, 91

Pesach and matzah, Vol.2:72–74, 76, 88, 122, 127–128, 131–133

types of, Vol.2:130

Masoretic text, Vol.1:164–165

matriarchs, Vol.1:128

matzah, Vol.1:28

blessing over, Vol.2:110, 114, 122, 124

broken, Vol.1:125

commentary on, Vol.2:74, 78, 88–91, 117, 119–120

Festival of Matzot, Vol.1:122

Kabbalah, Vol.1:204

link to *maror*, Vol.2:80–81

Pesach and *maror*, Vol.2:72, 76, 88, 127–128, 131–133

reasons for, Vol.1:135

Seder plate, Vol.1:39–40

yachats, Vol.1:140

Maxwell House Haggdah

distribution, Vol.1:85–86

layout, Vol.1:88

neutrality in text, Vol.1:89–90

Passover certification, Vol.1:86–87

translation, Vol.1:88

typesetting, Vol.1:89

mazal, Vol.1:134

Meiri, Vol.1:157

Melito, Vol.1:33

memory, Vol.1:30

Menachem Nachum of Chernobyl, Rabbi, Vol.1:173, 203, 205

messiah, Vol.1:172, 177, 186–187, 198

metaphors in prayer, Vol.2:165

Metatron, Vol.2:57

Michael, Vol.2:112

midrashim of Haggadah, Vol.2:24–25

miracles in the Exodus, Vol.2:99–104, 107, 139, 152

Miriam, Vol.1:105, Vol.2:11, 69, 77, 139, 142

Miriam's cup, Vol.1:72, Vol.2:152

Mishnah

Haggadah, Vol.2:225–234

Passover Seder, Vol.1:15, 16–18

search for leaven, Vol.1:102

mnemonic devices

letters of, Vol.2:63

listed, Vol.2:39

reasons for using, Vol.2:53, 59, 65–66

Seder order, Vol.1:109, 132–133, Vol.2:196

spilling wine for, Vol.2:30–31, 58

on staff of Moses, Vol.2:44, 48

Moses, Vol.1:225

encounter with God, Vol.2:9

mention of in Haggadah, Vol.2:48–49, 70

as redeemer, Vol.2:12–13, 44

rescue of from Nile, Vol.2:11–12

role in Ten Plagues, Vol.2:44–45, 52, 66, see also staff

motsi, Vol.2:110, 114, 117

murder, Vol.2:19

N

Nachor, Vol.1:214

Napoleon, Vol.1:53

nationhood, Vol.1:61, 63, 143

Nazis, Vol.2:26

ner, Vol.1:115, 129

New Haggadah for the Pesach Seder, Vol.1:82

The New Union Haggadah, Vol.1:82

New Year's festivals, Vol.1:12–14

night, comparison to exile, Vol.1:191–192

night, metaphors, Vol.1:203

A Night of Questions: A Passover Haggadah, Vol.1:82

Nile River, Vol.2:2, 8, 11, 18, 28, 46, 52

Nimrod, Vol.2:222–223

nirtsah, Vol.2:187–197

Noah, Vol.2:10

nullification of leaven, Vol.1:97–100

O

offerings. *see* sacrifices

Olat Tamid, Vol.1:81

Oral Law, Vol.1:22

Orthodox Judaism, Vol.1:65, 67, 69
    Haggadah, Vol.1:84

P

pakod pakadeti, Vol.1:220
paschal sacrifice, Vol.1:10, 12, 23–24, 28, 31,
    32, 172, 176, 197
    chavurah, Vol.1:25, 142
    commentary on, Vol.2:75, 78, 80–81
    eating, Vol.1:200
    Hallel, Vol.2:106, 164
    history of, Vol.2:85–88
    matzah and *maror*, Vol.2:72, 74, 127–128,
        131–133
    as a mitzvah of redemption, Vol.2:10, 12,
        17, 27
    nirtsah, Vol.2:187, 192–193
    offerings, Vol.2:126
    Shulchan Orekh, Vol.2:133–134
    tsafun, Vol.2:135
Passover Haggadah (Silverman), Vol.1:83
Passover Haggadah: The Feast of Freedom,
    Vol.1:83
Passover story, recounting, Vol.1:190–191,
    Vol.2:73–76, 79–80, 83, 91–92, 112,
    177–178
    Abarbanel, Don Isaac, Vol.1:187
    Abudarham, David, Vol.1:187
    B'nai Brak, seder in, Vol.1:188, 191, 197
    to children, Vol.1:172, 186, 181
    obligation to, Vol.1:140–141, 172, 173, 190
    paschal sacrifice, Vol.1:183–184
    praise of, Vol.1:176
    women's role in, Vol.1:144
Paul, Vol.1:25
peoplehood, concept of, Vol.1:52–53
    Haggadah, Vol.1:69
    Kaplan, Mordecai, Vol.1:63
Peretz, Y. L., Vol.1:151–152
Pharaoh
    comparison to God, Vol.2:46
    comparison to Laban, Vol.2:16, 24–26
    decrees of, Vol.2:1, 4, 10–11, 18–19, 28
    plagues affecting, Vol.2:46–49, 56–57
Philo, Vol.1:15, 150
Pilgrims Prayer, Vol.1:11, 18
Pithom and Rameses, Vol.2:2, 7
Pittsburgh Platform, Vol.1:57, 58

plagues, ten. *see* Ten Plagues
Plaskow, Judith, Vol.1:74, 207
Plato, Vol.1:200
Plutarch, Vol.1:17
population of Children of Israel (ancient
    Egypt), Vol.2:1, 6, 8–9, 13–15, 17,
    20–22, 28
"Pour out Your Wrath", Vol.1:61
praise of God, Vol.2:93–94, 96–108, 154–162,
    164–185, 206
prayer, Vol.1:18
    blessing over leaven, Vol.1:100–101
    Conservative Judaism, Vol.1:60
    daily, Vol.1:25–26
    interfaith relations, Vol.1:35
    metaphors, Vol.2:165
    Reconstructionist Judaism, Vol.1:63
    Shabbat, Vol.2:184
    vocabulary, Vol.1:30
Puah, Vol.2:28, 70
Purim, connection to Passover, Vol.2:98

Q

Quartodecimans, Vol.1:24
questioning, theological, Vol.1:148, 152

R

Rabbinical Assembly, Vol.1:61
Rachel (matriarch), Vol.1:215, 219, Vol.2:11,
    28, 69
Rachel (wife of Akiva), Vol.1:207–208
Rambam. see Maimonides, Moses
Ramban, Vol.1:229, Vol.2:18, 19, 59, 102
Rashbam, Vol.1:152, 153, 155, 156, Vol.2:18,
    80, 81, 127
Rashbetz, Vol.1:188, 189, 214, 217–218
    covenant between God and Israel,
        Vol.1:222, 229
Rashi, Vol.1:114, Vol.2:89, 123, 135, 183
reclining during Seder, Vol.1:153, 155–157
Reconstructionist Haggadah, Vol.1:62–64, 82
Red Sea, Vol.2:44–45, 47–48, 56, 60, 65, 77
redemption, Vol.1:31–32, 128–129, 185
    belief in, Vol.1:222, 224
    blessing of, Vol.2:109, 112–114, 116,
        121–123, 125–126
    Exodus story, Vol.1:143
    God, Vol.1:165–166, Vol.2:44

Jewish identity, Vol.1:192–193
messiah, Vol.1:186
promise of God, Vol.1:222, 230
Serach's role, Vol.1:219–220
women's role in, Vol.1:143
Reform Judaism, Vol.1:56–57
Haggadah, Vol.1:59, 80, 81–82
rejoicing on festivals, Vol.1:141
repentance, Vol.2:46, 49–50, 55, 60, 67, 85
Ritba, Vol.1: 127,167, 189, 218
ritual purity, Vol.1:13, 138–139
rituals, Vol.1:15, 49
rivit, Vol.1:137
rochtsah, Vol.2:110, 113–114, 116–117, 122,
     124, 130
Roman rule, Vol.1:173, 196, 222, Vol.2:18, 45
Rosh Chodesh, Vol.1:132–133, 186, 208
Rosh Hashanah, Vol.2:164
Rubinstein, Richard, Vol.1:227–228
Ruth, Vol.1:222

S

sacrifices, Vol.1:10, 31, 135, Vol.2:49; *see also*
     paschal sacrifice
Sadducees, Vol.1:22
salt water, Vol.1:143–144
sanctification, Vol.1:115, 123, 131, 137;
     see also Kiddush
Sarah, Vol.2:182
Saul, Vol.2:56
Seder
    calendar, Vol.1:178
    conclusion, Vol.2:186–197
    Conservative Judaism, Vol.1:60
    creativity, Vol.1:19
    customs, Vol.2:51
    definition, Vol.1:94, 100
    egg, Vol.1:38, Vol.2:133–134
    faith, Vol.1:165–166
    feminism, Vol.1:105, 109–110
    food, Vol.1:38–42
    historical change, Vol.1:200–201
    identity, Jewish, Vol.1:47–48, 67–68
    kadesh, Vol.1:111–112
    karpas, Vol.1:113
    Last Supper, Vol.1:23–24
    learning aids, Vol.1:67
    legal detail, Vol.1:53–54

meal, Vol.2:111, 115, 118, 133–134
mnemonic devices, Vol.1:108, 109
modern innovations, Vol.1:42–43
order of, Vol.1:107
origins of, Vol.1:16
origins of plate, Vol.1:37–38
personal preparation for, Vol.1:95, 101
plate, Vol.1:43–46, 103–104
Rabbinic law, Vol.1:200
rituals, Vol.1:48
shank bone, Vol.1:38
urchats, Vol.1:113
vegetarian seder, Vol.2:215–216
women's resource books, Vol.1:72
women's role in preparation, Vol.1:145
yachats, Vol.1:113
Seder Rav Amram, Vol.1:126, 219, Vol.2:146, 254
sefirot, Vol.1:45–46
Septuagint, Vol.1:164, 185, 202
Serach, Vol.1:219–220, Vol.2:9
seraph, Vol.2:29, 36–38, 57
Shabbat
    commandment of, Vol.2:46
    Dayyenu, Vol.2:33–34, 42–44
    during the Exodus, Vol.2:54
    feminism, Vol.2:69
    Hagadol, Vol.2:196
    prayers, Vol.2:184
    singing *Eliyahu Hanavi* , Vol.2:149
Shabbetai Zevi, Vol.1:186
Shakdiel, Leah, Vol.1:159
shank bone, Vol.1:38
Shapiro, Hava, Vol.1:158
Shapiro, Kalonymos Kalmish, Vol.1:205
shehecheyanu, Vol.1:113, 134, 138
Shekhinah, Vol.1:222, 231
    in Egypt, Vol.2:29
    enslavement, Vol.2:44
    feminism, Vol.2:69
    reference to "awe", Vol.2:52, 57–58
    at Sinai, Vol.2:37–38, 60–61
    in the Temple, Vol.2:214
Shibbolei Haleket, Vol.1:114, 127, 229
Shifra, Vol.2:28, 70
Sh'ma, Vol.1:176, 184, 188, 198
Shmuel ben Meir; *see Rashbam*, Vol.1:152
signs, relationship to staff, Vol.2:29–30, 36,
     38–39, 44, 52, 58

Silverman, Morris, Vol.1:83
simanei haseder, Vol.1:109
simple son, Vol.1:204–205
Sinai, Mount
    covenant at, Vol.2:16
    Dayyenu, Vol.2:33–34, 42–43, 68
    Exodus as preparation for, Vol.2:37
    mitzvah of *Hallel* given at, Vol.2:102
    spiritual cleansing at, Vol.2:60–61
    Torah given at, Vol.2:54
Sinclair, Jo, Vol.1:158
Six-Day War, Vol.1:59
slavery, Vol.1:125–126, 128, 145, 167
    Abudarham, David, Vol.1:166
    disgrace of, Vol.1:214, 217
    history, Vol.1:163, 167
    Holocaust, Vol.1:164
    idol worship, Vol.1:219
    Kabbalah, Vol.1:230
    length of time, Vol.1:225, 226, 229
    Midrash, Vol.1:162, 164
    personal, Vol.1:191–192
    as a punishment, Vol.1:224, 226
Solomon, Vol.2:55
Soloveitchik, Joseph B., Vol.1:141
Soloveitchik, Yitzchak Ze'ev Halevi,
    Vol.1:136–137
Soloveitchik, Yosef Dov, Vol.1:179
song(s)
    blessing of, Vol.2:184
    concluding the seder, Vol.2:198–204,
        206–224
    Dayyenu, Vol.2:49
    Eliyahu Hanavi, Vol.2:149
    and feminism of *Hallel*, Vol.2:97, 99, 101,
        107–108
    of Miriam, Vol.2:69, 152
    of praise, Vol.2:45, 177
    of redemption, Vol.2:120, 126, 129, 191
    of the sea, Vol.2:56, 177
    in the Temple, Vol.2:102
Soviet Jewry, Vol.1:43, 59, 121, Vol.2:120
speech, relationship to hearing, Vol.2:15–16
splitting of the sea, Vol.2:32–34, 41–43, 45,
    49
staff, Vol.2:29–30, 36, 38–39, 44–45, 52, 58, 66
statehood, Vol.1:181–182
strangers, Vol.1:224–225

Strikovsky, Arie, Vol.1:155
strong hand and outstretched arm,
    Vol.2:29–30, 36, 38–39, 43–44, 52,
    57–58
suffering, Vol.1:226–227, 228
A Survivors' Haggadah, Vol.1:164
swarms, plague of, Vol.2:30, 39, 46, 59, 62, 66
sword, Vol.2:29–30, 36, 38–39, 43–44, 52,
    57–58
symposia, Vol.1:25, 154, 199–200
Szold, Benjamin, Vol.1:82

T

tahor, Vol.1:138
Temple
    construction of, Vol.2:55
    Dayyenu, Vol.2:33–34, 42–43, 59–60
    destruction of, Vol.2:138, 140, 144–145
    Hallel, Vol.2:106, 164–165, 176
    Hebrew terms for, Vol.2:65
    history of, Vol.2:67
    laws in absence of, Vol.2:49–50, 133
    nirtsah, Vol.2:193, 196, 220, 222
    rebuilding, Vol.2:214
    remembering, Vol.2:118, 120–121,
        126–127, 132
    sacrificial system, Vol.2:85–87, 112
Ten Commandments, Vol.2:46, 60
Ten Plagues. *see also* specific plague
    commentary on, Vol.2:44–48, 52–56,
        62–67
    and Israeli-Palestinian conflict, Vol.2:36, 50
    of Jewish Women, Vol.2:69–70
    listed, Vol.2:39–40
    spilling wine for. *see* wine, spilling
Terach, Vol.1:218
testament, Vol.1:31
Tetragrammaton, Vol.2:44
t'fillin, Vol.2:84
theological vocabulary, Vol.1:30
theology in Haggadah, Vol.1:227
Thirteen Principles of Faith, Vol.1:162
time bound commandments, Vol.1:156
Torah, Vol.1:184, 188, Vol.2:33–34, 42–43,
    54, 60–61, 68–69
Tosefta, Vol.1:206–207
    Haggadah, Vol.2:225–234, 225–234
    Passover Seder, Vol.1:16, 16–18

translations, Haggadah, Vol.1:79–80
Trupin, Sofie, Vol.1:94, 96
tsafun, Vol.2:111, 115, 118–119, 125, 134–136
tum'ah, Vol.1:138

U

Unheroic Conduct, Vol.1:210
Union Haggadah: Home Service for the Passover Eve, Vol.1:81–82
urchats, Vol.1:113, 120, 123, 138–139
    women's role in, Vol.1:143
Uzza, Vol.2:48

V

vegetarian seder, Vol.2:215–216
Vital, Hayim, Vol.1:45

W

Wasteland, Vol.1:158
wealth, Vol.1:221, 222, 230, Vol.2:32, 34, 41–42, 45, 47–49, 54, 64
Weisberg, Ruth, Vol.1:182
Wellhausen, Julius, Vol.1:10–11, 11
Wengeroff, Pauline, Vol.1:145
When Bad Things Happen to Good People, Vol.1:227
wicked son, Vol.1:179–180, 182, 187, 202
Wiesel, Elie, Vol.1:228
wine
    fifth cup, Vol.2:126, 138–139, 145–147, 149–151, 183
    four cups, Vol.1:115, 128, 136, 136–137, Vol.2:116, 129, 147–148, 183
    laws of, Vol.1:137
    libations, Vol.2:102
    obligation during Seder, Vol.1:115
    spilling for Ten Plagues, Vol.2:30, 45, 50, 55–56, 58, 59, 65
    symbolism, Vol.1:27, 118
    women's obligation, Vol.1:142
wisdom, Vol.1:205
wise son, Vol.1:183, 203–204
    Abudarham, David, Vol.1:189
womanhood, Israel compared to, Vol.2:26–28
women. *see also* feminism
    Jewish literacy, Vol.1:206, 208
    maggid, Vol.1:144

ordination, Vol.1:206
    Orthodox Seder commentary, Vol.1:72
    reclining during seder, Vol.1:153, 156
    ritual purity, Vol.1:143
    role in Haggadah, Vol.1:75–76, 77, 206
    role in redemption, Vol.1:143
    Seder resource book, Vol.1:72
    Serach, Vol.1:219–220
    time bound commandments, Vol.1:142
wonders, relationship to blood, Vol.2:29–30, 36, 38–39, 45, 52, 58
World War II, Vol.2:119

Y

yachats, Vol.1:113, 123, 125, 126, 140, 144
YaKeNHaZ, Vol.1:133
Yocheved, Vol.1:144, Vol.2:9, 70
Yom Kippur, Vol.2:193
Yom Kippur War, Vol.1:59

Z

zakhor, Vol.1:140–141
Zionism, Vol.1:xiv, 210, 223, Vol.2:120
    Haggadah, Vol.1:180–182
    Reform Judaism, Vol.1:58, 69
Zipporah, Vol.1:109
Zuckoff, Aviva Cantor, Vol.1:73–74

The editors are grateful to the following for permission to reproduce the material listed below. This page constitutes a continuation of the copyright page.

Page 3: From *Masechet Pesachim* (Heidelberg and Munich: The Rabbinical Council of Ashkenaz [Germany] in the American sector with the assistance of the Military Government of the United States and the Joint Distribution Committee, 1949), frontispiece. Reprinted with permission from the American Jewish Historical Society, Newton Center, Massachusetts, and New York, New York.

Page 9: From *The Moriah Haggadah*, illuminations by Avner Moriah (Philadelphia: Jewish Publication Society, 2005), p. 39. Reprinted with permission from Avner Moriah.

Page 35: From *Haggadah Shel Pesach*, illustrated by Otto Geismar (Berlin: Yalkut, 1927). From the collection Lawrence A. Hoffman.

Page 71: From *The Haggadah of Passover* (New York, 1944); a gift of the Labor Zionist Committee for Relief and Rehabilitation, Inc. Nota Koslowsky, illustrator. From the collection Stephen P. Durchslag.

Page 73: From Ms. Hebr. 1333, 19 verso, from the Bibliothèque nationale de France. Reprinted with permission.

Page 95: From *A Survivor's Haggadah*, written designed and illustrated by Yosef Dov Sheinson with woodcuts by Miklos Adler (Munich: The U.S. Army of Occupation, 1946), leaf 18v. Reprinted with permission from the American Jewish Historical Society, Newton Center, Massachusetts, and New York, New York.

Page 136: From *Haggadah Shel Pesach* (Mantua, 1568). Reprinted with permission from Klau Library, Cincinnati, Hebrew Union College–Jewish Institute of Religion.

Page 137: From *Haggadah* (Baghdad, 1908). From the collection Stephen P. Durchslag.

Page 141: From *Haggadah, Battalion 403, Water Carriers from the Land of Israel* (Benghazi, Libya, 1941). From the collection Stephen P. Durchslag.

Page 146: From *Israel Passover Haggadah* by Menachem M. Kasher (New York: American Biblical Encyclopedia Society, 1950), p. 84.

Page 153: From *The Moriah Haggadah*, illuminations by Avner Moriah (Philadelphia: Jewish Publication Society, 2005), p. 113. Reprinted with permission from Avner Moriah.

Page 163: From *A Sephardic Passover Haggadah* (Hoboken, NJ: KTAV Publishing House, 1988). Reprinted with permission. Translation reprinted with permission from Alan D. Corré.

Page 204 and 205: From *Haggadah, Surveyors Battalion 524 of the Land of Israel* (Italy, 1946). From the collection of Stephen P. Durchslag.

Pages 231 and 232: From Ms. Kaufmann A.50, pp. 122 and 123. Reprinted with permission from the Library, Hungarian Academy of Sciences.

Every effort has been made to trace and acknowledge copyright holders of all images included in this book. The editors apologize for any errors or omissions that may remain, and ask that any omissions be brought to their attention so that they may be corrected in future editions.